# THEY FOUGHT FOR
# THE MOTHERLAND

# THEY FOUGHT FOR THE MOTHERLAND

## Russia's Women Soldiers
## in World War I and
## the Revolution

LAURIE S. STOFF

UNIVERSITY PRESS OF KANSAS

# ACKNOWLEDGMENTS

Although scholarly work often seems a solitary and lonely process, there are many voices that contribute to its production. I wish to express my sincerest gratitude to those who helped me undertake and complete this work. My research was made possible through several funding sources, including the American Council of Teachers of Russian/American Council for Collaboration in Education and Language Study Research Scholar Program Grant, the Department of Education's Title IV Foreign Language Area Scholarship, and travel grants and research awards from the Department of History at the University of Kansas. While writing the dissertation that was the original impetus for this book, I was provided with financial support through the University of Kansas Graduate School of Arts and Sciences Dissertation Fellowship.

The assistance of a number of scholars was invaluable throughout the processes of preparation, research, and writing. In particular, I would like to thank my adviser, Norman Saul, and the other members of my dissertation committee. Bruce Menning of the U.S. Army Command and General Staff College was extremely helpful in securing for me initial entrance into vital Russian military archives and in providing much support and constructive advice along the way. Maria Carlson, of the University of Kansas Center for Russian and East European Studies, was extremely generous, not only with her expertise but also with advice and support. Carl Strikwerda provided me with valuable commentary and always helped me look at the "big picture." Anna Cienciala offered many helpful suggestions as well. In Russia, Vladimir Posniakov, of the Moscow Academy of Sciences World History Institute, assisted me greatly in obtaining permission to work in collections and archives in Moscow. He and his wife also offered their friendship and moral support during my numerous stays in Russia. In the Russian State Military-Historical Archives, Valerii Mikhailovich Shabanov provided extensive assistance in locating information and materials required for my research, and his patience and helpfulness seemed

unlimited. Denise Youngblood and Reina Pennington provided extremely helpful suggestions for improvement. I would also like to thank my colleagues in the
Department of History at the University of Vermont, all of whom extended extraordinary kindness and collegiality to me.

I would also like to thank those who gave me support and encouragement
throughout the process of completing my research and writing. I would like to
thank Shona Schonning, an extraordinary person, for giving me the chance to
come to Moscow as often as I needed for research and study, as well as for being a great friend and supporter. My family, particularly my parents, grandpar-
ents, and parents-in-law, also gave me much support and assistance throughout
my graduate study and in the process of writing this book. I am extremely grateful to Tatyana and Nikolai Matusov, to Vadim and Elena Zvezdov, and especially to Benjamin and Veronika Franchi, who not only provided me with
invaluable assistance but also opened their hearts and homes to me in Moscow
and California. There were many people, too many to name in this short space,
with whom I shared the grueling experience called graduate school and who
made the process much more humane, and to whom I am very grateful. And finally, I would like to express my unending gratitude and love for my most pa-
tient, understanding, and supportive husband, John Benschoter, who gave me
boundless encouragement necessary to see this project through to the end, and
who, despite my own misgivings and lack of confidence, never doubted my
abilities.

# TECHNICAL NOTES

In transliterating Russian words and names I have used the standard Library of Congress system, with the exception of certain names that are used familiarly in anglicized form (for example, "Maria" as opposed to "Mariia"; "Kerensky" as opposed to "Kerenskii"). Names of personages are provided in as complete a form as I was able to locate, but contemporary reports often failed to include names of persons (particularly first names) and places and to give precise (or any) dates, and they frequently neglected to identify military units, often for reasons of wartime security. Thus, where only first initials or last names are provided in the text, it is because the full names were unavailable. The abbreviations used in the text and notes for Russian governmental agencies and Russian document collections and depositories are given according to their Russian acronyms:

GARF    State Archive of the Russian Federation (*Gosudarstvennyi arkhiv Rossiiskoi Federatsii*)
GPBSS   Saltykov-Shchedrin State Public Library (*Gosudarstvennaia publichnaia bibliotekta imina Saltykova-Shchedrina*)
GUGSh   Main Directorate of the General Staff (*Glavnoe upravlenie generalnogo shtaba*)
RGVIA   Russian State Military Historical Archive (*Rossiiskii gosudarstvennyi voenno-istoricheskii arkhiv*)
RGAVMF  Russian State Archive of the Navy (*Rossiiskii gosudarstvennyi arkhiv voenno-morskogo flota*)

Abbreviations of other Russian words in notes:

d.    *delo* (file or box)
f.    *fond* (collection)

l.    *list'*, ll.: *listi* (page, pages)
ob.   back of page
op.   *opis* (inventory)

Since nearly all the action described in this work took place prior to 1918, dates are given according to the Julian (Old Style) calendar that was in use in Russia during this period, which lagged thirteen days behind the Gregorian calendar used in the West. The various fronts referred to in the text are on what the Western powers labeled the eastern front, but in Russia they were designated as the northern, western, southwestern, and Romanian fronts, stretching, in order, from Riga to the Black Sea. Geographical locations are given according to their contemporary Russian names. More prominent places in formerly Russian-held areas now parts of Poland, Lithuania, Belarus, and Ukraine are, at the first mention, followed in parentheses by their current, linguistically appropriate names, when these are known—for example, Ivangorod (Deblin) and Vilna (Vilnius).

# INTRODUCTION

This book focuses on the experiences and significance of the women who became soldiers in Russia during World War I. This is the first major study to investigate these women in detail and to answer a number of important questions. Who were these women soldiers and what were their motivations for joining the fighting? How was it possible for so many women to cross into such a distinctly masculine realm, from which women were customarily restricted? To what extent does this phenomenon demonstrate "exceptionalism," both in terms of the women's gender transgression and in relation to Russian society's uniqueness? What effect did women's participation in combat have on the army and on the rest of society? Did their military activity contribute to any change in traditional gender roles in Russia or elsewhere? In what ways do these women inform our understanding of the relationship between women and war? And finally, what is the legacy of Russia's women soldiers of the Great War? This study seeks to provide answers to these questions while establishing the significance of these women within the context of the war, revolution, and Russian society during this critical time of change.

During World War I, thousands of women in Russia donned military uniforms and set out to defend their nation. Women have participated in war since the beginning of history, but this Russian experience was exceptional. Russia's involvement in the Great War fostered an explosion of female participation in combat, far surpassing the numbers of women soldiers in previous armed forces or in other armed forces at the time. By 1917, the number of women who became soldiers most probably exceeded 6,000, an unprecedented number.[1] Moreover, in the history of modern warfare, Russia was the first country to employ women systematically in sexually segregated military formations. The creation of separate, all-female military units in 1917 was a completely new method of utilizing women in war.

passed, however, the traditional roles of men and women are reasserted as part of a "return to normalcy" that usually follows the upheavals of war.

This work seeks to fill a conspicuous gap in scholarship on Russia during World War I and the revolutions. Russia's female soldiers have been largely forgotten by history, despite their striking actions. They were conspicuously left out of subsequent historiography for a number of reasons, the most prominent being that they ended up on the losing side of the upheavals of 1917. Organized in an effort to carry out the war aims of the Provisional Government, the women's military units were associated with the "bourgeois" elements that the Bolsheviks were determined to sweep away when they assumed power. As a result, the women were mocked and vilified, but were mostly brushed aside and ignored by both Soviet historiography and popular memory. Western scholarship has similarly failed to incorporate the women soldiers into the picture of Russia's World War I and revolutionary experience. Despite having been neglected by historiography, these women are important. Their stories must be told if we are to understand more fully World War I and the Russian Revolution and gender roles and women's experiences both inside and outside Russia. They are also important sociologically, for their actions demonstrate that women are able to perform combat roles in modern warfare, while illustrating the problems connected with their use in such activity.

Although the women soldiers were not incorporated into the subsequent historical record of World War I, a conscious attempt was made during the war to include women in the heroic narrative, a highly unusual phenomenon in the creation of the war myth. Russia's women soldiers received extensive attention from contemporaries. Observers expressed a ready fascination with the Russian female soldier, and books and articles from this period reflect this keen interest. Journalists quickly recognized the sensational value of such a striking phenomenon and covered their exploits extensively in publications from Petrograd to New York. In fact, Russia's women soldiers became temporary media stars all over Europe and in the United States. Although these women soldiers were displaying decidedly unconventional and unfeminine behavior, and thereby threatening the traditional gender system, they were often lauded for their active patriotism and sacrifice. But there were detractors as well. Many commentators criticized the women for becoming soldiers, perceiving their actions as damaging to the social order. Their reactions are equally important to understanding the phenomenon of female soldiers. This study examines public perceptions of women in combat in detail in an attempt to better comprehend the effects they may have had on gender roles in early twentieth-century society.

## WOMEN AND WAR

Understanding women's participation in the fighting of World War I in Russia is also important to the overall attempt to incorporate women's experiences into the historiography of war and contributes to our understanding of the relationship between women and war. This work establishes the place of these women in the narrative history of World War I and contributes to discussions on the effect of war on women and what social changes, if any, result from women's experiences in war. War and military activity have traditionally been male preserves from which women were intentionally excluded. Literary critic Nancy Huston has argued that "the defining characteristic of war is its masculinity."[3] This does not mean that society excludes females entirely from the process of war. Wars have always affected women, and women's activities have always had an impact on wars. In fact, in times of war, many women participate in public life to a far greater extent than in peacetime. This is particularly true in modern mass warfare, when the mobilization of the civilian population is as important as the mobilization of armed forces. Yet female roles during armed conflicts were historically expected to be limited to moral support on the home front and care and comfort for the ill and wounded, in contrast with the active frontline service expected of males. A woman in a combat capacity controverts this assumed "natural" role and challenges a man's conception of war itself.

In reality, however, these conceptions are in no way universal and rigid; not all men and women fit neatly into these prescribed categories. War often presents a direct challenge to conventional gender consciousness. As Alfred Meyer states:

> Wars may reveal the folly of the stereotype. Many men are sensitive, averse to violence, brutality, and killing, and many women may have all the traits of the activist, the capable manager, or even the warrior. The shock of battle experiences can bring into the open men's sensitivity and aversion to war as well as create opportunities for women to prove themselves as fighters.[4]

Female participation in war thus raises a number of issues vital to understanding socialization and gender roles. It questions the essentially masculine nature of war while similarly challenging conventional notions of female social roles. Historian Linda Grant De Pauw affirms the idea that "war is the most powerful cultural intervention which serves to define gender."[5] In many ways, women's relationship to war is more complex than that of men. Men's roles in war have been clearly defined by conventional gendered divisions of labor as those of defenders. Women's wartime roles, although traditionally prescribed as passive, are in reality more fluid and varied and assume aspects outside conventional social boundaries. This is particularly true of women's participation in combat. According to historian Nicole Ann Dombrowski, "women's entrance into combat not only reconstructs combat and its institutions but also reconstructs women in the process."[6] The traditional conception of femininity centers on the creative, caring, and nurturing forces of humanity. Full of violence, destruction, and death, war presents itself as the absolute antithesis to these energies; thus, a woman taking part in such activities seems to stand in stark contradiction to her so-called natural capacities. A woman in combat controverts socialized female roles and challenges a man's conception of war itself. Therefore men have found it difficult to accept the inclusion of women in soldiering.[7]

World War I is no exception. Scholars such as George Mosse contend that "a variety of motivations were at work as the generation of 1914 rushed to the colors at the outbreak of the war, but the quest for masculinity cut across them all."[8] The idea that the war was being fought in order to preserve "hearth and home," and thus was a defense of women and children, was used extensively by belligerent governments to motivate men to fight.[9]

At the same time, the war involved millions of women in capacities outside the maintenance of the home. Despite much debate among scholars concerning the ways that World War I affected women's lives and gender roles, no consensus has been reached. Some contend that the war had an emancipating effect on women, citing the vast increase in female employment in the workforce and the achievement of suffrage for women in some of the belligerent nations. Others assert that the war radically altered relations between the sexes and reconstructed notions of "femininity" and "masculinity." Still others argue that the war had little positive effect on women; despite new opportunities, they still earned less than men and were expected to return to prewar roles following the achievement of peace.

Regardless of this lack of agreement, there is significant evidence that World War I affected the lives of women considerably, both directly and indirectly. In Russia, the war "blurred gender boundaries and undermined traditional society . . . bringing hundreds of thousands, perhaps millions, of women into public life for the first time," historian Barbara Alpern Engel proclaims.[10] The greatest changes occurred in the economic sphere. Although there had been some increase in women's work activity prior to 1914, the war signaled a great intensification of women's participation in the labor force. Millions of able-bodied men were sent to the battlefields, creating serious labor shortages. The belligerent nations were ultimately compelled to employ vast numbers of women in the war effort. Furthermore, the nature of their involvement differed distinctly from past experience. Women began working in areas that under normal circumstances would have been deemed unsuitable for them. Millions of women went to work in industries producing the necessities of both military and civilian life. Others replaced men in vital public service jobs.

Without female involvement in the labor force, the warring nations would have suffered devastating shortages and work stoppages and undoubtedly would have been unable to prosecute the war. But aside from small gains in terms of independence, women did not benefit much from their wartime participation in the labor force. Women still earned significantly less than men performing similar work. Some countries repealed legislation designed to protect women (and children) from overwork and dangerous conditions. After the war, men coming home from the battlefields displaced many of the women who had been employed during the conflict. In many instances, the labor market rapidly restored its gendered division of labor.[11]

In terms of political and civil rights and equality, some historians, such as Arthur Marwick, argue that women effectively proved their worth to society and defused subsequent opposition to female suffrage through their contributions to the war effort.[12] Russian women were given the right to vote in 1917, and British women over the age of thirty received the suffrage in 1918. There is no question that many progressive women engaged in and supported women's war work in all forms as a means to achieve rights and opportunities. Yet regardless of women's war work, it seems likely that many countries would have granted female suffrage and other rights just the same. The British suffrage movement had a long history of fighting for women's rights, and this undoubtedly gave more momentum to the passage of suffrage legislation than did four years of war work. Despite their efforts in the war, women in other belligerent countries, such as France, did not receive the right to vote until much later. In Russia, where women had also been working long and hard for the vote, women's suffrage (which accompanied universal male suffrage) and other emancipatory legislation were largely the result of the ideological commitment to women's rights of the Provisional Government that was established after the fall of tsarism in 1917. Women's contributions to the war effort were, however, not completely without influence on the distribution of political rights.

Demographic changes in belligerent populations caused by the absence of large numbers of men led to fears that appropriate gender roles were undermined during and after the war. In Great Britain, many believed that the Great War had dramatically altered relations between the sexes. Some men complained that the wartime economy had resulted in the supremacy of women over men. Others criticized what they viewed as excessive influence by women schoolteachers and worried that these women were undermining "manliness" through their control over the physical development of young boys.[13] The intrusion of women into war work was not widely welcomed; one reaction was the attempt to protect the masculinity of war. In France, a great effort was made to ensure a strict separation of women from the realm of war. To many French, World War I represented a chance for France to regain its masculinity, which had been damaged by its defeat in the Franco-Prussian War. Historian Margaret Darrow summarizes the attitude: "What was the point of the war at all if women's war experience undermined men's?"[14] As a result, women's contributions to the war effort were often regarded with suspicion and accused of emasculating the conflict.

Although there is no agreement about the extent to which the war affected women's lives and gender roles in the long run, during the period of the conflict women's lives and gender roles were significantly altered. Historian Penny Summerfield asserts that bringing women into war work, including into various "masculine" occupations, not only caused a change in perceptions of gender roles but blurred the "visual boundary between masculinity and femininity" as women "took off dresses and put on trousers."[15]

Over the past several decades, scholars have begun to rectify the general neglect of women in the study of war. Both military and social historians have initiated serious and vibrant discussions about the relationship between women and war. Those who study women's military history have made great progress, creating new foundations in the historical discipline and in public discourse. Significant work has been done to incorporate the experiences of women into the history of war. This work hopes to build upon the existing infrastructure while exploring new ground through a case study of women soldiers in Russia during World War I. In particular, it strives to fill a gap in scholarship on Russia during the war and revolution, as well as on the relationship between women and war, by exploring these women combatants in depth, creating a narrative of their experiences, and analyzing the implications of their existence and the consequences of their actions.

The book is arranged thematically and so does not always follow a linear chronology, but it does generally progress from the beginning of World War I in 1914 to the cessation of Russian participation in the war in 1918. The first chapter describes several aspects of Russian history, culture, and society that may have contributed to making it possible for women to become soldiers, even if only temporarily, despite the strict patriarchal nature of early twentieth-century Russian society. It examines the themes of gender roles, the presence of a "strong woman motif" in Russian culture, and a number of historical precedents of women serving as soldiers throughout Russian history.

Chapter 2 begins with an overview of women's participation in World War I in a variety of activities. It then focuses on the experiences of women who entered the Russian army as individuals or in small groups prior to the creation of the all-female military units in 1917. It describes the methods they employed to gain entrance into male units, their motivations for going to war, their efforts to assimilate into the male world of combat, and their actions as part of the fighting forces.

Chapter 3 provides the historical context for the creation of the women's battalions, describing the situation that arose as a result of the February Revolution, the attempt to enlist the support of every available citizen in the war effort and to create a volunteer army, and the role of women and women's organizations in pressing for greater involvement of their sex in the war effort. The chapter then examines the formation of the first all-female combat unit, the 1st Russian Women's Battalion of Death under the command of Maria Bochkareva, and looks at the women who enlisted in its ranks.

Chapter 4 details the development of a women's military movement advocating the formation of additional women's military units. It examines the creation of such units both as a result of grassroots initiatives and under the auspices of the Ministry of War. It describes the measures taken to form, equip, supply, train, and utilize the units and the numerous problems encountered in the process. It follows the military authorities' efforts to satisfy popular demand for the expansion of female participation in the war while simultaneously attempting to bring the private initiatives under its direct control. The chapter also details the experiences of Bochkareva's 1st Russian Women's Battalion of Death at the front, including its "baptism of fire" in battle, the litmus test for the experiment of using women in combat.

Chapter 5 closely examines four of the official women's military units created in the summer of 1917. It describes their formation; efforts to properly equip, supply, and train them; and numerous obstacles in the path of these goals. It also looks more closely at how many women enlisted in these units and at their social and educational backgrounds and other pertinent information.

Chapter 6 follows the growth and further development of the women's military movement and the efforts to expand it at the grassroots level. Simultaneously, it demonstrates how the military authorities worked to maintain control over the movement's activities and bring all women's military formations under the military authorities' auspices. When this proved unsuccessful, the government

attempted to change the movement's focus (away from combat and toward auxiliary services), and to restrict and ultimately drastically reduce the movement. It
also examines the participation of women soldiers in the defense of the Winter
Palace during the Bolshevik Revolution in October 1917 and works to dispel
much of the rumor and misinformation concerning this controversial event.

Chapter 7 analyzes the contemporary responses to the women soldiers, both
as individuals and in all-female units, through an examination of numerous media reports and personal writings. It examines foreign and domestic, male and
female, and military and nonmilitary views and attitudes and attempts to draw
conclusions about the extensive commentary on Russia's women soldiers.

Chapter 8 draws important conclusions about the meaning of the women's
military movement for Russia and the place of women in war in a broader context. It analyzes the specific way in which the women's military units were used
and why and discusses the legacy of the phenomenon.

# 1

## THE RUSSIAN CONTEXT

In examining the participation of women in combat, we must consider the nature of their society, for the women soldiers of World War I did not exist in a vacuum. Several aspects of Russia's unique historical development created an atmosphere that may have made it more feasible for women to become soldiers in that country when they were prevented from doing so in others. In this chapter, we look at factors such as social constructs, gender roles, relations between the sexes, family structure, and historical precedents to help us better understand the phenomenon of women soldiers in Russia during World War I.

### GENDER ROLES IN RUSSIAN SOCIETY

Throughout most of its history, Russia's social and political structures were highly patriarchal and hierarchical. Similarly, the Russian family was patriarchal and hierarchical—in fact, the Russian state took its form from the model of the patriarchal family, in which a benevolent but authoritarian father figure dominated obedient and subservient women and children. The tsar was a political extension of the good father, ruling sternly and absolutely, but with the best interests of his people in mind.[1] Women were subordinate to men, as women's historians have asserted, as "an imperative justified by a definition of a women's nature that was applied to all women regardless of social rank."[2] Patriarchy had been a central feature of Russian society since its conversion to Christianity in the tenth century. The state and the church worked to subordinate women to male authority and insisted on their status as dependent beings.[3]

Women were generally excluded from public life and relegated to the domestic sphere, although there are some notable exceptions, prominent upper-class and royal women who took on public roles and activities. Some peasant women were allowed to represent their households in the village commune assembly, but only when no competent adult male was present. Married women had no legal status independent of their husbands; they did not even have their own passports (identification documents required for movement within and without the country). Legally, they had no right to live separately from their husbands, although unmarried women could establish their own residences at the age of twenty-one. Women by law had to obey their husbands and submit to their authority without question. In essence, the Russian woman's life was almost entirely dependent on the dominant male in her life; this figure was her father before marriage, her husband after. Even when educational opportunities began to appear for women in the second half of the nineteenth century, a woman's attendance at school was dependent on the goodwill of the man in her life. In order to escape domineering and restrictive fathers, young women in the late nineteenth century often arranged sham marriages with sympathetic young men who would allow them to control their own passports and fates.[4]

As was the case in other European societies, gender roles in prerevolutionary Russia were based upon strictly defined behaviors and a sexual division of labor. Men and women had specific tasks, responsibilities, and spheres of influence and activity, and they rarely, if ever, crossed into each other's areas. Women's lives were defined by and revolved primarily around marriage, childbirth, and domestic responsibility. Yet social status was also significant in determining male and female roles and played a decisive part in defining Russian women's behavior and activities. Although patriarchy and male dominance still governed in all the classes, life for a Russian noblewoman was vastly different than it was for a woman of the peasantry or working class.[5] Among prerevolutionary Russian noble families the male head of household was the unquestioned authority, and a strict sexual division of spheres of activity and competence existed. Upper-class girls' and women's behavior, work, and options for the future were strictly limited to those activities deemed acceptable for females. Most young women remained in their parents' home until marriage and were educated primarily by their mothers, who prepared them for a life of domestic work and subordination to and dependence on males. Noble girls lived almost exclusively in a realm dominated by other female figures, whereas boys from approximately the age of seven came under male control.[6] Accordingly, women's activities were restricted to the private arena of the home and family. Without male protection, they were not supposed to venture into the public sphere. They were to ensure that their husbands and children were properly fed, clothed, and cared for while overseeing the day-to-day operations of the household. In practice, women of the upper classes played important roles in running estates, particularly when their husbands were away.[7] Beginning in the mid-nineteenth century, Russian women began to take part in affairs outside the home, but this involvement was limited primarily to charitable work, primary education, and nursing/midwifery. Even this limited and decidedly feminine activity was frowned upon by some who believed women should not operate in the public sphere in any capacity.[8]

The Russian peasant household was similarly organized around the authority of the dominant male figure (the *bol'shak*). Although the head of the household was usually the father, grandfather, or eldest son, widows sometimes assumed this role in the absence of competent adult males. There was a corresponding vertical line of authority extending from a dominant woman (usually the wife of the *bol'shak*) over all other women in the household. But women's roles in the working and peasant classes were quite different from those of the nobility and bourgeoisie. It was common for women in lower social strata to engage in heavy physical labor, both inside and outside the home. They worked in the fields, in factories, and as servants to the upper classes, and they often earned wages. However, the inclusion of women in burdensome manual work, especially where men and women toiled side by side, did not imply gender equality among the Russian working classes and peasantry. Nor was such labor unique to Russia; women in the predominantly peasant societies of most eastern European countries also performed hard physical labor. Moreover, there was a distinct sexual division of labor. Russian society valued male labor more than female work, both socially and monetarily. Certain jobs and even entire industries were reserved solely for men (usually the more skilled and higher-paying work). Other tasks (mainly unskilled and underpaid jobs) were regarded strictly as women's work. As with the upper classes, the sexes by and large did not intrude into each other's designated realms. And while it was acceptable—in fact, necessary—for women to work outside the home, they were also expected to take care of the household. Domestic tasks were regarded as the exclusive domain of women. Women were solely responsible for growing food in household plots, food preparation and preservation, cleaning, caring for livestock, collecting wood and water, cultivating flax and wool, and making and mending clothing. Peasant and working-class women who labored outside the home for additional wages thus had a double burden, toiling in the fields, factories, or sweatshops, then returning home to complete their domestic duties.[9]

Patriarchy in Russia was not absolute, however, and it did allow some limited freedoms and opportunities for women. "Russian women were able to reconcile themselves to the patriarchy by maximizing their power within the roles assigned to them," argues historian Christine Worobec.[10] Women had complete control over childbirth practices and were key players in arranging the marriages of their children. Russian legal tradition had long guaranteed women certain property rights. A wife's immovable property was considered separate from that of her husband, and she could do with it as she saw fit without interference from males. This was a right that Western women did not enjoy until the twentieth century.[11]

There were other exceptions to the strict prescriptions of gender roles and sexual spheres in Russia. From its earliest history, a few notable women were able to act in ways that were clearly outside the purview of social conventions that dictated female behavior. History is sprinkled with such examples, beginning with the first Christian princess of the Kievan state, Olga. Following the death of her husband, Igor, in 945, Princess Olga ruled the Kievan Rus' lands as regent for her underage son Sviatoslav. During her rule, she waged battle against a number of enemies and organized the defense of Kiev from invading nomads of the steppe. In fifteenth-century Novgorod, during the last decade of the city's independence from Moscow, Marfa Boretskaia, widow of the mayor, organized military campaigns to expand the city's territorial holdings. She was defeated as she led Novgorod's struggle to resist control by Moscow. Women's historian Natalia Pushkareva demonstrates that "Marfa Boretskaia was not the only Novgorodian woman who 'took on male strength,' as medieval sources describe forceful women. Novgorodian chronicles are full of the names of militant women, such as the boyarina Anastasia Grigorieva, who participated in uprisings and conspiracies that shaped the city's political history."[12] Peter the Great's older half-sister, Sophia, who reigned as regent during his minority, was a very strong figure noted for her "masculine attributes" of adept politicking and sound strategizing.

Peter's reforms had a profound impact in bringing exceptional women to the fore during the imperial period. He was followed by a succession of female rulers that lasted until the end of the century, including empresses Catherine I, Elizabeth, and Anna Ivanovna. The last, Empress Catherine II, "the Great," proved to be one of the most important political leaders of the eighteenth century. She was also an able military commander (although she did not participate in the field). In fact, the eighteenth century was one of overwhelming female domination of the autocracy. The empress's close friend, Princess Ekaterina Dashkova, also wielded a considerable amount of power and influence, becoming the first woman president of the Russian Academy of Sciences.[13]

Many other women, as well as some men, refused to accept the limitations placed upon women by the patriarchy of Russian society. In the nineteenth century, a movement advocating greater freedom and opportunity for women and equality of the sexes gained prominence in Russia. During the 1850s, the

"woman question," already in full circulation in western Europe, was introduced in Russia, and many, both women and men, began to consider ways to
improve women's position.[14] Those who supported this movement pressed for
greater access to higher education and professional opportunities for women,
and in the next decades they achieved a considerable amount of success in
these areas. Many women were able to travel abroad and study subjects previously off limits to them. Russia itself began to offer professional courses and
higher education for women in the later part of the century. Russia produced
some of the world's first women doctors, scientists, mathematicians, and other
outstanding scholars and professionals. With better education came an increasing unwillingness to submit to the restrictions placed upon them.

Women in Russia also became important members of the radical intelligentsia
and the revolutionary movement, even assuming significant leadership positions. They sought not only to improve the conditions in Russia through radical
and revolutionary political activity but also to create conditions of sexual egali-
tarianism. Many engaged in decidedly nonfeminine, aggressive, and violent activities as part of the terrorism that accompanied the revolutionary movement of
the late nineteenth century. Radical activist Vera Zasulich shot the governor
general of St. Petersburg after he had a political prisoner illegally flogged. Sofia
Perovskaia, leader of the revolutionary organization called the People's Will,
participated directly in the assassination of Tsar Alexander II in 1881.

Significant economic and social changes that affected Russia at the end of
the nineteenth and the beginning of the twentieth centuries also had an impact
on patriarchy. In particular, industrialization and urbanization brought changes
to traditional peasant life, to family structures, and to women's activities and
behaviors. Prior to World War I Russia was seemingly suffering from what historian Karen Petrone labels a "crisis of patriarchal authority."[15] The Russian
pattern of industrial development began with the temporary or seasonal migra-
tion of men to urban cites of industrial labor. There men found new opportunities for earning that gave them significant independence from the household.
This, coupled with agricultural reforms in the early years of the twentieth century that encouraged peasants to leave the control of the village commune and
establish independent farmsteads, led many young peasants to emerge from the
control of their parents and establish their own households. When young men
challenged the authority of their fathers, their wives often supported them, similarly desiring to be free from the domination of in-laws that put them at the
bottom of the family hierarchy. Moreover, with many men absent from the countryside, women were left primarily responsible for agricultural production. With
increased workload also came the opportunity for increased authority.

Women also began to move increasingly into urban areas in order to work in the factories. Some women found the means to achieve financial independence (although they simultaneously lost the protections afforded by the patriarchal household) and were able to engage in activities heretofore inaccessible to them.[16] Furthermore, as the working class became increasingly politicized, so too did many women laborers. Despite ambivalence and even hostility from male workers, women increasingly participated in the workers' movement as it grew in late nineteenth- and early twentieth-century Russia.[17] Barbara Clements affirms that "women of all ranks of Russian society were actively involved in the social and political turmoil caused by Russia's entry into the modern world . . . [and] the instability caused by rapid social change also made resistance [to patriarchy] more possible than ever before."[18]

It is also important to understand that while Russian patriarchy was similar in many ways to that in the West, there were some significant cultural differences in gender and sexual mores and attitudes. Most importantly, as Laura Engelstein demonstrates, Russian society was not permeated by prudish Victorian sexual values: "Victorian notions of sexual respectability and danger were questioned before they had a chance to take root."[19] Nor was the ideology of domesticity strongly present in prerevolutionary Russia. It had just begun to permeate the upper levels of Russian society at the end of the nineteenth and the beginning of the twentieth centuries. Yet it had not become ingrained and did not dominate the Russian outlook as it did that of western Europeans, and it had little impact on the lower social strata, the vast majority of the Russian population.

## THE STRONG-WOMAN MOTIF

Another important factor that contributed to the high number of women soldiers in Russia is the prevalence from earliest times of the strong-woman motif in Russian culture. Admiration for the powerful female is well documented. Vera Dunham explains that "'Russian womanhood' is remarkable in that it is a perceptible motif" that "extols that coherence and strength of the woman in a historical sequence and in divergent class settings."[20] By contrast, no such consistent tradition lauding male heroism can be detected in Russian culture. From earliest times, the image of the strong woman permeated Russian folklore, evidenced by the frequent appearance of the Amazon theme. Epics and popular ballads sing the praises of mighty female *bogatyrs* (warrior heroes) and warrior maidens who could even defeat men. For example, a popular ballad tells of Ilya Muromets, one of the greatest Russian epic heroes, being beaten by his own daughter. As historian Dorothy Atkinson confirms, "Folk literature preserves a whole rank of warrior heroines, the *polianitsy*, who might have been modeled on the Amazons. Some of these vigorous females, early Russian prototypes of women 'in black leather jackets,' are shown as possessing great physical strength. These are clearly positive heroines, but there are times when admiration of them seems tinged with masculine uneasiness."[21]

Throughout Russian history, peasant women in particular were valued for their strength and endurance. A young *muzhik* (male peasant) seeking a wife would invariably consider physical prowess and robust health among the desired characteristics in a mate, above those of beauty and feminine charm. The image of the strong peasant woman, in particular, the *boi-baba* (battle-woman)—the energetic, manlike woman—was a common female representation in Russian culture. This virago was a positive figure attributed with "a practical quickness . . . , a strong will, and a large dose of pluck and even cunning."[22]

Modern Russian literature is also replete with strong, independent heroines, women who possess moral superiority as well as the will and ability to act, set against male protagonists who are often indecisive and impotent. Although some authors presented their "strong" women merely as foils to male ineffectiveness, as literary scholar Barbara Heldt maintains, "the inadequacies and weaknesses of some male protagonists find their complementary awesome strengths in the young heroines of Russia."[23] One can find models of female power and will in characters such as Fedor Dostoevsky's Nastasia Filippovna, Leo Tolstoy's Anna Karenina, and Maksim Gorky's Pelagea Nilovna. Heldt further comments that "the Russian heroine is generally taken as a marvelous given of nature, a being in whom not only her own and her family's future, but the future hope of Russia resides."[24] Russian authors such as Nikolai Nekrasov, Dostoevsky, and Aleksandr Blok perceived and portrayed women as "a vital source of national salvation," according to Dunham.[25]

The facts that strong women were valued in Russia and that Russian women were afforded some freedoms and opportunities undoubtedly made it easier for some to become soldiers. Yet the limitations on women still existed. Even the strong woman was restricted within the patriarchal structure of Russian society. The positive aspects of the strong *boi-baba* figure were limited to the context of the family. Outside this context, she was seen as a disruptive force, challenging traditional social structures and patriarchy. Thus, when she pursued her own interests of individual preservation or development, she became an evil figure.[26] Women's strength was very often portrayed in Russian literature through the endurance of great suffering rather than through positive and heroic action.[27] The power and authority of women did not extend far outside the boundaries of familial concerns, and although their influence may have been felt indirectly through the men they reared, few were able to become players in politics or public affairs. Gender lines were still distinctly drawn, and most women remained excluded from many areas of Russian life. Combat was unquestionably one such area.

HISTORICAL PRECEDENTS

Another important factor that may have contributed to the large number of women soldiers in Russia during World War I is the existence of a number of historical examples of women serving in combat roles in that country's history. The woman soldier in Russia did not make her first appearance during the Great War. There are numerous examples of women participating in war and violent activities in Russian history, folklore, and oral tradition. The first references to women in the Russian lands are to Amazons.[28] Recent archeological excavations have provided significant evidence for the existence of women warriors in Pokrovka, on the Russian border with Kazakhstan, perhaps the originals on which the Amazons of Greek myth are based. Archeologist Jeannine Davis-Kimball found numerous women's bodies buried with weapons in Neolithic kurgans (burial mounds), some possessing wounds suggesting death in battle, leading her to surmise that women warriors roamed the steppe nearly 2,500 years ago.[29]

The Amazon tradition did not fade, asserts Barbara Walker: "In the Amazon's territory around the Black Sea, women retained certain Amazon customs up to the eighteenth century: dressing in men's clothes, riding horseback astride, and fighting beside the men in war."[30] Popular legend, reflected in Sergei Eisenstein's 1938 film *Aleksandr Nevskii*, features a young woman warrior, Vasilisa, fighting in the Novgorodian campaign against the invading Teutons in the thirteenth century. American historian John Alexander points to the frequent use of Amazon imagery and attire in the reigns of Catherine I, Anna Ivanovna, Elizabeth I, and Catherine II. He even goes so far as to label Russia's eighteenth-century female rulers "Amazon Autocratrixes."[31] Russian scholar Evgenii Anisimov perceives two primary female types in early modern Russian history: the Amazon and the suffering woman.[32] While this may be a convenient oversimplification, it does attest to the potency of the Amazon myth and the influence of the strong-woman image in Russian culture. In 1787, Prince Grigorii Potemkin formed an Amazon Company from a group of local noblewomen in the

Crimea. Although the function of the unit was strictly decorative, aimed at impressing Catherine the Great and the visiting Austrian emperor, Joseph II, its members were appropriately uniformed and armed.[33]

Aside from semilegendary associations and manifestations, there are a number of very real women combatants in the annals of Russian history. Russian military historian Iulia Ivanova asserts that women served as warriors from the earliest times in Russian history, hiding their true sex by wearing men's clothing and calling themselves by male names.[34] Some of the earliest accounts of Slavic society describe their females as warriors and hunters. Byzantine historians claimed that Slavic women dressed in masculine clothing and fought alongside their men in battle, and this has been substantiated by archeological findings of weapons in female gravesites.[35] Women such as Princess Olga were involved in the military affairs of early Russia at the highest levels.

The modern period offers us further examples of militant women. Aside from the empresses who engaged their nation in expansionist wars, many women participated directly in combat. Under Catherine the Great, a young Don Cossack woman named Tatiana Markina shed her female dress in exchange for a military uniform and joined an infantry regiment in Novocherkassk using the name Kurtochkin. Energetic and strong-willed, she managed to reach the rank of captain in a short period. Her brilliant military career was interrupted by the complaint of a colleague, who accused her of being a woman and threatened to bring her up on charges of breaking imperial law, which prohibited women from participating in the army as combatants. She appealed to the empress, who called for a medical examination. The woman captain was pardoned, but this ended her military service. She received a discharge and a pension and returned to her village.[36] Another woman, Aleksandra Tikhomirova, served in the Russian army at the end of the eighteenth and beginning of the nineteenth centuries. Her brother, an officer in the guards, was killed, and she, closely resembling him, took his place as company commander. She served for approximately fifteen years, until she was killed in 1807. Only then did her comrades in arms find out that she was a woman.[37]

During the Napoleonic Wars, numerous peasant women fought as partisans against the invading French armies. The best-known female participant in these hostilities is undoubtedly Nadezhda Durova, who became the first woman in the Russian Empire to hold an officer's rank as a woman. After a childhood spent dreaming of the romance and prestige of military life, in 1806 Durova, disguised as a man and using the name of Aleksandrov, entered the ranks of a passing Cossack regiment. She quickly mastered military skills, including shooting and reconnaissance. Between 1807 and 1812, she served with several

units, including the Polish uhlans of Grodno, the Mariupol' hussar regiment, a
Lithuanian uhlan regiment, and the armies of Alexander I. During her service,
her true sexual identity became known, but she was allowed to remain in the
army. She participated in a number of battles and important campaigns, and
news of her accomplishments soon reached Tsar Alexander I. She was given an
audience with the tsar, at which she requested the right to bear arms and serve
the fatherland. He allowed her to remain in the active army and conferred upon
her a medal of excellence for military service. Durova fought in the Battle of
Borodino, where she was wounded in the leg. Following her recovery, she was
promoted to the rank of staff captain and served as aide to Field Marshal
Mikhail Kutuzov until 1816. She retired with a military pension, and when she
died at the age of eighty-three, she was buried with full military honors.

Durova left a detailed account of her experiences in her memoirs; excerpts
were first published in the journal *Sovremenik*, with a foreword by Aleksandr
Pushkin.[38] Her story has since become part of Russian popular culture, being
the subject of numerous books, an opera (Anatoly Bogatyrev's *Nadezhda
Durova*), and a film (*Ballad of a Hussar*).[39] A popular novella entitled *A Daring
Life*[40] was based on Durova. Historian and translator of Durova's memoirs Mary
Zirin contends that the novella "set a generation of girls longing for adven-
ture."[41] It and a biography[42] of Durova were published in the years just prior to
World War I and probably influenced young women to join the fighting.
Durova's story was resurrected, although hurriedly and with many errors, by So-
viet authorities during World War II in an effort to attract women to military ser-
vice during that conflict.[43]

Women's participation in war reached new heights during the Crimean War
(1854–1855), when women were used for the first time as nurses both at the
front and in the rear. Although women had been employed in medical capacities during wartime since the time of Peter the Great, they had been restricted
to working as orderlies and housekeepers. Upon the initiative of Countess
Elena Pavlovna, sister-in-law of Tsar Nicholas I, and under the supervision of
noted surgeon and educator Nikolai Pirogov, auxiliary units of female nurses
were sent to the front during the Crimean conflict. Although there was much
opposition from the male military establishment to the presence of women in
the theater of war, even in the decidedly feminine capacity of caring for the
wounded, the exemplary performance of the female nurses won over most detractors and established a new precedent for the use of women in medical capacities during subsequent hostilities.[44]

There are also accounts of women fighting during this conflict, dressed as
men in order to enter the active army without opposition. Similar reports exist

concerning the Russo-Turkish War (1877–1878) and Russo-Japanese War (1904–1905). During the latter conflict, a woman calling herself Mikhail Niko-laevich, the daughter of one soldier and the widow of another, dressed in a Cir-cassian overcoat, trousers, boots, and an Astrakhan hat and volunteered for a Cossack detachment. Being proficient in Chinese, she proved instrumental in reconnaissance in Manchuria, as well as in negotiations with bureaucrats and suppliers. The wives of the commander of the 22nd Regiment named Gromov, of an officer of the mountain cavalry battery named Shchegolev, and of the su-pervisor of a division hospital named Makarov also served in this war.[45] A woman named Olga Jehlweiser also reportedly fought under General Pavel Rennenkampf during the Russo-Japanese War and later went on to participate in World War I.[46]

Women in prerevolutionary Russia also had a tradition of engaging in other kinds of violent activities, as previously mentioned. Numerous women played important roles in the Russian revolutionary movement, dating back to the 1860s. The women of the All-Russian Social Revolutionary Organization, who lived, worked, and propagandized in Moscow's factories, came to be known as "the Moscow Amazons."[47] Women's involvement in the revolutionary move-ment often assumed an acutely violent and nonfeminine character. Female rev-olutionaries often handled explosives and smuggled weapons, and many did not hesitate to use them in terrorist campaigns. Some, such as Ekaterina Breshko-Breshkovskaia, Vera Zasulich, and Maria Spiridonova, even carried out assas-sination attempts against officials of the tsarist government. The participation of several female revolutionaries, including Sofia Perovskaia, was vital in the assassination of Tsar Alexander II in 1881. Perovskaia, according to Richard Stites, was "the coolest and best fitted to oversee and carry to completion the long-sought murder of the tsar. On March 1, she arranged her look-outs and bomb-throwers in their proper places, and, from her post on the canal, gave the final signal for the fatal bombs to be hurled."[48] She was the first woman to be executed by the Russian government for a terrorist act. With a long history of female involvement in war and violence in Russia, it should not be altogether surprising that women fought during World War I.

Russia, moreover, is not the only country that possessed female soldiers. While social convention in most nations excluded women from combat partici-pation, many women chose not to accept these restrictions. In times of war, some women have understood their utility beyond the needle and the bandage, believing they could do more good with rifle and bayonet. Nearly every coun-try's history possesses cases of women, primarily disguised as men, entering the hostilities. During World War I, women in other belligerent nations participated

fields in great numbers. When millions of peasant men left for the front, female laborers quickly dominated agricultural work. By 1916, women made up an estimated 72 percent of the workforce on peasant farms and 58 percent on landowner estates.[4] This "feminization" of agriculture was threatening to many men. Although in Russia women had always performed agricultural labor, certain tasks were considered the exclusive domain of men. With the absence of so many able-bodied men from rural areas, women were left to do most of the traditionally "male" labor in the fields, denying men their special and unchallenged tasks in rural life.[5] Moreover, the absence of men left women in positions of authority in the village community.

Women entered the urban workforce as well, although at a slower rate and with more resistance from men. Initially, women found employment only in unskilled jobs, but soon necessity dictated their use in skilled areas as well. Thousands of women went to work in the production of armaments and military provisions. Thousands more became metalworkers. Women workers came to dominate in areas such as transportation and utilities. In Moscow, the number of female office employees increased by 80 percent.[6] Women became messengers, mechanics, chimney sweeps, streetcar conductors, mail carriers, police, janitors, carters, foresters, and truck drivers and filled other so-called men's jobs. In an attempt to facilitate the use of nontraditional labor in industrial production, the Russian government relaxed restrictions on labor by women and children (ironically, these restrictions had been designed to protect them). The number of women workers in Russia's industries increased by 38.8 percent during the war years, and by 1917 women composed nearly one-half of the labor force.[7]

Despite their vital contribution to production and labor, women in Russia continued to be severely underpaid, earning as little as 35 percent of male wages.[8] Moreover, they were exposed to "proletarian anti-feminism" from male workers who resented their presence in the labor force, especially those men in essential industries who saw female employment as a threat both to their jobs and to their exemption from conscription.[9] Using women workers was seen as a temporary measure required during a time of crisis. It was expected that women would return to more suitable female occupations, or even end their wage labor altogether, as soon as the war ended and men could adequately replenish the labor supply.[10]

In most of Europe, there was an initial outpouring of patriotic enthusiasm, at least among the educated classes, and many women, even traditionally pacifist feminists, expressed their support for the war effort. While some questioned the wisdom of embarking on such a destructive path, most women believed in their duty to support their nation in time of crisis, as well as their male loved ones who were fighting and dying. Advocates of the women's movement supported the war, perceiving their war-related activities as opportunities to demonstrate their worth to society and thus as a path to rights and equality.[11] In Russia, the scene was similar. Most women of the educated and higher social strata joined the initial nationalistic fervor, including a large portion of the women's movement, which had maintained a decidedly pacifist character prior to the outbreak of war.[12] Only a small portion of radical socialist women, primarily Bolsheviks, expressed staunchly antiwar sentiments.

Progressive women tended to view the war, which they expected to be short and not terribly destructive, as a positive event that could provide opportunities for greater activity by women in the public sphere. Like their counterparts in the West, they assumed their contribution to the war effort would have social, political, and legal rewards. Seeking to "present themselves as responsible citizens who recognized their obligations as well as their rights," women's organizations such as the Mutual Philanthropic Society and the League for Women's Equality were quick to express their support for the war.[13] The league called for a "women's mobilization" that sought to involve all of the women of Russia in war work. The organization's leader, Dr. Poliksena Shishkina-Iavein, appealed to the "daughters of Russia" to join the war effort: "We women have to unite: and each of us, forgetting personal misfortune and suffering, must come out of the narrow confines of the family and devote all our energy, intellect, and knowledge to our country. This is our obligation to the fatherland, and this will give us the right to participate as the equals of men in the new life of a victorious Russia."[14] Contemporary women's periodicals resounded with patriotic themes and appeals to their readers to devote themselves in service to the nation.[15] Response to such calls came primarily from middle- and upper-class women and female members of the intelligentsia, but some working-class women also contributed to the nation's war efforts. In this atmosphere, thousands of women undertook activities that they believed would meet the needs of Russia in its time of crisis.

Russian women worked in various capacities for the war effort. They joined voluntary organizations created to meet wartime needs. Women's groups around the country organized committees dedicated to "women's war work." The major women's organizations engaged in a variety of war-related endeavors, from military supply to caring for war victims, refugees, orphans, and prisoners of war. More than 30,000 women worked for the Union of Zemstvos (an organization of local government bodies that assisted in the war effort in the rear).[16] An entire journal dedicated to the topic of women and the war was established under the editorial direction of A. I. Iakovleva in March 1915.[17] Women volunteered their time, energy, and resources in activities such as sewing soldiers' clothing and linens, cutting bandages, making care packages for troops, staffing travelers' aid stations for soldiers in transit, and working in shelters, soup kitchens, orphanages, and other facilities for the homeless and disabled. Many of these efforts were hindered, however, by the lack of support and even hostility of the Russian government and bureaucracy to community efforts and grassroots participation. Suspicious of citizens' initiatives, authorities were "slow to appropriate funds to cope with immediate emergencies and showed themselves reluctant to relinquish bureaucratic control over Zemstvo and other civic organizations." Moreover, "the bureaucrats' distrust of all citizens' participation frustrated any attempt to solve pressing problems."[18]

One of the most popular forms of female service during the war was nursing, a tradition that had begun during the Crimean War but exploded in 1914. Upon the outbreak of the Great War, women rushed to volunteer their services as Sisters of Mercy, as Russian war nurses were called. Approximately 18,000 women served as nurses in Russia during the Great War.[19] The Empress Alexandra and her adult daughters, nieces, and cousins became nurses and even had a wing of the Winter Palace in Petrograd converted into a military hospital. Following the royal trend, many of the fashionable women of Russian society went to work as nurses, as did others from a variety of backgrounds: doctors, journalists, writers, students, and even Bolsheviks. In fact, the initial female response to the call for volunteer medical personnel was so overwhelming that many had to be turned away.[20] Enlistment in the Russian Red Cross as Sisters of Mercy was limited to literate women with at least some secondary education. Women's organizations strongly supported female participation in medical service because it was consistent with conventional conceptions of feminine nature: caring, nurturing, healing, and compassion—working to preserve rather than destroy life. Although officially nurses were supposed to remain three or four miles from the frontline positions in mobile field hospitals, many worked close to the trenches in regimental aid stations. Some even ended up serving in the trenches and on the battlefields. As stretcher bearers, female medical personnel were sent into no-man's-land to retrieve wounded soldiers, and many became casualties themselves.[21]

Women also performed a number of vital auxiliary services in the rear and at the front. Such women were not attached to the army but worked through civilian governmental organizations such as the Union of Zemstvos, which recruited them for war work. Peasant women were recruited to dig trenches for the troops. Women worked as cooks, supply clerks, drivers, and scouts both behind the lines and in the advanced positions. Women requesting to enlist in the active army were often given auxiliary duties rather than being assigned to combat service. Presumably the men making such decisions felt these positions to be less dangerous and somewhat (although only slightly) more suited to women than direct combat. For the most part, however, these activities were just as demanding and hazardous as combat.

In early 1915, the Zemstvo Union organized a Special Automobile Department to coordinate its work in automobile service. In May, the department established a school to train military drivers to serve at the front. In mid-July, the school began admitting women to its courses. Despite warnings from the union concerning the dangers involved in working so close to the fighting, 430 women applied to the courses. The physically unfit, undereducated, and underage were rejected, but 58 women were accepted (compared with only 28 men). After two months of instruction, the trainees had to take an exam. All of the female students passed. The test results more than justified the experiment of allowing women to become drivers: Although the men had slightly better physical skills, the women demonstrated superior technical understanding of the work and displayed enthusiasm and diligence that greatly impressed their instructors.[22]

Other women not affiliated with the union school also served as military drivers at the front. One such woman was E. P. Samsonova, who was Russia's first female pilot. Samsonova had a high aptitude for things mechanical, and she had left the Bestuzhev Higher Courses for Women in Petrograd in order to learn automobile operation and maintenance in Warsaw. After becoming an accomplished driver, Samsonova entered Russia's first school for pilots and quickly mastered flying as well. She then decided to devote herself entirely to flying, and in 1912, after much wrangling with the authorities, she was admitted to the military flight school at Gatchina. There she became a fully trained pilot and was soon thrilling audiences at the Moscow aerodrome. Her flare attracted much public attention.

When the war broke out, she immediately began training to become a Sister of Mercy. Simultaneously, she submitted a petition to the minister of war asking permission to serve in the active army as a military pilot. Her request was denied on the grounds of her sex. As a result of this rejection, Samsonova began work in a Zemstvo medical organization in Warsaw, but she soon became dissatisfied with nursing. Seeking to utilize her automotive skills, she went to the Galician front and convinced the commander of a motorcycle unit to accept her on a trial basis. After proving her abilities, she was soon admitted to an automobile detachment.[23] Over the course of four months, Samsonova served as a military

with invaluable information about their activities and reveal the war from a woman's perspective. Yet even these works are sometimes problematic as historical sources. In a number of instances, the women themselves were guilty of glossing over or leaving out elements they may have considered embarrassing or unfavorable. At other times, they exaggerated, euphemized, and even fabricated certain things in order to present themselves in a more favorable light. Nevertheless, they are still extremely useful in giving us insight into the experiences of the women soldiers.

As a result of the limitation of sources, uncorroborated by archival evidence, the task of making an accurate count of the numbers of individual women soldiers is very difficult. A contemporary account from the London *Graphic*, quoted in *Literary Digest*, put the number at 400 by mid-1915 but failed to reveal the source of this count.[30] There are no fewer than 50 recorded cases of such women, but the total number was most likely several hundred, perhaps even close to 1,000, as historians Ann Eliot Griese and Richard Stites estimate.[31] However, since the majority of these women soldiers fought disguised as men, most records that document the existence of female combatants reflect only those whose true sex was discovered, which usually occurred only after they had been wounded and were examined by medical personnel. Those who fought and were never wounded, or who died undiscovered, remain unknown to us. Therefore, one can only assume that there were others who served with the Russian armies but were never documented.[32] There were sufficient numbers of women soldiers whose true sexual identity was known to warrant reports from both Russian and Western commentators that the sight of female soldiers had become relatively common.[33]

Prior to May 1917, women entered the fighting as individuals or in small groups, becoming part of male regiments. As imperial law prohibited women from participating in the army as combatants, the majority became soldiers by cropping their hair, donning male clothing, and using masculine pseudonyms in order to pose as male volunteers. Those who enthusiastically requested to join the army voluntarily may have been accepted to compensate for less-than-eager conscripts, especially as the war dragged on, shortages of manpower worsened, and victory seemed to slip further away. The existing systematic recruitment regulations and mandatory medical examinations prior to enlistment were not always uniformly applied. As a result, it was possible for women to enter the Russian armed forces in male guise. Most avoided examination altogether by joining troops already en route to or at the front rather than signing up at enlistment centers. What is even more remarkable is that a number of women were admitted into the ranks without having to assume male identity.

The imperial statute prohibiting women from serving in the active army was not universally enforced. Enlistment was often left to the discretion of individual commanders, and women desiring to become soldiers were sometimes able to convince command personnel to allow them to join a particular unit. Even when women were discovered in male guise, they were often allowed to remain at the front by decision of the commanding officer.[34]

When all other attempts to gain entrance to the armed forces failed, one could always appeal to a different or higher authority. Petitions, letters, and appeals were submitted to the military authorities by hundreds of women desiring to fight alongside the men throughout the war. Numerous requests were sent to military commanders and high-ranking officials by women desiring to enter the ranks of the Russian armies. Some even appealed directly to the tsar for permission to enlist.[35] One such request was sent by a peasant woman from Siberia, Maria Bochkareva, who would become the most famous of Russia's female soldiers of World War I by commanding the 1st Russian Women's Battalion of Death in 1917.[36] Another petition came from Elena Iost, who explained in her letter to the tsar asking for his permission to enlist in the army that she burned to serve her country as a soldier because this vocation seemed most natural to her, despite its strangeness for most women. Invoking the historical figure of Nadezhda Durova, Iost wrote,

> I pray to Your Imperial Majesty to allow me to join the ranks of the troops with the same kind of noble and radiant outburst for the MOTHERLAND, with which the heart of Durova was filled and with which my own soul, filled with courage and fearlessness and unwomanly boldness, burns. . . . When I hear soldiers' song or see troops (the cavalry, I so, so love horses), I am transformed, everything inside brightens and rejoices, and at the sight of dashing soldiers my soul wants to leap out of my body, and I want to be among them and also be a defender of the Motherland, the sacred, dear, and unceasingly loved Motherland.[37]

Despite the somewhat lax and arbitrary enlistment procedures employed by the Russian army and the instances where exceptions were made, many women faced great obstacles in fulfilling their desires to become soldiers. They wrote letters and made personal appeals to the authorities asking for permission to enlist. They cajoled and threatened, used influence, and even begged. They sold the last threads of their own clothing in order to purchase uniforms and equipment. They risked and often endured arrest and prison in their attempts to join the active army. The significant numbers of women seeking enlistment did not, however, convince the military authorities to consider a change in policy toward female service. Instead, they generally continued to adhere to an arbitrary system by which requests by women were evaluated and decided on an individual basis.

The women who volunteered to defend Russia during the Great War came from every class, socioeconomic background, and educational level. They were aristocrats, upper- and middle-class students of secondary schools and higher-education courses, members of the urban proletariat, and peasants. They served in a variety of capacities, including in the infantry, cavalry, artillery, medical service (medics, stretcher bearers, and other frontline medical positions reserved for male soldiers), and reconnaissance. Military reconnaissance and frontline medical service were particularly common areas of service for women.

It is important to point out that most of the accounts of women soldiers detail their participation in activities that were largely supportive in nature. They carried shells and ammunition to male soldiers, they helped wounded soldiers off the battlefield, they performed reconnaissance and information gathering, and they were even assigned to medical duties despite lack of training in this area. While all these activities required the women to put themselves in very dangerous situations and risk their own lives, few reports speak of women actually carrying out violent actions against others. It may have been somewhat less disconcerting, both for the women themselves and, when their true sexual identity was known, for male personnel, to have women perform supporting tasks. Perhaps more importantly, it was undoubtedly somewhat easier for those reporting about the women soldiers to discuss their heroism in such terms. They were able to avoid directly confronting the issue of women in destructive, life-taking roles—which would have been very difficult for many journalists and their readers to accept—and incorporate women soldiers into the heroic narrative. Furthermore, those women who were awarded medals of distinction for courageous actions were mostly recognized for supportive roles. Thus, even in this decidedly male sphere of combat, women's activity and heroism were often framed in terms somewhat more compatible with traditionally supportive roles.

It is also important to note that contemporary newspapers and journals consistently related stories of women who were young and unmarried or who, if married, had accompanied their husbands to the front. Rarely do they speak of women with children or other familial responsibilities. Again, this self-censoring would have made female military service somewhat more palatable to readers. The public would have found it difficult to celebrate the heroism of a woman in the capacity of a soldier if they knew she had "abandoned" her duties as mother in order to take up arms. Yet there were women who did leave children or elderly parents behind to become soldiers. Tatiana Aleksinskaia, a Russian-born doctor who had emigrated to the West prior to the war but returned to help her native countrymen, reported encountering one such woman who had left two children in the countryside with her mother in order to join the ranks of the active army with her husband and her brother.[38]

Accounts of female combatants relate some remarkable stories. Russia's women soldiers were often portrayed as more enthusiastic, better disciplined, more courageous, and more self-sacrificing than their male compatriots. Command personnel frequently used high praise in describing their female soldiers. While men hesitated, women were often cited as volunteering for dangerous missions or being the first to rush from the trenches during attacks. Many were even awarded high military honors for their courage, including the coveted St. George's Cross. Those who served disguised as men may have felt compelled to perform especially well in order to avoid detection of their true sexual identity. Those whose true sex was known may have been careful not to err or malinger in their duties in order to escape gender-based criticism and rejection. Those who were reporting about them may have believed it necessary to show the women in the best, most heroic light in order to justify their precarious existence. Undoubtedly, women soldiers wanted (consciously or unconsciously) to demonstrate that they could successfully fulfill this traditionally male role and that they were "worthy" of being called soldiers. Perhaps even more significant is the fact that all women who participated in the Russian armed forces were volunteers. They willingly chose to risk their lives in the war, unlike the vast majority of conscripted males, who lacked the same zeal for the cause.

The primary motivation for most of the individual women to become soldiers was patriotic. Many displayed a strong sense of devotion to the homeland and passionately desired to defend their nation. One young woman soldier professed, "I have a strong, passionate desire to become a volunteer in the active army for the defense of our dear tsar and Fatherland."[39] These were common sentiments among Russia's female warriors. War propaganda that made the enemy appear demonic and bent on the destruction of everything they held dear contributed to their desire to fight.[40] "I must stand up for the motherland. . . . my heart burns for this," proclaimed another young woman soldier, Anna Alekseevna Krasil'nikova, the daughter of a miner from the Ural Mountains.[41] When the war began, Krasil'nikova asked the governor of her region for permission to enlist in the army. Her request was denied, so she decided to enter the ranks without official authorization. She cut off her hair, donned military attire, and boarded the first available military train bound for the front. Along the way she was discovered and had to disembark at the Vilna (Vilnius) station. Eventually, she reached Ivangorod (Deblin) in central Poland, where she managed to enlist as a volunteer in the 205th Infantry Regiment, using the name Anatolii Krasil'nikov.

Initially she was assigned to serve as an orderly, but she was sent to the trenches shortly thereafter. Krasil'nikova described her activities in the war theater as extremely arduous and dangerous but proudly proclaimed that she had never lagged behind and performed all duties required of the male soldiers. During the course of her service in the summer and fall of 1914, she fought in nineteen battles. On November 7, 1914, she was seriously wounded in battle. Her unit had been ordered to attack, but heavy artillery fire from the enemy caused the men to hesitate. Krasil'nikova dashed out of the trenches, which inspired the rest of the company to follow her onto the battlefield. She had not run more than a dozen steps, however, before a bullet struck her in the hip. Taken to a nearby field hospital and examined, her true identity was discovered. For her heroic actions she was awarded the St. George's Cross. She longed to return to the front after recovering from her wounds, expressing a strong desire to defend the homeland.[42] Many women were unsatisfied by the traditional roles of passive support or behind-the-scenes work assigned to women in wartime. "Women have something more to do for Russia than binding men's wounds," stated another female warrior.[43] They were convinced that they could serve their country better in combat.

The desire for excitement also inspired women to become combatants. For women who had spent their lives sheltered by parents and husbands and for girls living in all-female institutions, going to war provided a chance for independence and freedom of action that women could never experience in civilian life. Bored with their restricted lives, the war also offered them the opportunity to travel to places far from home. "I so wanted to see something different, a different forest, sky, city. . . . I wanted to go abroad, to see German cities," proclaimed one woman soldier.[44] Such motivations were not uncommon for many young women (and men) who volunteered for military service during the Great War. Many had overly romanticized conceptions of war and believed it would provide them with an escape from mundane, everyday life. At the same time, they felt the need to be useful to their country.

Some of Russia's youngest female soldiers fell prey to idealistic notions of war and the desire for adventure. Early in the war, a group of twelve Moscow schoolmates between the ages of fourteen and seventeen made up their minds to join the fighting by the eighth day of mobilization. They expressed the desire to "see the world and ourselves kill the Germans!"[45] At the end of July, the girls ran away from their homes without bidding their parents farewell. They reached the suburbs of the city, where they managed to convince soldiers of a passing unit to conceal them on a train bound for the front. The men complied and even provided them with military uniforms. When they reached the Austrian front, the regimental authorities were baffled and disturbed by the presence of these young girls in soldiers' attire. The girls were steadfast in their desire to fight and could not be convinced to return home. As a result, they were allowed to remain with the regiment.

One of the girls, Zoya Smirnova, gave a vivid and compelling account of their experiences at the front to a correspondent of the Russian daily, *Novoe vremia,* which was later published in the *New York Times.* While their first battle proved to be quite terrifying, especially for the younger ones, they soon adjusted to life in the trenches under heavy artillery fire. The young women spent fourteen months fighting together, and during this time they participated in a number of dangerous battles. They "shared with the men all the privations and horrors [of war] . . . and discharged the duties of ordinary privates." According to the Russian correspondent,

> The regiment traveled the whole of Galicia, scaled the Carpathians, incessantly participating in battle, and the girls never fell back from it a step. . . . The battles in which the regiment participated were fierce and sanguinary, particularly in the spring, when the Germans brought up their heavy artillery and began to advance upon us with their celebrated phalanx. Our troops underwent a perfect hell and the young volunteers endured it with them.[46]

Not all the young women survived the ordeal; one was killed by a German shell in front of her schoolmates. Smirnova herself was wounded twice; the second time she was left unconscious on the battlefield and was only found accidentally by stretcher bearers. Her wounds were so severe that she had to remain in a base hospital for over month. She was promoted to junior noncommissioned officer (NCO) and received the St. George's Cross for her bravery.[47] When she returned to the trenches after her convalescence she could no longer locate her regiment, which had already departed for another front. Smirnova now encountered strange faces in the trenches, and she became disoriented without the support and familiarity of her unit and her schoolmates. She lost her composure and began to weep, which soon gave away her sex. The officers of the new regiment persuaded her to exchange her soldier's uniform for that of a nurse. She never found out what had become of the rest of the young women in her former unit.[48]

Smirnova reported that the male soldiers treated the girls with ample respect and a heavy dose of protective paternalism. One gets the impression that these young women became something like mascots for the regiment. With their heads shaved and clothed in army fatigues, the female soldiers passed for young boys, and the men came to accept them as soldiers. At one point, Smirnova asserts that their assimilation into the male world was so thorough that the women adopted male surnames and even forgot their past lives in the feminine sphere. The men, however, never completely forgot that they were girls, continuing to guard their conduct in front of the female soldiers.[49]

Finding sympathetic men to assist them was often the key to successful enlistment in the active army for a number of women who became soldiers. In addition to the twelve girls described above, other women found male protectors and supporters to aid them in this process. An officer named Yakovlev acted in such a capacity for a young woman who wanted to join his unit, which was being sent to Galicia to participate in the fighting. He, along with the young woman's cousin, a lieutenant in the regiment, acquiesced to her persistent pleading to be taken with the unit to the front, despite what Yakovlev described as the difficulties associated with fulfilling such a request. He and his fellow officers were ambivalent about allowing the woman into their ranks, but they agreed to bring her along and not to reveal her true identity to the commander of the unit. They properly uniformed and outfitted her for service, and she accompanied the soldiers to the frontline positions. She soon found herself participating in combat and proved herself to be a courageous soldier. She even risked her life to return for a wounded soldier after her unit had retreated. Her brave deeds were reported to the commander, who soon learned of her true identity. Shortly thereafter, she was wounded by an enemy bullet and sent to the rear for medical treatment. The commander, however, agreed to allow her to return, despite her sex, after she had recovered.[50]

It was not uncommon for women-turned-soldiers to join the army in order to be with a loved one or family member. Women went to the front with or following the men in their lives: husbands, fathers, brothers, and lovers. Alexandra Braiko, a young peasant woman, volunteered for service in the regiment in which her two brothers had been conscripted when the war broke out.[51] Marfa Malko, the wife of a junior officer, fought alongside her husband until he was killed and she herself was captured by the Germans. She took part in three battles, captured a German flag at Sokhachev, Poland, and shot the two enemy soldiers who pursued her.[52] Another woman soldier, discovered in a Moscow infirmary in March 1915 lying next to her husband, had also followed her spouse into the army. When her husband, a student, was called up for service, she disguised herself as his brother and was accepted into his company as a medic. Their unit pursued the Austrians through the Kozenitsk forest and spent two days in the trenches under heavy enemy fire outside Czestochowa in southwestern Poland. When the unit went on the attack, this woman soldier followed the men into battle. Both she and her husband were wounded and were sent to Moscow to recover. It is interesting to note that although the other members of their company were well aware that there was a woman in their midst, they accepted her and even welcomed her presence as a source of encouragement and moral support.[53]

Some women who wanted to become soldiers clearly understood the social implications of their participation in combat and were thus motivated by the desire for greater opportunity for female action. In early 1915, a young woman named Vasia Fedorenko sent a letter to the Ekaterinoslav military commander requesting to enlist as a volunteer and to be sent to the front. She desperately sought to prove that "women also can fight, and just as well as men." In the letter, Fedorenko wrote, "Why are men given all the important responsibilities while women are assigned to kitchen work? Why does society so mistrust the intentions of women? Thousands of women could be fighting in the ranks of the Russian army. Why don't they trust that we, like men, can also take up arms and go to the defense of our motherland with honor and pride?"[54] Fedorenko's appeal was refused, along with those of two other young women from the Ekaterinoslav intelligentsia seeking entrance into the army, Lenia Matlakhova and Valia Shad'ba. This rejection did not deter them. The three decided to go to Tiflis (Tbilisi, Georgia) to appeal to the regional governor general of the Caucasus, Count Vorontsov-Dashkov, for permission to enlist in the ranks of the Russian army. They had read an article in the newspaper about the wife of a private who had written a letter to the governor general, stating, "I possess a deep, passionate desire to join the army, and I respectfully ask you to enlist me. I will faithfully serve."[55] Moved by this expression of patriotism, the governor general had allowed her to enlist.

The young women took up sewing garments in order to fund the journey. They finally managed to accumulate enough money to reach Tiflis and appealed to the military commander, who sent them off to the headquarters of the Caucasian Army. Fedorenko, Matlakhova, and Shad'ba were given an appointment with the duty general, who offered to enlist them as "frontier guards" but denied their request to be sent to the front lines. They were given Cossack accoutrements and equipment, and they cut off their hair and changed into soldiers' uniforms. The next day they took the first medical train headed for the front lines, but they were recognized on the train and arrested by the guards. They were released after relating their stories, but the next day the young women once again found themselves in the hands of the police. They had been standing on the main prospect during the tsar's arrival in Tiflis, but someone in the crowd noticed them and objected to their presence. They were arrested and held until the commander of the Palace Guard, Colonel Spiridonovich, freed them and took them to see the tsar. The three asked the tsar for his permission to be sent to the front, and he promised to review the matter. It is not known whether their request was granted or denied.[56]

A number of the individual women who joined the fighting were members of Russia's upper classes. The Petrograd women's journals were particularly fond of printing stories about society women turned soldiers. Women in higher social positions often used their influence and connections to enter the ranks of the active army. There were even some from the most prominent aristocratic families in Russian society, including princesses. One of the most interesting examples of an aristocratic woman who served in the Russian army was Princess Kati Dadeshkeliani, who published a memoir detailing her experiences in the war disguised as a male officer.[57] The princess was a member of the ruling family of Svanetia, a small province of Georgia. Her motives for joining the army were more personal than patriotic: She was seeking adventure and excitement in order to escape the depression caused by the murder of her father and the suicide of her younger sister. She entered the army using the pseudonym Djamal Dadeshkeliani, under the protection and tutelage of a family friend, Colonel Edik Khogandokov. She was assigned to the 4th Squadron of the Tatar Regiment, which was part of the Grand Duke Mikhail's so-called Savage Division, as an aide-de-camp to Khogandokov, who commanded the regiment.

Khogandokov taught Princess Kati the rudiments of military etiquette, and as a result she was able to pass for a young male officer. She was assigned as a cavalry courier stationed at regimental headquarters in Czortkow, in Galicia. Dadeshkeliani, with her lifelong experience with horses, had little difficulty performing the services required of her. In fact, she soon became bored with delivering messages and documents, despite the danger involved in these missions, which were often conducted under heavy enemy fire. She requested that she be transferred to the trenches for combat duty. Khogandokov was hesitant to send a woman to the front lines, but Dadeshkeliani persisted, and he finally relented. She spent a week in frontline positions in mid-1915. The princess's experiences in the trenches proved short-lived and disenchanting. It seems that

her perceptions of warfare prior to experiencing it firsthand were highly romanticized, and when confronted with the brutal realities of combat, she suc-
cumbed to fear and suffered from "paralyzing constraint."[58] She ascribed her
poor performance in the trenches to her sex and returned to regimental headquarters with relief after this short term of combat duty.

After returning from the trenches, Dadeshkeliani was assigned to an ambulance company stationed at Borszczow. She felt much more comfortable with
her duties in this capacity. "I never felt the same feeling of uselessness, of pow-
erlessness, or failing of duty, for in this work there was an abundant scope for
my womanly faculties as well as for my energy and my will-power."[59] She maintained her male guise, however, and continued to function successfully in this
role, serving in a medical capacity until mid-1917. A royalist, Dadeshkeliani
was quite unnerved by the February Revolution and refused to take the oath to
the Provisional Government. She eventually left the army in August 1917 and
rejoined her family in Petrograd.

While in the army, the princess had little difficulty emulating male behavior
and convincing others that she was a young man. She even managed to fool the
Dowager Empress Maria Fedorovna, with whom she had been granted an audience and who never suspected the young Georgian officer of being a woman in
disguise. Despite her inability to adjust to life in the trenches, she was not
averse to using violence. When threatened, she did not hesitate to use her fists
or her weapons to resolve conflicts. Although she retained her male disguise
throughout the war, she never seemed to relinquish her belief in separate
spheres for men and women. As Prince Djamal, Dadeshkeliani assumed a
conventional "gentleman's" role in her relations with women, acting as protective escort under the traditional presumption that women needed such
safeguarding.

Perhaps the irony that the "protector" was actually a woman did not occur to
the princess, as she never questioned the validity of her role. Nor did she seem
to realize that her military activities defied ideological conceptions of the sexual division of labor. She continued to attribute her failures in the trenches to
her membership in the "weaker sex," despite her ability to perform other male
tasks and cross gender-defined lines with relative ease. Dadeshkeliani never
resolved this underlying contradiction in her memoirs, but she made it clear
that she did not believe that women should participate in combat, declaring
that "a woman is not in her place in the fighting ranks, even when she is disguised, there is an atmosphere of weakness about her and the men will be in-
stinctively encouraged to spare her, to protect her, and their own action will
thereby be impeded."[60]

Dadeshkeliani was not the only woman officer in the Russian army during
the Great War. A twenty-nine-year-old woman identified only as Citizen Andreeva reached the rank of second lieutenant after participating in six battles
on the Austrian front. Motivated by a strong feeling of patriotic duty, she had
joined the army when the war broke out. She served in the same infantry unit as
her husband, the company commander. Arriving at the Minsk railway station in
mid-1915, she drew a large crowd of curious spectators, who barraged her with
questions. Andreeva was well versed in military tactics and made a positive impression on the crowd.[61]

Another woman officer of the Great War was Aleksandra Efimovna Lagareva
of Kiev, who enlisted in a regiment of Don Cossacks shortly before her eighteenth birthday. Lagareva, herself from a Don Cossack family, was reported to
have achieved the rank of lieutenant and was given command of a small detachment of men.[62] She and seven members of her unit were captured by the
Germans in the spring of 1915 and locked in an old church. While confined,
Lagareva overheard her captors discussing the fact that she was a woman and
feared abuse. She decided it was necessary to escape. She broke the window of
the church, climbed out, and killed the enemy sentry with a large stone. She
then released her men, recovered their horses, and, together with the small detail, captured a patrol of eighteen German uhlans near the Polish town of
Suvalki (Suwalki). The capture yielded some important military documents being held by one of the enemy soldiers, which Lagareva delivered to a Russian
general. For this feat, she was awarded the St. George's Cross. Unfortunately,
the sources of Lagereva's story made no mention of how the male soldiers responded to the authority of a female commander. But one report did relate that
upon discovery that he had surrendered himself to a woman, one of the uhlans
became extremely distraught.[63]

Many of the women who participated in the fighting in Russia during World
War I were students and members of the intelligentsia. L. P. Tychinina was a
student at the Kiev Higher Women's Courses who joined the war shortly after
the Russian mobilization. Her first request to join the active army was rejected,
despite her male disguise. Determined in her desire to go to the front, Tychinina engaged an orderly to tutor her in military matters. He taught her how to act
like a soldier and ensured that her second request for enlistment was successful. Entering the army under the pseudonym of Anatolii Tychinin (her brother's
name), her true sex was not suspected, although she looked rather young. She
boarded a train full of reserve troops headed for the German border and joined
an infantry company in the trenches. She took part in several important battles
as a medic. Her duties required her to go into no-man's-land to help wounded

soldiers, coming under heavy enemy fire. While performing this dangerous act, Tychinina was wounded six times and eventually was captured by the Austrians. Unconscious, she was sent to an enemy hospital for treatment. When she awoke, there was a crowd of medical personnel around her bed, staring in amazement at what they had just discovered to be a young woman. When the Russians counterattacked, the Austrians retreated, and Tychinina was rescued and sent back to Moscow to recover from her wounds. As she was recovering, she desired nothing more than to return to the front when her wounds had healed.[64] Her younger sister Natalia, a student at the Kiev gymnasium, also enlisted, and for her heroic part in the Battle of Opatov she was awarded the St. George's Cross.[65]

Kira Aleksandrovna Bashkirova, a sixth-class student of the Vilna Mariinskii Higher Women's Courses, also served as a soldier in the Russian army during World War I. She disguised herself as a scout in order to be accepted into a reconnaissance detachment. She participated in several important and dangerous reconnaissance missions but was not satisfied with this kind of service. Bashkirova volunteered for a Siberian infantry regiment in December 1914, maintaining her masculine guise and using the pseudonym Nikolai Popov. She was assigned to cavalry reconnaissance and after her courageous performance in a mission on the night of December 20, she was awarded the St. George's Cross. Soon afterward, however, the officers of her regiment discovered her true identity, and she was sent home to Vilna with a letter of commendation that allowed her to retain her medal despite her sex. Yet Bashkirova would not accept this as the end of her military career, and instead of returning home she volunteered for another regiment. After fighting several battles with this new unit, she was wounded and sent to a field hospital, where her true sex was once again revealed.[66]

Maria Smirnova, a graduate of the Novocherkassk Women's School, also participated in the fighting, serving on the East Prussian front. At the beginning of the war, Smirnova decided to join the army in order to defend her country. She disguised herself in male clothing and presented herself to the military commander of Novocherkassk as Sergei Smirnov, asking to enlist in the active army. Thanks to her masculine appearance, she was able to enlist as a male volunteer and became an infantry soldier. Smirnova participated in many battles and bayonet attacks. During one particularly fierce engagement with the Germans, she was wounded and evacuated to Rostov for medical treatment. Physical examination revealed Sergei Smirnov to be a young woman, but this did not deter Maria from desiring to return to the front as soon as she recovered.[67]

Other women soldiers came from the peasantry and working classes, and their stories appeared in the pages of contemporary periodicals together with the reports about the society women who served. One such was Ekaterina Alekseeva, a nineteen-year-old domestic servant of peasant origin. Alekseeva sold her clothes to buy a soldier's overcoat and presented herself to the commander of her local reserve battalion as Aleksei Sokolov, requesting permission to join the fighting. A strong and stocky physique allowed her to pass for a young man, and she was accepted into the ranks without question. She was soon sent to the front, where she participated in a number of battles. During one such engagement, she suffered a severe head wound, and when she was examined in the hospital, her true sex was discovered. In the course of her conversation with a reporter from *Zhenskoe delo,* Alekseeva provided insight into her motivations for joining the army and becoming a soldier. The young peasant woman revealed that, in addition to strong patriotic sentiments, strong religious beliefs provided an impetus for her to fight with Russia's "Christ-loving army." She maintained that it was her faith that gave her the strength and determination to go into battle.[68]

Another young peasant girl, sixteen-year-old Alexandra Ivanovna Shirakova, also served in combat and was wounded in battle. Shirakova was working in a tailor's shop in Moscow when the war broke out. Having access to the necessary materials, she made herself a set of male clothing. With her hair shorn and wearing masculine dress, she was able to pass for a teenage boy despite her small build. She joined an echelon en route to the front, enlisting under the name of Sasha Shirakov. On the way to the front lines, she was taught basic combat maneuvers and how to use a rifle. She was assigned the task of delivering shells to the company. On numerous occasions she was required to carry out this activity under heavy enemy artillery and gun fire. As a result, the male soldiers came to regard her as brave and deft.

After serving at the front for three months, she was traveling with her unit to a new position when she fell from an unstable bridge into a stream. She became ill and was evacuated to Moscow for medical treatment. When she was examined by the medical personnel, her true sex was discovered, and she was placed in a separate ward. Interviewed by a correspondent of the Russian daily *Russkiie vedemosti,* Shirakova reported that none of her comrades in arms had guessed her true sex. When asked about her combat experiences, she replied that "at first it was frightening, but then it was nothing to be surrounded by falling bullets, with the hissing of shrapnel in the air, with the explosion of 'suitcases' [artillery shells] nearby, but then you stop paying attention to them, it becomes such a common occurrence."[69]

Antonina Tikhonovna Pal'shina was another representative of the lower classes who served in the Imperial Russian Army during World War I. Born in the Sarapul' region to poor peasants, Antonina held a variety of jobs until the war broke out in 1914. At the age of seventeen, she disguised herself as a man, calling herself Antonin Pal'shin, and went to the Turkish front, where she enlisted in the 2nd Caucuses Cavalry Regiment. After basic training, she was dispatched with her unit to the front lines and participated in a number of battles until she was wounded and, upon medical examination, her true sex was revealed. She did not give up her desire to fight, however, and after recovering made her way to the Austrian front. But before she could join a new unit, she was apprehended at the railway station and accused by the gendarmes of being a female spy. She managed to escape this predicament and returned to Sarapul', where she enrolled in medical courses to become a nurse. She completed this training in April 1915 and was sent to the southwestern front to serve outside the city of Lvov. Unsatisfied with this work, and unable to stand the frivolity of her fellow nurses from the privileged classes, Pal'shina decided to make her way back into the active army. She took the uniform and equipment of a male soldier who had died in her care, cut off her hair once again, and made her way to the front, where she was accepted into a new unit. She was wounded twice in the course of her service with this second unit and received four military awards, including two St. George's crosses, fourth class, one of which was pinned upon her personally by the commander of the southwestern front, General Aleksei Brusilov. She was also promoted to the rank of junior noncommissioned officer. After her second wound, she was recovering in a rear hospital near the city of Kiev when the February Revolution occurred. She did return to military service, but after the establishment of Bolshevik power, Pal'shina went to work for the new regime. She served in the Sychevsk executive committee beginning in 1918, and then in 1920 she went to work in the Cheka (Extraordinary Commission), the first incarnation of Soviet political police.[70]

Many of the women who joined the fighting were athletes, and others were naturally inclined to physical prowess. One such woman was a famous sportswoman, Princess Kudasheva, who served on the front lines in the capacity of a military scout. Kudasheva was highly regarded in Siberia and central Asia for her sporting skills and enlisted in the active army, bringing her favorite horse with her.[71] In fact, a number of the women who joined the armed forces were experienced equestrians, making them good candidates for cavalry reconnaissance. M. N. Isaakova was another accomplished sportswoman who fought with the Russian army. Her athletic skills included climbing, fencing, and horseback riding, and she was credited with great physical strength. When the war began, she decided to join the cavalry. After obtaining a good horse, she applied to one of the standing Cossack regiments in Moscow for acceptance in the ranks of the volunteer regiments but was refused. Isaakova then acquired the necessary soldier's paraphernalia, including a rifle, and went to Suvalki in Poland. She requested permission to enlist in a Cossack regiment stationed there, and this time was accepted.

While participating in an attack on a German cavalry unit, Isaakova was wounded and evacuated to Petrograd, to St. George's Hospital, where her wounds required surgery. After recovering, the young woman soldier went directly back to the theater of war and joined a Cossack reconnaissance unit. She spent days in the saddle, riding through rain and sleeping on dirty straw, and took part in six important reconnaissance missions. During a battle at Łódz in late 1914, the Cossack unit in which Isaakova was serving received an order to reconnoiter in the region of Skernevitsa (Piskierniewice), where a unit of German dragoons attacked the Cossacks. A skirmish followed and the Germans were pushed back. In an attempt to protect their own men, a German battery opened fire. Isaakova lost consciousness after being hit by a piece of shrapnel and was taken prisoner at Łódz. After three days, the Germans made a hasty retreat from Łódz, leaving the wounded Russian prisoners behind. Safely back among Russian troops, Isaakova was evacuated to Moscow and awarded the St. George's Cross, fourth class, for her brave deeds.[72]

A number of women volunteers came from military families and must have been no strangers to the martial life. The daughters of Colonel Tomilovskii were given soldiers' uniforms and sent to the advanced positions after requesting to serve on the front lines in September 1914.[73] One of the colonel's daughters distinguished herself in battle on the East Prussian front near Augustowo. She was hit by enemy fire on three occasions, but she remained at her post despite her wounds. Tomilovskaia was charged with command of a squad of men to carry out reconnaissance. In this capacity she managed to intercept a telegram from a German commander that detailed the time and place of an impending attack, and the Russians were thus able to thwart it.[74] Olga Petrovna Khabich, the wife of a colonel in the Russian army, served in an artillery unit and received two St. George's crosses for her brave soldiering.[75] The daughter of the commander of another artillery unit, identified only as Citizen B., went off to join her father's troops dressed in the uniform of a private. She participated in several battles under heavy bombardment in the Augustowo forest and was also awarded a St. George's Cross for her courageous feats in combat.[76]

For some women, the desire to become a soldier was the result of masculinized socialization—such as being the only girl in a family of men, losing their mothers and being raised by their fathers, or similar circumstances—that led them to feel more comfortable in the male sphere. Such was the case with Aleksandra Pavlovna Alekseeva. Alekseeva had been trained to tame wild animals and had learned to shoot very well, to climb, and to engage in other outdoor activities. She wore male clothing and had a number of male affectations. She had desired to serve as a soldier in the Russo-Japanese War but was unsuccessful in attempting to enlist. When World War I began she was in Rostov and volunteered for a local regiment. Her male dress and characteristics enabled her to enlist under the name of Alexander Alekseev.

For Alekseeva, it seems the transition to military life was not very difficult. She was assigned to reconnaissance duty and quickly proved herself very adroit in this capacity. Her bravery and ability soon became renowned. A journalist from the newspaper *Vremia* heard a tale of a courageous scout named Alekseev, considered to be one of the best in the army. "Alekseev" had been wounded in a battle with the Turks, and so the journalist went to the field hospital where "he" was being treated. Upon his arrival, he was astounded to discover that "Alekseev" was actually a woman. She appeared masculine, however, with her hair shaved off and a weather-beaten, pockmarked face. Her demeanor was also decidedly male, and she used the masculine grammatical form when speaking about herself. When asked whether she was afraid of being captured by the Turks, Alekseeva answered, "Afraid of what? What could the Turks do with me?" This is one of the few references to potential capture in the stories of the women soldiers, but there is little indication that the idea that female prisoners of war would possibly be subject to gender-specific treatment was of great concern. The journalist then asked her whether she would return to the front after recovering from her injuries, to which she replied, "Where else would I go? I am already used to it there."[77]

Some women found retaining the masculine guise difficult, and as a result, a number were discovered or revealed their true sexual identity without being wounded. The story of a young soldier named Vasilii is demonstrative: "Vasilii" had carried out all the necessary functions of a soldier, and his brave actions in some extremely perilous reconnaissance missions had earned him the St. George's Cross as well as other medals. After one particularly dangerous assignment, he was lying in the trenches when suddenly he jumped up and exclaimed, "Oh, mama, mama, a rat!" This caused his comrades to burst into laughter. "Here is some hero," they jeered, "heroic cavalryman, but afraid of rats!" Vasilii went into hysterics and was taken to the infirmary, where it was discovered that "he" was actually an eighteen-year-old woman who had taken her fiancé's documents to enter the army. After recovering, she was sent to the

nearest Red Cross post to be trained as a medical assistant.[78] Anna Khrisanfova, a twenty-one-year-old peasant girl, ran away from the Kazan convent
where she was a novice in order to join a passing echelon of soldiers on its way
to the front. Khrisanfova was discovered, despite her shortly cropped hair, soldier's uniform, and military bearing, and sent back to her native village of
Nodlenov.[79]

Even after being discovered, women tried to remain in the ranks. Although
they persisted in their attempts, many were turned away by the military authorities. However, rejection by the authorities did not necessarily mean women
were unable to serve. Sometimes they merely needed to make their requests to
another official or to try to slip into the ranks of another unit unnoticed. In the
fall of 1914, Alexandra Danilova, the wife of a reservist from Kazan, cut her
hair short, dressed in soldier's attire, and appealed to the mayor of Baku for
permission to enlist in a local regiment. Her request was denied, but apparently
she did not let this failure deter her. She was discovered in the ranks of another
unit after fighting and being wounded in a battle in Galicia.[80]

Upon being discovered, many of the disguised women soldiers were sent
home or were encouraged to take up a more "feminine" war service, such as
nursing. In April 1915, three young women were discovered in an infantry regiment on the western front disguised as male soldiers. They were disarmed and
sent back to their homes. One of the women was Alexandra Rodianova, the sixteen-year-old daughter of a gold miner from Tomsk. Another was seventeen-
year-old Alexandra Bykova, the daughter of a bureaucratic official from
Kostroma. The third was Alexandra Latkova from a Petrograd petit bourgeois
family. Dressed as scouts, they had entered the regiment as it passed through
Warsaw en route to the front. Before being discovered, the young women had
gone through the full course of combat training and had engaged in several battles.[81] Private Ivan Lomov, a machine gunner in a Siberian regiment, was revealed to be Ekaterina Lomova. Another machine gunner, Private Ivan Gubin
of the Tiflis Grenadier Regiment, was not who "he" appeared to be but was, in
fact, a young woman named Natalia Gubina.[82] In Odessa, authorities found sixteen-year-old Vera Besedina, the daughter of a clerk, in a reserve regiment
dressed in her brother's military uniform. She had run away from home and entered the unit with the intention of joining the active army. As they marched to
the front she had dislocated her foot, and when the young soldier was given
medical attention, her true identity was revealed. She was sent to the Odessa
Regional Society for the Defense of Women, which sheltered her until she
could be returned to her home.[83]

Not all the disguised women were removed from combat positions upon discovery of their sex, however. In many cases, since they had proved themselves

worthy and capable soldiers, such women were allowed to remain in the ranks. Some women managed to conceal their true sexual identities for the duration of their service. There were also those, such as Elena Konstantinovna Shutskaia, serving under the name Leonid Shutskii, who remained undetected until being killed in battle.[84] Furthermore, significant numbers were accepted into units and served as women.[85]

It was not uncommon for the women who became soldiers in Russia to come from Cossack families, particularly of the Don, Zaporozhian, and Kuban groups. Cossacks were warriors by tradition, and their militaristic culture influenced both men and women. Strength, courage, horsemanship, and combat skills were highly valued by both men and women in Cossack communities. Moreover, women in Cossack society often enjoyed greater freedom of action and participation in the public sphere than other women in Russia. Because Cossack men were often away on military campaigns, women had long been responsible for making decisions and acting independently of their husbands in many aspects of community life, from defense to agricultural production to village governance to property ownership.[86] As a result, Cossack women often had the skills and opportunity necessary to become soldiers. Likewise, many of Russia's women soldiers served in Cossack units, which may have been more inclined to accept female volunteers into their ranks than others because of the difference in women's roles within their society.

Examples of Cossack women soldiers abound, including Elena Choba, a Kuban Cossack, who began the war serving as a nurse. When her husband was called up in the initial mobilization, she herself applied to enlist in military service as a volunteer. Choba was known in her village as a dashing horsewoman, displaying great bravado at trick and fancy riding, experienced at handling swords and daggers. Cutting off her hair and dressing in a Cossack uniform, she went to Ekaterinodar, where she appealed for permission to enlist. Her request was granted by the ataman in the fall of 1914, and she was sent to the frontline positions.[87] At the end of September 1914, another Cossack woman, from Astrakhan, eighteen-year-old Tatiana Grigoreevna Kaldinkhina, appeared before the military commander of Astrakhan with the request to enlist as a volunteer. Initially he refused to grant Kaldinkhina's request but later agreed, and she was sent to frontline positions. Having lived among German colonists, she had a good command of the German language, and as a result she was often sent to take part in reconnaissance missions. Kaldinkhina was awarded two St. George's crosses, third and fourth classes, for her excellence in reconnaissance. After her last mission, she was promoted to the rank of senior NCO. While scouting, she was wounded by shrapnel in the left leg and sent for treatment to a rear hospital.[88]

The story of another Cossack woman soldier, Margarita Romanovna Kokovt-seva, circulated in fashionable circles of Petrograd and Moscow and even reached the pages of the American press.[89] In an interview with a correspon-dent of *Birzhevyia vedemosti*, the young woman explained that her desire to serve her homeland in battle was so strong that she ignored the admonitions of her family, dressed herself in male clothing, and set out for the eastern front early in the war. Having reached the headquarters of a corps, she presented her request to join the army and, appealing to the general, was allowed to enlist as a volunteer. She brought her own horse with her, and when the officers saw her skill on horseback, she was assigned to a Cossack reconnaissance unit. As she commented to the correspondent, "I love to ride and at home I had my own horse which I alone cared for. . . . A Cossack is a Cossack! Horses are part of us."[90]

Kokovtseva was awarded the St. George's Cross after being wounded in a bat-tle at close quarters with a group of German cavalry. She and nine other Cos-sacks faced more than twenty enemy troops. During a volley of shots between the two groups, Kokovtseva was shot in the head and taken back to the regi-ment by her Cossack comrades. She refused medical treatment until she could make a full report of her reconnaissance and then was sent to a nearby field hospital. "In order to keep my spirits high I sang my favorite song, which imme-diately ended the pain." After a few days recovering from her wound, she de-sired to return to the frontline positions. She was now even more determined "to struggle against the enemy together with the Cossacks."[91]

Kokovtseva told a Russian reporter in mid-1915 that among Cossack soldiers she felt "equal among equals." Her relations with the men were quite good. "Oh, don't you believe," she told the correspondent, "what people say about the frivolity of Cossacks, about their rudeness in relations with women—it's just a fairy tale—about the possibility of offending the weaker sex." The Cossacks, she reported, treated her politely and straightforwardly.[92] Kokovtseva's motives for fighting did not include any desire to integrate women into the military. When asked about the idea of creating units of "amazons" for the war, the young Cossack woman responded negatively. "Well no, I am against this. . . . first of all they [women] quarrel too much among themselves. A woman lieu-tenant would never accept the authority of a woman colonel. Second, military formation was not like dancing a quadrille." Kokovtseva was no feminist; she seemed to possess no inclination toward the expansion of women's rights and opportunities in general. The reporter explained, "She was not one of those who believed that the redemption of women lay in equal rights, and she considered herself to be an accidental exception in the kingdom of women."[93]

Another Cossack woman who fought in a male unit was Marina Iurlova. A Kuban Cossack from the Ekaterinodar area, she left a detailed memoir of her experiences in both World War I and the Civil War.[94] Although it may be suspect as a historical source, since it was published a number of years after the events, her account provides an interesting portrait of her life as a young girl in wartime. She joined a Cossack regiment in the Caucasus at the age of fourteen in the early days of the war, in 1914, after the first mobilization calls. Making no attempt to hide her sex, she did conceal that she was the daughter of a colonel, for fear she would be sent back to her family, and therefore used the name Maria Kolesnikova. Iurlova joined the army almost by accident, without any premeditation. Swept along with a group of women who wanted to follow their conscripted men during the initial mobilization, she ended up on one of the military trains headed to a training camp. She convinced the commander of a Cossack *sotnik* (hundred) to allow her to stay on in the unit as a sort of mascot, on the pretext that she had come to the front to find her father, an enlisted man. Under the wing of a large Cossack named Koslov, who became her protector, she remained in the company caring for the horses. With her hair shorn and in uniform, she was accepted as a boy, although she did not consciously try to disguise her sex. She drilled with the men and trained to be a soldier.[95]

Remarkably brutal in its depictions, Iurlova's account, although somewhat sensationalized, is unlike the romanticized pictures painted by others; it portrays all the horrors of war and its devastating effect on human beings. She openly criticized the senseless waste of life, as she watched the rank and file used as cannon fodder by command personnel as if they were nothing more than expendable beasts of burden. The male soldiers are alternately described as crazed with the taste for blood, numb to the horrors they witnessed and carried out, frightened of being killed themselves, and resigned to their fate. Why she wanted to join the army, or why she stayed after enduring hardship and depravation, she never explained.

During her military service, Iurlova was awarded the St. George's Cross twice for acts of bravery. She dismissed her military honors as undeserved, since on both occasions she was commended for experiences in which she did little but survive when most of the men around her were killed. In the second incident, in late 1915, she was buried alive while shells rained down on her comrades in arms. Although she came out of this horrible experience alive, she was in severe shock. Forced to lie still for hours under piles of dirt and manure, she listened to the screams of those dying around her, paralyzed with fear that she would be killed as well. Following two months of recuperation in the hospital, Iurlova enrolled in an automobile school in Tiflis. Although the male students were amused that she was a girl, they treated her with respect because she possessed two St. George's crosses. While completing her studies, she often moonlighted as a chauffeur for officers to earn extra money. The officers of the upper classes found her an interesting conversation piece and introduced her as a curiosity to high society. Iurlova found this attention unwanted and resented being treated as a party novelty.

After completing the automotive courses, Iurlova went to Erevan, Armenia, in mid-1916 to join the Red Cross. Her experiences were bleak and gruesome, as the town was suffering from a severe famine. Most of her time was spent burying the dead in mass graves. During the spring of 1917, she heard a rumor that the tsar had been overthrown, but she had no confirmation of its veracity. Other rumors claimed that the Russians were being sold to the English to fight as slaves and that the war was being deliberately lost. In August 1917, her unit went into battle, still unaware of events in the capital.[96] By this time, she reported in her memoirs, she had seen so much horror and bloodshed and had become so detached and disillusioned that she was indifferent to what was happening around her or what might come to pass. She was shelled while transporting wounded men to a field hospital and lay deaf and paralyzed in her hospital bed in Baku. From there she was sent to Moscow for further treatment. Her journey to Moscow was secured by another soldier-protector, Mikhail Vereshchenko. Recognizing that she was a woman, he ensured her a place on the crowded train and escorted her all the way to the doors of the hospital. She spent a year in the Moscow facility and was evacuated to Kazan in September 1918. In Kazan, surprisingly enough, her name appeared on a list of soldiers that the Bolsheviks compiled for training in the Red Army. After refusing to declare her loyalties to the new government, stating instead that she had no party affiliation and took no sides in the political disputes, she was arrested and imprisoned.

Iurlova was freed from imprisonment by Czechoslovak troops, who had joined the White forces and driven the Bolsheviks from Kazan. She served with the Czechoslovaks and was shot in the shoulder and sent back to the hospital in Kazan. Once again, she was forced to evacuate when the Bolsheviks retook the town. She ended up in a hospital in Omsk, Siberia. One of the Czechoslovak officers with whom she had served had taken a liking to her and "rescued" her from the Omsk hospital. He gave her some money and sent her on to Vladivostok to be treated in an American hospital. She made her way to Kharbin and was admitted to a hospital where she was placed in the women's ward for the first time in her military career. She felt very ill at ease and was not sure how to act around other women. Eventually, she left Kharbin and moved on to Vladivostok, where she finally reached the American hospital.

Iurlova describes her relations with male soldiers as rather brusque. For the most part, they seemed to want to have little to do with her, aside from the few who served as her protectors and the even fewer that took romantic interest in her. Nor did they treat her with any disrespect. Only after she began to develop noticeable feminine physical attributes did she receive some degree of sexual attention, although even this was rare. The experience of puberty was quite difficult for the young girl, having no other women available to help her through the confusing changes she underwent. She was extremely naïve about sex and did not develop a conception of herself as a female until much later in life. When an officer made a pass at her, she was baffled by his actions. "I was a soldier. Not a girl," she commented.[97]

This thought seems to encapsulate the experience of the majority of women who joined the army during World War I. Even when they did not disguise themselves, they seemed to at least temporarily abandon their female identity when they became members of male units. They invented new genderless or even masculine conceptions of themselves. They cut their hair, donned military uniforms, and abandoned all outward indications of their femininity. A number of these women soldiers reported that their transformation was so pervasive that they themselves "forgot" their true gender. They even began to refer to themselves by their male pseudonyms and used the male grammatical form in their speech. The essential masculinity of war dictated that these women temporarily became men in order to function successfully in the realm of warfare. Moreover, their combat activities seemed more acceptable to the public when they sublimated their femininity, making it possible to celebrate them as heroes despite their gender transgressions.

The relative ease with which a number of the women soldiers assimilated into the male realm may have been indicative of their sexuality. One can only assume that at a least some of these women were homosexual. Of course, none of the sources address this issue directly, making any conclusions regarding sexuality purely speculative. There are a few subtle hints, however, in some of the memoirs left by women soldiers. Maria Bochkareva reported visiting a brothel with her comrades in arms, urged on by the men, who exhorted her to "be a real soldier." To their great surprise, Bochkareva accepted their invitation, ostensibly out of "curiosity" and a desire to "learn a soldier's life so that I understand his soul better." At the brothel, Bochkareva allowed a prostitute to sit on her lap and even to be left alone with her. Her encounter was cut short, however, by an officer who was supposedly policing the premises for soldiers who had broken barracks discipline by leaving without permission.[98] She further relates an incident in which she openly "flirted" with a middle-aged peasant woman and even tried to kiss her, ostensibly for the amusement of her fellow soldiers.[99]

As the war dragged on, especially after 1915, stories about women combatants become less and less prominent in the press, perhaps because they lost sensation value as the frequency of encountering such women increased. As the presence of women in the ranks of the Russian army became more common, the press may have lost interest. One may also speculate that the military authorities may have tightened their control of the enlistment process after finding that so many women had been able to slip into the ranks unlawfully. The continued losses and hardships of the Russian army and concomitant waning of patriotic enthusiasm for the war as the conflict dragged on could also have influenced women's desire to enlist. The decrease in media coverage may indicate that the movement by women to enlist in the army had lost momentum and had begun to taper off somewhat, but it does not mean that women in Russia ceased combat participation. Although fewer in number, reports of individual women soldiers continued through 1916 and into 1917. The February Revolution and its consequences precipitated a renewal of patriotic spirit and desire to aid the war effort. The women's military movement, as well as media interest, would be revitalized in a new form in the summer of 1917 with the creation of all-female military formations. At that point, most women desiring to serve their country as soldiers became part of these units. But the phenomenon of individual women soldiers in male units continued throughout 1917, and was carried on into subsequent conflicts in Russia and the Soviet Union.[100]

# 3

## RUSSIA'S FIRST ALL-FEMALE COMBAT UNIT

By the spring of 1917, the phenomenon of individual women joining existing army units would give way (though not completely) to the creation of separate, all-female military formations. The formations were established both through the efforts of grassroots women's groups and under the auspices of the Russian military administration. More than fifteen such units were created in the spring, summer, and fall of 1917, and more than 5,000 women volunteered for their ranks.[1] The organization of these sexually segregated units can be partly attributed to the activities of Russia's women soldiers who served as part of male units. Indeed, a number of experienced female veterans who believed strongly in the power of women on the battlefield were involved in these formations. Yet it was the distinct political and social conditions that arose after the fall of the imperial government that made the creation of all-female military units possible. In particular, the increasing instability of the army, which the ruling powers seemed unable to curb, and the introduction of new political and social freedoms provided fertile ground for the development of the women's military movement in Russia in 1917.

### THE STAGE IS SET: THE FEBRUARY REVOLUTION

On February 23, 1917 (March 8 by the Western calendar), the women of Petrograd took to the streets for International Women's Day. Their march soon turned into a widespread bread riot as workers from the city's factories turned out to join them. Tsar Nicholas II ordered the disturbances put down by force, but the troops called on to subdue the upheavals turned against their imperial master and sided with the protestors. By February 28, the capital was experiencing a full-scale revolt, as hungry and war-weary citizens voiced their dissatisfaction with the autocracy. The tsar had little choice but to abdicate, for both himself

and his young son, in favor of his brother, the Grand Duke Mikhail. The grand
duke refused to accept power. Thus ended over 300 years of autocracy. Historian William H. Chamberlain described the collapse of the Romanov dynasty in
Russia as "one of the most leaderless, spontaneous, anonymous revolutions of
all time."[2]

Following the abdication Russia was proclaimed a social democracy. As
such, the Russian people were to determine their own future through the convening of a Constituent Assembly, composed of democratically elected representatives. The Constituent Assembly was delayed until internal conditions
could be stabilized and the population had sufficient understanding of their
rights and responsibilities as free citizens. This required time, but in the in-
terim it was necessary to make arrangements for some kind of acting government. A new, Provisional Government was therefore formed, comprising the
left-leaning and centrist parties of the former State Duma (parliament). This
government, as its name suggests, was intended to be temporary and transi-
tional. All but one of its members came from the liberal bourgeois parties;
Alexander Kerensky, who became the new government's minister of justice,
was the only socialist. The other members of Russia's radical and revolutionary
parties initially refused to participate in what they perceived to be a "bourgeois
government." Instead, they simultaneously created the Petrograd Soviet of
Workers' and Soldiers' Deputies, modeled upon the organization established
during the 1905 Revolution.[3] The executive committee of the Petrograd Soviet
was initially dominated by Social Revolutionaries and Mensheviks and included a small number of Bolsheviks. Since Marxist ideology held that there
would be a period of "bourgeois democracy" prior to the achievement of the socialist revolution, the majority of socialist members (Mensheviks and Social
Revolutionaries) of the Petrograd Soviet tolerated the existence of the Provisional Government. The Soviet agreed to support the Provisional Government
as long as it adhered to a socialistic program. The two entities were to coexist in
an arrangement of "dual power," wherein they would cooperate and share the
responsibilities of governance.

Yet "dual power," remarks historian Sheila Fitzpatrick, "proved an illusion,
masking something very like a power vacuum."[4] Although the situation was not
ideal, the Provisional Government recognized its dependence on the Soviet for
support from soldiers and workers and thus accepted the arrangement as a part
of the revolution. The Provisional Government and the Petrograd Soviet dis-
agreed on many key issues, and each exercised authority independently over
various areas of Russian society. While the Provisional Government held sway
over the ministries and executive organizations, the army high command, for-

eign trade, and war production, the Petrograd Soviet had extensive control over the garrison troops, railways, post and telegraph offices, factory committees, unions, and local housing authorities.[5]

In addition to the political uncertainties that followed the fall of the monarchy, Russia was facing a number of other tangible problems that proclamations of freedom and democracy could not resolve. The Russian economy was faltering badly. The country suffered from rampant inflation, labor shortages, work stoppages, and deficiencies of food and fuel. Much of the population, particularly in Petrograd, was embittered by years of autocracy and rebellious against authority in general. All of this contributed to general unrest and seemed to push the nation close to the brink of anarchy.

The most pressing problem facing the new leadership was the all-encompassing war in which Russia had been embroiled for three long years. The members of the Provisional Government, as well as most of the Russian elite, were convinced of the necessity to continue prosecution of the war. They believed that Russia could still emerge from the war victorious and in fact that this was necessary to ensure the survival of the country. Historian John Thompson affirms this view: "At the time, inertia, the lingering effects of patriotism, a concern for national survival, and a sense of duty to Russia's allies all combined to make it unthinkable, both for the leaders of the new government and for many among the revolutionary crowds, that Russia should withdraw from the war."[6] Many were convinced that Russia's previous failures in the war were a result of the tsarist government's incompetence and mismanagement of the war effort. Now that Russia was "free" and had a representative government that truly stood for the interests and the will of the people, they believed that the war could be conducted effectively and successfully.

The Provisional Government essentially adopted the war policies and aims of the previous tsarist regime, including the territorial annexations and war indemnities laid out in previous agreements between the Great Powers. For the Petrograd Soviet, the issue of the war was more complex. At heart, many of its members opposed what they considered an imperialistic war. Yet only the Bolshevik minority condemned further participation in the war outright. The Mensheviks and Social Revolutionaries, who controlled the Soviet at this time, supported the war effort. They believed that the struggle had to be continued, since a withdrawal from the war before a general peace was achieved might facilitate the victory of the Central Powers in the West and leave Russia vulnerable to be overrun by the kaiser's armies. Moreover, they reasoned that the internal stability of the country would be jeopardized should Russia withdraw from the war, for they worried that without the external conflict the army would be transformed into what historian Richard Abraham terms a "meaningless mob, useless, restless, irritable, and therefore capable of all sorts of excesses,"[7] and anarchy would ensue.

The Petrograd Soviet recognized that "the weakening of the army and a decline in its fighting efficiency would be a most serious blow to the cause of freedom and to the life interests of the country."[8] The members of the Soviet were unwilling to leave Russia defenseless against attackers and thus saw the need to at least hold the line until Germany stopped its attack or had a revolution of its own. The Soviet did not support Russia's original war aims, which had included territorial and monetary compensation to a victorious Russia, and instead pressed for a policy that renounced annexations and indemnities and hoped for a speedy conclusion to the hostilities. The Soviet did, however, agree with the Provisional Government that the best way to end the war was to deliver a final, decisive blow that would rout the enemy and allow Russia to withdraw from the hostilities as victors.

It was questionable, however, whether the Russian army was in condition to undertake a new offensive. The military structure had been seriously compromised and had been experiencing disintegration long before 1917. Relations between officers and soldiers were severely strained, a problem that had long existed in the Russian army, coming to the fore during the Russo-Japanese War and the subsequent Revolution of 1905–1906 and indicating that the potential for mutiny was very real.[9] The soldiers' disaffection was largely the result of the patriarchal structure of the army, which made sharp social distinctions between officers and soldiers. Reflecting the nature of the tsarist hierarchy, soldiers were treated like children by officers and were denied privileges such as smoking in public, riding trams, attending theaters, going to parks, and eating in restaurants. The paternalistic role of officers was even reflected in the way they addressed their soldier charges, using the familiar form of the pronoun "you" (*ty*) rather than the respectful form (*vy*), further reinforcing the soldiers' inferior and childlike position.[10]

The Russian army continued to suffer from strained officer-soldier relations during World War I, and this problem was accompanied by numerous other serious difficulties. Elements such as war-weariness and declining morale had existed for some time among much of the rank and file. The majority of conscripted peasant-soldiers had failed to identify with the government's war aims from the very beginning of the conflict. Nor did they share the patriotic fervor initially displayed by the upper levels of Russian society. In general, they entered the war with low morale and skepticism about the conflict. Although there was little resistance to mobilization in the summer of 1914, most scholars agree this was more due to peasant resignation to a lifetime of service than to patriotic conceptions of defense as national duty.[11] Even the elite's original enthusiasm for the war had begun to wane by the end of 1915, following the demoralizing defeats suffered by the army and once it became clear that the war would not be short and victorious.

The retreats of 1915 and the heavy losses incurred as a result of the Brusilov Offensive in the summer of 1916 further contributed to the army's troubles. Desertion was a particularly serious problem. It has been estimated that more than 500,000 men deserted in the first year of the war alone.[12] Insubordination had reared its head more than a few times in the Russian army prior to the February Revolution. "Entire companies, like some in the 55th Siberian Rifle Regiment in December 1916, simply refused to go into battle and 'fled to the rear' when ordered to do so," maintains historian Allan Wildman.[13]

Despite these problems (some of which, it should be noted, were also being experienced in the armies of other belligerent nations), the Russian army maintained its cohesion even through the political turmoil of early 1917. In fact, certain areas and units were largely unaffected by the forces of disintegration. Following the February Revolution the majority of Russia's soldiers retained an essentially defensive stance, unwilling to abandon their positions and allow the enemy to break through the front.[14] This attitude allowed the command structure to retain some semblance of authority, albeit temporarily, and in a truncated, democratic, and representational form, in areas where discipline had become problematic. The soldiers were willing to hold the line while the new government negotiated a peace settlement to end Russia's participation in the conflict. But they were much less willing to go on the attack. And as time went on with no sign of peace, many soldiers' patience began to wear thin. By the late spring, the situation had begun to deteriorate dangerously in some areas of the front. Problems were particularly serious on the northern front, where the troops became increasingly radicalized and were influenced by Bolshevik antiwar agitation. Attempts to restore order had been largely ineffectual with most of these troops, among whom lack of discipline, declining morale, collapse of authority, and fraternization with the enemy were significant problems.

In March, the Petrograd Soviet issued Order Number One. This resolution, which historian Bruce Lincoln has called "the most fateful document of the February Revolution," was produced as a power play by the Petrograd Soviet in order to win the support of the soldiers of the Petrograd garrison. It promised the soldiers better treatment and greater representation, gave them rights as citizens, allowed them to create committees to represent their interests, outlawed corporal and capital punishment for insubordination and desertion, and gave the soldiers' committees control over all weapons. Moreover, it ensured soldiers' loyalty to the Soviet by declaring that orders of the Provisional Government could be carried out only when they did not conflict with those of the Soviet.[15] Although initially intended only for the soldiers of the Petrograd garrison, the order was soon spread throughout much of the army. The dissemination of Order Number One significantly changed the relations between soldier and officer and the nature of the hierarchical structure of the military. Soldiers were no longer required to address their superior officers with traditional terms of respect such as "Your Excellency," and officers were forbidden to use the familiar grammatical form "*ty*" with their underlings. Command personnel could not use traditional methods of enforcing discipline, which now were either illegal or proved ineffective once soldiers were granted the rights guaranteed by the new order.

While the order sought to eliminate many of the soldiers' strongest grievances and the most hated elements of the patriarchal structure of the army, it created conditions in which discipline and cohesion in the ranks became increasingly difficult to maintain in some units. Highly mistrustful of their officers, who tended to come from the upper classes, many soldiers, who were by and large conscripted peasants, were quick to condemn their commanders for sympathy with the old regime. Violence against officers became a serious problem after the February Revolution.[16] The institution of soldiers' committees was also troublesome to internal order and discipline. Although these committees were intended to represent soldiers' interests in all matters but military operations, they were sometimes used to question superiors' orders and avoid participation in dangerous maneuvers. So while the troops maintained their "defensist" stance, willing to hold off attacks against Russia, many were not willing to go on the offensive themselves.

This attitude was not pervasive throughout the army, but in certain areas it was significant enough to warrant serious concerns on the part of command personnel as to whether the soldiers would fight when the time came to go on the attack. Many of Russia's soldiers were "uncharacteristically reluctant," asserts historian Louise Heenan: "The army had changed: its institutions had been altered, its regulations drastically modified, and its soldiers distracted by thoughts of land and peace."[17] In some areas, desertion rose as soldiers interpreted their newly granted rights and freedoms as a chance to leave the war and return home in search of new opportunities. The strongest impetus behind the peasant-soldiers' abandonment of the front was to obtain land of their own, to which they believed they were entitled now that the old order had been overturned. Mutinies in certain units became more frequent, sustained, and violent. As General Mikhail Alekseev, commander in chief of the Russian Army, commented shortly before his dismissal in mid-May 1917: "The internal rot [in the army] has reached its ultimate limit. . . . The troops are no longer a threat to the enemy, but to their own fatherland. Admonitions and appeals no longer have any effect on the masses."[18]

Some units, particularly some Caucasian and Cossack regiments on the southwestern front, retained their internal integrity and continued to obey commands, but other units were experiencing this decomposition to a serious degree. News from the capital was often slow to reach the front, but the troops were neither isolated from nor indifferent to the political situation in the rear. The reaction of the peasant-soldiers varied by region, with those in the north becoming more radicalized than those in the south, but many perceived the February Revolution as a force that would free them from the oppression of tsarism, which included forced conscription into the army.

During the months following the February Revolution, contemporary public opinion interpreted the military situation as extremely dangerous. The army was thought to be teetering on the brink of total disintegration. In particular, as Wildman asserts, desertions created tremendous "public anxiety over the health of the army . . . primarily because the consequences of desertion were visible (or thought to be so) in every major center." This perception existed even in the early spring of 1917, when units at the front "barely noticed desertion, and in percentage terms it had little effect on fighting strength."[19] There was great anxiety over the seeming inevitability of a new German offensive against Russia, which many believed the army in its weakened state would be unable to repulse. Pro-war forces often purposely exaggerated the problems at the front to make the situation seem more desperate and enlist greater public support for the war effort. At the same time, however, many citizens hoped that, with a new government supposedly working for the "true" interests of the Russian people, the spirits of the troops could be raised sufficiently to allow offensive to proceed.[20]

Despite these serious problems facing the army, the Provisional Government resolved to follow through with the new offensive intended to crush the enemy once and for all and to extract Russia from the war "with honor." The offensive had been planned in collaboration with the Allies prior to the fall of the tsarist government, when Allied leaders met in Chantilly, France, in November 1916. In fact, the Russians had been actively preparing for the attack, strengthening the front in the early months of 1917.[21] The new ruling powers in Russia were determined to live up to their commitments, despite the Allies' failure to deliver on promises of financial and material support. Originally, the offensive was to have been carried out in early spring 1917, but Minister of War Alexander

Guchkov cautioned that it would be impossible for the army to be ready for such an undertaking even by May. The offensive was therefore postponed until mid-June. It was clear, however, that the entire effort would be a colossal failure unless the morale of the troops was extensively revitalized and command obedience was restored.

But morale in the army was not the only problem facing the new government's war policy. Having to share dual power with the Soviet severely limited the Provisional Government's ability to act. The tenuous political situation was exacerbated by the public release of Minister of Foreign Affairs Pavel Miliukov's April 18 note to the Allies in which he reiterated that Russia's war aims still included annexations and indemnities. This sparked angry protest from the Soviet, which had insisted that the war be concluded without "domination over other nations, or seizure of their national possessions, or forced occupation of foreign territories."[22] The note also set off a wave of protest demonstrations in the capital that took on an antiwar and anti–Provisional Government character. This so-called April Crisis led to the resignation of Miliukov and Guchkov and threatened the existence of the Provisional Government. To salvage itself, the Provisional Government agreed to a coalition with some members of the Soviet, which, on May 2, voted to allow its members to participate in the cabinet. On May 5, a new coalition government was formed. Alexander Kerensky was appointed the new minister of war. His primary task was to rebuild the army's fighting capacity and prepare Russia for the upcoming offensive. As Kerensky himself explained, "For the sake of the nation's life it was necessary to restore the army's will to die."[23]

It was clear, however, that significant preparations to ensure the army's fighting capacity had to be undertaken in order for the offensive to be successful. The government and military authorities now made the revitalization of the army their top priority in the months preceding the June offensive. They embarked on a massive pro-war propaganda campaign at the front and in the rear. They printed agitational literature, held pro-war demonstrations and rallies, and distributed gifts to the soldiers in the name of the Supreme High Command staff. In speeches and printed appeals, they invoked the "sacred" duty of every Russian citizen to participate in the defense of the nation. Even the All-Russian Congress of Workers' and Soldiers' Deputies appealed to the nation to organize all available resources to aid the homeland.[24] The progovernment press published article after article seeking to raise public support. Volunteers were trained as "lecturer-enlighteners" and sent around the country and among the troops to boost morale. A host of leading public figures, including deputies of the State Duma, ministers of the Provisional Government, heroes of the war and revolutionary movement, and other prominent individuals, were enlisted to make rousing patriotic speeches at the front. Minister of War Kerensky personally went to the front on numerous occasions, along with other emissaries of the Provisional Government, imploring the soldiers to obey their commanders and continue the struggle.

Despite his great skill as an orator and his political credibility among the soldiers as the only socialist minister in the government, Kerensky's effect on the troops was limited, and he was not able to motivate the troops to engage in any sustained action. His patriotic speeches and impassioned pleadings managed only to generate ephemeral bursts of patriotic zeal. Such enthusiasm rarely lasted longer than Kerensky's brief visits to the front and dissolved quickly once enemy fire was felt again. The desire for peace seemed to overwhelm any and all attempts to inspire the army to action, and the troops could not be sufficiently motivated to engage in sustained fighting.[25]

As it became apparent that these efforts were not having any prolonged success and as the matter became more urgent with the offensive drawing closer, the authorities became increasingly willing to resort to more unconventional methods to achieve their goals. Special shock units composed of the most dedicated and enthusiastic officers and soldiers at the front were created in the spring, designed to be the first troops to go over the top and lead others into battle. General Aleksei Brusilov, commander in chief of the southwestern front, had successfully used shock units as a strategy to break through enemy lines during the 1916 offensive. Therefore, he believed they could be successful in providing leadership and examples of heroic action for those soldiers who were hesitant to fight. In mid-May, Brusilov also proposed the formation of "revolutionary" units, including special "shock" detachments and "battalions of death," from volunteers drawn from the rear. He had been pitched the idea by a groups of soldiers and sailors associated with the Left Socialist Revolutionary Party who were convinced that units composed of the most dedicated and patriotic volunteers, taken from the rear as well as the front, would be effective in "leading by example" and demonstrating to the wavering troops the true meaning of duty.[26]

These units were to be composed of officers and soldiers from service, auxiliary, reserve, and other units located in the rear as well as from military schools and academies. Civilians were also to be included in these volunteer units. In fact, recruitment for the revolutionary units was to be extended to a wide segment of the rear population, including students, workers, members of the intelligentsia, and all Russian citizens who had not yet been called to service or who had been exempt.[27] To coordinate these activities, the All-Russian Central Committee for the Organization of Volunteers for the Revolutionary Army was

BALTIC

SEA

ESTONIA

*Lake Peipus*

■ Pskov

NORTHERN FRONT

LATVIA

●Riga **TWELFTH ARMY**

Dvinsk ● **FIFTH ARMY**

LITHUANIA

Smolensk ●

Vilno ●

Smorgon
Krevo ☼ **TENTH ARMY**

☒ Molodechno

Mogilev
■ **STAVKA**

Petrograd ●

*Masurian Lakes*

■ Minsk

**WESTERN FRONT**

**SECOND ARMY**

● Warsaw

● Brest-Litovsk

**THIRD ARMY**

POLAND

**SPECIAL ARMY** Kiev ●

**THE RUSSIAN FRONT, SUMMER 1917**

Front in June 1917

■ Front Headquarters

☒ Tenth Army Headquarters

☼ Location of battle of 9-10 July, in which Bochkareva's battalion participated created in the spring of 1917 under the leadership of a Socialist Revolutionary, Captain Mikhail A. Murav'ev.[28] This organization also had seventy separate regional committees that were charged with recruiting volunteers for the revolutionary units. The central committee received funds from the treasury to carry out agitational activities in order to attract enlistees.[29]

The creation of revolutionary units, particularly the shock and death battalions, received widespread support on the home front, where many believed that such formations could provide the necessary impetus to restore the fighting spirit of the army. But members of the military establishment were more skeptical as to the value of these units. A number of prominent representatives of the Russian military leadership believed that the creation of volunteer units from the rear was unwise. Supreme Commander in Chief Mikhail Alekseev and others were worried that taking troops from other units would compromise those units' staffs and make them ineffective. Alekseev also did not want to siphon badly needed resources away from existing units to create these new ones. Using civilians further vexed him, as he considered them politically and military unreliable and unprepared for frontline service.[30] Even the use of shock units formed from frontline soldiers and officers created opposition.

Among the soldiers at the front the reaction to such units appears to have been somewhat negative as well. The futurist writer Viktor Shklovsky was a soldier in an armored-car regiment during the war, and he attested to the general dislike of such units by the troops. In a view reflecting the persistence of social antagonism in the army, he complained that shock units "hurt the unity of the army and made the highly mistrustful soldiers fear that now certain special units were being created to act as policemen. The most loyal committee members were against the shock troops. They got on the soldiers' nerves; it was said that they received a big salary and had special privileges."[31] Shklovsky further expressed his belief that such units were counterproductive, as they removed the best, most enthusiastic, and often most intelligent men from the ranks of regiments experiencing problems of decay, which was exactly where they were needed most, in his opinion.[32]

Despite his concerns, Alekseev allowed Brusilov to experiment with such unit on his front.[33] Minister of War Kerensky approved their use in the upcoming offensive, and when Brusilov was appointed supreme commander in chief he ordered such units to be created throughout the army.[34] These revolutionary volunteers and shock troops were to be organized into special battalions, strictly disciplined, highly trained in special "storming tactics," intensely loyal to superior officers, and sworn to fight to the death.[35] They were also supposed to refrain from drinking while in service.[36] Such formations would lead attacks in an attempt to "arouse the revolutionary, offensive spirit in the Army" and would "carry along the wavering elements inspired by their example."[37] They would bear their own insignia: black-and-red chevrons on their sleeves and skull-and-crossbones emblems on their caps, symbolizing dedication to the revolution and willingness to die for the motherland. All members of the revo-lutionary battalions swore undying loyalty to their superior officers, accepted the strictest of discipline, and took an oath to fight until death for the freedom of Russia. These special volunteers were to be dispatched to the front as soon as possible, in order to have maximum effectiveness in the offensive.

A number of the new revolutionary units were given the designation of "bat-talions of death," indicating both that they would be fatal to the enemy and that they were willing to fight until they lost their own lives. The volunteers swore "never [to] be taken prisoner alive," "never [to] fraternize with the enemy," and "never [to] allow their spirits to fall, believing that my death for the motherland and for the freedom of Russia is happiness and the justification of my oath."[38] Preexisting units were also designated as units "of death" when they pledged similarly to fight to the last drop of blood and to be the first into battle when called. In all, during the summer and fall of 1917 approximately 100 such units were created.[39]

The civilian population, particularly the liberal-democratic members of the educated elite, also sought to assist in this effort of revitalizing the army and augmenting it with dedicated revolutionary troops. A number of quasi-military and grassroots volunteer organizations were created with the goal of revitalizing the fighting spirit of the army. Such organizations were intended to reinforce the troops as well as to carry out propaganda work and boost the morale of sol-diers at the front. The League of Personal Example was established to carry out propaganda for the newly forming volunteer army. Its leaders, veteran revolu-tionaries Lev Deutsch and Vera Zasulich, traveled the country with an en-tourage of pro-war agitators, distributing propaganda and delivering rousing patriotic speeches in order to drum up support for the war among both the civil-ian population and the army. The eminent British scholar of Russia, Bernard Pares, was in Russia attached to the British diplomatic mission and was one of the league's founding members. Most of the other members were, according to Pares, "young volunteers who had been in charge of so much of the most daring work at the front and in No Man's Land."[40] This organization appealed to citi-zens of Russia to give their service for the nation:

Save the motherland—she is being killed! Save the army—it is falling apart! The troops are dwindling! There is no discipline. The military spirit is dying! Soldiers! What will you say to your children when they ask you,

"Father, where were you when the Germans enslaved Russia?" All who do not want to be slaves must fight to the death for the freedom of the motherland. We call upon you to devote yourselves to strict discipline, to go to the enemy and defeat him![41]

The All-Russian Central Committee for the Organization of Volunteers for the Revolutionary Army similarly aimed its efforts at "everyone who holds dear the fate of our motherland."[42]

As part of the effort to create a revolutionary army, volunteer military formations of various compositions were created all over the country. There were units made up of escaped prisoners of war, disabled veterans, members of non-Russian nationalities, and holders of the St. George's Cross, among others.[43] The idea was to enlist the support of every citizen, able-bodied and even not so able-bodied. Everyone was expected to contribute to the war effort, and this included women. Therefore, such organizations sought to actively involve women in war work. Another group that actively sought to involve women in military affairs was the Military League. This organization established a Women's Volunteer Committee in charge of organizing "women's war-work detachments" to employ women in specialized auxiliary military functions, for example, as telephonists, telegraphists, drivers, electrical technicians, clerks, topographers, and medics.[44] Those behind such organizations believed that women had a special role in the effort to revitalize the army and that they had a great moral influence that would be strongly felt by men.

Women formed their own quasi-military organizations as well, such as the Women's National Military Union of Volunteers, and similarly appealed to members of their sex to put their energies into the war effort. The newly established Women's National Military Union of Volunteers encouraged women to go to the front to assist in the all-important task of raising national consciousness among the soldier masses. The group addressed Russian women with the following call, published in a number of prominent Petrograd periodicals:

Women citizens, all to whom the freedom and happiness of Russia is dear, hurry into our ranks—hurry while it is still not too late to stop the collapse of our dear motherland. By directly participating in military activity, we women citizens must raise the spirit of the army and carry out educational-agitational work in its ranks, so as to convey a logical understanding of the duty of free citizens to the homeland.[45]

Women's participation in the war effort increased considerably during this period of renewed dedication to the war. The February Revolution had given a boost to women's organizations, which had been revitalized and were expanding since the beginning of the war. These groups appealed to women throughout the country to devote their energies to helping the war effort. Progressive women's organizations such as the League for Women's Equality and the All-Russian Women's Union (Anna Shabanova's former Mutual Philanthropic Society) became involved in various war-related activities. A number of prominent women lobbied the government to create a Women's War Work Commission within the Ministry of War.[46] A proposal to relieve the massive shortages of medical personnel by calling on all women doctors under the age of forty-five for military service was submitted to the Ministry of War.[47] Publications about women heroes from the past, including Nadezhda Durova, the woman officer of the Napoleonic Wars, appeared in bookstores all over the country in an effort to inspire women to similar patriotic activity.[48] In this atmosphere, serious consideration of recruiting women for military service began to circulate in Russian society.

The idea of creating women's military formations had been discussed in certain women's circles from the very beginning of the war. A number of advocates of women's military service and female soldiers had proposed the use of all-female units in the Russian army. In the fall of 1914, S. P. Iureva attempted to organize a unit of women in Petrograd with the intention of joining the army in the theater of war. Iureva received letters daily from women desiring to enlist in her formation.[49] In October 1914, the somewhat conservative women's journal *Zhenskaia zhizn'* reported talk of the creation of a women's guard unit.[50] In March 1917, the idea was implemented on a limited scale when a mounted women's militia was used to guard a mass demonstration organized by the League for Women's Equality as they paraded through the streets of Petrograd demanding suffrage.[51] In the spring of 1917, the idea of using women at the front gained credence among significant numbers of Russian society. The notion circulated among women's and military organizations, which now began to consider it both desirable and possible.

The movement to create women's military formations was part of this larger volunteer effort to utilize all available resources in the war, even those previously considered unacceptable for military service. The creation of units of disabled veterans, beginning in May 1917, may be particularly significant in understanding why many Russians now found it somewhat acceptable to use women in combat capacity. Many of the members of these "invalid" units had serious wounds and handicaps, including missing arms and legs.[52] A number of these volunteers had been fitted with prosthetic limbs. They were being drilled and prepared to join the active army at the front for participation in the upcoming offensive. The main purpose of such units was to provide an example of undaunted courage and to shame the wavering soldiers into returning to their combat duties. Fighting prowess was secondary to inspirational power.[53] If the new government and military authorities were willing to use these "damaged" men, the use of "weak" women in combat could similarly be justified.

The political circumstances in Russia following the February Revolution were equally important in making the creation of women's military units possible. The extension of various rights and freedoms to the general populace and to the army after the fall of autocracy and the establishment of social democracy played a particularly significant role in making it feasible for women to serve in military capacities. With the proclamation of social democracy, women would achieve advances in rights, freedoms, and opportunities during this period. Many believed that women would finally be given the equality for which they had long aspired. In particular, many women were convinced that the government could not ignore all they had done for the war effort.

Immediately following the formation of the Provisional Government, feminists and progressive women began working to ensure that their war work was recognized and rewarded, pressing the new government to grant women rights and equality, especially the vote. The Provisional Government declared its commitment to women's equality. Women were given new opportunities to work in many areas of the public sphere from which they had previously been excluded. They were granted the right to serve as attorneys at the bar and to become jurors; they were to be given equality of opportunity, pay, benefits, and titles in the civil service; and on July 20, 1917, Russia would become the first great power to grant women the vote.[54] As such, the new Russian government established an agenda for women's emancipation and laid the political groundwork, at least in theory, for women's right to participate in all aspects of public life, including combat.

Furthermore, over the course of the long conflict, significant numbers of women in Russia had become disillusioned by the large-scale mishandling of the war effort by men. They questioned men's ability to bring the conflict to a victorious end. Although their fears may have been exaggerated, many shared the perception that the army was in a state of serious disintegration. In a metaphor reflective of women's traditional roles as caring nurturers, many women perceived the army as "sick," in need of a strong dose of morale to recover its fighting prowess. They were distressed by perceived cowardice and irresponsibility on the part of male soldiers who refused to fight. Convinced that the involvement of women in active combat was necessary in order to stem the tide of demoralization and restore the fighting capability of the army, many believed that wavering men needed to be reminded of their duty as soldiers and that the presence of women in combat would serve to "heal" the troops, that is, to jolt them out of their complacency and shame them into fighting again. Some were even persuaded that only through women's efforts could the country be extricated from the devastating situation in which it now found itself. Others saw the need to use women to augment the dwindling numbers of available men.[55]

The Russian women's movement readily embraced the notion of using women in the defense of the nation, believing they would serve to shore up the morale of the army and shame the men into fighting. At a meeting of the All-Russian Women's Union on May 26, the notion of creating women's reinforcement companies for the defense of the nation was discussed at length. The union produced an appeal directed at the women of Russia:

> We, as citizens with equal rights, are required to raise our voices, to gather and offer all our strength to aid the motherland in this critical moment. . . . civic duty calls Russian women to support the united will of our armies, to raise the fallen spirits of the troops, to go into their ranks as volunteers, to turn the passive stance at the front into an active attack, so that the honor, virtue, and freedom of Russia will not be ruined.[56]

Anna Shabanova, chairman of the union, gave a ringing endorsement of this idea. She, as well as other members of the women's movement, clearly saw women's military participation not only as a way to aid the homeland in its time of need but also as a means to advance women's position in Russian society. The government, they were certain, would reward the sacrifice and valor of women with greater rights and equality.[57]

Beginning in the spring of 1917 a number of individuals and women's groups from around the country sent petitions to the government seeking permission to organize all-female military formations. One such request came from a woman volunteer and recipient of the St. George's Cross, Valentina Petrova, who had fought with the 6th Siberian Infantry Division, 21st Siberian Rifle Regiment, since 1916. She had already organized a number of women into a unit she dubbed the "Black Hussars of Death," and she wanted to meet with Minister of War Kerensky to discuss the possibility of expanding the unit into a woman's battalion that would be sent to the active army.[58] Another petition came from a women's group in Minsk that had organized a women's guard legion and was requesting permission to be included in the ranks of the army as a rear defense unit.[59] In Petrograd, a Committee for the Organization of Women's Military Detachments was organized, headed by a student of the Bestuzhev Higher Courses for Women, O. Fomlenko. This group sent a memorandum to the minister of war proclaiming, "The situation at the front has sounded an alarm in the soul of every Russian. It is impossible to remain inactive in these difficult times. Love for the motherland and the desire to introduce fresh, intelligent forces into the ranks of our troops, who are tired by the long war, summons us [women] to become defenders of Russia."[60]

The Committee for the Organization of Women's Military Detachments aimed to create special detachments of women and requested that the Ministry of War assign them experienced command personnel. The goal of the women's units was to "raise the spirit of the army and create iron discipline." Like Brusilov's revolutionary battalions, these detachments were to demonstrate by example "the necessity of attack in order to save the honor and freedom of Russia," as well as to counter antiwar agitation in the army with propaganda and "enlightenment-education."[61] Representatives of the women's movement similarly urged the new government to allow women to participate in the active defense of the nation. They established organizations such as the Women's National Military Union of Volunteers and the All-Russian Women's Military Union of Aid to the Motherland. These groups appealed to the Ministry of War for permission to form women's military units and for the inclusion of such units in the ranks of the active army.[62] The members of the union expressed their desire "to take the places of the fainthearted soldiers at the front, who, valuing their lives more than that of the motherland, are prepared to quit their posts." The women further promised that should they be allowed to take up positions in the trenches, they would not ask why Russia was fighting.[63]

Despite some reservations about the use of women in such capacities, Kerensky ultimately gave his permission for the creation of the first women's military formation in late May 1917. He entrusted the organization and command of the unit to a formidable young female NCO and veteran of the war named Maria Bochkareva.

## MARIA BOCHKAREVA AND THE 1ST RUSSIAN WOMEN'S BATTALION OF DEATH

Maria Leont'evna Bochkareva is the most famous of Russia's women soldiers of World War I. She was hailed by admirers as a great hero and patriot and condemned by detractors as a tyrant and a dupe of the bourgeoisie. The patriotic, progovernment public viewed her as a Russian Joan of Arc, out to save the nation from destruction. The war-weary masses of soldiers reviled her for attempt-

Maria Bochkareva, the most famous Russian woman soldier of World War I, drilling recruits of
the 1st Russian Women's Battalion of Death (courtesy Museum of the Revolution, Moscow)

ing to prolong the hated hostilities. Even her physical appearance and bearing
caused strong reactions—stocky, with short-cropped hair and a pockmarked
face, she smoked, drank, spat, and swore. Regardless of the epithets, she was a
key figure in the story of women's soldiering in World War I. She served for two
years (1915–1917) as part of a male combat unit, enduring all the privations of
war, including multiple wounds. Her strength of body was matched by an
equally notable strength of character. Although numerous sources claim otherwise, she did not originate the idea of creating the women's battalions, but she
did play a pivotal role in getting the units off the ground, championing the
cause among Russia's highest military and civilian officials in the spring of
1917. She served as the commander of the first such unit and successfully led
them into battle in July of that year. Despite her humble peasant origins, she
associated with the elite of Russian society, government, and the military, as
well as with several foreign leaders and other important personages of the period. She was even given audiences with King George VI of England and President Woodrow Wilson in 1918.

Fortunately for us, Bochkareva left a detailed record of her experiences in
the war and revolution in the form of an "as-told-to" memoir in English, written
by a Russian émigré journalist, Isaac Don Levine, and published in New York
in 1919. Although this account embellishes and even fabricates some facts of
her life while altogether ignoring others, the book presents an insightful look
into her life as a woman soldier. It also provides extremely valuable commentary on the seldom-recorded firsthand experiences of a Russian peasant during
the war and the revolutions of 1917. Subsequent research has distilled much

fact from fiction, and we are thus able to present a more accurate portrait of this remarkable woman.[64]

Born Maria Leont'evna Frolkova in 1889, Bochkareva came from humble origins, the daughter of a poverty-stricken peasant family from Nikolskii Kirilovskii district in the province of Novgorod. When she was six years old her family moved to Tomsk in Siberia in the hopes of receiving a plot of land. Her father was an abusive alcoholic, and in an effort to escape his cruelty Maria married a local peasant, Afanasi Sergeevich Bochkarev, at the age of fifteen. She soon discovered that her husband was also a heavy drinker, inclined to violence when intoxicated. Once again she fled brutal treatment at male hands and ran off with a local petty criminal, Yakov Buk. She lived with Buk for three years, working in a butcher shop they set up with the proceeds of Buk's larceny, until he was arrested in May 1912 and sent to Yakutsk.[65] Bochkareva followed him into exile, and the couple settled in Yakutsk and established another butcher shop. Buk found old habits hard to break, however, and after being caught buying and selling stolen goods, he was sent further out into the wilds of Siberia, to the remote settlement of Amga, in 1913.

Maria accompanied Buk to Amga, but life there proved far from idyllic, as Buk began to gamble and drink heavily and also became physically abusive. The young woman sank into a deep depression and contemplated suicide to escape these hardships. The outbreak of war in the summer of 1914 provided her with a new reason to live and an opportunity to escape her dreary life. She decided to enlist in the army. "My heart yearned to be there," she proclaimed, "in the boiling cauldron of war, to be baptized in its fire and scorched in its lava." She had patriotic as well as personal motivations, declaring, "The spirit of sacrifice took possession of me. My country called me."[66] Returning to Tomsk in November 1914, she appealed to the commander of the 25th Reserve Battalion to admit her as a volunteer. The commander laughed at her strange request, explaining that it was illegal for women to serve in the imperial army. Bochkareva was persistent, however, and when the commander facetiously suggested that she ask the tsar for permission to enlist, the illiterate young woman convinced him to help her draft a telegram to Nicholas II. She sent the appeal with the commander's personal recommendation, and to the great amazement of all, including Bochkareva herself, she received a positive response from the tsar.

Having secured the tsar's permission, Bochkareva, now twenty-five years old, entered the 4th Company of the 25th Tomsk Reserve Battalion and began military training with the men of the unit. Initially, the male soldiers were quite confused by the presence of a young woman in their midst. Some mistook her for a prostitute, placed in their ranks for their entertainment. As a result her first few nights in the barracks were spent fighting off the advances of a number of the men, but after delivering strong blows to her pursuers, she was left alone. Bochkareva excelled in military training, and upon demonstrating her abilities in this area, she earned the respect of her male comrades in arms. Over time, and through common experience, she developed camaraderie with the other soldiers, and they came to treat her as an equal. In fact, Bochkareva seems to have had little trouble assimilating into the male realm.

Becoming a soldier was not Bochkareva's first foray into the male world. She had held several jobs traditionally reserved for men prior to enlisting in the army. In Irkutsk, she and her husband Afanasi had worked on a road-construction crew. She had even been promoted to assistant foreman as a result of her skill and hard work, while Afanasi remained a mere laborer. Despite the hostility and derision of her subordinates, the young woman had performed her duties very well. As a butcher while in exile with Buk, Bochkareva had entered and mastered another almost exclusively male occupation. Her successful emulation of male behavior in the civilian world undoubtedly eased her transition into the male military realm. She seems to have felt more comfortable functioning in the world of men and readily adapted to male behaviors. She smoked, drank, spat, cursed, and, as previously mentioned, even visited a brothel with some male soldiers of her regiment (merely out of curiosity, she claims). The nickname she acquired when she became a soldier, "Yashka," was a male diminutive form of "Yakov" (the name of her former lover). By the time she took command of the 1st Russian Women's Battalion of Death, she regularly used male grammatical forms when speaking in the first person.[67]

The process of assimilation was not always a smooth one, however. In a drab, shapeless uniform and with her hair cropped short, Bochkareva's true sex may have been readily overlooked. Yet she could not remain fully dressed at all times. Living in the barracks with the men, she had to dress and undress in their presence. Moreover, she had to bathe with them, as there were no separate facilities for women. Eventually, the filth of ever-present mud and vermin overwhelmed her modesty. Although initially the men teased her, they did not molest her, having been sufficiently threatened by the commander. But after a short time, Bochkareva reported, both she and her male comrades became accustomed to her presence in the bathhouse. It seems that she nearly completely abandoned her femininity and convinced those around her to ignore it as well.[68]

In February 1915, Bochkareva's unit was sent to the Russian western front, assigned to the Second Army, V Corps, 7th Division, 28th Regiment, headquartered in Polotsk, in Belorussia. Once she was at the front, word spread that there was a woman in the ranks, and Bochkareva's presence attracted much attention. While most men accepted her, there were a few who could not come to terms with a woman in the role of a combatant. Some of the male soldiers initially expressed hostility toward Bochkareva. When the challenge was great enough, she did not hesitate to deliver blows to soldiers who derided her. Objection to her presence in the ranks more often emanated from officers than from rank-and-file troops.[69] This seems consistent with conventional conceptions of gender roles and behaviors in early twentieth-century Russia, since officers, who by and large came from the upper classes, would have held notions of separate sexual spheres wherein women were strictly relegated to the domestic realm. The soldiers, by contrast, were mostly peasants and working-class men, who were accustomed to seeing women perform arduous and even dangerous work.

Despite protests from some officers, the young woman, armed with imperial permission, was sent into the trenches with her unit to fight in battle. Bochkareva quickly proved herself a brave and valuable soldier. During her first combat experience, although she had not been designated as medical personnel, she spent most of the battle helping rescue wounded men who had been left to die in no-man's-land, dragging them off the battlefield under heavy enemy artillery fire. For her efforts she was awarded the first of her military honors, a medal "for distinguished valor." In the spring of 1915, she was wounded in battle and evacuated to a hospital in Kiev, where she spent two months recovering. During her convalescence, she longed to return to the front. When she finally rejoined her unit, the men greeted her with enthusiasm, as now they respected her as a seasoned veteran and treated her as such. Over the course of the next several months she rescued many more men left for dead on the battlefields, and as a result of her courageous service she was recommended for a St. George's Cross. She was denied this honor because, she claims, she was a woman, and she bitterly resented this rejection.[70]

In the fall of 1915, Bochkareva received a gold medal, second degree, was promoted to the rank of corporal, and was placed in charge of a detail of eleven men. The men seemed to accept her authority without resistance, having come to see her as one of them. In March 1916, a bullet shattered the bones of one leg, and she was taken to a Moscow hospital, where she spent nearly three months recovering. In June, she returned to the front and caught up with her regiment, which had been transferred to Lutsk in western Ukraine on the southwestern front. Her time there was cut short by another injury: A shell fragment lodged in her spine and left her paralyzed. She managed to recover from this wound as well, learning to walk again, and after six months of convalescence she returned to the front in the winter of 1916. She was promoted to junior NCO and finally received her long-coveted St. George's Cross in December 1916.

By this time, conditions in the army had deteriorated significantly. Bochkareva reported that the mood among the soldiers was bad. "The soldiers had lost faith in their superiors," she asserted, "and the view that they were being led to the slaughter by the thousands prevailed in many minds. Rumors flew thick and fast. The old soldiers were killed off and the fresh recruits were impatient for the end of the war."[71] Despite small victories, the situation in her regiment degenerated. The men could not understand why the war continued, nor did they know what they were fighting for, and by February 1917 Bochkareva described them as "depressed in spirit, discouraged and sullen in appearance."[72]

Much of their indignation and dissatisfaction was directed against the government, which they believed to be working against the true interests of Russia. When the soldiers received word of the February Revolution and the fall of tsarism, they were overjoyed and quickly swore allegiance to the new government. Bochkareva claims to have been exhilarated by the end of the "oppressive autocracy," but she believed in the necessity to continue the fight against external aggressors. The men, however, did not share this opinion. They lacked zeal for the cause, despite the replacement of the old regime with seemingly sympathetic leaders. Interpreting freedom and democracy as license without responsibility, they became insubordinate and undisciplined. Fraternization and demoralization rose, and men began to desert. Bochkareva blamed this degeneration primarily on the abolition of the old army discipline, particularly as accomplished by Order Number One. Her unit, stationed on the Russian western front, soon dissolved into a disorganized mob that could not be motivated to do much of anything aside from convening meetings of the soldiers' committees, let alone fight a war.

In May 1917, Bochkareva was "discovered" by Mikhail Rodzianko, former president of the State Duma, who was at the front on a morale-boosting mission for the Provisional Government. Impressed with Bochkareva and recognizing her potential propaganda value, he convinced her to return with him to Petrograd. In the capital, Rodzianko showed off the woman veteran in various quarters, hoping her example would prove inspirational. At a soldiers' meeting at the Tauride Palace, Bochkareva proposed the idea of forming women's military units in an attempt to stop the decay in the army. She believed, as did other proponents of women's military participation, that the presence of women soldiers in the trenches would shame the men into fighting again and would revitalize morale by providing an example for those who were faltering.

Using women to shame men into going into battle was not a novel concept. In London, young women handed white feathers, as symbols of cowardice, to men

New recruits of the 1st Russian Women's Battalion of Death (courtesy Museum of the Revolution, Moscow)

walking the streets in civilian clothes.[73] One British propaganda poster that circulated during the Great War depicted a young Irish woman demanding of her man, "Will you go or must I?"[74] Women were encouraged to reject with contempt any man who was able but not willing to give his life in defense of his homeland.[75] In Russia, the women's units were supposed to demonstrate to the men that their failings—that is, their hesitation and refusal to fight—made it necessary for women to come to the defense of the nation. This was intended to inspire feelings of shame that would spur the men back into action.

Although in her memoirs Bochkareva claims she originated the notion of an all-female combat unit, the idea was already circulating in Petrograd society, including among women's groups and in the volunteer military movement. However, it was Bochkareva who ensured that the idea would come to fruition. With Rodzianko's backing, the veteran woman soldier sought official consent for the formation of women's military units. According to Bochkareva, the leader of the State Duma escorted her to Stavka (Headquarters of the Supreme Commander of the Russian Army) at Mogilev (Mahiliou) in mid-May. There she met with General Brusilov, who had recently replaced General Alekseev as supreme commander in chief of the Russian Army. Bochkareva reported that Brusilov was receptive to the notion of creating a women's "battalion of death," which he probably saw as consistent with his own efforts toward organizing

Volunteers of the 1st Russian Women's Battalion of Death getting their heads shaved (courtesy Museum of the Revolution, Moscow)

shock units and other revolutionary units as part of his plans to revitalize the army. Armed with these endorsements, Bochkareva claims that she and Rodzianko went to Minister of War Kerensky to obtain final approval on May 20. Kerensky agreed after she had assured him that she would be personally responsible for the "moral integrity" of the unit. He may have visualized the stalwart woman as the command figure specifically requested by those pressing him for the creation of women's military units. Kerensky assigned her to command the 1st Russian Women's Battalion of Death.[76]

It is difficult to ascertain the veracity of Bochkareva's version of these proceedings, particularly of how these prominent figures were personally involved. Neither Kerensky nor Brusilov nor Rodzianko mention anything about these events in their own accounts of the revolution.[77] Bochkareva did send a letter to Kerensky, dated May 28, 1917, stating that a women's detachment had been recruited and assembled, consisting of 500 volunteers. She requested that the unit be given barracks, uniforms, weapons, and instructors and that it be attached to the active army at the front in order to participate in the upcoming offensive.[78] Whether she had obtained permission from the military authorities prior to assembling the unit we may never know, but it seems very unlikely that she would have initiated its formation without at least some nod of approval from Russian officials beforehand. In response to Bochkareva's telegram, Kerensky approved her request on May 31, ordering that the matter be handled by the commander in chief of the Petrograd Military District and the Mobilization Section of the Main Directorate of the General Staff (*Glavnoe Upravlenie Generalnogo Shtaba;* GUGSh) of the army.[79]

The organization of the 1st Russian Women's Battalion of Death began in late May 1917. The Petrograd Women's Military Organization assisted in its formation, launching a publicity campaign to attract women volunteers. Posters, featuring Bochkareva's photograph and declaring, "The duty of every woman is to join the general effort for victory over the enemy," appeared around the city.[80] Announcements published in the periodical press appealed to women to join the unit and publicized the time and place of informational meetings and recruitment sessions. The results of this campaign were very successful; thousands of women attended the meetings and assemblies, held in late May and early June, in various locations around the city, both in prominent places such as the Mariinskii Theater and in private quarters. At these meetings, Bochkareva and other speakers made impassioned pleas for women's help in saving Russia from destruction. Kerensky is reported to have attended some of these gatherings.

During an assembly sponsored by the Women's Union for Victory on May 21, Bochkareva transfixed an audience of thousands of women. Among them was an eighteen-year-old student named Nina Krylova, who was captivated by Bochkareva's words. "I have decided to form a women's Battalion of Death," Bochkareva declared, "to create real soldier-women and to go with them to the front. . . . it must serve to shame those male deserters, who, on the eve of final victory over the enemy, run away from their civic duty. . . . And so, comrades, I call upon you to join my battalion."[81] The spectators were so moved that several thousand registered for the unit immediately following the meeting. Registration for the women's unit was completed quickly. Approximately 2,000 women volunteered to join the first all-female military formation.[82] Nina Krylova was among them. Her experiences with the 1st Russian Woman's Battalion of Death were documented in a manner similar to Bochkareva's. She related them to a writer, Boris Solonevich, whom she met in a Belgian prison while they were being held by the Nazis during World War II and who published them as a "slightly fictionalized" memoir in 1955.[83]

The battalion was open to enlistment by women aged eighteen and older, but those under twenty-one were required to have permission from their parents to join. As a result, the eighteen-year old Krylova and her best friend Lilia, who also signed up to join the unit, had to secure their parents' reluctant approval in order to official register. The recruits were given medical examinations, performed by a commission of female doctors, and were only accepted if they were

in good health and were not pregnant.[84] Bochkareva commented that among the
female recruits there were "very few perfect specimens of health," but only
those with serious illnesses were rejected. All volunteers were obliged to sign a
document pledging their unquestioning obedience to the commander and the
discipline she instilled and promising to go faithfully to the front once training
was complete. The members of the battalion also swore an oath of loyalty to the
Provisional Government and were bound by all existing military laws. Additionally, they were supposed to follow a strict set of rules established by the
Petrograd Committee for the Organization of Women's Military Detachments, a
strange mix of military conduct and social niceties:

1. The honor, freedom, and well-being of the motherland is the first priority.
2. Iron discipline.
3. Steadfast and unwavering spirit and faith.
4. Courage and valor.
5. Accuracy, neatness, persistence, and quickness in execution of all duties.
6. Irreproachable honesty, and a serious attitude toward work.
7. Cheerfulness, happiness, kindness, hospitality, chastity, and
   fastidiousness.
8. Respect for the opinions of others and full faith in one another.
9. Quarrels and personal scores are intolerable, as is the degradation of
   human dignity.[85]

The social backgrounds of the women recruits were quite varied. Of the original volunteers, many were literate and urban. Between 40 and 50 percent possessed a secondary education, and approximately 25–30 percent were students
at the higher women's courses (kursistki), including a number from the
Bestuzhev Higher Courses for Women and approximately 200 from the Women's
Polytechnic Institute in Petrograd.[86] One Russian journalist commented,
"There is no military unit in the world which has a greater percentage of soldiers with higher and secondary education than the women's battalion of
death."[87] There were professionals such as lawyers and doctors in the ranks,
and some wealthy, prominent, and even titled women of aristocratic households,
including the young Princess Tatuieva and Magdalena (Maria) Skrydlova, the
twenty-year-old daughter of Admiral Nikolai Skrydlov, former commander of the
Black Sea Fleet, and goddaughter of the tsar. Skrydlova had served as a nurse in
the Red Cross since the outbreak of war. After the February Revolution, she left
the Red Cross and in May joined the 1st Russian Women's Battalion of Death,
explaining to her father that "women have something more to do for Russia than

Maria Bochkareva and volunteers of the 1st Russian Women's Battalion of Death (courtesy Museum of the Revolution, Moscow)

binding men's wounds."[88] A number of volunteers came from the petite bourgeoisie and working classes, including clerks, stenographers, dressmakers, factory workers, domestic servants, and peasants. Krylova asserted that the mixed social composition gave the unit a democratic character, as "many girls and ladies from well-to-do and well-known families found themselves in the battalion with their former cooks and chambermaids."[89]

The majority of enlistees were ethnically Russian, but a small number were Polish, Estonian, Latvian, or Jewish; there was one Japanese woman and one English woman. The women ranged in age from eighteen to thirty-five, with the exception of a young girl from Warsaw who was only fifteen (it is unclear how she managed to get around the age restrictions) and a doctor who was over forty. Among the older women, some were married and a few had children, but most were single and childless and were not constrained by familial responsibilities.[90] A number of the enlistees had served in the war as medical and other auxiliary personnel, including one doctor and more than thirty nurses. At least ten women were experienced soldiers who had fought in male regiments during the war.[91] Nearly thirty had been awarded military honors for their brave feats at the front, including at least eight who had received St. George's crosses.

The women who enlisted in the 1st Russian Women's Battalion of Death did so for various reasons. Patriotism, at least in a rudimentary form, and the desire to aid the motherland in its time of need were undoubtedly the leading

General Petr Polovtsev, head of the Petrograd Military District, reviewing the 1st Russian
Women's Battalion of Death (from Donald Thompson, *Blood Stained Russia*)

motivations. These women supported the idea that Russia had to continue the
war to a victorious end.[92] Fear of German domination, fueled by wartime propaganda, often accompanied patriotic sentiments. Following the overthrow of the
autocracy in February, they had no desire to exchange Russia's hard-won freedom for the "Teutonic yoke." A number had lost loved ones in the war and desired to avenge them, ensuring that their deaths had not been in vain by
achieving victory for Russia. They recognized that the army needed help in accomplishing this goal. Many believed that the troops suffered from a "sickness
of the soul" and that their presence at the front would raise the morale of the
troops and reinstate the desire to fight. Bochkareva constantly reminded the recruits that their mission as members of the women's battalion was to serve as an
example for the male soldiers. When men faltered, she proclaimed, it was the
responsibility of women to take up arms and fight in their places. Some of the
volunteers were outraged by men refusing to fight, shirking their obligation to
the nation. Believing these men had betrayed them, the women aimed to shame
the men into resuming their duties as warriors.[93]

Despite extensive discussion of the women's willingness to sacrifice themselves for the sake of the nation, there seems to have been very little discussion
(or at least such discussion was not recorded) of the fact that they, in taking on
the role of soldiers, would be required to kill as well as die. The fact that scant
attention was given to the killing aspect of soldiering may be a result of its ex-

treme contravention of gender roles. To emphasize that the women would be required to take others' lives might have made the whole venture too difficult to swallow for the general public. Certainly, the women were aware of the strong possibility they would have to inflict harm on the enemy, but this was not the main purpose of their experiment. Therefore, the topic may have been consciously avoided, and instead, stress was placed on the impact the women would have on the male soldiers.

Although Bochkareva herself cannot be labeled a feminist by any stretch of the imagination, there were a number of progressive women who joined the battalion. Such women regarded the unit as a unique opportunity to prove themselves worthy of greater rights and responsibilities in public life by demonstrating their self-sacrifice to the nation. For them, women's entrance into combat would be a great advancement in the struggle for sexual equality, allowing them to enter a realm previously impenetrable by their sex. Krylova, who shared these views, summarized them in her memoirs:

> Those of us who possessed knowledge of culture, began to feel more clearly that we women had already begun to withstand an unexpected historical test, and that even in the military sphere, the centuries-old prerogative of the male sex, we cannot be inferior. If not in physical force, then in organizational and spiritual strength. . . . And indeed, what of male objectives? Haven't they kept us from studying, from advancing, haven't they kept us only as mothers, housekeepers, and dependent slaves? How is it possible to advance, to enrich one's mind and one's spirit, when it is normal for a girl to be forced at eighteen to marry and reproduce—to have a child every year and a half? . . . But the revolution had already occurred— woman had won for herself the rights of which she had been deprived during the course of millennia—THE RIGHTS OF AN EQUAL MEMBER OF SOCIETY. Woman would never again forfeit her rights to education, to her own life, to her own heart, to choose the time when SHE wants to have children, to make her life according to her own plans, and not by the plans of men. And soon the world would see which was truly higher: man, with his rude and vulgar mind and dark soul, or woman, with her sensitivity, humanity and emotion.[94]

Although not all members of the unit shared Krylova's feminism, they did believe in their ability as women to make an impact on the army.

As ordered by Kerensky, the Petrograd Military District, headed by General Petr Polovtsev, assisted in the formation of the women's unit. The district headquarters provided accommodations, uniforms, equipment, weapons, and training instructors. The women were given the Kolomensk Women's Institute as barracks and training grounds. Twenty-five male military instructors, junior officers from the Volynskii Regiment, were assigned to provide the women with appropriate military training before they were sent to the front. They did not have their own field kitchen but shared one with a nearby guard unit. The uniforms distributed to the female recruits included special insignia designed for the battalions of death: black-and-red chevrons and skull-and-crossbones emblems. As standard military issue, the uniforms were not designed for women, and the female volunteers were forced to make do with the ill-fitting clothing.[95] Boots were particularly troublesome, since men's feet were significantly larger than women's. Trousers also presented problems for women with more generously female shapes.[96] After a week of training, the women's battalion was equipped with 500 rifles.

Once the recruits were assembled at their new training grounds, Bochkareva separated the unit into two battalions of about 1,000 women each. Each battalion was further divided into four companies, and the companies were subdivided into four platoons. She selected a number of the better-educated volunteers, particularly those who came from military families, to be subordinate command personnel. Krylova impressed Bochkareva with her knowledge of military order, learned from her father, an officer and decorated veteran of the Russo-Japanese War, and was made a platoon leader. Princess Tatuieva was chosen as a company commander. Bochkareva appointed Maria Skrydlova to be her adjutant. Skrydlova's talents proved very useful to the illiterate Bochkareva, since the adjutant spoke five languages and often served as interpreter when foreign journalists and dignitaries visited the women's unit.[97]

Because the military authorities regarded the women's battalion chiefly as an instrument of propaganda in their campaign to raise the army's morale, they did not invest it with much beyond the basic necessities. After supplying the unit with all the requisite equipment and armaments, the Petrograd Military District maintained a rather hands-off policy toward the internal management of the women's battalion. As a result, aside from the occasional parade review (given more for photographic opportunities than for military assessment), Bochkareva was largely left to her own devices in commanding her recruits. This was not altogether unusual, however, for Russian military units.

Bochkareva insisted upon maintaining the strictest possible discipline in the unit and subjected her volunteers to a stringent training regimen and a Spartan military lifestyle. The recruits were required to rise at 5:00 AM, engage in morning prayers, and eat a simple breakfast of tea and bread. They drilled intensively until 11:00 AM, when they broke for the midday meal, and then they

Female NCOs of Bochkareva's battalion; her adjutant, Magdalena Skrydlova, is at the center (courtesy Museum of the Revolution, Moscow).

A section of the 1st Russian Women's Battalion of Death doing exercises, part of an intensive training regimen (from Donald Thompson, *Blood Stained Russia*).

continued training until 9:00 PM. They slept on bare boards laid on metal cots, covered only by thin bedsheets.[98] Their daily training consisted of strenuous physical exercises, marching drills, hand-to-hand combat practice, and, most importantly, rifle training. Bochkareva personally supervised nearly every aspect of the military instruction and kept a close eye on the women's conduct at all times. She was intent upon transforming the volunteers into capable warriors: "I will make strong those of you from the 'weaker sex.' . . . Forget that you are women, you are now soldiers."[99] In so doing, she attempted to strip away all aspects of their femininity, which, she was convinced, had no place on the battlefield. Thus, all the women were given crew cuts and were dispossessed of personal hygiene items, even their toothbrushes. The slightest hint of femininity was considered frivolity and grounds for removal from the unit. She strove to "beat the domestic foolishness out of them."[100] Bochkareva had a particular dislike for giggling and interpreted even the slightest smile in the direction of a male instructor as flirtatious behavior. Both actions resulted in severe punishment, usually ending in expulsion from the ranks. The commander encouraged, and herself practiced, such "masculine" behavior as smoking, spitting, and swearing in order to facilitate the process of transformation into "real" soldiers.

Bochkareva's strict discipline applied to all areas of battalion life and was of the old tsarist army form, since she rejected the new democratic military practices encouraged after the February Revolution. She severely punished even the most minor transgressions, often subjecting offenders to corporal punish-

The women of the 1st Russian Women's Battalion of Death undergo rifle inspection (courtesy Museum of the Revolution, Moscow).

ment. The women were denied leave but were allowed occasional visits by family members. In addressing the volunteers the veteran woman officer used first names and the familiar form of "you"; she peppered her language with curses and the salty language of soldiers and went around slapping the recruits on the back. Initially, this offended many of the more cultured women, but eventually those who remained in the unit became accustomed to Bochkareva's brusque manner. She had little sympathy for the complaints or discomfort experienced by some of the more sophisticated women, who cringed at her language and found the crude soldiers' food hard to swallow. She admonished them for their priggishness:

That's nothing! Get used to it—the front is the front—you are now soldiers! It is impossible to say anything in Mother Russia without strong words!

What do you think, the tsar never shouted curses? And you've never heard
how well Count Lev Tolstoy can swear? And what about Peter the Great?
And Suvarov? If I call someone a fool, this cannot possibly offend. . . . you
are no longer women, you are soldiers. I'll tell you later how topsy-turvy it
was for me when I first joined the ranks . . . Or the first time I had to bathe
with the men. But a soldier is a soldier; you cannot make an exception for
yourself. It was much worse than the way you have it now—and I withstood
it. It's nothing—get used to it. Don't put up your noses![101]

Bochkareva's insistence that members of her battalion adhere to the discipline of the old army caused problems with some volunteers. From the inception of the unit, misunderstandings and disagreements over the commander's
methods were heard from the more educated recruits.[102] Bochkareva was a
somewhat megalomaniacal leader, unable to accept any form of criticism or to
adopt any means of command other than those she had learned as a soldier in
the prerevolutionary army. Those who could not or would not accept her iron
regime were deemed "unreliable" and dismissed. Others chose to leave on
their own accord as a result of their disillusionment with Bochkareva. As a result of her stringent regime, several hundred "unreliable elements" were
weeded out from the ranks of the women's battalion within the first few days of
instruction. The commander was unperturbed by the depletion of the ranks.[103]
More interested in quality than quantity, she was determined to prepare them to
withstand the hardships of the battlefields and life in the trenches.

Bochkareva insisted that all volunteers sign a waiver of their rights as soldiers granted by Order Number One upon enlisting. This meant there were no
soldiers' committees in the battalion and therefore no form of representation.
Yet despite the fact that they had waived their soldiers' rights and sworn obedience to Bochkareva, many contended that such discipline was excessive and
outdated. While it may have been appropriate at the front, in the rear, the commander was merely "first among equals."[104] The commander's harsh methods
drew criticism from her superiors as well. When complaints reached his office,
Kerensky insisted that soldiers' committees be formed. Bochkareva claimed
that he had promised her free reign in her battalion and refused to comply with
his demand. Believing that the democratization of the army was the root of the
problems at the front, she would not allow the creation of representative organizations in her unit. This did not sit well with many of the more educated
women, who were outraged by the commander's behavior and demanded more
democratic treatment.

Eventually, this conflict led to an irrevocable split between those advocating
a more "conscientious" discipline and those willing to submit to Bochkareva's

strict rule. Even after being dressed down by the minister of war and confronted by an angry mob of disgruntled women enlistees and belligerent Bolshevik sympathizers demanding the institution of soldiers' committees, the commander stood her ground. She chose to dismiss the group of "rebels" rather than conciliate them with measures she believed would be contrary to her aim. As a result, she lost more than half of her remaining volunteers.[105] When those ousted protested, she ordered the entrances to the barracks blocked and guarded at gunpoint. Refusing to accept Bochkareva's decision, the outcasts took their complaint to General Petr Polovtsev, commander in chief of the Petrograd Military District. The general failed to persuade Bochkareva to change her ways, and the obstinate commander threatened to abandon the entire effort if her authority was further challenged. Polovtsev was content to have the matter resolved internally rather than risk losing what he and his superiors saw as a valuable source of propaganda. Bochkareva was thus allowed to have her way, despite complaints from Kerensky. She was left with approximately 300 women, extremely dedicated to their commander and willing to withstand her strict discipline and rough treatment. Although some, such as Krylova and Skrydlova, stayed in the unit, most of the more educated and higher-class women were purged as a result of this break. Of those who were left, Krylova commented that there were many "whose faces and figures so resembled Bochkareva that there could be no doubt of their peasant background."[106] Determined to carry out her mission of making soldiers out of the "weaker sex," Bochkareva immediately resumed intensive military training, preparing the volunteers for their upcoming activity at the front.

In addition to these internal difficulties, this first women's military unit experienced serious problems from without. There were many who opposed the formation of the battalion. Bolsheviks in particular were very hostile to the battalion. They perceived it to be a tool of the bourgeoisie, helping to continue an imperialistic war that benefited only the upper classes. They strongly objected to Bochkareva's implementation of old army discipline, her complete disregard for the Declaration of the Rights of the Soldier (issued by Kerensky in early May), and her refusal to create representative soldiers' committees.[107] Groups of soldiers, students, workers, and other Bolshevik sympathizers agitated among the women soldiers and pressed them to demand their rights from Bochkareva, which undoubtedly played a role in the rebellion against the commander. Some displayed their hostility by more violent means, protesting at the gates of the unit's barracks, throwing rocks through their windows, and threatening the women verbally and physically. The women were forced to post guard around the clock to protect themselves from these disturbances. One evening, nearly 200 protesters gathered outside the women's barracks and harassed the female volunteers. They were only dispersed after the women's guard unit fired two rounds of shots over their heads.[108]

The women's battalion received much attention from the public and the media.[109] Whether they approved of it or not, observers recognized how extraordinary it was, and stories and photographs of the women's unit filled the pages of both domestic and foreign publications. The women were held up as examples of patriotism and bravery by many in Russian society, as well as by observers in the Allied nations. The unit was visited by prominent and varied personages such as Princess Kikuatova (one of Bochkareva's high-society sponsors), veteran revolutionary Ekaterina Breshko-Breshkovskaia, and British suffragette Emmeline Pankhurst. Sent to Petrograd by the British government on a morale-boosting mission aimed at ensuring that Russia remained in the war, Pankhurst visited the battalion in June 1917 with an entourage of British journalists and representatives of the women's movement. She addressed the women soldiers with a stirring speech, which Nina Krylova recalled in her memoirs:

> We all, millions of women, must fight for our rights in life, even for the right to defend one's own homeland and for the right to die for it. The creation of the Women's Battalion of Death is the greatest page written in the history of women since the time of Joan of Arc. I believe that at the front your example will carry the tired Russian soldier, demoralized by the enemy and by Bolshevik propaganda. Be brave. A million women's eyes filled with tears will follow you to victory, and a million women's hearts will be beating with hope, as one with yours. And our spoken prayers will help you to fulfill your difficult but honorable role.[110]

Bochkareva was also invited to several social gatherings in the capital, attended by prominent public figures such as Anna Shabanova, the chairperson of the All-Russian Women's Union, and Minister of War Kerensky. She claimed that at one such evening at the Astoria Hotel in mid-June, Kerensky (putting aside his personal differences with the woman commander) told her that the very existence of the woman's unit was exerting some degree of positive influence on some of the troops. He reported that a number of men expressed the desire to go to the front, including units of disabled veterans, reasoning that if women could fight, they could do so as well.[111]

Needing loyal units to bolster the Provisional Government and counter Bolshevik agitation in the city, Kerensky asked Bochkareva to allow her women soldiers to march in a progovernment demonstration. She consented, despite the dangers of exposing her unit to crowds of Bolshevik supporters massed in the streets. Although Bochkareva's main purpose was to help the motherland repel the external enemy, she was highly aware of the political value of her women's battalion. She frequently reminded her charges that they were not just warriors, but political soldiers.[112] The situation at the rally was tense, and as a result, the officers and instructors of the women's unit were armed with revolvers. The demonstration erupted into violence when Bolshevik sympathizers blocked the path of the progovernment forces on their way to Mars Field. They became engaged in a heated argument. According to Bochkareva, a volley of shots was fired, and several of the women soldiers were wounded in the fray, including the commander herself.[113] This incident did not deter them, and they continued preparing for their true test at the front.

After training for combat for nearly a month, the women's unit received word from the Ministry of War that it would be dispatched to the front at the end of June. The summer offensive was already under way on the southwestern front, having been launched on June 18, but the first phase had not gone as well as planned.[114] The female soldiers were to be sent to the Russian western front, to an area that had been experiencing problems with morale, and assigned to a regiment scheduled to take part in the offensive. The women awaited with great anticipation their chance to prove themselves on the battlefield.

# 4

# THE WOMEN'S MILITARY MOVEMENT

Arise brave women!
Take the bayonets from the hands of men,
And show them quickly
How life must be given for the children.
The country has forgotten the honor of soldiers,
They run in the blood of the homeland
They take up places in the huts at the washtubs
Behind our women's backs.
They are cowards, they are afraid
To defend us with their bayonets.
They have already made peace with the enemy,
To become his hired hands.
Arise then for your freedom,
While it is not too late to fight.
You can bring happiness to the people,
Let the men do the washing![1]

While Bochkareva's unit organized and trained in Petrograd, women around the country were participating in the formation of various other all-female military formations. The creation of the 1st Russian Women's Battalion of Death inspired a flurry of activity in the effort to organize women for military service. Some of these women's units were officially sanctioned and organized by the Russian military authorities, while others were initiated and formed through private efforts. Activities connected with women's military service continued to gain momentum throughout the summer of 1917, enlisting thousands of women in various cities throughout Russia. Fifteen women's military formations were established by the Russian military authorities between May and October 1917.[2] At least ten additional units were organized by women's grassroots initiatives.[3]

These activities were not random or sporadic actions by disparate groups with differing aims. Rather, they were part of a widespread organizational effort spearheaded by women with clearly definable goals. Each unit had its own organizational committee with executive powers. Many of the women involved in these activities also possessed strong social and political motivations, believing that women's military service to the homeland would be rewarded with rights and equality. Moreover, this movement was a socially significant phenomenon and was readily recognized by contemporaries, who referred to it as the "women's military movement" and understood the greater social and historical implications of its actions. In short, women's military activities of 1917 can justifiably be considered a social movement.

## GRASSROOTS INITIATIVES

Beginning in May 1917, organizations devoted to women's participation in the military were established in many cities. Thousands of women became involved in these private efforts to organize women desiring to go to the front and defend their country. Many interpreted the official sanctioning of Bochkareva's 1st Russian Women's Battalion of Death by the Ministry of War as carte blanche to form similar units. Local women's groups began to assemble and train female volunteers on their own initiative, without official approval, and during the spring and summer of 1917 women's quasi-military units appeared all over Russia. The presence of hundreds of individual women in the ranks of the active army from the beginning of the war undoubtedly contributed to and facilitated the creation of women's military units. A number of female veterans, such as Bochkareva, played essential roles in their promotion and organization.

With enlistment for Bochkareva's unit closed, the Petrograd Women's Military Union, headed by a veteran Sister of Mercy, Elizaveta Molleson, orchestrated recruitment efforts for another battalion of female volunteers in the capital. This unit would include many women who had been rejected by Bochkareva or who could not accept her strict, old army discipline. The Military League, one of the organizations created following the February Revolution as part of the volunteer movement, assisted in these efforts, creating a women's volunteer committee under its auspices, which undertook the registration of women desiring to serve in combat and auxiliary units.[4]

In Moscow, the All-Russian Women's Military Union of Aid to the Motherland, headed by M. A. Rychkova, was established to organize activities by women in the war effort in that city. The goal of the union was to unite "the

**Cities with women's military organizations 1917**

SWEDEN

FINLAND

*Baltic Sea*

ESTONIA

● Petrograd

● Viatka

Perm ●

URAL MOUNTAINS

Ob

● Ekaterinburg

*Volga*

● Tver

LITHUANIA
Minsk ●

● Moscow

Simbirsk ●

POLAND

BELORUSSIA

Saratov ●

GALICIA

Kiev ●
UKRAINE
Poltava ●
● Kharkov

*Dnepr*

Odessa ●
● Mariupol'

*Don*

*Volga*

ROMANIA

*Black Sea*

● Ekaterinodar

CENTRAL ASIA

BULGARIA

GEORGIA

*Caspian*

Tashkent

AZERBAIJAN
Baku ●

OTTOMAN EMPIRE

ARMENIA

*Sea*

PERSIA

0        miles        500

women of Russia who stand for the interests of the government . . . independent of nationality, class, and party differences, and who have as their goals to render active help to the motherland in the battle with German militarism, for freedom, honor, and the very existence of the motherland itself."[5] To achieve this, the Moscow Women's Military Union wanted to create women's battalions of death, women's war-work militias, and medical detachments composed of women doctors, Sisters of Mercy, and medics.

Calls for women's participation in military endeavors were issued in public forums all over Russia, urging women to defend the hard-won freedom and democracy of the "new" Russia against the external aggressor. The journal *Listok voiny* in Ekaterinodar published a call to create military formations of female volunteers in order to instill "fresh spirit and gallantry into the hearts of the cowardly soldiers."[6]

Many women took their demands for inclusion in military activities to the minister of war. Petitions requesting permission to organize military units of female volunteers flowed into the ministry throughout the spring and summer, both from individuals—such as Bochkareva and Valentina Petrova—and from women's groups around the country. The Organizational Committee of the Women's Volunteer Army sent a letter to Kerensky declaring, "In these difficult times it is impossible to remain inactive. Love for the motherland and the desire to introduce fresh, intelligent forces into the ranks of our homesick, war-weary troops has called us to the defense of Russia."[7] The All-Russian Women's Military Union of Aid to the Motherland wrote to Kerensky expressing their patriotic motivations to help the motherland in its time of crisis. The telegram sent by the Petrograd Women's National Military Union of Volunteers expressed similar sentiments but also contained an element of universal female solidarity. "We are not deaf," wrote the women, "and the groans of torture of our sisters in Belgium, Serbia, and Poland have reached us, and we know that if our soldiers falter it will be up to us." The drafters of the telegram also added a political dimension to their appeal, reminding Kerensky, "You, citizen-minister, have promised us civil rights and equality, but now, when our homeland is suffering, give us equality of death for her. . . . Give us that which we ask, that we demand, from you."[8]

The activities of the women's military movement in Petrograd inspired women all over the country to action. There were even a number of Russian women residing in England who requested permission to join the women's units.[9] Even before Bochkareva had begun to organize her battalion, a women's circle in Minsk had already undertaken efforts to create a women's "legion of defense."[10] In early June, Moscow women's activist R. P. Slug initiated the creation of a women's battalion of death, assisted by the All-Russian Women's Military Union of Aid to the Motherland. A delegation was dispatched to Petrograd to solicit the minister of war for the necessary accommodations, equipment, and training.[11] Simultaneously, a women's military detachment of more than 300 volunteers was organized in Kiev. This unit sent representatives to the capital to lobby Kerensky for official sanction and inclusion of the unit in the active army. The organization also appealed to Stavka to speed their training and dispatch them to the front as soon as possible.[12] In mid-July, another 120 women joined together in Kiev to create a women's *kurun* (a Zaporozhian Cossack unit) of death, and they asked the Poltava General Military Committee for assistance in organizing and training.[13]

In Ekaterinodar, efforts to create a women's military unit were undertaken by a local Kuban Cossack, Matriona Leontevna Zalesskaia, in early June.[14] Zalesskaia issued an announcement to the press calling all "women-citizens," free from familial responsibilities, to join with her, "a daughter who deeply loves her homeland," in forming a women's combat unit. "The spirits of our husbands, brothers, and sons are in confusion, and it is our duty to support them and place in their hearts the strength of courage and valor through our example."[15] In a statement published in the local newspaper, Zalesskaia outlined the goals and regulations of her unit. Her motivations included strong patriotic elements but were accompanied by an equally resolute commitment to sexual equality. "The goal of the Organization of Women-Volunteers," she explained, "is, on the one hand, to raise the spirit of courage and boldness in the hearts of the dispirited soldiers and, on the other, to restore the equality and equal rights of women in electoral reform and political life lost under absolutism."[16] By June 25, 800 female volunteers had enlisted in her organization.[17]

Following these examples, more than 200 volunteers gathered in Saratov to form the Saratov Women's Shock Battalion. Its organizational committee petitioned Kerensky for the assistance of the military authorities in the formation and training of their unit.[18] The governing board of the Viatka Women's Union sent a letter to the minister of war thanking him for allowing the formation of the Petrograd Women's Battalion of Death and requesting permission to organize a similar unit in Viatka.[19] Sixty women applied to join the unit in Viatka, and they were then dispatched to Petrograd to join the 1st Petrograd Women's Battalion.[20] In Tver, thirty-four women had gathered to form a women's battalion of death.[21]

In Odessa, an experienced woman combatant named Lebedeva created a women's unit consisting of approximately 500 volunteers from the southern regions of Ukraine.[22] In Tashkent, the local women's union created an all-female unit in June. The women were receiving military training and appealed to the local military authorities for acceptance into the active army. The commander of the Tashkent forces decided to admit some of the women to the local training program for reserve troops, including an officer, Sublieutenant Gaby, but asked permission of the chief of the General Staff to dispatch the rest of the women to Petrograd to join the Women's Battalion of Death there.[23] A similar unit created in Simbirsk also requested permission to join the Petrograd battalion.[24]

In Ekaterinburg, the local chapter of the League for Women's Equality established a group called the Union for the Defense of the Motherland and began to register women who desired to go to the front as soldiers. By June 14, thirty women had been successfully recruited, and the organizer, Tiusheva, requested instructions from the minister of war on how to proceed.[25] Even women in the Russian community in far-off Kharbin, Manchuria, desired to join the women's battalions and appealed to the local authorities to be dispatched to one of the women's units forming in Russia.[26]

Occasionally male military personnel would assist in the formation of women's military units. In Poltava, the 1st Detachment of Volunteer Women Scouts was organized under the aegis of a Lieutenant Ilovaiskii.[27] A Private Novitsin, of the 24th Infantry Regiment, organized a women's battalion of death in Mariupol' in which more than 300 registrants displayed their "strong conviction to die for the benefit of the motherland."[28] A schoolteacher and veteran revolutionary, E. K. Petrova, organized a women's battalion of death in Baku in July. She enlisted the support of the local garrison commander, Major General Sokolovskii, as well as that of a member of the Executive Committee of the Soviet of Workers' and Soldiers' Deputies in that city. This unit carried a banner that read "For the freedom of Russia—the Women's Battalion of Death" and bore the symbol of Russian death battalions: a skull and crossbones.[29] Once the formation was complete, an application was sent to the Ministry of War requesting that the Baku unit be allowed to join the women's battalion in Petrograd.[30] Some women attempted to join the various special male shock units and revolutionary units formed during the spring and summer of 1917. In Pavlgrad, a number of women registered for service in Captain Kratsepinov's shock battalion after the example provided by the Petrograd Women's Battalion of Death. The regimental commander was unsure what to do with these female volunteers and requested instructions from GUGSh.[31]

The Minsk Women's Legion undertook the formation of a women's guard unit intended for active duty assignment and appealed to the commander in chief of the western front for official sanction and assistance. The commander agreed, as long as Stavka offered no opposition.[32] Aided by the staff of the front headquarters, the women's legion drew up staff lists and regulations for the formation of the Minsk Separate Guard Militia of Women-Volunteers: The unit was to admit women no younger than nineteen, in good health, without criminal records, and possessing "irreproachable morals."[33] The staff was to consist of 172 soldiers, 2 clerks, 4 medical personnel, 22 NCOs, and 3 commissioned officers. Volunteers were forbidden to belong to any political party, and each was required to "forget her personal interests, staunchly remembering that she, above all, is a defender of her motherland from a terrible enemy, and must be prepared to give her life, if demanded, at any moment to save the motherland." Once their training was complete, they were required to swear the following oath of loyalty:

> I, the undersigned, do swear to give my life in order to save the motherland, for which I am obligated to
> I. serve according to all the conditions of the militia;
> II. endure all burdens and deprivations of military service without complaint;
> III. not abandon my unit, even under fear of death, until the end of the war.[34]

Strict discipline was to be maintained in the unit, and all orders of the command personnel were to be obeyed immediately, without discussion. Officers were given full discretion to control the behavior of their subordinates, who, in turn, were to afford officers the utmost respect. The militia was to be outfitted as an infantry unit and issued appropriate uniforms, equipment, and armaments by the headquarters of the commander of the western front.[35] When delegates from the committee undertaking the formation process appealed to the military authorities to allow the women's unit to be assigned to active guard service, their request was denied. Lieutenant General Anton Denikin, commander in chief of the western front, advised the commander of the Tenth Army that employing this women's unit was "premature and undesirable."[36] Denikin argued that the best course of action was to await the outcome of Bochkareva's unit's participation in battle and thereby "see how well they hold up in combat." No further actions seem to have been taken to complete the formation of the Minsk women's guard unit.

Other grassroots women's formations dispatched themselves to regional army posts and headquarters, appearing before command personnel with requests to be assigned to active duty at the front. Military authorities were baffled by these groups, which were often armed and outfitted through their own fundraising efforts, and did not know how to proceed. The central military authori-

ties failed to provide procedures on how to handle them, and command personnel were left frustrated and confused. Such was the case when Lebedeva, the
organizer of the Odessa women's unit, appealed to Major General Gavrilov, the
chief of staff of the Odessa Military District, in August 1917. She requested appropriate accommodations, equipment, and money from the war fund to cover
organizational expenses. She also asked that upon completion of training, the
100-woman-strong unit be dispatched to the Romanian front. Gavrilov was dismayed by the disorderly unit and applied to GUGSh for instructions on what to
do with Lebedeva and her unit, but he never received a response.[37] In the absence of official policies and regulations regarding women's military formations, commanders were left to handle them according to their own discretion,
as they had done with individual women who attempted to enter the ranks prior
to the spring of 1917.

## OFFICIAL EFFORTS

The flurry of activity throughout the country on the part of women desiring to
serve as soldiers in the active army convinced the Russian government that the
women's military movement could not be ignored. The flood of petitions and appeals made to the Ministry of War and the General Staff by women wanting to
join in the defense of the nation was beginning to overwhelm the authorities.
There were even applications to join the women's units from foreign citizens,
including some who were citizens of Russia's enemies.[38] Thus, on June 1, 1917,
Minister of War Kerensky authorized the formation of additional military units
composed of female volunteers to be attached to the active army. He entrusted
the Department of Organization and Service of Troops within GUGSh with executive authority over all activities related to the organization of women's units.

   Immediately following the minister's approval, the army administration began to formulate a consistent policy on organizing and using these units. On
June 8, GUGSh determined that in order to make optimal use of the diversity of
age, social background, level of education, and health among the volunteers,
the women's units should be designated for three types of military service. The
first category would be formations intended for combat assignments. For this,
two separate infantry battalions, each consisting of 1,000 to 1,400 women,
would be created. These all-female combat units would be established in Petrograd and Moscow, where the greatest number of volunteers had assembled. The
second would include smaller auxiliary units, primarily communications detachments, composed of approximately 100 women. The third category would

take in those women whose health precluded them from frontline service, assigning them to medical services as replenishment forces. The detailed practical considerations connected with the implementation of this plan would be settled later.[39] GUGSh informed the staffs of the military district headquarters of Petrograd, Moscow, Kiev, Odessa, Kazan, Minsk, Omsk, Tiflis, Irkutsk, Dvinsk, Tashkent, and Khabarovsk of the decision by the minister of war to allow the formations of the women's units.[40]

The women's battalions were to be organized in the same manner as other (that is, male) volunteer units, according to the separate Turkestan Rifle Battalion Provisional Table of Organization, issued on November 28, 1916. The all-female units would be allotted the same personnel, equipment, and support services as male units. As such, the women's battalions included all auxiliary units necessary for combat participation, including machine-gun, communications, cavalry scout, and sapper detachments. The staffs of the battalions consisted of 19 officers, 5 administrative personnel, 1,083 combatants, 85 noncombatant soldiers, 127 horses, and 58 transport carts.

GUGSh designated that the four separate women's communications units be structured according to the basic communications detachment of the Infantry's 4th Battalion Regiment, with a staff of 2 officers, 99 soldiers, 11 transport carts of various types, 15 horses, and 6 motorcyclists. The personnel of the women's units were to consist entirely of female volunteers, with the exception of command, training, and senior medical personnel. Because of the insufficient number of women with the appropriate training and education required for such positions, these were to be filled by male officers. Eventually, however, these men were to be replaced by women volunteers. The army's main supply administration was responsible for providing uniforms, arms, ammunition, and all other required equipment. Financial support for the women's units came from the war fund of the state treasury. To cover unforeseen expenses associated with formation, each combat battalion was to receive 1,500 rubles, and each communications unit was allotted 200 rubles. The female volunteers would also receive the same pay as male rank-and-file soldiers.[41]

GUGSh ordered the commanders of the Petrograd and Moscow military district headquarters to supervise the formation and training of the women's units in their respective cities.[42] The local women's military organizations in each city also played important parts in the creation of the women's units. In Petrograd in mid-June, the Organizational Committee of the Women's Military Union assisted in the registration of female patriots desiring to enter the newly forming 1st Petrograd Women's Battalion (not to be confused with Bochkareva's 1st

Russian Women's Battalion of Death, also organized in Petrograd). The union was rumored to have among its members such prominent women as Olga Kerenskaia, the estranged wife of the minister of war; Nadezhda Brusilova, wife of the commander in chief of the Russian armed forces; and Countess Sofia Panina, the only female member of the Provisional Government.[43] In Moscow, a similar organization, the All-Russian Women's Military Union of Aid to the Motherland, had already begun efforts to create the 2nd Moscow Women's Battalion of Death. Now, with official support, the union lent assistance to the Moscow Military District in its efforts to complete formation of the unit.[44]

## ATTEMPTS TO CONTROL AND EXPAND THE MOVEMENT

After beginning the process of officially forming women's military units, GUGSh now worked to bring all activities associated with the women's military movement under its control and to implement standard regulations for all the women's military units. This became especially important following the serious difficulties encountered in Bochkareva's unit, whose internal management was left to the discretion of its commander. This was no easy task, however, considering the numerous private women's quasi-military organizations operating on their own agendas. It was extremely difficult for the authorities to determine the nature and intent of these units, whether they were properly trained, armed, and equipped, or whether the women in their ranks were healthy enough for military service. This caused significant commotion and confusion in the military establishment and prevented the army from utilizing the privately organized women's formations in a systematic matter.

Various suggestions were put forward for bringing the women's military movement under a single governmental authority. General Romanovskii, of the Department of Organization and Service of Troops, recommended the creation of a single administrative agency under the auspices of GUGSh to regulate women's military activities. The chairwoman of the Petrograd Women's Military Union, Elizaveta Molleson, urged the minister of war to establish a special "Commission on the Formation of Women's Combat Units" under GUGSh in order to manage the formation of women's military units, expedite all executive work, and consolidate the various grassroots women's military organizations throughout Russia. The Organizational Committee of the Women's Military Union suggested the creation of a "Central Committee of the All-Russian Women's Military Union" that would serve as a liaison between official agencies and organizations involved in the women's military movement.[45] The Military League appealed to the Ministry of War for the establishment of a "Committee of Women's War-Work Units," whose aim would be to organize the creation of women's volunteer auxiliary and special service units in order to replace men as telegraphists, telephonists, drivers, electrical technicians, clerks, topographers, and medical personnel.[46]

The Ministry of War acknowledged the need to mobilize women in the war effort and desired to find "a solution to the problem of utilizing the ability and capacity of Russian women (whose rights have already been recognized in principle)."[47] Yet it rejected the idea of creating an organ that would only treat issues pertaining to women's military service. Instead, Kerensky decided to establish a special commission within GUGSh to oversee the broad range of war-related activities in which women were involved. The Commission on Women's Labor Conscription, created in late June 1917 and chaired by women's activist Olga K. Nechaeva, head of the Russian Union of Women's Democratic Organizations, was charged with the task of deciding whether the conscription of women for war work was possible or practical. All the women's organizations, including Nechaeva's own union, were to cooperate in the commission.[48]

Although the Ministry of War had authorized the creation of the six official women's units in Petrograd and Moscow, this was insufficient to satisfy the large numbers of women desiring to participate in military service. Appeals from those desiring to enter the ranks of the active army continued to flow "uninterruptedly" into the Ministry of War. Women also appeared before the Central Executive Committee on the Formation of Revolutionary Battalions, under the auspices of Stavka, with requests to volunteer for women's military units.[49] The military authorities complained that they did not "have the time or ability to satisfy each volunteer with an exhaustive response."[50] As a result, General Kamenskii recommended that the Ministry of War release a statement to the press regarding the registration process. Accordingly, a press release was sent out at the end of June explaining the decision by the minister of war to allow the formation of the women's units in Petrograd and Moscow. The statement instructed volunteers to address their requests for enlistment to the military district headquarters of either city or to the Organizational Committee of the Women's Military Union in Petrograd, now headquartered at the Engineers' Palace.[51]

The press release was too little and too late. Throughout June and July, the central Russian military authorities continued to be inundated with women's requests to join the fighting. Aside from letters and telegrams flooding the Ministry of War, several delegations of women from cities around Russia pressed for the expansion of the women's military movement within the military establishment.[52] As a result, GUGSh resolved to increase the number of women's military units. On July 29, the Department of Organization and Service of Troops approved the formation of one additional combat infantry unit and seven more communications detachments.[53]

In expanding the women's formations, the military administration targeted areas with substantial grassroots activity initiated by private citizens and women's organizations. In Kiev and Saratov, several women's units had been organized by private initiatives. The military authorities believed it advisable to make use of preexisting formations rather than to create entirely new units. On July 14, GUGSh presented the Military Council with a proposal to form seven additional communications units, five in Kiev and two in Saratov. The Military Council approved this proposal on July 29 and allotted 200 rubles to each unit from the war fund for organizational expenses.[54] Ekaterinodar was also singled out as a location for expansion of official women's military units. There, as noted above, Matriona Zalesskaia had been successful in harnessing women's energies for the war effort by organizing a women's combat unit. The unit, consisting of nearly 800 women from the Kuban region, with many Kuban Cossacks and Caucasians among them, was to be used as the base for the organization of an official women's infantry battalion in Ekaterinodar. GUGSh recognized the desirability of utilizing these women, who "fervently expressed their desire to give their strength and life for freedom and for the hard-won revolution."[55]

The formation of these additional all-female units did not, however, put an end to the grassroots women's military movement and the unofficial women's units in other parts of Russia. Nor were the military authorities successful in bringing all of these efforts under GUGSh's control. The existence of these independent organizations made the task of formulating a consistent policy regarding the use of women in the armed forces extremely difficult. GUGSh expressed its misgivings in a memorandum issued on July 31: "At this time, a whole range of different formations and organizations [composed of women volunteers] of an unofficial nature have arisen in Petrograd and elsewhere in Russia, and the military authorities remain totally uninformed about their political platform, their military program, their sources of recruitment and equipment, their staffs, and the personnel comprising their instructors."[56]

The unofficial women's units were more than just an administrative headache for the authorities. They caused real concern for an unstable government, whose authority over the armed forces was precarious at best and was dependent largely on the goodwill of the Petrograd Soviet. The government did not welcome the establishment of independent armed groups of citizens over which it could not maintain direct control and whose allegiance could not be assured. Although the grassroots women's units avowed their intent to fight solely against Russia's external enemies, there was no way to guarantee their loyalty. The government was uncertain of the influences upon the women's units. Nor did it know whether the preparation they received was sufficient to allow them to carry out combat duties, which made it nearly impossible to utilize them effectively in the active army. Furthermore, the idea of bands of armed women was unsettling to many men in the administration. GUGSh thus demanded that all unofficially formed organizations either submit to the military authorities or cease their "irresponsible and unsanctioned"[57] formation. All women desiring to establish new military units composed of female volunteers were now required to obtain the official consent of the Ministry of War before undertaking any organizational measures. Most importantly, units without official sanction would be unable to tap the patronage and resources of the military administration.[58]

Although GUGSh prohibited any unsanctioned women's military formations, it was not willing to turn its back on the aid being offered by these women. Therefore, instead of disbanding the unofficial women's units and completely sacrificing their potential usefulness, GUGSh undertook to bring the existing private women's units under its authority by using the grassroots formations to augment the staffs of its official women's units. Accordingly, the Baku Women's Battalion of Death, organized by the local women's union in that city without official permission, was to be sent to Petrograd to join the 1st Petrograd Women's Battalion.[59] When a privately initiated women's shock battalion was organized in Mogilev, its leaders were instructed to apply to the Organizational Committee of the Women's Military Union in Petrograd. The Ukrainian Women's Battalion of Death, formed in Mariupol', was dispatched to Kiev to be added to the official communications detachments created there.

While the Ministry of War made some effort to satisfy the women's demands to serve in the armed forces, its commitment to the women's military movement was rather weak. The military authorities tended to regard the movement with trepidation and skepticism, at least partially as a result of their uncertainty of the value of the women soldiers at the front. There were those in the military establishment who agreed with General Denikin, commander of the western front, who asserted that the creation of any additional women's units would be, as noted above, "premature and undesirable" until their frontline performance and their effect on the male troops could be assessed.[60] The general would not have to wait long for the results he was seeking. Just as Denikin was making these comments (on July 8–9, 1917), Bochkareva's 1st Russian Women's Battalion of Death was readying itself for its baptism in battle. It had not been an understatement when Bochkareva told her volunteers that the eyes of the country would be upon them. Not only were these women soldiers to be a model of inspiration for the wavering soldiers, but they were also to serve as the experimental test case that, if successful, would determine the future course of the women's military movement in Russia.

## THE TEST: THE 1ST RUSSIAN WOMEN'S BATTALION OF
## DEATH AT THE FRONT

After training for nearly a month in Petrograd, Bochkareva and her troops received orders sending them to the front. They were scheduled to depart at the end of June and were to be sent to the western front to join the Tenth Army (see map, page 62). The summer offensive was launched on June 18 on the southwestern front, but the first phase had not been as successful as hoped, despite the massive preliminary artillery bombardment and high troop concentration involved. Shock units often led attacks, but many of the regular troops followed only reluctantly.[61] Kerensky blamed this less-than-satisfactory performance on increased German reinforcements, the army's insufficient organization, and Bolshevik influence, which was significantly dampening morale. The psychology of the army was key, he reasoned, and therein lay the intended purpose of the women's units.[62] This was the opportune time to put the women soldiers into action.

On June 21, 1917, the 1st Russian Women's Battalion of Death marched through the streets of Petrograd in a grand procession to St. Isaak's Cathedral. The women were outfitted in full gear and marched in perfect parade formation. According to one observer, each volunteer also wore a small pouch around her neck containing a capsule filled with cyanide, which she had been commanded to consume immediately upon capture by the enemy.[63] They were led by a unit of St. George's Cavaliers and were accompanied by the 9th Reserve Cavalry, the 4th and 1st Don Cossack Regiments, cadets of the Mikhailovskii Artillery School, reserve guard battalions of the Preobrazhenskii and Volynskii Regiments, and several echelons of the Baltic Fleet. Thousands of curious spectators watched as the women entered the cathedral to receive their banners and have their colors blessed. The ceremony was presided over by Metropolitan Veniamin of Petrograd. Bochkareva was promoted to the rank of sublieutenant and given a revolver and a gold-handled saber. The women's unit was presented with a red-and-black banner with the figure of St. George the Victorious on one

The 1st Russian Women's Battalion of Death marched through Petrograd to a ceremony at St. Isaak's Cathedral, June 21, 1917 (courtesy Museum of the Revolution, Moscow).

side and the skull-and-crossbones emblem, along with the words "Women's De-tachment of Death of Bochkareva," embroidered on the other.[64] The metropoli-tan blessed the standard, and Bishop Andrei of Ufa presented Bochkareva with an icon of the Tikhvin Mother of God. The First and Third Armies also sent icons as gifts to the women soldiers.[65] A privately initiated gathering was also held, where donations were accepted on behalf of the battalion to help pay for its necessities. In all, 1,540 rubles and 15 kopeks were collected from the crowd for the support of the women's unit.[66]

The conferral of colors on the unit was more than a ceremonial honoring of the women soldiers. The entire event was a large pro-war demonstration or-chestrated by the government to drum up public support for the offensive. A full army orchestra played the revolutionary theme song, "The Marseillaise." Prayers were said for those who had fallen in the initial phases of the offensive. Strategically dispersed among the crowd were people carrying banners that read "Long Live Kerensky and the Revolutionary Army," "Forward for the Homeland," "Glory to the Victorious Regiments of June 18," and "Down with Traitors to the Motherland." Inside, the cathedral was overflowing with people. A number of prominent officials and personages attended, including General Polovtsev, commander of the Petrograd Military District, representatives of the

The 1st Russian Women's Battalion of Death receives its standard, blessed by Metropolitan Veniamin of Petrograd in the ceremony at St. Isaak's Cathedral (from Donald Thompson, *Blood Stained Russia*).

Provisional Government, members of the Allied missions, and a delegation of leading figures of the women's movement, headed by British suffragette Emmeline Pankhurst. Kerensky, Rodzianko, and the newly appointed commander in chief of the Russian Army, General Lavr Kornilov, were also present.

Following the ceremony at St. Isaak's Cathedral the procession moved on to Mars Field. Along the way people threw flowers at the women soldiers and shouted, "You are our defenders, we are all counting on you!" and "Hurrah for the valiant warriors!" En route the procession met with opposition from the Pavlovskii Regiment, one of the more revolutionized units in the capital, with strong antiwar sentiments. But the pro-war forces greatly outnumbered the Pavlovtsy (members of the Pavlovskii Regiment), and the crowd booed them with cries of "cowards" and "traitors." When the procession reached its final destination, the square in front of the Winter Palace, the St. George's Cavaliers formed ranks with their banners in their hands and with loud cries of "hurrah" sent the women's unit back to their barracks.[67]

Bochkareva and her women soldiers were given a few days to get their affairs in order before they left for the front on June 23.[68] Most of the women remaining in the battalion were very anxious to begin their combat service. Some,

Review of the 1st Russian Women's Battalion of Death on Mars Field (courtesy Museum of the Revolution, Moscow)

however, seem to have suffered from cold feet and did not return from the twelve-hour leave they were granted the night before leaving for the front. Their reasons for doing so may never be known, but we may surmise that some may have suffered from fear of combat that was actualized only at the last moment, while others may have been restrained by concerned relatives and friends. Krylova thought this desertion was shameful, but Bochkareva rationalized that it was better that those who were unsure left then rather than in battle. The commander's observations concur with opinions of other Russian officers concerning male desertions, particularly in regard to those recruited from the rear, who were considered potentially unreliable in combat. As a result of these last-minute desertions, the 1st Russian Women's Battalion of Death was reduced to fewer than 300 dedicated female volunteers.

On June 24, the women's battalion marched to the Kazan Cathedral to receive a final blessing before entraining at the Warsaw Station and heading to the western front. Metropolitan Veniamin addressed a large crowd gathered to see the women's unit. "Weak women have been transformed into warriors. The place of unworthy men has been occupied by selfless women."[69] Along the way they were flooded with the greetings and flowers of well-wishers, as well as the jeers and insults of detractors. At the station, antiwar agitators attempted to prevent the women from boarding their train, accusing them of working for "capitalist bloodsuckers." Bochkareva pressed them through the crowd, and they managed to get on the train without violence. The journey to the front lasted several days, and at each stop large crowds gathered at the stations to witness the curious spectacle of women soldiers of whom they had heard rumors. Initially, the crowds were friendly, offering the women flowers and gifts, with only occasional jokes made at the women's expense. As they got closer to the front, however, the spectators were composed more and more of disgruntled soldiers and antiwar sympathizers, who often expressed hostility toward the women soldiers. Bochkareva answered their disparaging remarks with strong language that often inspired smirks of begrudging respect from seasoned troops.[70]

The women's battalion finally reached its destination on the Russian western front after two days of train travel. In early June, Stavka had decided to send the women soldiers to this particular area of the front because it was suffering from dangerously low morale, high desertion rates, fraternization with the enemy, and insubordination.[71] The army groups on this front were preparing to undertake their part of the new offensive. The women's battalion was assigned to the Tenth Army, I Siberian Army Corps, 132nd Infantry Division, under the command of Colonel V. I. Zakrezhevskii. When their train reached its destination on June 27, the headquarters of the Tenth Army at Molodechno, in northeastern Belorussia, a crowd of curious male troops met the women's unit. The men were anxious to see this anomaly for themselves and reacted with amused bewilderment at the presence of uniformed, armed women. The male soldiers' curiosity was so intense that they surrounded the train in throngs. As they strained to get a glimpse of the women soldiers, they shouted mocking insults and gender slurs. Bochkareva, first off the train, returned their derision with salty curses and forced the men to clear a path and allow her women through. The crowd retreated to the sides of the road and provided passage for the detraining women, but they followed close behind as the women made their way to their new camp. A crowd of spectators remained during the women's entire stay at Molodechno, subjecting them to continuous unwanted attention and derision. The unit was assigned to bunk in two rickety wooden barracks, empty except for two long rows of planks that served as beds.[72]

The first night at Molodechno was rather unpleasant for the women soldiers. They had only the wooden boards to sleep on. Their attempt at sleep was interrupted late that night by a group of male soldiers who harassed the women by shouting insults, pounding on the walls, shattering the windows of the barracks, and thrusting their arms through the broken glass and grabbing at the women. Krylova even reported that a shot was fired at the barracks; it ricocheted off the tin roof of the building. The battalion sentries tried to fend off the harassers but were unable to do so. Bochkareva ordered the unit to form ranks and aim their weapons, hoping this would scare the men into retreat. She argued for nearly an hour, as curses were hurled back and forth. Finally, the men dispersed when Bochkareva threatened to open fire on them.[73] This episode would be one of numerous hostile encounters with male troops at the front.

The women's battalion spent a week drilling outside Molodechno, awaiting the order for dispatch to the trenches. During this time, General Valuev, commander of the Tenth Army, reviewed the unit. Valuev was quite impressed by the highly disciplined and well-trained female volunteers. The women were then sent to the headquarters of the I Siberian Army Corps, at Redki. General Kostaev, chief of staff of the corps, inspected the women's battalion and was also very pleased by its military polish. "Magnificent!" the general exclaimed as he pumped Bochkareva's hand and congratulated her. "I would not have believed it possible for men, let alone women, to master the game so well in six weeks."[74]

Despite these favorable reports on the women's accomplishments, Kerensky was still displeased that the unit lacked a soldiers' committee. According to Bochkareva, upon meeting her at corps headquarters in early July, Kerensky once again berated her for her intransigence in this matter. He ordered that a committee be formed immediately. Bochkareva's response was to tear off her epaulets and threaten to resign. Kerensky in turn promised to court-martial her, but he never carried out his threat. Bochkareva returned to her troops with no intention of changing her style of command.[75]

After a week encamped outside Molodechno, the women's battalion was dispatched to the division headquarters at Redki in southeastern Lithuania. They arrived on July 3 and were assigned to join the 525th Kiuruk-Dar'inskii Regiment, stationed outside the town of Smorgon on the Vilna-Dvinsk highway. The women's unit was provided with eight machine guns, along with a crew consisting of six male noncommissioned officers to man them, and small-arms ammunition. Bochkareva addressed the women soldiers prior to their departure for the trenches: "Don't be cowards! Don't be traitors! Remember that you volunteered to set an example for the laggards of the army. I know that you are of the stuff to win glory. The country is watching you set the stride for the entire front."[76] A shock battalion greeted the women and expressed gratitude for their arrival. The overwhelming majority of male soldiers, however, were not as welcoming. In fact, many expressed open hostility to the presence of fresh troops, ready and willing to continue the war they considered futile.[77]

The entire corps was preparing to undertake an offensive against the Germans. Kerensky had personally addressed the troops of the 132nd Division on July 5 in an attempt to raise their spirits and inspire them to action.[78] Beginning on the night of July 6, the corps began a heavy artillery barrage of the enemy.[79] The reliability of the troops in this area, however, was less than certain. While some units, including the 1st, 2nd, 4th, and 7th Siberian Rifle Regiments, performed their duties satisfactorily and maintained good morale, others, such as the 16th Siberian Division and the 62nd and 63rd Regiments, had no desire to continue fighting, and many of them refused to carry out orders.[80] Only a few days prior to the arrival of Bochkareva's battalion, the 703rd Infantry Regiment had been forced to disband due to massive desertions.[81] The 525th had come to replace this disintegrated unit in the trenches. Antiwar agitation had become rampant in this part of the front. It was here that the women's unit was to test the notion that their presence would help stem the demoralization and remind the men of their duty to fight for the homeland.

On July 7–8, the 525th Regiment (of which the women's unit was now a part), moved to the village of Sin'ki in preparation for the coming attack. The women arrived in the village at midnight and were quartered there until morning. The I Corps' orders were to attack and capture the positions held by the enemy in the Novospasskii and Begushinskii forests and nearby villages. The 132nd Division's assignment was to help the 1st Siberian Division take the western section of the Novospasskii Forest, to strengthen the position, and to persist in its defense.[82] The Russian troops were facing an estimated eighteen German battalions.[83] The corps' offensive was launched on July 9, and it was then that the 1st Russian Women's Battalion of Death received its baptism in battle.

On July 9, the women soldiers crouched in the trenches awaiting orders to begin their offensive. The portion of the trenches that the women's unit occupied was almost a mile long. The enemy trenches were a mere 800 feet away, and the women could clearly see movement in them.[84] Finally, the order was given to attack. But no one moved. The officers of the male units begged the hesitant rank and file to act, but to no avail. The troops of the 1st, 62nd, and 63rd Siberian Regiments refused to fight.[85] Instead, they convened their soldiers' committees and debated the necessity of engaging in such a dangerous maneuver. The futile debates went on for hours; the opportune time for attack was quickly passing. The women soldiers, anxious to prove themselves in battle, decided to proceed with the advance, with or without the support of the male troops. This was the opportunity for which they had been waiting since the inception of the women's battalion. A few hundred male volunteers joined the female soldiers, and as the sun's first rays filtered into the trenches, they rushed over the top. They went with the hope that the waverers would be inspired by their example and would follow them into battle. These dedicated soldiers were not willing to believe that their Russian compatriots would allow them to be slaughtered alone in no-man's-land.[86]

A small force of women volunteers, officers, and male soldiers thus rushed into a hail of enemy fire. They managed to advance across the battlefield with few casualties. Their success inspired some of the reluctant soldiers to come out of the trenches. Eventually, more than half the corps joined the advance, and the Russian troops were able to take the first and second lines of German trenches. The 525th Regiment occupied and secured the western and southwestern sections of the Novospasskii Forest. But this success proved short-lived. Upon reaching the third line of enemy trenches, some of the Russian soldiers found stores of alcohol left behind, perhaps deliberately, by the retreating Germans. Weary of war, they found this temptation too great to resist. The women tried to stop the men from stealing and drinking the alcohol by breaking as many bottles as they could before the men could get to them.[87] The volunteers beseeched their conscripted comrades to continue the attack, but these entreaties had little effect on the troops. By evening, the Russian advance had come to a standstill. Large numbers of individual men and then entire companies retreated without being ordered to do so, reasoning that they had done enough and deserved a rest. The withdrawal threatened to become a general retreat.[88]

The Germans, who had regrouped, now launched a counterattack. The women and a number of male soldiers from the neighboring units attempted to hold their position until morning. They had been promised relief from the nearby 527th Regiment, but this relief never arrived. Bochkareva appealed to the 9th Division of the X Corps, also in the region, asking for 100 troops to assist them, but this support did not materialize either. Some soldiers of the 528th Regiment came to their aid on the left flank but retreated as soon as the Germans intensified their attacks. Once again, the woman commander asked the 9th Division for help, and the 9th finally responded by firing a volley of machine-gun fire over the women's heads and toward the Germans, who returned fire. Despite the lack of support, the women managed to repel six German attacks. But with each attack, greater numbers of male soldiers deserted the position. Eventually, the women's battalion ran out of cartridges and was forced to retreat under fierce German gun and shellfire. They scattered into the forest.[89]

The Russian troops lost all the ground they had gained, and their casualties were heavy, but the women managed to capture a number of German prisoners, including two officers, and two enemy machine guns.[90] The captured Germans were astonished at being seized by women. Some of the distraught prisoners could be heard crying out: "Good God! Women!" "Damn! What disgrace! Captured by women! Damn!" One of the officers was so overcome with shame that the women soldiers were forced to bind his hands so that he could not attempt suicide.[91]

The women's unit suffered a number of casualties as a result of their participation in the events of July 9–10. Official sources list two deaths, two missing in action, and thirty-six wounded.[92] One of those listed as severely wounded died shortly thereafter.[93] Bochkareva fell unconscious in the forest after a shell exploded close to her. She and the other seriously wounded soldiers were evacuated to a Petrograd hospital for treatment. The rest of the women soldiers were placed under the command of the 1st Siberian Rifle Division and were sent back to reserve billets to rest. Bochkareva's adjutant, Magdalena Skrydlova, was placed temporarily in charge of the women's unit.[94]

The actions of the female soldiers of the 1st Russian Women's Battalion of Death in the battle of Novospasskii Forest proved definitively that women were capable of carrying out combat duties and could indeed fight as well as men. Command personnel who witnessed their performance in combat were thoroughly impressed. The commander of the 525th Regiment reported that the soldiers of the women's battalion

conducted themselves heroically in battle, consistently maintaining their position in the front lines, carrying out service on par with the [male] soldiers. Under attack from the Germans, the volunteers rushed to counterattack by their own initiative. . . . the battalion provided an example of courage, bravery, and composure, raised the spirits of the soldiers. . . . The volunteers inspired feelings of respect and confidence in many of the soldiers.[95]

Sublieutenant Kervich, commander of the 6th Company of the 525th Regiment, to whose command thirty members of the women's battalion had been assigned, was also very impressed with the performance of those women in his charge. He reported to the commander of the 525th Regiment,

Despite the heavy fire from the enemy they remained at their posts and carried out their duties on a level equal to the [male] soldiers. The five persons ordered to carry cartridges to the machine guns performed their duties conscientiously, although they were under fire from the enemy. One of them went on reconnaissance and the others set up listening posts. Through their work the women's detachment proved that they deserved the name of warrior in the Russian revolutionary army.[96]

The commander of the 132nd Infantry Division was equally pleased with the combat performance of the women's battalion, noting that the women soldiers "underwent all hardships of life in the field without complaint, bravely going into battle in front of others, and fulfilling the most dangerous and difficult assignments."[97] The commander of the 1st Siberian Rifle Division further commended the women, stating, "They deserve the highest of all possible praise: they acted courageously."[98] The chief of staff of the I Siberian Army Corps added,

> Outside of combat, the [women] volunteers conduct themselves commendably as well . . . without any reproach, modestly. The unity of their strong discipline makes them irreproachable, as does their service, fulfilling the most unskilled labor without showing any kind of pretensions to improvement of their positions, being content with their inclusion in the tasks they are assigned and their inclusion with the rest of the soldiers.[99]

Colonel Zhelenin of the command staff of the 132nd Infantry Division proclaimed,

> Based on the experience of the current action, the future recruitment of women into the troops of the division is definitely desirable. It is desirable to assign women volunteers to the ranks to carry out combat service, as the courage and high spirits that they display in battle has the greatest influence on the soldiers.

He also reported that the relations between men and women soldiers were quite good, and that although the men displayed an inordinate amount of curiosity toward the women, they generally were well disposed toward them and respected them.[100]

Despite this evidence of the women's capabilities in combat and the extensive praise lavished upon them by command personnel, the military authorities remained unconvinced that women could be effective soldiers. In fact, the women's success in combat was ultimately irrelevant. Instead, they were much more concerned with the influence of the women on the male soldiers, since the intent of the experiment had been to raise the morale of the dispirited army. In his report on the battle of July 9–10, the chief of staff of the I Siberian Army Corps summed up the general opinion of male military personnel: "On the whole, all command personnel recognized that 'in view of the moral influence exerted on the rest of the combat units by the women's combat units, it is useful to enlist more of them [women] into the army, but in small numbers, since, as a result of their physical weakness, they cannot carry out serious fighting.'"[101]

Unfortunately, the women's positive influence was exaggerated. While they had provided a model of courage and fortitude in battle, the effect of the example was limited and ephemeral. They had convinced some of the men to go into battle, but this drive could not be sustained under the pressure of an enemy counterattack and the temptation of the bottle. Nor did it have an effect on more than a small minority of conscripts, especially in the face of enemy attacks. Moreover, reports by command personnel stating that relations between the male and female soldiers were largely amicable were euphemistic. In reality, there was much antagonism on the part of the men toward the women volunteers, as attested to by Bochkareva, Krylova, Dorr, Beatty, and other observers. The men's hostility and aggression toward the women would only increase over time and would ultimately lead the military authorities responsible for the women's units to reassess their usefulness. Like all Provisional Government attempts to inspire men to continue fighting, the use of women soldiers failed to provide sufficient and sustained impetus to men who desired peace more than anything else. Yet for the next several months, the Russian government would continue its efforts to organize all-female combat units in the hopes of stemming the tide of decomposition in the army.

# 5

## THE OFFICIAL WOMEN'S
## COMBAT UNITS

The Russian Ministry of War authorized the creation of sixteen separate all-female military formations between May and October 1917. Four, including Bochkareva's unit, were designated specifically as infantry battalions slated for active combat. Eleven were assigned as communications detachments to support combat units. And the Ministry of the Navy allowed for the formation of a women's naval detachment. Thousands of volunteers from all over the country enlisted in these women's military formations. After organization and training, the units were meant to join the ranks of the active army and navy and to participate in active defense of the homeland. Ultimately, only one of the women's military units, that under Bochkareva's command, was able to fulfill its intended mission of participating in battle at the front. All, however, were uniformed and armed, engaged in official military organization and training, and were committed to waging war against Russia's external enemies. This chapter will detail the experiences, from initial organization to disbanding, of the three women's infantry units—the 1st Petrograd Women's Battalion (a unit entirely apart from Bochkareva's 1st Russian Women's Battalion of Death), the 2nd Moscow Women's Battalion of Death, and the 3rd Kuban Women's Shock Battalion, formed in Ekaterinodar—and of the only women's naval unit, the 1st Women's Naval Detachment.

### THE 1ST PETROGRAD WOMEN'S BATTALION

The 1st Petrograd Women's Battalion may be the best known, as well as the most controversial and misunderstood, of Russia's all-female military units of World War I. Its fame derives largely from the participation of members of the unit in the siege of the Winter Palace during the October Revolution in 1917.[1] Their renown was largely transformed into infamy by Soviet historiography as a

Registration for recruits to the 1st Petrograd Women's Battalion (Courtesy Museum of the Revolution, Moscow)

result of their allegiance to the Provisional Government and opposition to the Bolsheviks. Much inaccuracy and distortion surrounds this unit, stemming from misrepresentations of both the facts of the events and the intentions of the women. Moreover, this unit is often confused with Bochkareva's unit, the 1st Russian Women's Battalion of Death, due to the similarity in their titles and the shared locus of their formation. Even the unit's name is somewhat misleading, for it was actually the second women's battalion to have been formed in Petrograd. Complicating matters further, the name of the only woman known to have left a memoir of her experiences with the 1st Petrograd Women's Battalion, Maria Bocharnikova, is similar to that of the woman commander of the 1st Russian Women's Battalion of Death, Maria Bochkareva.[2] Despite these challenges, the following pages attempt to draw a clear picture of this unit.

The 1st Petrograd Women's Battalion began its formation in early June, shortly after Kerensky had given his authorization for the creation of women's military units but after the creation of Bochkareva's unit. The facts about the organization of the unit have been garbled by reports that the bulk of the membership of this battalion was derived from the remnants of Bochkareva's unit following its participation in the battle at Smorgon. These assertions are clearly controverted by indisputable evidence that proves that the latter unit remained largely intact following the battle, save for a few wounded who were recovering in hospitals, and was stationed on the Russian western front near Molodechno until late October.[3] It is possible, however, that some of the members of Bochkareva's unit who were expelled or left during the fight for committee rule during the formation in June may very well have found their way into the ranks of this other Petrograd women's unit.

Initially, formation was undertaken by private initiative, through the Organizational Committee of the Women's Military Union in Petrograd. Once the unit became officially sanctioned, it was placed under the authority of the Petrograd Military District. The Women's Military Union, however, remained pivotal in the formation efforts, carrying out much of the logistical organizational work on behalf of the military authorities. Recruitment for the unit was conducted through public announcements and press releases appealing to women to participate actively in the defense of Russia. The response was tremendous; thousands of women applied for enlistment. The battalion accepted women between the ages of eighteen and forty; those under twenty were required to provide proof of parental permission. All volunteers wishing to enlist were required to undergo a complete medical examination, and those deemed unfit for service were rejected. Enlistment and initial training were conducted in the Engineers' Palace in Petrograd. The women soldiers were housed there until August 5, when the entire unit moved to an encampment near the Levashovo Station on the Finland Railroad, where the women completed their field training.[4]

As ordered by GUGSh, the 1st Petrograd Women's Battalion was formed in the same manner as male volunteer units, according to the organizational structure set out by the Turkistan Rifle Battalion staff regulations of November 28, 1916. This table of organization allotted for a complement of 1,163 personnel, including all officers and noncombatant auxiliary functions. The battalion was divided into four companies, each company was further separated into four platoons, and each platoon consisted of four squads. The combat battalion included a number of specialized subunits, including a machine-gun detachment, a cavalry-scout detachment, a sapper detachment, a communications detachment, and a transport detachment. A training detachment was assigned to the unit, consisting of 3 officers, 12 NCOs, and 125 soldiers. A reserve company aimed at replenishing forces lost in battle was also to be created, comprising 6 officers, 1 doctor, 6 clerks, 2 medics, 6 orderlies, 2 first sergeants, 42 NCOs, 40 corporals, and 368 rank-and-file troops.[5] The battalion was designated to have a complement of 1,168 women soldiers, and it achieved this number by early August. As in other units, command, training, and senior medical personnel included men.

Our information about the 1st Petrograd Women's Battalion has been greatly enriched by the unpublished memoirs of a member of the unit, Maria

1st Petrograd Women's Battalion clerk (courtesy Museum of the Revolution, Moscow)

Bocharnikova.[6] Much of the information she provides is corroborated by another member of the unit, identified only as "S.," whose story was preserved in an unpublished manuscript.[7] Bocharnikova was a young Russian woman from Tiflis who enlisted in the battalion in June 1917 and served with the unit until it disbanded completely in early 1918. Like many other Russian women soldiers of World War I, Bocharnikova had, from a young age, taken great interest in things military. Her younger brother, a cadet in the Vladikavkaz Cadet Corps, schooled her in military affairs, including formation marching and rifle drill. He thrilled her with stories of Russia's great war heroes. Upon the outbreak of war in 1914, she left home to become a Sister of Mercy after unsuccessfully attempting to enlist as a soldier. She was working as a nurse in Persia when, in May 1917, she learned from a local newspaper of the formation of the women's unit in Petrograd. Bocharnikova jumped at the opportunity to become a soldier and journeyed to Petrograd to enlist. The newspaper had listed an address on Mytninskaya Quay as the place where the unit was being organized. Upon arrival in the capital, however, she was directed to the Engineers' Palace. She soon learned that Mytninskaya Quay was the enlistment point for Bochkareva's battalion. The chief clerk of the organizational committee adamantly emphasized that this unit had nothing to do with Bochkareva's. Bocharnikova was nearly rejected from enlistment, as she was still two months shy of her eighteenth birthday. Ultimately, she was allowed to enter the battalion, after consideration of her

Field kitchen of the 1st Petrograd Women's Battalion (courtesy Museum of the Revolution, Moscow)

service as a Sister of Mercy and the promise of a telegram of permission from her parents.

Bocharnikova provides us with extensive detail about the internal life of the battalion. While housed at the Engineers' Palace, the women slept on piles of straw on the bare floor. When they moved to the encampment at Levashovo, initially they were put up in tents. This option proved less than desirable in heavy rain, so they sought shelter in nearby dachas. The volunteers were fed simple food, mostly bread, kasha, and borscht. They spent their days in intense drill and training exercises. Training for the day ended late in the evening with roll call and the singing of the Lord's Prayer and "God Save Us." Some of the women from more comfortable backgrounds found it difficult to adjust to the Spartan military life of the battalion and left the unit during training. As in Bochkareva's battalion, the women of the 1st Petrograd Women's Battalion had their hair cut short. One of the women in the battalion turned a tidy profit by acquiring a clippers and comb and charging the volunteers fifty kopeks a head for haircuts. The women were issued uniforms, equipment, arms, ammunition, and other necessities of military life, including 1,176 rifles, so that all the members of the battalion were appropriately armed.[8]

Despite the fact that the women's battalion was supposed to receive all necessary financial and material support from the district military authorities, shortages of funds and resources, coupled with a general inattentiveness on the part of military officials, meant that the unit experienced difficulties outfitting its members. Volunteer S. reported that while the women were immediately issued uniforms, they had to wait for boots, and for several weeks, many of the women wore their own shoes.[9] In fact, the Organizational Committee of the Women's Military Union in Petrograd did much work to secure necessary materials for the unit.[10] In order to supplement the women's needs, the union held several public benefits to collect money for the cause of the women's battalion. Such events featured variety show (*estrada*) celebrities who provided entertainment for the public at Luna Park and an American-style auction to raise money for the women soldiers. The centerpiece of the auction was a personally autographed portrait of Kerensky, which inspired an intense bidding competition lasting over forty minutes. The portrait was ultimately sold for more than 20,000 rubles to a Moscow attorney named N. M. Vainberg. In all, nearly 60,000 rubles were reportedly raised from the public for the benefit of the 1st Petrograd Women's Battalion.[11]

As there were no sufficiently trained female officers, the officers of the women's battalion were mostly men. Staff Captain A. V. Loskov of the Petrograd Military District was placed in command of the battalion. Loskov, the son of a hereditary nobleman who had been a lieutenant colonel in the tsarist army, was a graduate of the Kiev Military Academy and had served in the guards of the Keksgol'mskii Regiment.[12] The battalion commander's adjutant, the company commanders, and the training staff were drawn from the district headquarters and other Petrograd units, including the Alexander Nevskii, Semenovskii, and Preobrazhenskii Regiments. The company commander of Bocharnikova's 2nd Company was a young lieutenant of the Nevskii Regiment, Vladimir Somov, to whom she was completely devoted. "Somov was like a loving, caring father-figure," Bocharnikova doted. "I am not exaggerating when I say that at first command each of us would walk into fire or water for him."[13] Captain Shagal (who also left a brief account of his experiences with the battalion), an instructor of the 180th Infantry Reserve Regiment, was assigned to command the 3rd Company. Staff Captain V. N. Dolgov of the Nevskii Regiment was given command of the 4th Company.[14] These were the only male personnel in the unit. The company sergeants, platoon and squad leaders, and other NCOs were drawn from the women volunteers, selected primarily from those who had some knowledge of military affairs or who possessed some level of higher education.

Bocharnikova's background earned her the rank of corporal and command of a squad in the fourth platoon of the 2nd Company. Later she was promoted to junior NCO and made leader of the fourth platoon after the previous leader left

A group of female soldiers of the 1st Petrograd Women's Battalion and their male officers (courtesy Museum of the Revolution, Moscow)

to join the Women's Naval Detachment. Her company sergeant had originally been a young woman of the intelligentsia, but it seems she could not handle the responsibility of her charge. She was replaced by a twenty-three-year-old Cossack woman named Maria Kochereshchko,[15] a veteran of the war, twice wounded, and holder of the St. George's Cross, who was much cruder than her predecessor but who quickly brought the company in line.

According to Bocharnikova, the women who volunteered for this all-female combat unit came from a wide variety of social backgrounds. "There were women of every description—peasant women in bright summer dresses, Sisters of Mercy with their little pigtails, factory workers in their chintz print dresses, high-society ladies in elegant gowns, conservatively dressed office workers, maids, nannies."[16] Among the members of the battalion were sixty women who had been sent to the capital from Viatka after requesting that their local unit be allowed to join the 1st Petrograd Women's Battalion. According to volunteer S., approximately 60 percent of the women came from the intelligentsia; the remaining 40 percent were from the uneducated classes.[17] While the majority were ethnically Russian, Poles, Jews, and other nationalities and ethnic groups were also represented among them. Some had war experience, having served in various capacities, including combat, and there were even two nuns in the ranks of the battalion. Most joined the women's unit for patriotic reasons, but there were also those with personal motivations, including some who sought to escape abusive relationships with men. One woman recounted how her husband had beaten her and pulled half her hair out. As soon as she found out that women were being accepted into the armed services, she ran away and signed up. Her husband lodged a complaint with the draft board but was rebuked by the local commissar, who told him, "Too bad, now she's an apostle of the revolution and liberty. Don't you dare touch her, she's going to the front to defend Russia!"[18] Volunteer S. recalled that she joined to escape from the deep personal sorrow she suffered as a result of the death of her five-year-old son.[19]

The political views of the women volunteers were equally varied. Among their ranks were a number of vociferous monarchists who resented having to swear loyalty to the Provisional Government. They believed the latter had betrayed the tsar, their *batushka* (little father), as many in prerevolutionary Russia referred to the monarch. One volunteer, after seeing veteran revolutionary Ekaterina Breshko-Breshkovskaia speak, commented, "O, grandma, grandma! What a wonderful sweet old lady you are. But how I would delight in hanging every one of your comrades from the nearest tree for their 'Great Bloodless [Revolution]!'"[20] Despite their misgivings about their new government, they took the oath nonetheless and remained committed to carrying out any orders they were given. The oath taking had the significant symbolic effect of finalizing the women's psychological transformation into "true soldiers." The overall sentiment among them was that their job was to defend the motherland from external enemies, regardless of the internal political situation. In essence, their view was consistent with that of the ideal modern army: divorced from politics, but ready to obey commands from those in authority.[21]

In accordance with the regulations of Order Number One, the women's battalion possessed a soldiers' committee like all regular military formations. Bocharnikova was elected to the committee as a representative from her company. Indicative of its social mission, one of the committee's first actions was to implement a literacy campaign within the battalion. They began to tutor the illiterate members of the unit to read and write, but their efforts did not meet with much success. Many of the working-class and peasant women found it very difficult to learn these skills. Others misused their newfound abilities, such as the woman who, upon mastering the scripting of her last name, scrawled it all over the walls of their quarters. Her actions met with sharp rebuke and threats from other members of the company, who warned they would do the same to her posterior unless she ceased immediately. The company committee also set out to eradicate foul language among the women. Bocharnikova reported that this effort was somewhat more successful. They managed to eliminate cursing in the main unit, but in the transport detachment, which was composed mostly of women of the lower classes, many of the volunteers continued to use bad language, despite the committee's decrees against it and the officers' horror at hearing women "curse like sailors."

Unlike Krylova, in her account of life in Bochkareva's battalion, Bocharnikova did not include manifestations of progressive feminism, either on her own behalf or on that of the other volunteers. Nonetheless, it is evident that the women soldiers of this unit were very well aware of the gendered implications of their actions. When male soldiers advised them to return to their homes and their "womanly duties," the women volunteers were quick to retort that it was the men who were not fulfilling their obligations as defenders. "Allow us to give you a suggestion," Bocharnikova reported that the women of her platoon wrote to a soldier who had complained about their actions. "Why don't you dress yourselves up in our summer frocks, tie our scarves around your heads, make the borscht, wash the babies, braid the tails of the livestock, chew your sunflower seeds, and wag your tongues."[22] In another interesting play on their own gender transgression, after taking the soldiers' oath, the women began singing a traditional marching cadence, but reversed the male and female roles: "Soldiers, chums . . . where are your *husbands?*" sang the platoon leader. The volunteers roared back "Our *husbands* are our loaded guns, that's where our *husbands* are!" The original verse, of course, asks soldiers, "Where are your *wives?*" and answers that their *wives* are loaded cannons.[23] Furthermore, the influence of the Petrograd Women's Military Union, with its clearly feminist agenda, undoubtedly played an important role in the life of the battalion.

Relations between male and female personnel within the battalion were good for the most part, and Captain Shagal insisted that the officers were held to the highest standards in their dealings with the women. In fact, he asserted that the officers were particularly concerned about this issue, so much so that they immediately established a "court of honor" to address issues of misconduct on the part of male officers.[24] Bocharnikova, however, related several instances of sexual misconduct. One officer was overheard having sex with a woman soldier in his tent, and both offending parties were forced to leave the battalion immediately. Another male officer, one of the company commanders, was caught giving excessive attention to one of the female volunteers, and he too was dismissed. Bocharnikova reported that while they were training, a rumor went around camp that one of the women volunteers in another company of the battalion had become pregnant. In order to verify the truth, the entire company was subjected to medical examinations. Seven soldiers were found to be expecting, and the pregnancies were assumed to be the result of liaisons with male instructors

1st Petrograd Women's Battalion in camp at Levashovo (courtesy Museum of the Revolution, Moscow)

(since all of the women had undergone medical exams prior to enlistment). Both the male and female personnel involved in the "scandal" were discharged from the unit for their inappropriate behavior. Bocharnikova was appalled and disgusted, seeing such behavior as completely inappropriate for women as well as for soldiers. Despite her transcendence of gender roles, her attitudes about sex were quite conservative, adhering to traditional social mores. Perhaps more importantly, she believed such actions to be damaging to the honor and image of the women's battalion.[25]

The battalion trained throughout the summer and fall of 1917. In early October, the combat training became more intensive as the volunteers prepared for their scheduled departure for the front at the end of the month. On October 17, the quartermaster general of the Petrograd Military District reported to the chief of the Department of Organization and Service of Troops of GUGSh that the formation and training of the women's unit were complete and that it was prepared to be sent to join the active army.[26] Upon receipt of this information, Stavka ordered the 1st Petrograd Women's Battalion to be dispatched to the Romanian front on October 24.[27] The battalion would never reach its intended destination, however, as political events in the capital on the twenty-fourth would intervene and draw the female soldiers into the battle for control of the Russian government.[28]

## THE 2ND MOSCOW WOMEN'S BATTALION OF DEATH

The 2nd Moscow Women's Battalion of Death began its life as a grassroots-initiated organization in early June 1917 through the efforts of a private citizen named R. P. Slug. Slug had served in a medical detachment with a number of other women at the front, and she had witnessed great courage and valor on the part of women as nurses and as soldiers. As a result, she was a great believer in the power and abilities of women. She was convinced that the presence of women at the front provided great inspiration for the men and therefore that a women's battalion would awaken the "warrior spirit" in male soldiers who were refusing to fight and spur them into action. Slug was aided in her efforts to create a women's military unit by the Moscow women's military organization, the All-Russian Women's Military Union of Aid to the Motherland. The union's leadership included women's activists M. A. Rychkova, R. A. Popova, and N. A. Zubova.[29] This group was extensively involved in the war effort and already had organized women in a variety of areas. In addition to a division promoting the creation of women's military formations in the Russian armed forces, the organization possessed a department devoted to the care of volunteers' and soldiers' families, a medical division in which women doctors, medics, nurses, and other medical personnel were organized into ambulance and auxiliary units, a communications section, an organization that provided aid to wounded and disabled soldiers and to prisoners of war, and an agitation-propaganda section that worked to combat desertion and disintegration in the rear.[30] The union established an organizational committee dedicated to facilitating the formation of a women's military unit in Moscow.

In early June, the organizational committee of the All-Russian Women's Military Union of Aid to the Motherland began recruiting women for the battalion, initially registering them in Slug's own apartment on Tverskaia Street.[31] Committee member Nekrasova also offered her apartment on Troitskaia Street for the registration of female volunteers, and the Dresden Hotel on Skobelevskaia Square was used for this purpose as well.[32] Once official approval for the formation of the battalion had been secured through the Ministry of War, General Kamenskii, chief of GUGSh's Department of Organization and Service of Troops, ordered the chief of staff of the Moscow Military District, General Verkhovskii, to proceed with the formation of the women's infantry battalion.[33] The approximately 300 women who had already registered for the battalion through the women's union were accepted into the official formation. Efforts to find appropriate accommodations, uniforms, equipment, and arms were undertaken by the military district headquarters, with the assistance of the Moscow quartermaster and the Moscow Guberniia Committee. On June 27, the women's unit occupied the barracks of the 56th Infantry Reserve Regiment, and registration continued there.[34] As with the other women's units, enlistment was open to women between the ages of eighteen and forty, and women desiring to join the battalion were required to undergo a complete medical examination. Those who were deemed unfit for combat service had the choice of joining auxiliary medical or other noncombatant detachments. Women under the age of twenty were required to secure their parents' permission to enter the unit.[35]

As word spread of the formation of this women's battalion in Moscow, the unit grew significantly. By the end of June, more than 400 had enlisted in the battalion. The first two companies, consisting of 213 and 216 women each, were formed on June 25 and June 27, respectively. Two more companies, with similar numbers, were organized on July 9 and July 12, when the numbers of volunteers had swelled to over 1,000. Enlistment, as well as discharging, continued throughout the formation and training period, during the summer and fall of 1917, and personnel flowed in and out of the battalion. In all, by September, 2,746 women had applied to join the 2nd Moscow Women's Battalion of Death, but many of these had been rejected on grounds of poor health or had left on their own accord.[36]

The staff of the Moscow battalion, like that of the 1st Petrograd Women's Battalion, was arranged according to the staff regulations of the Turkistan Rifle Battalion.[37] In addition to the main infantry combat unit, the battalion included two communications detachments, a cavalry-scout detachment, a sapper detachment, a transport detachment, and a machine-gun detachment. The battalion was designated as an infantry unit exclusively for combat assignment. Colonel I. A. Chibisov was assigned to command the battalion, taking his post on June 21, 1917. As his adjutant, Chibisov selected one of the women volunteers, Ekaterina Cholovskaia. Two staff officers from the reserves of the district headquarters as well as four senior officers and twelve soldiers of the Aleksandrov Military College were assigned to aid in the formation and training of the battalion. The district medical examiner appointed a doctor to the unit as well.[38]

Chibisov insisted upon strict discipline in his unit, believing that "the stronger the discipline in the battalion, the more unified in force it will be."[39] Accordingly, he ordered austere internal order to be established in the barracks and the conduct of the women to be scrutinized closely, particularly in relation to their behavior with men. This did not, however, mean that Chibisov enforced the discipline of the tsarist army, nor was his discipline as ironfisted as that of Bochkareva. All the principles of the "newly constructed social-democratic republic"[40] were adhered to in this unit. Accordingly, the battalion elected soldiers' committees entrusted with all the authority vested by Order Number One in regulating the internal life of the unit.[41] Committee elections were deferred until such time as the volunteers became better acquainted with one another. Ultimately, they were held on August 20; six women were chosen as representatives and three additional volunteers were designated as alternates. The battalion's internal disciplinary court was also created at this time.[42] While as individuals the members of the battalion had the right to belong to any political party or association, the battalion as a whole was prohibited from pursuing any political goals that were not in accordance with the views of the Petrograd Soviet of Workers' and Soldiers' Deputies or that did not support the Provisional Government. This was a somewhat sticky requirement, considering that there were issues on which the two governing bodies undoubtedly conflicted.[43]

The daily activities of the members of the battalion were strictly regimented. The women volunteers rose at 6:30 AM and were required to say morning prayers. From 6:30 to 7:30, they cleaned their barracks for inspection by their platoon commanders and squad leaders. A sparse breakfast of tea and bread was their reward for passing inspection. Intensive training and work assignments followed until 11:00, when lunch was served. After lunch, the volunteers were given a break until 2:00 PM, at which time they resumed their training. At 6:00, the battalion members were given dinner, and then they engaged in marching and other military drills until 9:00. At 10:00, the women retired to the barracks and went to sleep after saying evening prayers.

The women soldiers were to have limited contact with the civilian world. Visits from family members or friends were only permitted with prior approval from command personnel. The volunteers were allowed short leaves from the battalion when they were free from duties, but they were required to return to their barracks by 10:00 PM. While in the city on leave or on official military duty, the women were instructed to conduct themselves flawlessly, never forgetting that they held the "high and honorable title of soldier" and "that even one improper action . . . will reflect unfavorably upon the entire battalion."[44]

The volunteers were schooled by male instructors assigned by the Moscow Military District Headquarters. Once enough women officers had been properly trained, these men, as well as the male command personnel, were to be replaced by female officers. For this purpose, twenty-five women from among those members of the battalion possessing higher education were chosen to attend the Aleksandrov Military College.[45] Upon completion of officer-training courses, these women were to be promoted to the rank of sublieutenant and assigned to command posts in the battalion. By late September, all twenty-five

Volunteers of the Moscow Women's Battalion of Death in officer's training (courtesy Museum of the Revolution, Moscow)

women cadets had completed their education and received officers' commissions.[46] They were never, however, assigned to command positions, their service being cut short by the Bolshevik Revolution in October.

The social composition of the 2nd Moscow Women's Battalion of Death was as varied as that of the other all-female military units formed at this time. A number of women volunteers possessed secondary and higher education, and some came from the nobility and middle classes. The great majority, however, were derived from the working classes and peasantry. Many were unskilled laborers, domestic and other servants, factory workers, or peasants. Most were unmarried and childless. Nearly all the women soldiers were Russian Orthodox, although there were several Roman Catholics, at least one Lutheran, and one Muslim among the ranks. Quite a few Cossack women were members of the battalion as well. Most of the women were not native Muscovites, having been born in places all over Russia, from Irkutsk, Siberia, to Lublin, Poland. A number of the women volunteers in this battalion had previous military experience, and several had been awarded military honors, including St. George's medals, for their heroism. Others were Sisters of Mercy or other medical personnel who had served in the war.[47] The average age of the enlistees was around twenty years old, but they ranged from as young as fifteen (despite the age minimum of eighteen) to as old as thirty-seven.[48] In fact, the unit attracted many young girls who, upon hearing of the formation of the battalion, had left home against their parent's will, or without their knowledge, and attempted to join. Their concerned families often appealed to the Moscow Military District Headquarters requesting that their runaway daughters be returned home.[49]

During its training, the 2nd Moscow Women's Battalion of Death was visited by a number of prominent personages. On July 2, the Moscow women's battalion was blessed by Archbishop Tikhon in a benediction ceremony held on Red Square. The battalion was presented with an icon of St. George the Victorious by the unit of St. George's Cavaliers.[50] Representatives of the Allied missions to Russia made a special point of coming to see the female soldiers in early August. The foreign visitors were much impressed by the women's unit. Pankhurst, who was among the delegation that reviewed the women soldiers, commented that she thought the women were "in perfect form." In a speech following the review, she told the Russian women that their efforts were demonstrating that women were equal to men not only in rights but in responsibilities as well. A member of the French mission, Colonel Luazon, was delighted by the seriousness with which the women occupied themselves in military tasks and was certain that the discipline of the women's battalion would serve as an excellent example for many male units. He praised the women volunteers in a heartfelt speech in which he exclaimed that in France there had been only one Joan of Arc, but in Russia, there were many.[51]

Not all observers held such high opinions of the Moscow women's unit. In fact, when Bochkareva visited the battalion in July, she was appalled at the unmilitary manner of the women volunteers. "When I arrived at the barracks . . . I nearly fainted at the sight of them. They were nearly all rouged, wearing slippers and fancy stockings, loosely dressed and of very nonchalant bearing. There were plenty of [male] soldiers around, and their relations with the girls were revolting." She accused them of resembling prostitutes and disgracing the army.[52] While these claims are undoubtedly exaggerated, they reflect the somewhat more relaxed discipline and less stringent control of the Moscow unit as compared with Bochkareva's own ironfisted Spartanism.

Bochkareva's comments referring to the women's dress are indicative of the problems the unit had securing uniforms and footwear. The Moscow district warehouses had been ordered to provide the women's unit with arms, equipment, and supplies, including uniforms, ammunition, weapons, and tools. The warehouse, however, did not deliver all the necessary items. One Moscow

Blessing of the 2nd Moscow Women's Battalion of Death colors on Red Square, July 2 (courtesy Museum of the Revolution, Moscow)

newspaper reported that the Moscow quartermaster refused the unit's request for uniforms, stating that those designed for men were unsuitable for women. This meant that the battalion was forced to procure many of the volunteer's uniforms by its own means.[53] Collections were taken up at public gatherings for this purpose. For example, on June 22, supporters of the women's battalion appealed to a crowd of 10,000, which had gathered to honor the soldiers who fell in the first phase of the June offensive, to assist the women volunteers. Over 5,000 rubles were raised for the unit.[54] When the Moscow women's battalion eventually did receive uniforms, they were standard issue rather than uniforms altered or made to fit women's physiques. The women's wearing of civilian footwear similarly was due to the fact that they had not been supplied with sufficient numbers of properly fitting army boots. A scarcity of leather in the city only aggravated this problem and delayed the order put in to the army for boots made to fit women's feet.[55] In addition, there were shortages of needed equipment and provisions. Thus, what Bochkareva perceived as blatant disregard for military regulations was probably the result of the central military authorities' inattentiveness to and inability to fulfill the needs of the Moscow women's battalion.

The battalion experienced other problems as well. Relations between male and female personnel within the unit were fairly smooth, but neighboring male units were not happy about the creation of the all-female battalion. Many of these men expressed their animosity openly. Male soldiers from units located in the nearby Khamovnicheskii Barracks harassed the women while they gathered for roll call, hurling insults and criticism at the female soldiers. They attempted to hinder command personnel as they gave orders and assignments. Others behaved indecently toward the women volunteers. These activities became so troublesome that the company committees of the women's battalion drafted a resolution to the committees of the military units of the Khamovnicheskii Barracks requesting the disciplining of the guilty parties and prevention of further disruptions on the part of the men.[56] It is interesting to note that the experience of this unit was similar to that of Bochkareva's unit, in that animosity was expressed most vociferously by male soldiers who had limited contact with the women. There was also hostility from some civilians.[57] During the course of their training, one of the members of the Moscow battalion was apparently killed after a fall from a moving streetcar. Although the source does not indicate violence, the woman soldier may have been intentionally pushed by a disgruntled fellow rider. The funeral was highly ceremonial, attended by members of the Moscow Women's Union, the command staff of the battalion, the commander of the Aleksandrov Military College, Major General Mikheev, and British suffragette Pankhurst. The woman soldier was buried with military honors, and the funeral procession was accompanied by a military orchestra.[58]

By September, the problems experienced by the 2nd Moscow Women's Battalion of Death seem to have become too great to overcome. Many of the women were highly dissatisfied with the unit and had become disillusioned with the attempt to create an all-female fighting force. Nearly 200 had already expressed their unhappiness by leaving the unit without being officially dismissed. Hundreds of others requested permission to quit the battalion and return to their homes. Inundated with requests for dismissal, Chibisov appealed to GUGSh for direction. The military administration granted permission for the dismissal of any volunteer desiring to be released from service.[59] Since no statutes existed regarding the status of these women as soldiers, the government had no conflict in allowing them to return to civilian life. Given the opportunity, volunteers poured out of the battalion, and by mid-September the unit could no longer maintain its internal cohesion. At this time, the commanding officers decided to disband the battalion. It is unclear, however, whether this decision served as the impetus for, or was prompted by, the mass departures of volunteers.[60]

In the wake of the dissolution of their unit, many of the remaining women asked to be sent immediately to the front lest they lose their long-awaited op-

portunity to fight for their country. Colonel Chibisov and the Moscow Military
District authorities decided to grant their requests. On September 26, 10
women were dispatched to the Romanian front, 5 were sent to join the 1st Siberian Artillery Division, and 5 became part of the 58th Pokravskii Regiment.
That same day, 42 female volunteers were sent to the southwestern front. On
September 27, 208 members of the 2nd Moscow Women's Battalion of Death
left for the (Russian) western front. A second echelon, consisting of 212 of their
comrades in arms, joined them on September 30.[61]

Their unanticipated arrival at army headquarters provoked the chagrin of the
front's command personnel, who did not know quite what to do with the female
volunteers. They had received no preliminary information about the women and
had no knowledge of the extent or nature of their military training or for what
kind of assignment they were intended. The chief of staff of the western front
armies appealed to GUGSh for instructions. After a month, GUGSh finally
replied that the volunteers had been dispatched by the Moscow Military District without its approval, in response to their own desire to join the fighting at
the front, but offered no guidance.[62] Not knowing exactly how to proceed, the
staff of the headquarters of the western front placed them under the authority of
the commander of the Tenth Army. They were then assigned to the 27th Infantry Division. The front command personnel was not pleased with this situation and explicitly requested that they be sent no more women's units. Stavka,
having been informed of the situation, ordered that all units that "do not affect
the battle situation" should be disbanded in an effort to reduce staff and con-
serve materials.

The military authorities undoubtedly believed that the women soldiers fit
into this category, for not only did they have serious reservations about the utility of women's military units, but their existence was viewed as "quite problematic" and "their formation and maintenance calls for extraneous expenditure
from the treasury, not to mention the excessive complications involved in their
organization."[63] As a result, a committee of representatives from the 27th Division voted to disband the women's companies and send the female volunteers
home in mid-November. The women soldiers were never given the opportunity
to prove themselves in battle.[64]

## THE 3RD KUBAN WOMEN'S SHOCK BATTALION

The creation of a women's military unit in the Kuban region was initially undertaken, as in Petrograd and Moscow, through private initiative. In early June
1917, Matriona Leontevna Zalesskaia, a Kuban Cossack, began gathering

women from around the region in the city of Ekaterinodar for the purposes of defending Russia against its external enemies. "In view of the fact that the homeland is enduring heavy trials in this terrible war," wrote Zalesskaia, "I, as a daughter who deeply loves her motherland, call upon all women in the city of Ekaterinodar, as well as the whole of the Kuban Oblast, who are free from familial duty, to unite and form a cadre of women able to actively carry out combat service in the active army."[65]

After recruiting several hundred women volunteers for the unit in June, Zalesskaia and the organizational committee of the battalion turned to the Ministry of War for official sanction and assistance in the unit's formation.[66] At this time, the central military authorities were looking for ways to accommodate the continued requests by women to join the fighting. In July, they resolved to expand the women's military movement by creating additional all-female military formations, including another women's infantry battalion designated for combat assignment. The activities in Ekaterinodar proved a convenient means to accomplish this goal, building upon private efforts that had already begun the organizational process. Thus, GUGSh gave its permission for the formation of the 3rd Kuban Women's Shock Battalion in July 1917 and designated it for combat service at the front.

The formation of the Kuban women's battalion was conducted in a manner similar to that of the official all-female military units in Petrograd and Moscow. The model for its organization was likewise the Turkistan Rifle Battalion staff regulations. The executive work connected to the formation of this unit was placed under the authority of the commander of troops of the Caucasian Military District. GUGSh assigned financial responsibility for the formation of the unit to the war fund and initially ordered the release of 1,500 rubles for this purpose. Any additional expenses associated with the women's unit were also to be covered by the war fund. All supplies and equipment were to be furnished by the army's main supply administration. Horses were ordered from the equestrian reserves.[67] Zalesskaia appealed to the Ministry of War in an effort to ensure that the equipment, uniforms, and supplies issued to the unit be compatible with the female physique. In particular, she was concerned that clothing be of appropriate sizes to fit women, especially the boots.[68] Uniforms, therefore, were to be specially made to fit the measurements of the members of the battalion.

As in other all-female units, command positions were to be temporarily filled by men until women had received officer training and could replace them. The organizational committee requested that the commander be a staff officer with battlefield experience and at least one military honor. They had a particular individual in mind, a Cossack staff officer serving under the ataman of Kuban Cossack Forces, Sergeant Major Andrian Sinchilo.[69] Sinchilo had served in the active army since the beginning of the war, as part of the 7th Cossack Infantry Battalion, 2nd Kuban Cossack Infantry Brigade, and held a number of honors and medals. Since the spring of 1917 he had been working together with the committee in order to bring the women's unit to fruition.[70]

In order to minimize the number of male personnel in the unit, the staff list called for the smallest officer complement necessary for the functioning of the battalion. All other personnel, including doctors, medics, and all combat and noncombat personnel, were to be female volunteers. The staff list of the battalion called for 1,000–1,200 combatant and noncombatant personnel. One-fifth were to be devoted to noncombatant service. The battalion was to be divided into four companies, and each company was to have four platoons. A fifth company was also to be formed from the surplus of women volunteers; it was to serve as a reserve company to replenish casualties once the unit was put into action. Company commanders were to be junior NCOs with previous battle experience. Each platoon was to have a leader with similar qualifications. Additionally, ten NCOs were to be assigned to each company for the purposes of training and instruction. These staff positions were to be filled by those with combat experience, preferably by women when possible. Two female doctors and five female medics were to be included in the ranks of the unit. The unit was to designate a clerk, treasurer, and armaments master from among the volunteers. Other noncombatant personnel, such as a priest, a rifle master and apprentice, two blacksmiths, two harness masters, and a cobbler, were also on the list of staff personnel for the battalion, but these positions could be filled from outside units, even by men. Zalesskaia was chosen to be an assistant to the commander, at the rank of junior staff officer, and was to serve as a mediator between the women volunteers and the command personnel.[71]

All women of adult age were accepted into the organization, as were minors who had secured the permission of their parents or guardians. Once registered, the volunteers were instructed to forget about their homes, families, and friends during their time of service and devote themselves fully to military life.[72] The majority of women volunteers for the Kuban unit were Cossacks and Caucasians, although enlistment was open to all residents of the Kuban Oblast. Many of the volunteers were soldiers' wives. A number of the enlistees had previous military experience, including several who had participated in combat as part of male units during the war.

The Kuban women's battalion seems to have been the most neglected of the Russian women's military formations of 1917, receiving very little support from the military establishment. The unit experienced a great deal of difficulty in organization, and the formation process moved extremely slowly. Although the Ministry of War had given its approval for the formation of the unit in July, by September, the organizers of the battalion had yet to receive the appropriate paperwork necessary to begin formation.[73] By October, little to no progress had been made in bringing the unit into existence. It is not clear why. The central military authorities seemed to have been completely unaware of what was going on in regard to this battalion. On September 26, 1917, GUGSh's Department of Organization and Service of Troops wrote to the Military Headquarters of the Kuban Caucasian Forces inquiring whether the women's battalion was prepared to be dispatched to the front, as called for by their combat designation.[74]

But the unit had barely moved beyond the initial steps of organization, and by mid-October, official formation had yet to be undertaken. On October 15, the organizational committee of the battalion appealed to the commander in chief of the Caucasian Army to immediately order the formation to be completed, since approval had been secured from all the appropriate authorities.[75] On October 21, Zalesskaia turned to the Kuban Military District, asking for immediate assistance in the formation of the women's unit. The unit was still lacking supplies, equipment, horses, and sufficient funds to proceed.[76] Nor had any of the unit's officers, other than the battalion commander, Sergeant Major Sinchilo, been appointed. The battalion had not even received the proper paperwork and documentation required to implement formation procedures and conduct official registration and staff assignment. On October 24, the military authorities in Kuban requested instructions on whether funds could be released for the formation of the women's unit. By this time, direct supervision of the activities associated with the unit had been transferred to the ataman of the Kuban Cossack Forces.[77]

It seems that only at this time did the actual formation of the 3rd Kuban Women's Shock Battalion get under way. On November 7, 1917, GUGSh issued a general order for the disbanding of all the women's military units with the exception of the 1st Petrograd Women's Battalion. The order appears to have been ignored in Ekaterinodar, as was a second resolution issued on November 30 reiterating the order. On December 10, although the unit now had personnel, it still had not received armaments, equipment, or supplies. At the end of that month, the Mobilization Department of the Caucasian Military District asked whether the women's battalion wished to be transferred to Tiflis to carry out garrison duty in that city.[78] The offer was accompanied by the promise that the battalion would be fully armed and equipped once it arrived in that city. But the battalion was never dispatched to Tiflis. Instead, it seems to have lingered on in

Ekaterinodar into the early months of 1918. Until this time, it had seemed desirable to maintain the formation of the women's unit, as one of those that retained "a consciousness of duty, patriotism, and honor."[79] But by late February 1918, the commissar of military-naval affairs of the Zakavkaz Commissariat decided that serious shortages made it impossible to arm and supply the women's unit.[80] There are no further mentions of the unit in official documents. One can only assume that it disbanded; without weapons and equipment, there would have been little point in retaining it.

### THE 1ST WOMEN'S NAVAL DETACHMENT

Efforts to create women's military formations in Russia during World War I were not limited to the army. At least one all-female unit was organized in the navy in the summer of 1917. Like all the other women's military formations of this time, the women's naval unit was initiated from within the private sector. The Circle of Women's Labor for the Motherland appealed to the Petrograd Military District, the Ministry of the Navy, and the Main Naval Headquarters to establish women's naval units for use "wherever there is need for responsible and essential work for the honor and benefit of the dear motherland."[81] The main organizing force behind the move to create a women's unit in the naval forces was a woman who called herself Marina Morskaia (using the Russian word for "naval" as her nom de guerre).[82] The pressure brought to bear by Morskaia and her circle, along with a general need for manpower, convinced the minister of the navy to authorize, on July 1, 1917, the formation of women's naval detachments for service in the rear.[83]

The first (and inevitably only) Russian women's naval unit was organized under the authority of the Naval Infantry Training Detachment in Oranienbaum. This unit, titled the 1st Women's Naval Detachment, had a proposed complement of 150 persons. Although the women were to receive combat training, upon completion of their military preparation they would be assigned to serve in auxiliary capacities in the coastal administration of the Kolsk Naval Base, where there was a great need for such services. This meant that the majority of women volunteers were intended for labor in bakeries, laundries, and mess halls and in cleaning capacities. A few who possessed the appropriate skills and training were to be assigned to accounting and clerical duties. Undoubtedly, the naval authorities viewed such assignments as more suitable for women.[84]

The commander of the Naval Infantry Training Detachment, Lieutenant Vladimirtsov, was responsible for the details associated with the formation of the women's naval unit. Upon receiving instructions from the Main Naval Headquarters to proceed with formation, he began making the necessary arrangements to fulfill this order. He requested that supplies be ordered and monies be released from the Kronstadt Port in order to equip the women's unit. Realizing that existing standard-issue uniforms and footwear would not fit women, he asked that a sufficient number of boots and caps be made in small sizes and that five or six experienced tailors be assigned to the unit, along with appropriate material and sewing machines, to make the necessary alterations to uniforms.[85] The Main Naval Headquarters approved all of Vladimirtsov's requests and told him to address any further needs to the captain of the Kronstadt Port.[86] Additionally, ribbons that read "Women's Naval Detachment" were ordered for the women's caps.[87]

Although the staff list of the 1st Women's Naval Detachment called for 150 volunteers, fewer than forty women actually registered to serve in the unit. There were no restrictions on those who could enlist, but because of the severe arctic climate of the region, only women of robust health were accepted.[88] All but two of the enlistees were working women who held paying jobs outside the home, engaged in both blue-collar and white-collar labor. Eight worked as clerks, typists, and general office workers; six were tailors, dressmakers, and seamstresses; five were agricultural laborers; three were cooks. Several of the women had medical backgrounds: Three were nurses, one was a medic, and another was a hospital orderly. Two were domestic servants and one worked as a server in a tavern. One volunteer worked as a telephonist, and another in a printing press. Another woman was an unskilled laborer. One worked as a nanny in an orphanage. The two who were not employed possessed secondary education. The only professional among the group was a teacher.[89]

The volunteers of the women's naval unit were required to rise at 7:30 AM each day and clean their quarters. After morning tea and prayers, the enlistees were subjected to inspection. Following inspection, the unit engaged in physical exercises for an hour and fifteen minutes. The rest of their day was filled by training drills, interrupted only by a short lunch and rest break at midday. They had dinner at 7:00 PM, and at 9:00 PM they were required to say evening prayers and go to bed. On Mondays and Thursdays, their afternoon drill included training to salute, and Saturdays were bathing days for the entire unit.[90]

Initially, Vladimirtsov was unclear about the kind of training the women volunteers were to receive. He queried the central naval authorities on July 19, asking whether the women were to be drilled merely in basic military affairs—that is, marching, forming ranks, and saluting—or whether their instruction would include rifle training (and if so, whether the necessary rifles would be

A group of young recruits to the 1st Women's Naval Detachment in uniform (courtesy Museum of the Revolution, Moscow)

distributed to them).[91] Ultimately, shooting would not be part of their military training. Literacy, however, was, and each afternoon at 4:30 the women had hour-long lessons in reading and writing. Two officers, Ensign A. Vasil'ev and 2nd Lieutenant Chuksanov, were assigned to the Naval Infantry Training Detachment for the purpose of literacy instruction among the women.[92] One must therefore assume that many of the volunteers in the women's naval detachment were illiterate or, at best, semiliterate.

The male sailors of the Naval Infantry Training Detachment did not welcome the creation of an all-female unit in their midst. The sailors' committee of the unit made a formal protest against the order issued by the Ministry of the Navy authorizing the formation of the 1st Women's Naval Detachment. The sailors, while welcoming the women's "great display of patriotism," considered the unit completely unnecessary. The men had clearly been insulted by what they perceived as a challenge to their masculinity and to their roles as defenders. Their remonstration was tinged with hostility and subtle threats. They described the introduction of women into their midst as "an intolerable act" that might have "entirely undesirable results." The sailors suggested that the women use their energies and strengths in labor at home rather than serving their country in a military capacity. They advised women to organize not battalions of death and shock detachments, but labor battalions to engage in auxiliary work where it was needed most—in the cities, towns, and countryside, helping the very old and very young.[93] This sentiment was shared by the members of the Central Committee of the All-Russian Navy (Tsentroflot). Yet despite their opposition, once the order was implemented, they did not hamper the formation or training of the women's unit. In fact, they even confirmed one of the women, Evdokiia Skvortsova, as an active member of the sailors' committee to serve as the representative of the women's detachment.[94]

The men, however, did not need to mount much resistance to the women's detachment. As of mid-August, only thirty-five women had enlisted in the unit, and therefore the main naval authorities decided to disband it on August 16, 1917.[95] The women who had enlisted in the detachment were given the opportunity to serve the navy in the capacity of hired laborers at the Kolsk Naval Base and wherever else need for their services existed.[96] Essentially, they would be assigned to the same types of service for which they had been designated originally, as part of the women's naval detachment, but now they would be considered civilians and would be paid for their work. The women would be provided with food and transportation vouchers for their journeys.[97]

Upon learning of the decision to disband the women's naval detachment, the women's circle that had initiated the organization of the unit was somewhat distraught, but the opportunity for employment in civilian service made available to the enlistees eased their distress. However, they insisted that the navy allow the women to retain their uniforms. Taking back the uniforms, they argued, would greatly offend the volunteers, who had been promised full rights as sailors until the end of the war, including the right to wear military dress. Initially, the naval authorities agreed to allow the women volunteers to continue wearing their sailors' uniforms, since many had no opportunity to obtain any other clothing.[98]

This decision, however, ruffled many feathers among the male naval personnel, who had a particular objection to outfitting the women volunteers in sailors' uniforms. It seems the men found it difficult to stomach the sight of women dressed as sailors. In order to satisfy both the men and the women, the naval administration ordered that the female volunteers' navy uniforms be replaced by army uniforms. The women were allowed to keep their underwear and boots, but they had to exchange the rest of their navy uniforms for army uniforms. Full winter army uniforms, including sheepskin coats, fur hats, and winter boots, were ordered for the women, but shortages prevented the delivery of all requested items.[99] Although the naval authorities considered the 1st

Women's Naval Detachment officially disbanded and the issue closed after August 16, the remaining women volunteers were allowed to remain in their accommodations in the Naval Infantry Training Detachment until they were dispatched to their civilian positions or returned to their homes.[100]

Despite its disapproval of the formation of women's naval units, Tsentroflot extended its protection to the women sailors after the detachment had been formally disbanded by the naval authorities. The committee, understanding that there were extenuating circumstances associated with the women's unit, even agreed to allow the continuation of the provision of all allowances and rights to the female volunteers and to permit the women to continue wearing provisional sailors' uniforms, until they could be replaced by army uniforms, as long as the women conducted themselves honorably. This sympathetic attitude may have been a combination of working-class affinity and male paternalism.

On the whole, it seems that the relations between the male and female sailors were more or less amiable. There is only one recorded case of a complaint by a female volunteer against a male sailor, but it is based upon a relatively innocuous incident. When one of the women volunteers, Mira Iofa, was visited by a male relative, a sailor from another command, named Ivanov, demanded the outsider leave, threatening them both and verbally insulting Iofa when she asked for an explanation. The committee declined to pursue the issue, judging Ivanov's words and actions to be less than criminal.[101]

Following the order to disband the unit, the volunteers of the 1st Women's Naval Detachment were dispersed to various locations where they could be put to work. The three members of the unit who were Sisters of Mercy, Vera Mikhailova, Pelageia Kosik, and Evdokia Ponamareva, were offered paid employment as nurses in the naval infirmaries at the Kolsk and Iokong bases. They were dispatched there on September 3.[102] Six other enlistees were sent to the commander of the Kolsk Naval Base on September 19 for domestic labor and clerical work.[103] Two volunteers, Vera Shopshina and Agrapina Kobiakova, were sent to the Commission on Women's Labor Conscription for assignment to service in medical units on September 19.[104] On September 21, ten volunteers were dispatched to the Women's Military Union in Petrograd.[105] The detachment representative to the sailors' committee, Evdokiia Skvortsova, left for Irkutsk on September 28, having secured documentation from the commander of the Naval Infantry Training Detachment, for her travel.[106] A number of the members of the women's unit seem to have remained under the command of the Naval Infantry Training Detachment until the Bolshevik seizure of power in late October. Their ultimate fate is unknown. There are no official records pertaining to the Women's Naval Detachment after October 1917.

# 6

## THE FATE OF THE MOVEMENT

### THE PINNACLE

By midsummer 1917, the women's military movement had grown significantly. The failure of the June offensive did not deter women from the cause of aiding their country militarily. Women from all over Russia continued to be involved in the efforts to create all-female military formations and to send women to the front to defend the homeland, and more joined these efforts as the summer progressed. There were attempts to organize women for military participation in more than fifteen cities, including Petrograd, Moscow, Kiev, Saratov, Ekaterinodar, Minsk, Odessa, Mariupol', Tashkent, Viatka, Pavlgrad, Baku, Ekaterinburg, Poltava, Kharkov, Tver, Simbirsk, and even Kharbin in China. In southern Russia and Ukraine, women's military organizations were particularly numerous, and a Black Sea Women's Military Union was formed. GUGSh commented in mid-July that "the lofty impulses of women-volunteers, having expressed themselves passionately in their desire to give their strength and their lives for freedom and the hard-won revolution, has begun to take on a mass character."[1] Yet the Russian military authorities were too preoccupied with other problems and too little convinced of the benefit of all-female units to give the required attention and resources to the development of the women's military movement.

Where official efforts were insufficient, private initiatives attempted to fill the gaps. Women's quasi-military associations worked to accommodate the large numbers of women wishing to serve their country as soldiers through a variety of efforts in the above-mentioned cities. Although all these groups aimed at achieving female participation in the active army, their actions were incongruent and disorderly. Their success in recruiting and organizing, their methods of formation and training, and the extent of their record keeping were equally uneven. As a result, it was nearly impossible to determine precisely how many women were involved and in what capacity they were serving. In an attempt to coordinate the disparate efforts of the various individuals and groups engaged in the women's military movement and to bring them together under a centralized authority, the Organizational Committee of the Petrograd Women's Military Union decided to convene a Women's Military Congress. In mid-July, the committee issued a statement to the press announcing the congress in Petrograd and inviting representatives from all the women's voluntary war-work organizations from around the country to attend:

> Women-citizens! The fatherland is in danger! The decisive hour has come. . . . The enemy, highly disciplined and technically strong, is threatening to take our fields and our very blood, to destroy that which took centuries to create, and to stamp out our young freedom. It is the duty of everyone to help the homeland out of this difficult situation. And we women cannot remain on the sidelines, indifferently observing while everything good and valuable we have is destroyed. But our separate actions, our individual efforts, are not significant in the great matter of helping the state. We must unite—in this there is strength. We must organize—in this there is power. The women's volunteer movement . . . must be unified, well-ordered.[2]

The Women's Military Congress was held at the Nikolaev Engineering School in Petrograd on August 1–4, 1917. More than fifty individual women soldiers and representatives of both official and grassroots women's military units and quasi-military organizations from all over the country, as well as of nursing and medical units, attended the gathering.[3] A small number of women volunteers from the 1st Petrograd Women's Battalion who excelled in rifle drill were selected to form an honor guard for the convention.[4] The meeting was "suffused with the spirit of feminism and Socialist Revolutionary style patriotism."[5] Speakers invoked images of self-sacrifice for the nation, coupled with progressive achievement for women.

Elizaveta Molleson, chairwoman of the Petrograd Women's Military Union, opened the congress on the evening of August 1, welcoming all the courageous women delegates. Captain L. N. Rostov, a member of the Petrograd Women's Military Union (and one of the few men actively involved in the organization of women's military formations), asked the attendees to rise in order to pay homage to the memory of those who had laid down their lives for the homeland. Rostov stressed the necessity of demonstrating the effectiveness and value of the women's military organizations in the face of the unfavorable, at times even hostile, response by some elements of Russian society. To bolster his remarks and buoy the spirits of the delegates, the captain read a testimonial from the commander of the 1st Siberian Infantry Division commending the courageous actions of Bochkareva's battalion in battle and praising the women soldiers for their positive impact on the morale of the male soldiers. Veteran revolutionary Ekaterina Breshko-Breshkovskaia, whose appearance on the stage was met with thunderous applause, commended the women warriors for their courage. She called on them to be proud and to ignore derision and insults from cowardly men. Comparing their efforts with her own revolutionary struggle against the tsarist autocracy, she urged the women to bravely go to the front and into battle with the enemy and reminded the attendees that equality of women and men included equality of responsibility. In honor of the "grandmother of the revolution," the guard detachment of the 1st Petrograd Women's Battalion presented arms, and the military orchestra played "The Marseillaise."[6]

The delegates selected Olga Nechaeva, leader of the Russian Union of Women's Democratic Organizations and head of the Ministry of War's Commission on Women's Labor Conscription, to chair the gathering. In her address, she reported on the activities of the commission, particularly its efforts to introduce a project for the recruitment of women into medical service. Breshko-Breshkovskaia was chosen honorary chairwoman. The head of the Black Sea Women's Military Union made a presentation on the organization of women's military units in the provinces. The delegates voted to send a telegram to Minister of War Kerensky in thanks for allowing the creation of the women's military units. The day's business closed with a parade and review of the 1st Petrograd Women's Battalion in the courtyard of the Engineers' Palace.[7]

Over the next three days, the delegates addressed issues concerning the Russian women's military movement. Molleson stressed the need to definitively determine both how many and in what capacity women were participating in military endeavors throughout the country. Bringing all the activities associated with the women's military movement under the control of a central authoritative body was of primary importance. The attendees resolved to create an All-Russian Women's Military Union to serve as a central agency, overseeing the various women's military organizations around the country. They also decided to hold periodic congresses of representatives of provincial women's military unions in order to regulate the development of the movement and to address issues concerning the formation and maintenance of women's military units around the country.[8]

Equally significant to the women participating in the congress was the status of women serving in military capacities. They adamantly insisted that all women serving in the military be afforded the same rights and treatment and receive the same pay, leaves, and privileges afforded to men in the services. The delegates discussed the necessity of providing assistance to women veterans and their families, equivalent to that afforded to male veterans and their families, as well as the establishment of a home for disabled women soldiers. As such, the congress participants were seeking to legitimize the participation of women in the armed forces, to make it a regulated and standardized aspect of military service and thereby of Russian society. They were also concerned with the legacy of female participation in military activities and, therefore, promoted the construction of memorials for those women soldiers who had given their lives on the battlefields for the sake of the nation.[9] They were especially concerned to achieve recognition for the women who had sacrificed themselves for Russia, so that their contribution would never be forgotten. In so doing, they were consciously attempting to include women's combat participation in the ritualized national myths of warfare.

On the last day of the gathering, the delegates voted to accept a resolution in favor of conscripting women for war work. The participants expressed full support for calling up women volunteers for the application of female labor in all branches of the military. The resolution stressed that women volunteering for any kind of military service, be it in the rear or at the front, should be granted the same status as male military personnel. The congress was closed on August 4, 1917.[10] Despite plans for future meetings, there is no evidence to suggest that additional women's military congresses were ever held in Russia.

## A REEVALUATION AND CHANGE OF FOCUS

The Women's Military Congress represented the height of the women's military movement in the private sector. But in official circles the movement was facing serious challenges. Although they sanctioned and oversaw the organization of women's military formations, the central Russian military authorities had never been fully committed to the idea of utilizing women in combat capacity. Even before the officially formed all-female units had completed their training, the military establishment began having second thoughts about the sagacity of deploying such units in battle. Despite the acclaim lavished upon the women soldiers of Bochkareva's battalion following their successful participation in the battle at Smorgon, the central military authorities remained wary of the women's units. Some among the military establishment even insisted that the accomplishments of the women in the battle of July 9–10 were anomalous and doubted they could be repeated. It is clear that many among official military circles remained unconvinced of the value of women soldiers and regarded the efforts to create all-female military formations as largely a waste of time and resources during a critical period in the war.[11]

Aside from philosophical misgivings, organizational problems persisted as well, as detailed in chapter 5, for the official combat units. The majority of the women's military formations lacked sufficient supplies, equipment, and money. Because of shortages and difficulties with distribution, military supply officials were often unwilling to send materials to women's units when men's units were lacking. Many of the items that were given to the women's units were inadequate or inappropriate, particularly in the case of uniforms. Even the Petrograd Soviet intervened to assist one of the Petrograd women's battalions. The Executive Committee of the Soviet sent three delegates, one Menshevik, one Bolshevik, and one Socialist Revolutionary, to the unit after receiving complaints that the women volunteers were being neglected by the military authorities. When asked why, in their opinion, they were being ignored, the women soldiers responded, "Because the quartermaster . . . does not consider our battalion of *babas* [the Russian colloquialism for woman] a military unit and does not put us on the list for supplies."[12]

Furthermore, the formation of communications detachments from women volunteers had not met with much success. Although the women's infantry battalions had no trouble attracting recruits—and in fact, the Petrograd and Moscow units were overwhelmed with volunteers—those units assigned for communications duties apparently lacked the same appeal for women desiring to aid their country in the military arena.[13] Hostility from male military personnel as well as civilians similarly caused trouble for the women's units. Perhaps most importantly, the inability to bring the women's military movement under its control continued to plague the Russian authorities. Numerous attempts on the part of GUGSh and the Ministry of War to obtain control over the women's military movement were unsuccessful. Even the creation of the All-Russian Women's Military Union, whose central committee was to direct all activities associated with the women's military movement, failed to stem the activities of grassroots organizations, which continued to engage in separate and individual efforts. The persistence of these elements, many armed and trained without official sanction and control, provided a constant source of aggravation and concern for Russian military authorities.[14]

It is important to understand that the military authorities were not weighing the value of the women's units only; they were seriously considering the utility of all the irregular military formations that had been created in the spring and early summer of 1917 as part of the effort to shore up army morale. These included the revolutionary and shock battalions formed from volunteers from the rear, units composed of non-Russians, and those created from disabled soldiers and veterans. In August, the Commission on the Reduction of Staff of the Army issued a statement reflecting its belief that such formations were excessively costly to create, supply, and maintain and recommending that Stavka seriously consider reexamining the necessity of such units.[15]

The military administration was now faced with the task of determining a course of action for the women's military movement. On the one hand, pressure from various women's military and quasi-military organizations and support from advocates within official circles encouraged continuation and even expansion of the movement. The presence of thousands of women desiring to serve their country in a military capacity was difficult to ignore at a time when it seemed Russia needed the assistance of all its citizens to weather the existing crisis. Groups such as the All-Russian Women's Military Union and the Commission on Women's Labor Conscription pressed for greater involvement by women in the war effort, proposing projects such as the creation of reserve regiments of female volunteers to provide replenishment forces for women's units sent to the front. On the other hand, skepticism about the value of the women's movement was leading many in the military establishment to believe it to be an unnecessary drain on limited resources.[16] However, once the women's military units had been formed, military authorities, while recommending that no further augmentation occur, simultaneously did not believe the best course of action would be to disband them entirely. In fact, they claimed that the circumstances of the war did not afford them the opportunity of even disbanding the women's units. Instead, they asserted that the women should be assigned to a different kind of service, defensive rather than offensive.[17]

As early as July, some leaders, including newly appointed Supreme Commander in Chief of the Russian Army General Lavr Kornilov, desired to discontinue the organization of female volunteers for combat purposes, believing that there were better uses for women's energies and strengths. Kornilov suggested changing the designation of existing infantry units from combat assignment to the defense of railway lines and stations.[18] The Department of Organization and Service of Troops also recommended that the women's communications detachments—whose organization, it claimed, had not met with much success—should also be utilized for the defense of railways.[19] The Ministry of War, pointing to the great need for personnel in this type of service, proposed that women also be recruited for the defense of railways.[20]

On the recommendations of its various officials, the Russian authorities ultimately decided that using women in the defense of railways would be the best policy. On August 22, the Provisional Government thereby resolved to allow the enlistment of women for this kind of service. Those women who were recruited for the defense of railways were to be accorded all the rights given to male recruits.[21] In September, Stavka ordered that the existing women's infantry battalions in Petrograd, Moscow, and Ekaterinodar each be assigned to a different sector of the front for the purpose of defending railway lines and stations, but the order does not seem to have ever been implemented.[22] Logistical difficulties, coupled with opposition to the use of women's formations in this capacity, prevented the plan from being executed. The chief of staff of the Priamurskii Military Region, Major General N. I. Efimov, complained that organizing women to defend the railways would be "impossible," since "all local social organizations definitively oppose women's military organizations."[23] The administration of the Eastern Chinese Railroad reported similar sentiments concerning the "undesirability of the formation of women's [railway defense] battalions" on the part of regional officials.[24]

Other areas of military service were considered for women as well. The extreme need for medical personnel, coupled with the greater "suitability" of such activity for women, convinced many to advocate that women be assigned to medical capacities in the Russian military. In particular, GUGSh suggested sending women to replace male medical personnel at the front, so that the men could be used as combat troops. The Commission on Women's Labor Conscription under GUGSh, charged with the task of preparing a report on the feasibility and possible ways of utilizing women's labor in the war effort, had submitted a proposal to Minister of War Kerensky advocating the recruitment of women for medical service in the active army, at the front as well as in the rear, in mid-July.[25] Kerensky approved the proposal, and the Provisional Government ratified it on August 20.[26] The commission designated the formation of three women's reserve medical battalions, one each in Petrograd, Moscow, and Kiev, and one women's medical reserve detachment in Kharkov. Recruitment for these units began in late August. In September, GUGSh approved the use of women as replacements for male medical personnel and accorded them the same rights as all servicemen.[27]

Despite the changes in focus and direction implemented by military officials, the difficulties associated with the women's military movement remained largely unresolved. There was a growing sentiment in military circles that the all-female formations were more trouble than they were worth. Military officials continued to be frustrated by the absence of a standardized policy concerning the use of women in military service. The "disorderly character" of the women's military formations seemed to present the military authorities with more problems than solutions to the army's multiple crises. GUGSh complained about the difficulties involved in "fighting" to control those women's units that had formed without governmental sanction and that remained out of its control. Even those units approved by the Ministry of War were causing significant problems and were not accomplishing their intended task of inspiring the male troops to continue fighting. The government and the army now seemed increasingly convinced that the women's military units would not be successful.[28]

The experiences of the 1st Russian Women' Battalion of Death at the front did not help prove to the military authorities that using women as soldiers would have a positive influence on the army. Following its initial baptism in battle, Bochkareva's unit remained at the front for several months. Although they had proved themselves in battle, the women soldiers encountered greater and greater hostility from the men around them, largely as a result of their continued zeal, which conflicted with the men's increasing unwillingness to fight. Moreover, the unit suffered from problems of internal cohesion and discipline. Bochkareva herself had been sent to Petrograd to recover from her wounds in the battle of July 9–10 at Smorgon. In her absence, her adjutant, Magdalena Skrydlova, had been placed in charge of the unit, and the battalion was sent back to reserve billets to rest. Apparently, some of the women found it difficult to accept Skrydlova's authority. Without their commander's stern regulation, they began to rebel. Threatened with disbanding by the army authorities, the unit settled down and returned to order.[29]

Perhaps more significantly, external problems were increasing as well. Male hostility to the presence of the women soldiers was becoming more pronounced. When Bochkareva returned from convalescence, her unit's position among the men further deteriorated. The women were accused of being counterrevolutionaries. The men's displays of anger were becoming increasingly violent.[30] The male soldiers' negative reaction to the women's unit only served to bolster criticism of the women's military movement in official circles. The positive assessment of the command personnel praising the actions of Bochkareva's unit seems to have been quickly forgotten or ignored. The Department of Organization and Service of Troops now assessed the abilities of the women soldiers quite pessimistically: "As fighting elements, the women showed themselves to be of little use, capable only of breaking through [enemy lines] in a short burst, but enduring the severe conditions and deprivations of war with difficulty."[31] Moreover, it appears that the unit was suffering from a lack of material support from the military administration. On October 20, the Women's Military Union to Aid the Motherland published an appeal to its members and to the general citizenry to help in securing winter clothing for the unit, still located at the front.[32]

Male soldiers' opposition to the general women's military movement was also being expressed more frequently. The executive section representing the soldiers' committees of the Romanian front issued a protest against the use of women in combat in August 1917. While the men recognized women's rights to sacrifice themselves for the good of the nation, they believed very strongly that there were more appropriate ways for them to do so. The complaint stated,

> [Since] women's battalions, as military units, do not augment in any significant way the battle capacity of the army, neither in relation to quantity nor quality, the section asserts that the formation of women's battalions as military units is not desirable and the energies of women can be used exclusively for auxiliary service in the rear and in the near front as, for example, telephone operators, and so on.[33]

In September, the Soldiers' Section of the Poltava Soviet of Workers' and Soldiers' Deputies expressed similar disapproval of the women's units. In fact, these troops were convinced not only that the women's military formations were useless but that they were in fact harmful because they were organized and trained by "counterrevolutionaries." They urged the commander of troops of the Kiev Military District to immediately dissolve the unit that had been created in Poltava by Lieutenant Ilovaiskii and to confiscate their arms and equipment, which they asserted had been taken from other units.[34]

Unable to resolve the myriad of problems associated with the women's military movement and facing mounting opposition, the Russian military administration began to withdraw its support for the all-female units. In late September, the Department of Organization and Service of Troops recommended that the organization of women's military units be ceased. It contended that the women's military movement was little more than a "sudden flash of fashion," that the problems associated with it were insoluble, and that in fact, the entire idea had been a failure. In September, it stated,

> The establishment of women's combat formations was based upon the idea of using the bellicose impulse of women in order to raise the spirits of the main male elements of the army. This assumption was not justified. The small number of women did not produce any kind of influence on the general mass of troops, the soldiers regarding them indifferently and sometimes even with hostility.[35]

The agency also criticized the organizational aspects of the women's military units, maintaining that staff lists for the units had not been fully developed:

They contained a number of significant errors and omissions and were too large for implementation in one battalion.[36] Moreover, the temporarily successful performance of Bochkareva's small band of women soldiers was not enough to convince the military administration that women were effective soldiers. When it became clear that the positive influence of the women was limited and that many of the men were hostile toward the all-female units, there was little incentive to continue the program.

Seemingly exasperated with the women's military units, in October GUGSh proposed that the government give them no more attention and especially no more financial or material support, thus leaving them responsible for finding their own means of support. GUGSh authorized the commanders of the women's units to discharge volunteers who desired to leave the ranks, on the grounds that regular rules of enlistment did not apply to them.[37] Considering that the military authorities never gave sufficient attention or material support to the women's military units, the withdrawal of official support is not altogether surprising. The women's military movement had been generated through private initiative, and from their inception, the all-female units had relied upon assistance from grassroots women's military and social organizations and from the private sector. When the units suffered from a shortage of supplies and equipment, they often turned to private sources. Bochkareva's unit enjoyed extensive sponsorship from private citizens, including several patrons from Russian high society, and was almost entirely organized through the efforts of the Petrograd women's military associations. However, this new official policy is somewhat puzzling in that it represented an abandonment of the previous driving concern to control unofficial armed military organizations and an apparent willingness to allow them to exist outside official auspices. Perhaps it was assumed that once official support was withdrawn, the movement would wither and die. Furthermore, it is likely that the Russian military establishment, despite being uncomfortable with the notion of women soldiers, did not actually believe women, even armed, were a real threat.

## THE END OF THE WOMEN'S MILITARY FORMATIONS

By October 1917, the general opinion among the military authorities seems to have been that the women's military movement had lost whatever value it had or could have had. At the start of the organization of the women's military formations, Captain Murav'ev, chairman of the All-Russian Central Committee for the Organization of Volunteers for the Revolutionary Army, warned that the women's volunteer movement would only be successful if their formation was to "proceed with the utmost intensity, happening over the course of two to three weeks," at most. He also cautioned that the women's military movement was attempting to undertake too large a project, and one that demanded extensive resources.[38] The military authorities arrived at a similar conclusion in mid-October, believing that the true significance of the all-female military units, that is, their moral importance (and therein their only worth to the army) was only valid temporarily and had been "strongly exaggerated by the press and by the petitions of individual persons and whole organizations at the beginning of the revolution."[39] In fact, the significance of the women's military movement had been "negligible and unused," as the moment when they would have been able to exert any positive influence had passed. Complications associated with formation and combat training, they surmised, had prevented most of the women's units from being deployed at the front when and where their influence would have been felt. This seemed paradoxical, but it was adequate reasoning for GUGSh to maintain that the movement "had not justified its own existence."[40]

Although the army and military authorities moved toward the position that the women's military movement was a dying and futile effort, the women's military and social organizations themselves did not share that opinion. The Commission on Women's Labor Conscription continued to plan for the creation of women's medical detachments. In September, the commission submitted several proposals to GUGSh concerning such activities, requesting 10,000 rubles for the purpose. The All-Russian Women's Military Union appealed to the government for permission to organize ten women's war-work militias. The Petrograd Women's Military Union, with the support of the district military headquarters, submitted a proposal to form women's reserve units to serve as replenishments for the existing women's combat battalions. Individual women continued to apply for acceptance into the women's military units and continued to join male combat units at the front. The military administration refused to approve such new requests, believing such formations to be superfluous and being unwilling to commit state funds to what they considered unnecessary and unjustified expenses. The army was looking for ways to reduce, not increase, its personnel. GUGSh recommended that the Ministry of War reject all future petitions concerning the organization of women for military service.[41]

Ultimately, the Russian military authorities must have realized that merely withdrawing official support was not enough to end the women's military movement. Although many of the women who had joined the all-female units had left the ranks, many remained in formation. Still others, as noted above, pressed for inclusion in the movement. On October 17, GUGSh proposed the disbanding of all the women's combat units, with the exception of the 1st Petrograd Women's

Battalion, which the military administration advised should remain in existence in order to "accommodate the quantity of women actually desiring to serve the homeland."[42] The central military authorities were under the impression that the Moscow battalion had completely disbanded, that the Kuban battalion had never completed formation, and that the various communications units had no personnel. They had no information about Bochkareva's unit, which was still at the front. With its combat training complete, the 1st Petrograd Women's Battalion would be allowed to go to fight the external enemy. The Department of Organization and Service of Troops set the date for the dispatch of the 1st Petrograd Women's Battalion to the front for October 25, 1917. But events in the capital would intervene on that day, and the women of this unit would never get the opportunity to serve at the front. Instead, these women soldiers would find themselves entangled in the internal political struggle that was about to envelop their country.

## THE DEFENSE OF THE WINTER PALACE

The participation of members of the 1st Petrograd Women's Battalion in the defense of the Winter Palace is undoubtedly the best-known and most controversial event in the history of the all-female combat units of World War I. It is this episode that is most often depicted in the historiography and mythology of the Bolshevik Revolution, and simultaneously, it is the most distorted and ideologically charged. Many accounts are based on rumor and hearsay, and inaccuracy and misinformation surround the memory of this women's battalion. Soviet sources have portrayed the women in unflattering terms: as dupes of the bourgeoisie manipulated into coming to the defense of the Provisional Government, and as ridiculous, incompetent, and hysterical, cowering in the back rooms of the Winter Palace and blubbering pathetically as they surrendered to the Red Guards and soldiers. Western sources and those unsympathetic to Soviet power are equally unreliable, alleging gross mistreatment, including rape and murder, of the women by their captors while affording no credit to the women themselves in the fighting. The truth lies somewhere in between, and while we may never have all the facts surrounding these events, archival sources along with several eyewitness accounts provide us with sufficient evidence to reconstruct the story of the women's participation with considerable accuracy.[43]

By late October, the situation began to look particularly grim for the Provisional Government and its supporters. Tensions in the capital were increasing, and rumors abounded concerning the Bolsheviks' plans to take over the government.[44] The Bolsheviks mobilized their supporters in the capital, particularly the Red Guards, and set out to weaken the Provisional Government's authority over the Petrograd garrison.[45] To accomplish this, they used the Military Revolutionary Committee, the Bolshevik-dominated military arm of the Petrograd Soviet of Workers' and Soldiers' Deputies. Red Guards combined with sailors, soldiers, and workers' militias to give the Bolsheviks a strong armed presence in Petrograd.[46] On October 22–23, Kerensky met with his chief advisers, who reported that massive public support for the Bolsheviks was evident all over the city. Fearful of a backlash of public opinion, Kerensky had previously hesitated to take decisive measures against the Bolsheviks, but at this point he had little choice but to act. He issued an order for the arrest of a number of prominent Bolshevik leaders on the night of October 23–24 and shut down two Bolshevik newspapers. The Bolsheviks responded with action of their own: Forces of the Military Revolutionary Committee began seizing key government institutions. In an effort to defend the Provisional Government, Kerensky attempted to gather loyal troops in Petrograd.[47]

On the morning of October 24, Major General Ia. G. Bagratuni, chief of staff of the Petrograd Military District, sent an urgent message to Captain Loskov, commander of the 1st Petrograd Women's Battalion, ordering the women's unit to the district headquarters in Petrograd.[48] Since August, the battalion had been in camp outside the capital, near the Levashovo Station on the Finland Railroad. There the women had completed their training and were awaiting orders to be sent to the front. The entire battalion, including the command personnel, believed they were being called to the capital to participate in a review ceremony and parade prior to their departure for the Romanian front, as ordered by Stavka on October 17. The unit arrived in the capital at noon of the twenty-fourth, fully armed and equipped, prepared for dispatch to forward positions. They marched through the streets singing soldiers' songs until they arrived at the Winter Palace, ready to be reviewed by the military brass. Positioned on the square in front of the palace, they were joined by several units of *junkers* (cadets) from various military schools around the city as well as Cossack units.[49]

When they arrived on the palace square, the women learned that they had been called to the Winter Palace not to be reviewed in a parade but to defend the members of the Provisional Government inside. The members of the battalion were distraught, since their goal was to fight Russia's external enemies at the front, and they "had no desire to become embroiled in the political struggle."[50] The women felt betrayed by a government that was asking them "to fight the revolution" against their own people. As one young volunteer commented,

1st Petrograd Women's Battalion in front of the Winter Palace, ready for review, October 1917 (courtesy Museum of the Revolution, Moscow)

"I am a woman soldier and I fight only imperialistic invaders."[51] In fact, many of the female soldiers were quite ignorant of the internal political situation. Despite their disinclination to take part in the internal conflict, the women were aware of the possibility of entanglement in such events. Prior to their dispatch to Petrograd, they had been warned that the Bolsheviks might try to attack them. As a result, they had loaded their rifles with one round before departing their camp, but they kept the safeties on. Their pockets and packs were filled with additional cartridges. They were ordered, "in case of trouble," to fire the first volley into the air. Should this be insufficient to stop any advances against them, they were to reload and fire a second round at the attackers.[52]

Loskov, believing it inappropriate to use his volunteers in this manner, ordered the majority of the battalion to return to their encampment at Levashovo. Apparently, he sensed the futility of attempting to defend the Winter Palace with so few troops against the Red Guards and the numerous Bolshevik supporters from the Petrograd garrison. Many called to the defense of the Provisional Government had already abandoned their positions, including the majority of Cossack troops. Of those that remained, most were young cadets with no military experience, described by one historian as little more than "boisterous adolescents" whose "image of war still remained romantically

Women soldiers of the 1st Petrograd Women's Battalion on the Winter Palace square, October 1917 (courtesy Museum of the Revolution, Moscow)

untarnished by reality."[53] The Petrograd Military District authorities managed, apparently by threat, to get Loskov to leave a small detachment of the women's battalion in the city under the pretext of protecting the delivery of gasoline from the Nobel factory.[54] Half of the 2nd Company of the women's battalion, consisting of 137 soldiers, remained in position on the Palace Square. Among them were Maria Bocharnikova and volunteer S.[55] Apparently Loskov chose this company for a particular reason, perhaps believing they were least likely to put up a fight in which they would get themselves killed. When Captain Shagal, commander of the 3rd Company, asked why Loskov had not assigned his company or Captain Dolgov's to remain behind, the battalion commander responded, "Well, you know, if you were left there you would probably support the uprising against the Bolsheviks."[56]

On the evening of October 24, the company commander, Lieutenant Somov, received orders from the headquarters of the Petrograd Military District to dispatch his forces to the city's bridges. The women were supposed to assist cadet units in raising the bridges and in preventing them from being lowered in a strategy designed to cut off the working-class regions of Petrograd from the center and thereby deprive the Bolsheviks of support.[57] A half platoon was assigned to the Nikolaev Bridge, a half platoon was sent to the Palace Bridge, and a full platoon went to the Liteinyi Bridge. The cadets had managed to raise the bridges, but before the women even got the chance to render assistance, the workers, Red Guards, and other Bolshevik supporters quickly overwhelmed them and lowered the bridges.[58] The women returned to the Winter Palace and took up positions on the first floor of the building. They were led into luxurious apartments facing the Palace Square and issued ammunition. Perhaps realizing the historic significance of the events they were involved in, each of the women stashed one or two of the shiny brass cartridges as souvenirs. They sat on the floor in rooms they were told had belonged to Catherine the Great, afraid to soil the opulent furniture with their dirty tunics. They spent the night there. In the morning, they were led to the private church of the palace, where they were blessed by a weeping priest.[59]

Through the night and into the next morning, most of the forces stationed at the palace deserted their posts and took with them most of the armored cars and machine guns, leaving behind two heavy guns and one disabled tank. By the evening of the twenty-fifth, all the Cossacks had withdrawn, refusing to shed blood in defense of the Provisional Government, to which they felt no particular loyalty. The government called in other units, such as the cyclists' battalion, but they ultimately defected to the side of the attackers. Throughout the day, those who remained at the palace had received reports that the Bolsheviks and Left Socialist Revolutionaries had seized a number of key buildings and sites around the city and were making their way to the Winter Palace. The situation, on both sides, was one of utter confusion and "complete mismanagement."[60]

As darkness fell, the women were ordered to take up positions on the barricades that they and the cadets had erected in the courtyard in front of the palace that afternoon. Sporadic exchanges of gunfire occurred between the besiegers and the defenders. The defenders numbered approximately 2,500, while the besiegers, between 10,000 and 15,000 strong, completely encircled the palace.[61] The Military Revolutionary Committee issued an ultimatum to the members of the Provisional Government demanding their surrender, but the ministers made no reply. At 9:30 P.M., the cruiser *Aurora*, which had been strategically placed on the Neva River near the Nikolaev Bridge, began shooting blank shells at the palace, and additional blasts came from the Peter and Paul Fortress. This signaled the beginning of the Bolshevik attack. The women tried to hold off the attack from the barricades, but they were being fired upon from many different directions: from the General Staff Headquarters, from the Hermitage, from the Pavlovskii barracks, and from the Winter Palace garden. In the course of the fighting, at least one woman was killed and one of the male officers was wounded. Overwhelmed by greatly superior numbers, surrounded,

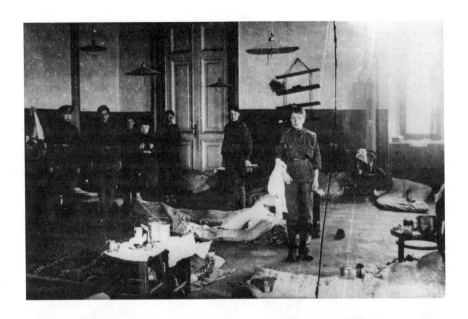

Members of the 1st Petrograd Women's Battalion inside the Winter Palace, where they had been ordered to protect the Provisional Government (courtesy Museum of the Revolution, Moscow)

with no place to retreat, the women found themselves in an increasingly hopeless situation. Because of their small numbers, the defenders were unable to create a solid line of defense around the palace, and as a result, groups of Red Guards and other armed Bolshevik supporters began to seep through into the courtyard. The women were ordered to retreat back into the building, which they did, shutting the gates behind them. The company's command personnel led the volunteers into an empty room on the second floor. A few minutes later, they were informed that the Provisional Government had surrendered and they were ordered to lay down their weapons.[62]

Despite the accounts demonstrating that the women "fought with the same valor displayed elsewhere by Russian women on the battlefield,"[63] detractors persisted in their claims of cowardice and ineptitude on the part of the female volunteers. The American socialist John Reed, who was present at the palace on October 24–25, was informed by Staff Captain Vladimir Artsibashev that the women remained inside the building "in the back rooms, where they [wouldn't] be hurt if any trouble comes."[64] Even recent assessments of the revolution by Western scholars continue to portray the women in this manner: "When the *Aurora* fired its first salvo the women became hysterical and had to be confined in a basement room," comments one historian in a 1997 tome.[65] One cannot but wonder why, if the women were so afraid to fight, they did not just leave their posts, as so many other units had done? The issue of surrender, however, was a sensitive one among the women soldiers themselves, some of whom wanted to continue fighting despite their inevitable defeat. Bocharnikova recalled being heartbroken when one of the woman volunteers from another company, upon meeting her years later, retorted, "If it were our platoon, we would've all died before we surrendered!" She insisted that it was the commanders who ordered them to lay down arms in order to avoid unnecessary bloodshed.[66]

What happened to the women following their surrender is a matter of great controversy and confusion as well. After their capture, tales of gross maltreatment, including torture, rape, defenestration, and murder, spread throughout the capital.[67] The majority of these rumors were unsubstantiated, but there were some instances of abuse. While the women were awaiting their fate in the palace, a crowd of Red Guards, soldiers, and sailors crashed into the room in order to get a good look at the famed female volunteers. They then led the women out of the palace, but on the way out the soldiers and sailors engaged in a dispute over who would take them into charge. The soldiers of the Pavlovskii Regiment emerged triumphant, and they led the women soldiers to their barracks. Along the way, some of the men tormented the women, hurling insults,

obscenities, and even blows at the volunteers. The women were taken to the
Pavlovskii barracks and enclosed in a small room. "They ogled us like caged
animals, laughing and taunting," Bocharnikova recalled.[68] The soldiers told the
women that all their officers had been killed and threatened them with sexual
violation and execution. They cursed the women for being "Kornilovites" and
"enemies of the revolution." When the threats escalated, two members of the
regimental committee intervened, ordering the soldiers to leave them alone.
The men complied, and the women were transferred to the barracks of the neu-
tral Grenadierskii Regiment. Bocharnikova reported that this unit fed the 137
female captives and treated them with respect.

The women were ultimately freed from their Bolshevik captors, largely
through the efforts of the British mission in Russia. The wife of Sir George
Buchanan, British ambassador to Russia, insisted on ensuring the safety of the
women soldiers and sent British military attaché General Alfred Knox to help
them. Knox went to the Bolshevik headquarters at Smolny and demanded that
the women be released.[69] The Bolsheviks consented, and the Military Revolutionary Committee issued an order for their immediate release on October 26.[70]
Some of the women, including volunteer S., immediately dispersed into the city,
obtaining female clothing and ending their military service.[71] The rest of the
women were dispatched back to their camp at Levashovo, accompanied by
guards of the Grenadierskii Regiment to protect them from the soldiers and
sailors who might attempt to molest them along the way. Although the women of
the 2nd Company had been told that their officers had been captured and killed
by Red Guards in the Winter Palace, the company commanders returned several days later. They were mostly unharmed, aside from Lieutenant Vernyi, who
had been wounded in the foot.

When the members of the 2nd Company returned to their encampment, Captain Loskov gathered the volunteers together and told them that they no longer
existed as a battalion. In what Captain Shagal considered to be an act of cowardice, Loskov announced, "I can protect you neither as women nor as soldiers.
Disperse yourselves," and he disappeared the next day. This caused a great
deal of distress among the members of the women's unit, and many refused to
leave the ranks. Shagal took command of the remaining volunteers and promised to defend them as women, but assured them, "As soldiers, you can stand
up for yourselves!"[72] It was announced that they would be disarmed and dismissed, but a few hundred remained nevertheless, intending to resist the disbanding.[73] Those women of the 2nd Company who had been disarmed when
arrested at the Winter Palace were rearmed with rifles from the armory. But
there was a severe shortage of ammunition.

Scouts were dispatched to assess the situation in the area surrounding the camp and in the city, as no one really knew what was occurring. They returned with information that four companies of armed Red Guards from the Aivaz, New Parviainen, Erikson, and other factories were moving toward the Levashovo encampment to disarm and disband the women's unit. When Lieutenant Vernyi learned of the approach of the Red Guards, he sent some of the volunteers out to find cartridges, hoping that, if fully armed, the battalion could resist them. When the Red Guard envoys arrived, they ordered the women to lay down their weapons immediately. The commander convinced the Red Guards to postpone any action, attempting to stall for time until ammunition could be obtained. After two hours, the Red Guards returned and, despite pleas for a further extension of the time limit, demanded that the women disarm in ten minutes or they would open fire. Without ammunition, the women were forced to capitulate. Instead of handing over their weapons intact, however, they disassembled their rifles and removed the bolts, rather than giving the Red Guards useful weapons. The envoys, after confiscating 891 rifles, four machine guns, and several other small armaments, seemed satisfied that the women would present no further problems. They declared the battalion disbanded and departed. Only half an hour later, the volunteers who had been sent out for ammunition returned with 10,000 cartridges. It was fortunate, however, that they arrived too late, for any confrontation with the Red Guards would have undoubtedly ended in bloodshed.[74]

Following their disarmament, the 1st Petrograd Women's Battalion began to break up, the remaining members of the unit dispersing to various locations. Some of them, however, did not have any other place to go. Others did not want to leave. Another major barrier in the disbanding of the unit was the lack of civilian clothing for the women soldiers to exchange for their military uniforms. Although the Military Revolutionary Committee instructed the Red Guards to allow the women free passage to and from Levashovo,[75] those who left the confines of the encampment, immediately recognizable in their military dress, were often harassed. Women who went on leaves to the city returned with horror stories of physical, verbal, and sexual abuse. Therefore, many of the women lingered at Levashovo even after the unit was disbanded.

Despite the fact that the women's unit had fought to defend the Provisional Government, the new authorities worked to ensure the well-being of the female volunteers. The Military Revolutionary Committee issued orders for the dispatch of trucks to deliver food from district warehouses to the women. On November 8, the Military Revolutionary Committee ordered the disbanding of the Organizational Committee of the Women's Military Union and the confiscation of the union's assets, to be used for the purchase of civilian clothing for the female volunteers.[76] Shagal reported that the Petrograd Committee of Public Safety and the Red Cross also helped them secure women's clothing.[77]

The disturbing stories concerning the treatment of the female soldiers circulating throughout the city raised concern among local government officials. The Petrograd Municipal Council sent a commission of three members to investigate the condition of the women. Representatives Mandel'berg, Fekkel, and Tyrkova went to the battalion's encampment outside the Levashovo Station to examine the condition of the women soldiers and to interview the remaining members of the unit. Their findings demonstrated that while there had been much derision and insult, as well as threats of sexual violation, the rumors of mass rape and suicide were untrue. Mandel'berg, the chairman of the Hospital Commission, reported to the council that numerous witnesses testified to the sexual violation of three of the women by the Pavlovtsy, but they were unable to find these women and talk to them directly. At least one of the women had been punched by angry soldier as they were being led to the Pavlovskii barracks.[78]

The commission's findings reported that none of the women had been killed or defenestrated by their captors.[79] Yet American correspondent Louise Bryant reported encountering one young female soldier living in a Petrograd slum who informed her that a male soldier of the Pavlovskii Regiment had pushed her out of a window during a heated argument, but that he had felt so guilty that he ran out of the building after her and carried her to a nearby hospital.[80] Another two volunteers reported having been attacked by soldiers while walking in Petrograd, taken to the Winter Palace, and thrown out of a second-story window. One volunteer landed on her head and died in the hospital, while the other suffered a broken leg but recovered.[81]

One volunteer committed suicide, but according to all observers and investigators, she did so for personal motives and not because of mistreatment or abuse. It was Bocharnikova's friend, Bazhenova, who took her own life in desperation, after her family disowned her for joining the battalion. She had nowhere left to turn, so she tied a rope to the trigger of her rifle, loaded it with a cartridge she had kept as a souvenir from the defense of the Winter Palace, aimed the barrel at her heart, and shot herself.

Bocharnikova relates the worst tales of mistreatment, but her account is largely unverifiable. She claims that upon leaving the unit to return to their homes, a number of the female soldiers, easily detected by their short-cropped hair, were molested, beaten, raped, and even killed by fellow Russian soldiers, sailors, and Red Guards whom they encountered along the way. Another group, composed of forty women, also on their way home, were reportedly abducted by sailors in Petrograd and taken to Kronstadt, their ultimate fate unknown. Thirty-six female volunteers made it as far as Moscow, where they were captured by soldiers, brought to their barracks, and presumably abused by the men.

On November 19, 1917, GUGSh submitted a proposal to the Military Council recommending the disbanding of any remaining women's military formations.[82] The Bolsheviks, now in control of the organs of Russian government, undoubtedly had little use for what were perceived to be "bourgeois" women with guns. Therefore, the Military Council resolved to disband the women's military units on November 30. All personnel attached to these units of women volunteers were to be released and allowed to return to their original status. All horses and equipment were to be returned to the main military administration.[83]

Although they had been disarmed and dismissed on October 30, the women volunteers of the 1st Petrograd Women's Battalion left the Levashovo encampment gradually, over a period of two months. Many had no other place to go, and some clung to the hope that they would still be given an opportunity to serve their country. Some of the male commanders also lingered in the hopes of receiving orders to be sent to the front. The ranks of the battalion diminished slowly, until by the end of 1917 there were no more than about ten female volunteers left. The last of the female soldiers left the encampment at Levashovo on January 10, 1918.[84] Those who were unable to return to their homes were sent to the former palace of Count Sheremetiev, now being used as a hospital and a dormitory for the women's battalion. They were given dresses and head scarves, as it was too dangerous for them to walk the streets in soldiers' uniforms.

While staying at the hospital, Bocharnikova became involved with anti-Bolshevik activists and was arrested for participating in counterrevolutionary activities. Eventually, she was released through appeals from the Red Cross. Through one of the battalion members she learned that General Kornilov was organizing a force to counter the Bolsheviks in the territory of the Don Cossacks. Bocharnikova and a number of her fellow volunteers desired to join, and they managed to secure passes to allow them to travel to the Don. She made her way to Tiflis, where she was reunited with her family, and then to the Don, where she joined the 1st Kuban Infantry Regiment and served as a sergeant major during the Civil War.[85] Captain Shagal also made his way south to join the army then being formed by General Kornilov, taking with him several of the women volunteers.[86]

Although by the time of the October Revolution the women's military movement was supposed to have been reduced to one infantry unit—the 1st Petrograd Women's Battalion—other women's formations remained in existence. At the time of the Bolshevik coup in the capital, the first of the women's battalions to have been organized, that under the command of Maria Bochkareva, was still at the front. The female detachment was located in reserve billets near the town of Olonets.[87] By now the animosity with which the majority of male soldiers regarded the women had grown so significantly that the danger from fellow Russian soldiers had become at least as great as that from the enemy. The male soldiers openly threatened the women's lives if they did not disarm and leave the front. The all-female unit now numbered fewer than 200 soldiers and could not resist the masses of male troops against them. In mid-December, the decision was made to disband the women's battalion. The remaining members of the unit desiring to continue their military service were offered entrance into the active army as part of male units.[88] Those wishing to return to their homes were granted permission to do so. The volunteers dispersed, and this signaled the end of the 1st Russian Women's Battalion of Death. Bochkareva, sullen and disappointed, commented that it was "a pitiful finale to a heroic chapter in the history of Russian womanhood."[89]

The 3rd Kuban Women's Shock Battalion also remained in existence after the October Revolution. In fact, it seems to have maintained formation until February 1918. This unit, located in an area not yet under Soviet control, seems to have ignored the official orders issued by the new Bolshevik government. Lacking equipment and arms, however, it was an insignificant force, and it dissolved once the impossibility of securing these supplies became apparent by mid-February 1918. It is possible, however, that some of the members of this battalion joined formations organized in the Kuban region that fought during the ensuing Civil War.[90]

The Russian women's military movement of World War I may have been short-lived, but while it was in existence during the summer and fall of 1917, there was an intense burst of formation, organization, and training of women for participation in the fighting. Most of these female soldiers never saw active duty, but they did undergo the rigors of life in the army, albeit briefly. While the government and army administration never devoted full attention to the matter, or even regarded it with complete seriousness, they did at least make an attempt to coordinate these women volunteers and prepare them for combat. Of the sixteen women's military formations designated by the Ministry of War, Bochkareva's small detachment is the only unit known to have carried the experiment through to its fruition by serving in combat against the external enemy at the front. The other women's units were never afforded the opportunity to demonstrate their effectiveness, either as soldiers or as inspirational symbols.

# 7

## IMAGING THE WOMAN SOLDIER

Russia's women soldiers of World War I received much attention both at home and abroad. Observers were fascinated by these female warriors, and publications from the period reflect this keen interest. The women became temporary media stars as journalists quickly recognized the sensation value of such a striking phenomenon. Their exploits received extensive coverage in newspapers and journals from Petrograd to New York.[1] Bochkareva in particular received much media attention, and her picture was featured prominently in numerous publications.[2]

Perceptions of these women warriors were diverse and divergent, even contradictory. The public was alternately captivated and repulsed by them. The overwhelming impression one gets from study of public images of Russia's women soldiers is that most observers, even many of their staunchest supporters, were equivocal about the presence of women in combat. This inherent ambivalence pervades much of the commentary made by contemporaries, both domestic and foreign. Russia's women soldiers were extolled for their patriotism and courageous actions, compared favorably to Joan of Arc by men and women, Russians and Westerners alike. Simultaneously, they were criticized for acting in such a decidedly unfeminine manner and significantly challenging the existing social order. Examining contemporary views of these women facilitates greater comprehension of the significance of the phenomenon. Debate concerning gender roles was at a critical juncture during the war years, particularly in regard to whether and how women would expand their participation in the public sphere. Reactions to women combatants are part of the larger conception of gender roles, and therefore they are extremely important to our understanding of those roles and the changes that occurred as a result of the Great War.

The attempt by the contemporary press to include women in the heroic narrative of the war is extremely interesting for the scholar of women and war, since women were traditionally excluded from war stories. There was an effort to include these women in the mythology of the war, despite their subsequent neglect in later historiography. This inclusion, however, does not reflect a straightforward acceptance of women as soldiers and thus should not be interpreted as an attempt to give women soldiers an equal place beside men in the war myth. One must look more closely at how these women were portrayed. In particular, it is important to differentiate between the portrayals of those who joined as individuals and became part of male units and of those who joined the all-female formations. By and large, the participation of the individuals who served with men was more acceptable to the early twentieth-century public primarily because they represented singular exceptions to gender roles. Most such women almost completely abandoned those behaviors that defined their femininity and surrendered their traditional roles without challenging the social order. These were women emulating men, and only temporarily and only occasionally. There are few, if any, implications for the female gender as a whole, and certainly no endorsement of widespread adoption of such behavior.

Although there were few women's combat units, their mass character proved disturbing to many observers, as they seemed to be more confrontational to the status quo of gender relations. Ironically, however, this was not the case (although progressive women certainly used the example of women bearing arms for the defense of the nation as proof positive of women's capabilities). While the individual women who joined male units participated in combat *despite* the fact that they were women, the women of the all-female units were used *specifically because* they were women. Their use in a form of female imagery designed to inspire men to fight was similar, though more extreme, to other such efforts, such as the "white feather" campaign in Great Britain. Essentially, the women's units were being used by the male military establishment to reassert traditional gender roles, that is, to get men to return to their roles as defenders. Once the men had done so, there would be no need, and certainly no desire, for women to continue to be soldiers. Thus, their entire existence was made necessary by the failure of traditional gendered behavior and the desire to reinforce it. Nearly all the commentary concerning the women's units is framed in terms of their usefulness in this capacity; very few observers acknowledge the effectiveness of the women's units in battle, which contrasts significantly with the commendations for combat action frequently given to individuals.

RUSSIAN IMPRESSIONS

## *The Russian Male Perspective*

Russian men's perceptions of women soldiers who fought as part of male units and of those who participated in the all-female military formations were varied. There were supporters and critics alike. In the early years of the war, the patriotic press fell in love with the image of the girl volunteer, disguised as a boy, seeking the adventure and romance of war, carrying out heroic deeds, and enduring the hardships of trench life. Newspapers and journals of every political and social persuasion published reports about such daring young women. Even the official publications of the tsarist government lauded the women soldiers. It is important to note, however, that all the portraits were of young women who were either unmarried or, if married, had gone to war with their husbands. No mention was ever made of children, elderly parents, or other domestic responsibilities left behind by women-turned-soldiers. Conventional social norms still dictated that women's primary responsibilities were to the family and the home, even during times of war. All the women were similarly portrayed as possessing a deep desire to serve the homeland, and their gender transgression was thus made somewhat acceptable by their patriotism.

It is further important to note that most of those who lauded the women for their heroism did not explore the deeper social implications of women's combat participation. These women were considered exceptions to the rules governing gender behavior and outside the purview of "female nature." They were more masculine than feminine, displaying traits and abilities that "normal" women did not possess. The great enthusiasm expressed by the public for their patriotic, heroic deeds did not indicate that Russian society condoned the participation of women in military endeavors in general. Furthermore, even the hundreds of individual women who became soldiers prior to 1917 were relatively few in Russia's army of millions. Therefore, they seem to have been perceived as a tolerable minority. Their presence in the ranks was an exceptional occurrence and certainly did not indicate widespread female integration. This tolerance is generally consistent with the policy of allowing occasional individual women to enter the Russian army, by personal prerogative of the tsar or commander, but maintaining a legislative ban on female military service.

Certain segments of Russian society may have found it more acceptable for women to carry out combat roles. It seems that some Cossacks were more sympathetic to and could even condone women who became soldiers. When Elena Choba, a Kuban Cossack and accomplished horsewoman, applied to be accepted as a volunteer in the army, she had the full backing of her village and was immediately given permission to enlist.[3] The Cossack military heritage, which extended beyond the male realm, undoubtedly made women's transition into the sphere of war much easier than in other communities within Russian society.

There were others, however, who could not tolerate women in the role of warriors. Some men were made highly uncomfortable by the gender transgression presented by women soldiers. Three young women dressed in soldiers' uniforms and attempting to join the army in Tiflis were met with disapproval from a crowd awaiting the tsar's arrival. "This is depravity! This is no place for you to put on such a masquerade!" shouted a disapproving man, and when the women retorted, they were arrested.[4] British commentator Victor Marsen claimed that despite the relatively frequent appearance of women on the battlefields, "the general sense of Russia was against them," although he provided no substantiation.[5]

The creation of the women's military formations in 1917 elicited a stronger response from Russian men. Support and opposition divided largely along political lines. Those who supported the women's military movement generally believed in the need to continue fighting the war to a victorious end and were convinced of the necessity of shoring up the army by whatever means possible. Those against the war also opposed the creation of units aimed at bolstering the army and prolonging the conflict. Yet, as with the individuals, resistance to all-female combat units also resulted from social values. Therefore, there were those who backed the war but could not accept the extreme transgression of gender roles. Social and political conservatives maintained that even during the exceptional circumstances of war, women were not to tread in the male sphere of military action; they were convinced that women's roles in wartime should remain passive, providing support at home for the men who were fighting at the front. For these men, women could best demonstrate their patriotism and willingness to aid the motherland by caring for wounded and dying male soldiers.

Acclaim for the women's military units emanated largely from the pages of periodicals published by and for the educated classes. Such publications supported the Provisional Government and the policy of continuing the war to a victorious end. Yet they had very large circulations and were fairly mainstream in their views. They recognized the significant propaganda value of the women's units and made use of them in their efforts to boost public support for the war. The idea that women could be used to inspire war-weary and demoralized men had much support in patriotic circles, where some believed that the moral influence of these heroic and self-sacrificing female soldiers would be so significant that the fighting spirit of the army would be restored and Russia would be "saved." A journalist for a popular Petrograd newspaper proclaimed,

"The Russian soldier would never remain lying in the trenches if he were to see that a woman, that same woman that he always considered to be beneath him, was not afraid of the fire and was the first to shout: Hurrah! and run into the fire."[6] Another commentator stated, "There is a feeling that a great turning point is to be achieved, that now begins the saving of Russia from great misfortune, from great disgrace. . . . And there is the desire to fall before the Russian women's battalion and to cry relieving tears of joy."[7]

There were those who extolled the women volunteers as models for free and responsible citizenship. "In this frightening, terrible hour, the Russian woman has bravely lifted up her head and entered the ranks of the frontline soldiers. Let this be an example, a supreme example of patriotism, a persuasive example of civic responsibility," exclaimed one Russian journalist.[8] The women's military movement was seen as the ultimate expression of women's desire to help the nation in its extreme time of need. All women were encouraged to participate in the war effort in some way, and those who did nothing were roundly criticized. A cartoon published in the popular journal *Ogonek* showed a "fashionable" woman, loaded with shopping and packages, transformed into a gallantly striding soldier.[9] A number of supporters of the women soldiers also saw them as testimony to women's ability to participate in every realm of public life. As one journalist professed, "The present war has brilliantly refuted the German prescription of women's duties: '*Kleider, Kinder, Küche.*' The war has removed the frying pan from women's hands and replaced it with . . . the gun. Russian woman, without rights, 'weak being,' 'prim creature,' slave, has come out of hiding from the kitchen to go to meet death."[10] In fact, participation in the war effort was contributing to the creation of an entirely new kind of woman-citizen in a new Russia.

Many Russian men who witnessed the women volunteers were impressed by their military aptitude. A correspondent from the popular journal *Sinii zhurnal* visited Bochkareva's unit while it was training in Petrograd.

> Before me on the drilling ground, harmoniously and gracefully beating time, pass a platoon of the first women's battalion in the world. . . . The battalion deftly and artfully fulfills all necessary aspects of military service. . . . The excellent bearing, the decisive and concentrated faces, the seriousness with which commands are carried out; it seems that one is present at the training of a true cadre of warriors.[11]

Another journalist who visited the women's battalion remarked, "The uncommonly well-composed and dashing platoon of 'soldiers,' neatly marching according to height, presented an extraordinary sight, moving to the point of tears."[12] The fact that he placed the word "soldiers" in quotation marks, however, reveals his inability to fully accept women in this role. Prince A. Lobanov-Rostovsky remarked that the women "were noticeable for the smart manner in which they saluted and for their disciplined bearing. I saw them marching down Nevsky on their way to the station where they embarked for the front. They had the appearance of crack troops and their crusading spirit was manifest in a huge golden cross on the unfolded colours."[13]

Public support for the women's military units was demonstrated by the thousands of people who came out to see Bochkareva's women's battalion receive its standard and benediction at St. Isaak's Cathedral in Petrograd. Although many came merely to catch a glimpse of such a novel and strange phenomenon, many others genuinely championed the women soldiers. A correspondent for the Russian newspaper *Novoe vremia* painted the scene:

> Since the first days of the Revolution, Petrograd has not experienced such
> an upsurge of joy as it experienced yesterday, June 21. On this day,
> Petrograd saw off its first women's battalion. . . . The street was completely
> full of people, and people filled the windows and balconies of the buildings
> along the Nevskii; from every quarter powerfully sounded unceasing
> "Hurrah!" From all sides they waved hats and banners and threw flowers.
> Many crossed themselves, and in their eyes tears of joy were visible.[14]

Similarly, numerous well-wishers appeared to see the women off as they departed for the front several days later, and as the battalion traveled, supporters appeared at stations all the way to Molodechno.

The Russian public expressed its support for the women's units with monetary and material assistance as well. At a number of public events, funds were collected for the women's military units. Not all of the thousands of rubles raised came from the bourgeoisie. At a fund-raiser in Moscow, a number of working-class men and women donated an average of 25 rubles each. One worker even pledged 150 rubles to the cause.[15] Other events featured famous entertainers who performed for the benefit the women soldiers.[16] Railway workers collected gifts and sent them to the volunteers of the 1st Russian Women's Battalion of Death.[17] Women's organizations solicited donations and voluntary assistance to secure winter clothing for the unit as well.[18]

Many within Russian society (as well as among the military establishment) worried that the women soldiers might not be able to withstand the rigors of combat. Indeed, there was much skepticism about the value of using women in combat capacities. After the successful participation of Bochkareva's unit in the battle at Smorgon, many seemed to "breathe as with relief," thankful that "nothing in the women's undertaking had proved to be comical" and that they "did not bring shame upon themselves."[19] From patriotic quarters, there was an outpouring of praise for the women soldiers following their first combat activity. "The Russian woman on the field of battle, in the ranks of heroes, has left a memorable impression of her selfless, devoted love for the motherland, sacrificing her life."[20] Some supporters even went so far as to excuse all past transgressions on the part of the entire sex once these women demonstrated their willingness to sacrifice themselves for the nation. For some men, the women soldiers became martyrs redeeming the entire female population. A writer for the popular monthly *Sinii zhurnal* expressed this sentiment: "One drop of this saintly blood compensates for all the mistakes, all the thoughtlessness, all the inconsistencies of 'the weaker sex,' representatives of which have gone to die for the homeland and freedom."[21]

Endorsement of the women soldiers was often coupled with anger toward soldiers who were refusing to fight. While women were being applauded for filling male roles, male shirkers were derided and sardonically advised to take up women's domestic functions. "It is horrible and wonderful to live in the days when women become men. When these men become '*babas*' as simple cowards, then it is only horrible," commented the author of an article on the procession of Bochkareva's battalion to St. Isaak's Square.[22] Labeling a man a "*baba*" (the Russian colloquialism for woman, usually indicating a peasant woman and roughly equivalent to "broad" in American slang) was a serious insult. A cartoon in a popular magazine depicted men wearing head kerchiefs, holding crying babies, and chewing on sunflower seeds (a common caricature of peasant women) while their wives, dressed in soldiers' uniforms, paraded smartly with their chins held high.[23] When criticized by men, the women soldiers themselves often responded by telling their male critics to go home and tend to the cooking and cleaning. Thus, it became acceptable, under these circumstances, for women to emulate masculine conduct, especially when men were not acting like "true men."

It was not, however, acceptable for men to emulate female behavior, particularly in regard to men's duties as soldiers. The male role of defender was essential for the survival of the nation in wartime, and men's refusal to carry it out was perceived as disastrous. Many men felt betrayed by those who valued their own lives over the benefit of the nation. The desire of some women to take up the fighting themselves was often seen as a natural reaction to this. "If desertion, cowardice, treason, and betrayal have dealt a blow to all the Russian people, so this blow has been especially felt by the Russian woman, and she has taken up arms not only so as to save the dying motherland, but also to save their faith in men, their faith in life."[24]

Although many Russian men admired the women soldiers for their dedication and self-sacrifice, they regretted that it was necessary to use women in such a manner. The priest who presided over a service for the fallen heroes of Bochkareva's battalion expressed this widely held sentiment: "This is a terrible and yet glorious hour for Russia. Sad it is, and terrible beyond expression that men have allowed women to die in their places for our unhappy country. But glorious it will ever be that Russian women are ready and willing to do it."[25] Even some more progressive elements in Russian society tempered their enthusiasm for the women's units with uneasiness about gender transgression. A backlash also developed against the Provisional Government for using young women in combat; there was considerable "public revulsion against those who had permitted boys as young as seventeen and girls as young as eighteen to face such ghastly possibilities."[26]

The view that women had no place on the battlefield, no matter how extreme the circumstances were, existed most strongly among conservative elements of Russian society. For them, the single demonstration by Bochkareva's volunteers in combat was not sufficient to prove that women would have any sustained success on the battlefield. Misogyny often informed opinions: "The devil himself could not defeat Russia, and he decided to send *babas* to the front," peasant villagers remarked.[27] The women soldiers made positive impressions upon many members of Russian society, but others were appalled by them. They saw Bochkareva as a megalomaniac tyrant, obsessed with petty details of military life but unable to maintain true discipline in her ranks. Many of her charges were no better: "They smoke *makhorka* [a poor quality tobacco], play leapfrog, fight, wallow in the dust of the square. . . . They emanate something unpleasant and repulsive."[28] Some even believed that there were women who had joined the battalion only because it was fashionable and cynically interpreted their actions as attempts to put themselves in the limelight. Moreover, it was difficult for men to take women soldiers seriously. The women's units were often seen as comical, and they were lampooned by many Russian men. A joke published in a popular journal asked whether the husbands of enlisted women were entitled to the same pensions as soldier's wives.[29]

Fear of potential sexual misconduct associated with the introduction of women into the male realm of the army was also in the forefront of many Russian men's minds. Civilian and military men alike wondered how it would be possible to prevent sexual interaction between males and females in the army.

Even Kerensky reportedly expressed initial trepidation regarding the ability to maintain high moral standards among a unit of female soldiers.[30] The onus of responsibility for maintaining sexual purity was often placed on the women, reflecting contemporary views of women as temptresses. Some men accused the female volunteers of being women of loose morals and even prostitutes. One citizen who supported the creation of the units remarked, "We were forced to hear the filthy suggestions about the intentions and future conduct of the women soldiers."[31] Interestingly, there was little discussion of potential sexual violence at the hands of the enemy should the women soldiers be captured in battle. However, the alleged distribution of cyanide capsules to the members of the 1st Russian Women's Battalion of Death is, if true, a good indication that such fears existed.

Sharp criticism of the women's military formations emanated from men on the left. A common contention from the socialist camp was that working-class and peasant women who had enlisted in the all-female units had been duped into serving the interests of the bourgeoisie. The Petrograd Soviet of Peasant Deputies stated that they found the organization of such units to be "not only an absolutely inappropriate and deceitful vaudeville show, but also another clear and deliberate effort of the bourgeoisie to use every means to prolong this horrible war until they get what they want."[32] They demanded that the women's units be disbanded immediately, as they were "shameful for the revolutionary army, which is currently shedding its blood at the frontline positions and which does not need a superficial boost."[33] The peasant deputies advised women who wanted to aid their country to go to the countryside and assist in agricultural labor instead of forming military units.

Not all radical and revolutionary elements opposed the women's military units, however, and some even expressed enthusiastic support. Veteran revolutionaries such as Lev Deutsch, Vera Zasulich, and Ekaterina Breshko-Breshkovskaia were unequivocal backers of the women's battalions. Deutsch and Zasulich, leaders of the League of Personal Example, believed the women soldiers would provide the much-needed inspiration to war-weary soldiers at the front and convince them to continue fighting. The positive assessment of the women's units by these elements is very closely connected with their stance on the war and their desire to use every available source of aid to shore up the army.

The most vociferous and caustic reproach against the women's military formations was launched by the Bolsheviks. Their negative stance owed little to opposition to gender transgression; rather, it was part of their efforts to disrupt any attempt to bolster the army and to discredit the Provisional Government.

They were similarly opposed to all the battalions of death and shock battalions composed of men that were organized during this period. The analysis by Nikolai Podvoiski, head of the Bolshevik Military Organization, sums up Bolshevik opinion well: "The bourgeoisie are playing on the patriotic feelings of women and are trying to demagogically use these feelings for their criminal goals."[34] Lenin called the female soldiers of the women's battalions "*kadetskii damy*" (meaning ladies of the Constitutional Democratic Party, one of the liberal political parties in the Russian parliament), implicating them as tools of the bourgeoisie. Yet, interestingly enough, he also remarked that "in Petrograd during the time of the battle against us [the women soldiers] displayed greater courage then the *junkers*."[35]

The Bolsheviks labeled the women's units "battalions of shame" and claimed they were a "dark spot on the revolution." "Why do they exist?" asked one Bolshevik journalist, adding, "In our civilized century, there is no more shameful women's work; is it really possible that she cannot bring benefit to society in a way other than ripping open the belly of her very brother?"[36] They fought against the formation of the women's units and encouraged protest once they were created. Bolsheviks infiltrated meetings of women's military organizations and attempted to denigrate the women soldiers in any way possible. They claimed that only "stupid" and misled students and those who were desperate, who had lost everything, joined the women's units.[37] One Bolshevik commentator even referred to Bochkareva as "some kind of psychopath."[38] Another Bolshevik agitator attempted to degrade the women's battalion by claiming that during the battle near Smorgon, the women's battalion had behaved like frightened girls.[39] The Bolsheviks similarly mocked the women's participation in the defense of the Winter Palace, portraying them as cowardly and misled. This image was perpetuated by the Bolsheviks even after the war, as demonstrated by the film *Oktiabr* by the Soviet director Sergei Eisenstein. In the film, the women soldiers are shown spending much of their time attending to their personal hygiene—including brushing their long hair—and acting in a generally frivolous manner.

In principle, Bolsheviks and other revolutionary groups did not oppose the use of women in a military capacity. In fact, radicals had employed women in a variety of violent activities since the 1860s, and many more women were armed for the cause of Bolshevism in the October Revolution and the ensuing Civil War than were employed by the Provisional Government. But gender was not the primary consideration for these groups. For them, the central concern was the purpose of the women's units, which they considered part of the effort to continue an imperialist war. Yet they found it convenient to use arguments against female participation in combat to bolster their opposition to the units. "No, we do not want any more crippled women; we do not want our future mothers to become depraved militarists. We do not want our mothers to bring up our children with feelings of hatred for other peoples. Woman, by her nature, by her assigned existence as mother, must be an opponent of the destruction of the producers of humanity."[40] The opinion that peasant and working-class women had been deceived by the bourgeois government persisted in Russian public opinion throughout much of the Soviet period.

## The Russian Military Reaction

Russia's women soldiers may have had the greatest impact on men in the military realm. It was here that women had the closest interactions with men, and it was here that some dramatic transformations of opinion regarding women in combat occurred. Relations between Russia's female soldiers and its male military personnel during this war were complex and changed over time. The military men's responses to the women soldiers are particularly interesting, as they highlight the general problem posed by women crossing such strictly defined lines of gender behavior. In order to assimilate into the military milieu, the women had to emulate the only models available to them, men. To become good soldiers, they essentially had to surrender their femininity. Furthermore, to be truly successful and avoid criticism, they had to learn how to be better soldiers than most men. Both aspects were highly disturbing to men. Opinions about women in combat were also heavily influenced by the politics of the time and at times even went against conventional social views. Moreover, there is a clear difference between the way many male military personnel viewed individual women entering male units and their perceptions of the women's military formations created in 1917.

The participation of individual women in the Russian army was irregular and sporadic, and male responses to their presence in combat were equally arbitrary. Initially, most men were skeptical that women could handle the rigors of warfare, and therefore many resisted women's efforts to become soldiers. Officers, who were primarily from the upper social strata of Russian society (at least until the February Revolution) and usually held conservative social and political views, tended to oppose women in combat as a fundamental transgression of the conventional gender order. Upon discovering women in the ranks of their units, Russian officers often sent them home or assigned them to more "suitable" medical or auxiliary services. But others allowed persistent women to enter their ranks, giving them an opportunity to prove themselves. Those who witnessed women carrying out military duties were impressed by their bravery, fortitude, and military ability.

The rank-and-file soldiers who came into contact with individual women combatants experienced a number of different responses simultaneously, including intrigue, confusion, shame, and arousal. Their initial reaction was often astonishment mixed with amused perplexity. Some seemingly could not resist the temptation of the presence of members of the opposite sex in such close proximity. As a result, some women who served in men's units, such as Bochkareva, reported that they were subjected to unwanted sexual advances. One cannot but wonder, however, whether the men were acting on true feelings of sexual excitement or in conformance with expected and conditioned responses to the presence of women. Moreover, aggressive sexual behavior may have been an effort to display power and dominance over women who challenged male prerogative in the military sphere. This had particular resonance considering the appearance of most women soldiers: decidedly unfeminine with shaved heads and male attire. These women, who tried to emulate male appearance as well as behavior, were perhaps being "punished" by men through sexual violence for their gender transgression.

Other female soldiers were treated benevolently by the men of their units from the very beginning of their military service. A number of women, particularly those who were very young, were taken under the protective wing of the male soldiers, who treated them with paternalistic concern and attention. Margarita Kokovsteva, who joined a Cossack regiment early in the war, reported that the men in her unit treated her with the utmost care. "They were surprisingly careful, extremely polite and related to me in a very straightforward manner, as if I was their child."[41] Some, like fifteen-year-old Zoya Smirnova and her friends, were aided by male soldiers in their attempts to join the active army. In many cases, men viewed female soldiers in their units as mascots, as was the case with Marina Iurlova. Often, when the men discovered that a disguised woman had been in their midst they were shocked but did not necessarily react negatively. Ekaterina Alekseeva, who had enlisted in male guise, remarked, "When they found out that I was a girl, they kissed me, fussed over me, asking over and over again how I was, what happened to me. What dears! . . . No one did anything to offend me."[42] (Alekseeva was referring to kissing in a nonsexual sense, implying an expression of affection for close friends or relatives.)

Eventually, the majority of women who participated in the fighting as part of male regiments came to be accepted, and many even earned the respect and admiration of the men with whom they served. These women endured all the privations and hardships of military life in the field and carried out all the duties required of soldiers. As a result, men came to regard them as their equals to some degree. Many of the women soldiers were given male nicknames, as a sign of their assimilation. This is not to say that the rank-and-file Russian soldier who served with a woman or two condoned general sexual integration of the military on the principle of gender equality. These women soldiers were still viewed as exceptions to the rest of their sex, and, as historians Ann Griese and Richard Stites comment, "If the men treated them as comrades in arms, it was not due to egalitarian ideology, but rather to peasant ethos (as the vast majority of soldiers were peasants) in which women had always been seen as doing hard physical labor."[43] Moreover, it was generally the men who had direct experience with the women soldiers who had the best opinion of their capabilities.

The creation of the women's military formations in 1917 triggered stronger reactions from male military personnel. Although individual women continued to serve in male units, beginning in late May most women who joined the Russian military did so as part of the all-female units. Instead of one or several young women, deemed exceptions to the general rules of gender behavior, there were large groups of women being armed and trained to fight as soldiers. This was a much greater encroachment upon the male military world. Moreover, politics now informed much of the opinion concerning the women's units, considering that they were created as part of the effort to bolster the army, continue the war, and thus effectively support the Provisional Government. Therefore, the reactions of many male military personnel to women combatants came to be determined less by perceptions of gender roles or even class empathy and increasingly by attitudes concerning the war. The facts that the women were volunteers and that they were organized under the auspices of the pro-war government are essential to an understanding of the male military responses to soldiers of the women's formations.

A number of military personnel had concerns about sexual interaction between male and female soldiers. At a meeting of soldiers' delegates discussing the idea of creating women's military units, an attendee asked: "Who will guarantee that the presence of women soldiers at the front will not yield there little soldiers?"[44] The male officers of the 1st Petrograd Women's Battalion were particularly concerned about the issue of sexual misconduct, making it a top priority in their officers' meetings. Captain Shagal, commander of the 3rd Company, expressed the worry that since the officers had been derived from varying units and did not know each other well, they could not vouch for each other's "honor." The onus of maintaining propriety within the unit, however, was firmly placed on the men, in Shagal's assessment. The women, according to the captain, were themselves above reproach: "The battalion was an association of the best, most honest, Russian girls and women."[45]

Despite Shagal's denial of any misconduct, as indicated previously, Bocharnikova reported incidences of sexual interaction between members of the 1st Petrograd Women's Battalion and male officers and training personnel. Nor, apparently, was the problem isolated to this unit. Rumors of sexual impropriety in the 2nd Moscow Women's Battalion of Death circulated in Russian society, and Bochkareva seems to have found evidence of its occurrence when she reviewed the unit in July.[46] She even admitted that despite her best efforts, her own unit was not immune to inappropriate interaction between male and female personnel. Bochkareva asserted that in the midst of the chaos of the battle at Smorgon, she discovered one of her female combatants engaged in sexual activity with a male soldier behind some bushes. The woman commander claimed she was so enraged by this transgression of her strict moral standards that she ran the unfortunate woman through with her bayonet, while the male soldier fled, barely escaping the commander's wrath. Although the truth of this incident is questionable, it speaks to the heightened sense of concern over improper sexual relations between male and female soldiers.

By 1917, the division in attitudes cut largely horizontally across the ranks of the Russian army. To some degree, the attitudes of male military personnel prior to the creation of the women's battalion were turned on their head. Officers who were trying to inspire their men to continue fighting maintained at least tacit support for the all-female military units, in the hope that the women soldiers would provoke action on the part of war-weary soldiers. In fact, the reactions of many of the officers who came into contact with the women soldiers were now quite positive. A number of male officers enthusiastically supported the women's military units. Captain L. N. Rostov was an active participant in the formation of the women's units, a member of the Petrograd Women's Military Union, and a delegate to the Women's Military Congress. Lieutenant Colonel Popov, convinced of the power of women to influence the demoralized army, spoke at a recruitment meeting for Bochkareva's battalion: "Drive them to the front! Shame them! And tell every man, women citizens, that you will allow those who have fought in the war and staunchly defended the fatherland to come near to your hearts."[47]

Male officers responsible for the formation and training of the all-female military units were impressed by the women's military aptitude. General Petr Polovtsev, commander of the Petrograd Military District, inspected Bochkareva's battalion during its training and was taken with the fortitude and persistence of the women, as well as with the perfection of their drill. In contrast, he lambasted those soldiers who were hostile to the women, accusing them of be-

ing "lazy and idle." "Well boys," he scoffed at members of the Petrograd garrison, "I hear none of you want to go to fight in your regiment at the front. Would
you like me to send my girls to your regiment instead of yourselves? They make
very good soldiers, so perhaps it would be an excellent idea for us men to stay
at home and send women to fight for us."[48] The general's remarks only served to
infuriate the men. In his final assessment of the women soldiers, Polovtsev
commended them highly: "Everything they did proved that they had a genuine
feeling of patriotism and a sense of duty of which few men could boast."[49] The
commander of the Tenth Army, General Valuev, who reviewed Bochkareva's
unit when it arrived at the front, was struck by their strict discipline and flaw-
less drill.[50] The commander of the I Siberian Army Corps, who also inspected
Bochkareva's volunteers at the front, was similarly impressed. "Magnificent!"
he exclaimed following the review, marveling at how well the women had been
trained, especially in such a short time.[51] Bochkareva's volunteers also made a
very positive impression on those who witnessed their performance on the battlefield. All the male officers involved in the battle at Smorgon offered nothing
but the highest acclaim for their actions in combat.[52]

The commander of the 3rd Company of the 1st Petrograd Women's Battalion,
Captain Shagal, recalled his experiences in very positive terms, declaring that
he had the "honor and good fortune" to serve as one of its instructors. He
praised the women for holding up well in the difficult work of training, as well,
in fact, as "young men" (undoubtedly a high compliment). He believed the volunteers to be "the best, most honest, Russian girls and women who wished to
serve, even infinitely more—to sacrifice themselves for the motherland." Shagal did not, however, believe the women would be effective in raising the fighting spirit of the army. But he did think the female soldiers worthy of a place in
history, especially those who had lost their lives: "Let you be light upon the
earth, my dear comrades, eternal remembrance and glory to you!"[53] As with individual women soldiers, the male military personnel who were closely associated with the all-female units, who saw them train and especially those who saw
them fight, had the highest opinion of the women soldiers; criticism largely
came from those who had little or no personal experience with them.

Not all officers were so approving. There were still those who objected to the
presence of women in the ranks of the military on the basis of conventional gender roles. General V. V. Marushevskii, commander of the White Army's Northern
Forces during the Civil War, met Bochkareva in the Northern Territories in 1918
and explicitly denied her request to enlist in the ranks of his troops. He did not
mince words in expressing his opinion about women as soldiers: "I consider that
the summoning of women for military duties, which are not appropriate for their

sex, to be a heavy reproach and disgraceful stain on the whole population of the northern region."[54] Others tempered their rejection of women in military endeavors with admiration for their willingness to die for their country. General Anton Denikin, chief of the General Staff, believed, "There is no place for women on the fields of death, where horror reigns, where there is blood, dirt, and hardship, where hearts are hardened and morals are crude," while in the same breath, he applauded the women who had fought and acknowledged that "we must repay that which is owed to the memory of these brave ones."[55] There were those among the military establishment who found it difficult to take the women's units seriously. The organ of the new Russian army, *Armiia i flot' svobodnoi Rossii,* maintained, "Now is not the time for petty gestures. It is necessary to take every measure to care for the men in the army, and not to form a musical-comedy army of women, who frighten neither the Germans nor those Russians who work for the destruction of our military strength."[56]

Rank-and-file soldiers often did not know quite what to make of the women's military units. "Young ladies amusing themselves," remarked some.[57] Others could not believe that female soldiers would actually be sent to the front. "They don't have the strength for it! They'll just run away!" a soldier commented when he saw Bochkareva's unit pass on the streets of Petrograd.[58] Many worried that the women would disgrace the Russian army. Expressions of "sorrow and humiliation that women had felt the necessity of enlisting," sentiments that revealed damaged male pride, were not uncommon.[59] Some soldiers appreciated the willingness for self-sacrifice displayed by the women but believed these women could better serve the country on the home front. The members of the Executive Soldiers' Committee of the Romanian Front recommended that women's energies be put to use behind the front lines, as telephone operators and other auxiliary, noncombatant, services.[60] The sailors of the Naval Infantry Training Detachment offered the following suggestion:

> Our advice and sincere request to you, Russian women: whomsoever of you who wants to carry out aid before the altar of the fatherland, unite yourselves not in a "women's naval detachment," or in "shock battalions," but in *labor* and *auxiliary battalions* and hurry, . . . while our brothers and fathers are struggling to defend the interests of the hard-won revolution, . . . to the villages, towns, suburbs, and settlements, where our elderly parents and young children remain alone.[61]

There were also men who perceived the creation of the women's units as a direct attack on their masculinity (which, of course, it was intended to be) and therefore deeply resented it. Viktor Shklovsky commented that he believed the idea to form female combat units was "thought up expressly as an insult to the front."[62]

As the conflict dragged on and as demoralization and war-weariness among the rank and file grew, perceptions of women as soldiers became more inimical. The most hostile and disapproving sentiment against the women's military units came from those who wanted an immediate cessation of the fighting. In Bolshevized units, disapproval of the women's formations was expressed, often violently. They mocked, derided, and verbally abused the women soldiers, accused them of being counterrevolutionary elements, and sometimes even physically attacked them. Many war-weary conscripts identified the women's units as tools of the upper classes, fighting for the cause of imperialism. Their antagonism was undoubtedly aggravated by the challenge to their masculinity presented by the women. Some appealed to the government to end these formations. For example, the Soldiers' Section of the Poltava Soviet of Workers' and Soldiers' Deputies requested that the Ministry of War immediately dissolve the all-female military formations established in Kiev.[63]

While all the women's military units came into contact with male military personnel, Bochkareva's unit undoubtedly had the most extensive and prolonged relations with the men of the Russian army. Their experiences provide us with vital information concerning the responses of male soldiers to female combatants. While training in Petrograd, the unit was continually harassed by male soldiers from neighboring units. At the front, the situation was not much better. Both Bochkareva and Krylova portrayed relations between the male soldiers and female volunteers at the front as being so antagonistic that the women were even fired upon by neighboring Russian units. American journalists Rheta Childe Dorr and Bessie Beatty, who spent a week with this unit at Molodechno, also told of enmity on the part of many male soldiers. The women of Bochkareva's unit were continuously confronted with throngs of curious but not very welcoming male soldiers and were assailed with curses and shouts of "Why did you come here? What devil brought you here? You want to fight? We want peace! We have had enough fighting."[64] Some of the men accused the women of having "imperialist intentions" and berated them for "stirring up the war again," a war with which they declared themselves to be "finished." Most were not inspired by the example of women fighting in the forefront. Some were sufficiently impressed once the women proved themselves in battle, but this positive assessment was fleeting and not widespread.[65]

Over time, the men's animosity toward the women grew to the point that there seemed to be greater danger from fellow Russians than from the enemy. It is important to note, however, that the negative treatment of Bochkareva's volunteers came largely from male soldiers who were highly politicized with a very antiwar stance. Such soldiers displayed equal enmity toward male revolutionary and shock units organized for the purpose of shoring up morale and leading the hesitant into battle. Thus, the criticism of the women's unit was not exclusively gender based. It was not, however, entirely free of gendered implications either. The fact that it was women presenting a challenge to the male role, and ultimately to masculinity, was indeed significant. Many male soldiers clearly resented the attempt to "shame" them by sending women.

Not all male rank-and-file soldiers had a negative reaction to the women's military formations. Those who were willing to continue fighting did not express hostility toward the women, and in fact, some male units were very welcoming. Soldiers of the First and Third Armies sent delegates to Petrograd to present Bochkareva's unit with icons and expressions of support for the heroic women.[66] The 2nd Railroad Battalion sent a positive message to Bochkareva's women soldiers: "We, conscious soldiers, standing on guard over the revolution, send greetings to these warriors and brothers in arms. Let these free citizenesses know that all the bitterness and mockery that is directed toward them comes only from those of us who are in the darkness of ignorance."[67] Black Sea Fleet sailor F. I. Baktin, in his address at a public gathering in Petrograd to raise money for the women's battalions, called the female soldiers "saintly heroines" "who stand staunchly defending the homeland from the enemy, at this moment, when the country is shaken."[68] Even some soldiers of the 525th Kiuruk-Dar'inskii regiment praised Bochkareva's unit after its participation in the battle at Smorgon:

> You stood your ground firmly and did not let the enemy break through and take our positions. You bolstered the weak and the cowardly. You supported the courageous ones. It was your blood, shed in the Novospasskii forest, that mixed with the blood of our heroes. You were real heroines. The regiment, the army and history will never forget your act of heroism, unparalleled since the Crusaders.[69]

In August 1917, the soldiers of the Berestechskii regimental committee voted in favor of allowing three young women to join their ranks, welcoming the "patriotic impulse of the girls" and asking that the soldiers and officers of the unit treat them with complete respect.[70] This difference in attitude may have been a result of this unit's general position regarding the war, that is, their willingness to continue fighting. Or perhaps the participation of a few women in the ranks of male units was less threatening than that of entire formations of women. There is even evidence that the women's units did have some positive effect on inspiring some men to continue fighting. The soldiers of the 6th Company of the 33rd Mounted Reserve Regiment in Simferopol asked to be moved up to the frontline positions, asserting that they did not want to remain in the rear when women were being trained as soldiers.[71]

### Russian Women's Views

The women soldiers received a great amount of attention from other women; they were extensively publicized in the numerous periodicals written by and for women. By and large, the women soldiers obtained much support from members of their own sex. As with men, social and political views were important in the attitudes of Russian women toward female combatants. Yet with women, gender affinity was also significant, as was the fact that the women soldiers were demonstrating conclusively their ability to function effectively in the public sphere and to contribute to the national good. Moreover, unlike the views of Russian men, particularly male members of the military establishment, those of Russian women concerning female soldiers were fairly consistent throughout the war.

The individual women who entered male regiments were featured extensively in women's publications. In nearly every issue, women's periodicals featured segments focusing on the contributions made by women to the war effort. They invariably included reports of women serving, or attempting to serve, in military capacities. Numerous photographs of women soldiers were printed in their pages as well. As the incidence of women serving in military capacities became increasingly common, the social implications of their actions were readily recognized by many women. Women pressing for rights and equality applauded women soldiers not only for their patriotic self-sacrifice and courage but also for proving that women were capable of functioning in the most masculine of spheres. "If we meet many excellent, strong women-*bogatyr*s, then isn't it possible now that the war shows us with our own eyes all the certainty of women's valiance, not a bit inferior to men's?" remarked writer V. Ermilova.[72]

Some even imbued the actions of "unconscious" women soldiers—that is, women who fought without a true understanding of feminism—with great significance for the women's movement. In recounting the story of a young servant girl, Ekaterina Alekseeva, who entered the fighting disguised as a young man named Aleksei Sokolov, one woman journalist remarked, "This simple servant of a priest, Ekaterina Alekseeva, is a sign of the times—more significant than it would seem at first glance. Ekaterina Alekseeva, as her own will commands, was equalized in rights with Aleksei Sokolov."[73] The war had provided a means by which women could demonstrate their worth and their right to liberation and had shown women that they did not have to remain under the domination of men: "The confused face of yesterday's slave is now the peaceful and solemn face of the future freedom of women."[74]

Not all Russian women welcomed the participation of others of their sex in the fighting. There were those who found combat to be an unacceptable way for women to aid their country in time of war. For them, women's usefulness lay in their moral, not physical, strength. Although they did not deny that women might indeed be capable of carrying out the duties and enduring the hardships of a soldier, they were convinced that this was not the correct path for them. Women "must fulfill that which men are unable to do. . . . the strength of woman is in what she brings into the world, *that* which man is *unable* to bring."[75] Woman had a special role in society: She was a giver and nurturer of life. She therefore should tend to men's wounds, not inflict them herself. Not only did they see such activity as disruptive to feminine roles, but they believed it was damaging to the efficacy of the military, which was largely based on the male role of defender and the complementary female role of nurturer. As one woman journalist asserted,

> It is possible to say with certainty that not one warrior would go to the field of battle if he knew that on that very field would be his wife, his sister, that when he returned, his family would be broken up, his children would be dead of hunger, and no one would be there to heal his wounds, received in glorious battle with the enemy.[76]

She insisted that "first and foremost, women are obligated to maintain the value and sanctity of the family hearth."[77]

With the creation of the women's combat formations, Russian women took greater interest in women's military participation. Women who supported a continuation of the war looked enthusiastically to the women's units, not only as a means to bolster the demoralized army but, equally, as the ultimate way to demonstrate their patriotism and citizenship. They emphasized that during this time of crisis for the nation, women could not "remain indifferent and passive," that they had to "take part in the defense of the motherland, wherever they can, either in the rear or at the front."[78] Praising the activities of those such as Bochkareva, who worked to apply women's strength to the realm of combat, they encouraged more women to follow suit. Some women among the patriotic camp extolled the women's units to the point of rapture. The women's journal *Damskii mir* labeled the women martyrs and saints. They were certain the actions of the women soldiers would ensure their legacy as heroes. "The motherland and history will not forget those who during hard and bitter times engaged in an unusual activity—went to fight the enemy with weapons. . . . The ecstasy of love for the motherland, the charm of heroism, will surround the memory of these women with a bright halo," wrote a journalist in *Damskii mir*.[79]

Among Russian women, there was a resurgence of interest in heroic women figures of the past and an attempt to link the actions of women in the current war to past demonstrations of female devotion and patriotism. The author of one article recalled a historical incident in which, when the Tatars invaded an ancient Russian town, all the women cut off their hair in order to weave strings for bows and used all their jewels as tips for the arrows.[80] Another author asked, "Did not the women of Chernogori fight alongside their fathers and husbands?"[81] The legacies of Joan of Arc and Nadezhda Durova were most frequently invoked. The patriotism of Russian women, displayed throughout history, was also used in an effort to break up class antagonism. A writer for *Damskii mir* pointed out, "When our country is being torn by an exaggerated class struggle, women of very different social positions united to defend the motherland, inspired by their love." She believed that the example of Bochkareva, an uneducated peasant, and her adjutant, Skrydlova, a member of the highest social circle in the country, united together in the 1st Russian Women's Battalion of Death, was a clear demonstration of this class unity.[82]

While many women recognized that the women's units would not be able to augment the physical strength of the army, either in quantity or quality, they saw in them great moral value. The writer Sophia Zarechnaia proclaimed in the pages of *Zhenskoe delo*,

> The crux of the cause is not to form women's battalions in order to reinforce the thinning, thanks to desertion, ranks of men, to enlarge the quantity of armed forces at the front. Rather, the cause is one of moral influence, which presentation of women at the front must make on the cowardly men, who have lost their sense of honor and consciousness of civil duty and responsibility.[83]

For such women, the organization of all-female military formations was much more significant than individual women's enlistment in male regiments. "Only a collective female feat can attract for itself sufficient attention and have any influence on the psychologically disheartened man," she proclaimed.[84]

Admiration for the volunteers of the women's battalion also came from those who doubted their own abilities to become soldiers. Countess Olga Putiatina wept as she saw the 1st Russian Women's Battalion of Death depart for the front, knowing that "they were going to do a man's job and show the way to the waverers" but deeply uncertain whether she possessed the same courage and fortitude to withstand the rigors of combat.[85] She believed that the women who became soldiers were not typical representatives of their gender. They were able to do things that other women could not. Putiatina, like others, was also unwilling to undergo the degradation heaped upon the women's battalions by detractors and critics, but she deeply appreciated those who were. Sophia Zarechnaia praised the women soldiers but admitted that she was "completely unprepared to take upon myself this thankless role of the defense of female battle capability," particularly after hearing male soldiers heap insults upon the women. In particular, Zarechnaia commended the women for demonstrating their "civic maturity" and doing so "with the strength of consciousness of one's responsibility to the homeland."[86]

Feminists and progressive women tended to look favorably upon the creation of the women's military units, seeing their creation as a necessary measure and even seeing participation in them as a patriotic duty, to assist the nation in its time of crisis. Organizations such as the League for Women's Equality and the All-Russian Women's Union enthusiastically welcomed the development of the women's military movement. The leader of the All-Russian Women's Union, Anna Shabanova, was convinced that women had to play a role in the defense of the nation and was dedicated to the organization of the women's units.[87] Feminist Maria Pokrovskaia, editor of the women's journal *Zhenskii vestnik* and leader of the Progressive Women's Party, completely abandoned her pacifist stance to support the war effort and the women's battalions. During the Russo-Japanese War, Pokrovskaia had asserted that "women soldiers do not serve human progress." By 1917, she had fully reversed this position, extensively praising and promoting the women's military movement.[88] A journalist writing for Pokrovskaia's *Zhenskii vestnik* asserted the necessity of the women's military units:

> The homeland and freedom are threatened with deathly danger from without. Women cannot remain indifferent and passive. They must take part in the defense of the homeland, whenever they can, either in the rear or at the front.[89]

For many progressive women advocating greater rights for and participation by women in the public sphere, the example of women in combat represented a tremendous opportunity. Many feminists and progressive women embraced the female combatants as harbingers of a new era for women's rights and equality. Ariadna Tyrkova, women's activist and member of the Petrograd City Duma, asserted that the women's military movement was part and parcel of the greater struggle by women to expand their rights and activities. "The women's movement," she proclaimed, "on the one hand is creating the unprecedented regiments of women volunteers that exist nowhere else in the world, and on the other, demands the rights of women to serve the government."[90] Surely, if women were capable of becoming soldiers, the most masculine occupation, they would be able to perform any other task reserved for men.

Moreover, by fighting and dying for their country, women would prove their worth to society and would undoubtedly be rewarded with rights and equality. Indeed, the Provisional Government granted Russian women a number of important rights and opportunities during its short-lived existence, the most important being the long-coveted right to vote, which was passed on July 20, 1917. Whether these gains were the direct result of women's wartime service to the nation is debatable, but there is little question that contemporary Russian women seeking rights believed their contribution would probably be rewarded politically. The women's military units were an important way of making such a contribution and represented another avenue for women's inclusion in the affairs of the nation. Civic responsibility was an extremely important component in the support of the women's military movement. At the May 26, 1917, meeting of the All-Russian Women's Union, the delegates adopted a resolution appealing to women to join the war effort, stating that "imperative responsibility and civic duty call Russian women to support the united will of our armies, to raise the fallen spirits of the troops, and to go into their ranks as volunteers, to turn the passive stand of the front into an active attack, so that we will not allow the ruin of the honor, virtue, and freedom of Russia."[91]

Women were just as obligated to demonstrate their civic responsibility as men. And part of this obligation was to teach others their duties as citizens. Many women saw the refusal of many men to fight as being born largely from the lack of understanding of civic responsibility. Russia's citizens had only recently gained their rights and freedoms, but they had not been educated in their responsibilities and civic duties. Much work needed to be done if Russia was going to develop not only into a free nation but also into a society based upon mutual consent, equality, rights, and responsibility. The external threat presented by Russia's enemies in the war, and the internal threat of anarchy

and Bolshevism, meant there was no time to give citizenship lessons to the
masses of soldiers. The women's military units were interpreted as a means of
quickly infusing this sense of responsibility in the men by appealing to their
sense of duty as defenders, which, deep down, these women were convinced existed on the most basic level. "Our most prized possession—freedom—is now
located on the edge of demise, and women, like all those who cherish freedom,
understand that we cannot remain non-participating witnesses; every bit of
strength and energy is demanded from the motherland and must be given to
save her."[92]

However, this enthusiasm for the women's military units should not be interpreted as support for a general policy of sexual integration of the Russian military. Even the most radical feminists of the time viewed the activities of the
women soldiers as exceptional, the result of the drastic circumstances of the
war. In essence, their participation was a defensive posture, comparable to the
violent actions of a female animal protecting her young. "Women are strongly
for the side of peace and against war, but when the motherland and freedom are
threatened with danger, they will take up arms and sacrifice their lives," stated
a writer in *Zhenskii vestnik*.[93]

Moreover, much of the advocacy of female participation in military endeavors came as a result of women's frustration with men's seeming inability to successfully prosecute the war. Zarechnaia echoed this sentiment: "If man,
especially during this recent, postrevolutionary period, does not always demonstrate even the most elementary demands of his citizenship, then it is especially admirable to call the heroic presentation of the youngest, most publicly
inexperienced group of citizens—that of women."[94] For three years women had
watched as Russia suffered defeat and hardship while the efforts of men had
done little to improve the situation. Pokrovskaia blamed men for bringing the
war about in the first place. "If women had possessed a 'decisive voice' in the
affairs of the nation," she asserted, "this dreadful war would never have been
waged. But having precipitated Europe into the conflict, men had proved incapable of bringing it to a successful conclusion. It was left to women to take on
the responsibility."[95]

Similarly, women were dismayed by men's failure to fulfill the role of defender. This often led their advocacy of a temporary exchange of gender roles.
Although such a switch was now seen as necessary, it was not regarded as natural or desirable. As another journalist commented:

We are told that to take up arms is not women's business! Truly! But to lie
about all day in the grass, chew on sunflower seeds, bawl songs, and "join"

various organizations, . . . is also not men's business, and if men continue to act this way, then women need to take on male responsibilities themselves. We have taken them. Our place is at arms, the place of men is at home at the hearth. . . . The roles have been changed!"[96]

Furthermore, not all Russian women who advocated women's rights and equality could bring themselves to embrace the women soldiers with enthusiasm. Nor was all the acclaim from Russian feminists and progressive women uniform or unequivocal. Many were torn between the positive, the patriotic and civic connotations of the all-female military units, and the negative, the emulation of destructive male behavior. One needs only look at opinions expressed in the progressive women's journal *Zhenskoe delo,* the organ of the League for Women's Equality, during the summer and fall of 1917 to see evidence of this painful ambiguity. The journal printed both articles that questioned the appropriateness of women's participation in combat and articles that supported the women's units for displaying civic responsibility and patriotism. One writer proclaimed, "The appearance of the Women's Battalion of Death is the national voice of Russian women, which gives its life for the good of the homeland."[97] Meanwhile, the editors of the journal condemned the "Russian 'amazons' for abandoning their femininity," indicating that "women's calling is to be compassionate, helping and healing; hence when men become soldiers, women should become nurses."[98] Other women were unconvinced that the women's military units would have any influence on the mass of male soldiers. They saw the experience of Bochkareva's unit at the front as confirming this view. Writer Maria Ancharova explained,

> The catastrophe at the front occurred after the organization of the women's battalions, and, of course, their participation cannot bring even the most microscopic fraction of change. . . . Military units expected them with bewilderment and disappointment, believing that the "battalions of death" were worthless ventures, inexcusable in these harsh times. They met them with indifference; they did not pay any attention to them.[99]

Thus, there seemed to be no reason for the women's units to continue to exist. According to Ancharova, "The women want to raise the mood at the front. Did they attain this through the form of the 'battalions of death' or not? . . . The answer is categorically no, they did not attain this in any measure." The problems facing the Russian army were too great for a small group of women, who had questionable military value, to resolve, she continued: "The time of Joan of Arc has passed. In war now you practically don't see the enemy face to face. Iron discipline and iron weaponry—these are the modern necessities for military success. Delicate and sincere women do not bring these into the army."[100]

Much of the criticism leveled against the women soldiers was based upon social conventions that dictated a women's role be centered on the creative and healing aspects of life. It was, therefore, unacceptable to many women that members of their sex were involved in the realm of death and destruction. "All of the peace-related activities of women in the rear do much more to raise spirits at the front than their appearance there in full military readiness."[101] Women were encouraged to support the war effort in ways more suited to their gender socialization, by sewing undergarments and preparing food packages for soldiers or, if they insisted upon going to the front, by becoming nurses to care for wounded and dying men. Moreover, many women chastised the volunteers of the women's units for neglecting their domestic responsibilities, for "abandoning their families to the mercy of fate" (despite the fact that the majority of women soldiers were young, unmarried, and childless). To them, "every bit of strength and energy is demanded for the motherland and must be given to save her," but attempts by women to join the fighting were rash and thoughtless, spurred by passion and impulse rather than governed by logic and reason.[102]

Other women were critical of what they perceived as ulterior motives on the part of those who joined the all-female military formations. Although she praised the women's unit involved in the defense of the Winter Palace, Countess Kleinmichel was careful to distinguish this battalion from the other all-female units, whose members she claimed had joined for less-than-patriotic and self-sacrificing motivations. She essentially accused them of being prostitutes, pursuing a profession besides the military, one "far less glorious," and of being "attracted by good food, high rates of pay, and the dissolute life," and she claimed that they "became famous through their acts of perverse cruelty."[103] Here the concern for sexual impropriety is turned on its head, with the women being blamed for conducting themselves immorally.

Although they were not opposed to using women to fight for revolution, Bolshevik women lambasted the women's battalions in a manner similar to their male comrades. Aleksandra Kollontai called them a "toy, show-off women's army." She criticized them for being composed of naïve, bourgeois girls who joined the units in order to escape unhappiness in their personal lives and of a few confused and misguided working-class women. While she believed the women soldiers themselves to be politically ignorant, she denounced their organizers for being motivated solely by class interests. They were "sowing hate and enmity; . . . encourag[ing] the lowest passions in people; awakening the beast in man, defying all the laws of humanity, compassion, culture, and morality." As such, they were "leading Russia to a complete economic collapse and to a sure death from the extension of war."[104]

## WESTERN IMPRESSIONS

Women in the ranks of the Russian army attracted significant foreign attention from the very beginning of the war. Western journalists wrote numerous melodramatic tales of the feats of Russia's female combatants, many of which included photographs, to prove to any doubting readers that such "Amazons" really did exist.[105] There was even a British newsreel made featuring the women's battalions in Petrograd and Moscow. The film depicts the visit of suffragettes Emmeline Pankhurst and Florence Harper to Bochkareva's unit and the benediction ceremony for the Moscow battalion on Red Square.[106] Western opinion of Russia's women soldiers ranged from adulation to condemnation. Like their Russian counterparts, foreign observers could extensively extol the women for their heroism and courage while simultaneously criticizing the state of affairs that had made it necessary for women to go into battle. The disparity of opinion about Russia's women soldiers of World War I was not merely the result of political or social ideologies or biases. Rather, the pervasive ambivalence about Russia's female combatants was a reaction to their extreme challenge to gender roles and their simultaneous willingness to sacrifice themselves for the good of the nation. This commitment to continue fighting became increasingly important as Russia's participation in the war became more and more uncertain.

### The Western Male Perspective

Many Western men were made extremely uncomfortable by the idea of women with guns, especially women organized, disciplined, and trained to kill men. On the whole, most Western men were unable to fully reconcile themselves with this ultimate act of intrusion into such a distinctly and exclusively masculine sphere. Although they often cheered the women for their bravery and self-sacrifice, they were generally thankful that their own nations did not allow women to act in such capacities.

Some male observers were appalled at the entire notion of women fighters and attempted to downplay their significance. One British writer exclaimed that "in the early days of the war these cases [of women soldiers] were painfully common, but the general sense of Russia was against them."[107] By using language like "*painfully* common" and "general *sense*," the author suggests that the reasonable elements of the country had to bear the irrational whims of a few overzealous but misguided women. While he did admit that such women were "deserving of notice," the author attempted to dismiss the entire phenomenon by stating that "a few score among the millions of Russia's armies require no other explanation than the simple law of averages" and downplayed their accomplishments by asserting that "it was not in this direction that the women of Russia showed their worth."[108]

A number of Western commentators attributed the unusual phenomenon of women in combat to Russian exceptionalism. The Western world regarded the Russian Empire with a good deal of mystification and even suspicion. Many foreigners suffered from a dilemma that continues to shape attitudes about Russia to the present day: Was it Eastern or Western, Asian or European? The Russians were exotic, even barbaric, and the nation was backward and politically oppressive.[109] The average Russian was often viewed as sturdy and strong, able to withstand immense pain and recover from terrible wounds, but as not particularly autonomous or intelligent.[110] The Russian army was noted for its stamina, spirit, and ability to withstand appalling conditions, which compensated for its deficiencies in training, technology, and military skill. Commentary on the female combatants was largely consistent with such views: The women soldiers were said to be strong and physically fit, extremely dedicated and self-sacrificing, and able to endure the harshest conditions of war.[111]

Westerners also perceived gender roles and relations in Russia as being very different from those in the West. They noted that women in Russia were often engaged in heavy physical labor in the fields and factories, whereas in the West, such work was primarily reserved for men. Russian women had also shown extraordinary fortitude and had carried out masculine tasks in the revolutionary movement, serving as assassins and terrorists. Some Westerners saw the average Russian woman as physically stronger and able to withstand greater hardship than the average Western woman. Therefore, to many foreign observers, Russian women were better suited to combat than their Western counterparts. Gender relations in Russia were sometimes seen as more equitable. A journalist for the London *Graphic* accounted for the number of women in the Russian army by asserting,

> There appears to be no sex-antagonism in Russia. Indeed, the line of sex cleavage is of the very faintest. Men and women do not lead separate lives. They work side by side normally, whether in the fields, or as students of medicine, politics, and the like in the universities. And everyone knows,

there are . . . as many women Anarchists as men. It is only natural that the
lion-hearted and adventurous should desire to share in the great
adventure.[112]

While this writer interpreted the particular kind of gender integration present in Russia as an indication of a more progressive and sexually egalitarian society, others viewed the mixing of the sexes as a sign of Russia's less developed
level of civilization. Some observers were appalled when they discovered that
female soldiers were housed together with married male soldiers. One Englishman attempted to explain this by stating that "the Northern nations are not so
prudish in the matter of having the sexes together. Men and women sleep
promiscuously in one compartment in their cottages, farms, etc."[113] He clearly
believed that the phenomenon was a peculiar feature of a peculiar people. An
American observer was distraught to find that following the February Revolution, the intermingling of the sexes increased:

> The normally lax standards were even freer under new conditions and
> everywhere the traveler was impressed with the looseness with which the
> sex problem was considered—people bathing in public places without
> clothing. On trains men and women were placed together, as a matter of
> course, in the same compartment for long journeys, lasting days. A whole
> peasant family often lived in one large room, with the most intimate
> relationships of life as a matter of common knowledge. Among the higher
> classes the marriage vow was winked at, and there was such an abnormal
> amount of illegitimacy that the country was full of foundling societies. . . .
> Even the poverty stricken university students had their mistresses.[114]

His comments indicate the extent to which Victorian standards of sexuality
had failed to permeate Russian culture and society and therefore how much
easier it was for men and women to cross lines of gender distinction, lines that
in Western societies would have presented much more of a barrier. For such
Western observers, the presence of women soldiers in Russia was an indication
of its deteriorating condition.[115]

There were many male supporters of Russia's female combatants among
Western commentators. Foreign sources proclaimed that the female soldiers
were an advancement, one of the "latest achievements of the Russian woman,"
"defying all precedents in the history of womanhood."[116] Observers were impressed that Russian women had answered the call of their country in need
"with undaunted courage and almost fatalistic fearlessness."[117] Robert Liddell,

a British member of the 7th Group of Polish Red Cross Volunteers, who served
on the Russian front until 1916, was also impressed with Russia's women soldiers. He encountered a number of female combatants when they arrived at his
medical station after being wounded. Liddell remarked, "There are many
women soldiers in the Russian army, and very good soldiers they are. They are
strong as men and undergo all the same hardships."[118] A London *Graphic* journalist proclaimed that the "passion of the Russian women to fight side by side
with their men is not only patriotic, but symptomatic of a fine sense of comrade-
ship." Moreover, these female soldiers were "proving that the handling of a rifle
is not necessarily and exclusively a male accomplishment."[119]

The formation of the women's military units elicited an even stronger response from Western men. British professor and Russian specialist Bernard
Pares actively encouraged the use of women as combatants. He was a member
of the All-Russian Volunteer Revolutionary Army's Executive Committee,
which included women's units and actively recruited women for military service in 1917.[120] The American diplomatic community in Russia also supported
the female soldiers. In July, the U.S. ambassador, David Francis, gave 1,000 of
the 20,000-ruble donation of Edwin Gould for "Russian Military and Civilian
Relief" to one of the women's battalions in Petrograd (probably the 1st Petrograd Women's Battalion). He commended the women for their courage in battle
and remarked that their bravery and spirit "should have an effect of making the
Russians who refuse to fight ashamed of themselves." The ambassador also remarked that the young women looked "very handsome in men's uniforms."[121]
Senator Elihu Root, heading the American diplomatic mission to Russia in the
summer of 1917, on encountering one of the women's battalions in Petrograd,
declared, "Russian women are doing wonderful work in shaming the men into
fighting, and where necessary I hope American women will follow their
example."[122]

Not all members of the Allied diplomatic mission were as impressed, however. Ambassador Francis's comments stand in stark contrast to those of
France's ambassador, Joseph Noulens, who, in referring to the 1st Petrograd
Women's Battalion on October 24, 1917, stated, "I saw these unfortunates when
they passed under the windows of the French Embassy . . . on their way to take
up their position. They marched in step, affecting a martial spirit which was ob-
viously contradicted by their plump figures and their feminine waddle."[123]

A French journalist was greatly inspired by the creation of the women's unit
and compared the women volunteers to Joan of Arc: "Once again that saintly
mission falls to the lot of woman: to save the homeland and the people!"[124]
American correspondent William Shepherd was won over by the women's units:

"It had never occurred to me before that women ought to go to war, but I am convinced now that in any country . . . women ought to step into the breech, guns in hand. It is their country as much as the men's."[125]

American sociologist Edward Alsworth Ross, of the University of Wisconsin, traveled to Russia in 1917–1918 and expressed great enthusiasm for the women's military units. "No finer assertion of moral personality in daughters has been witnessed than the self-dedication of the young women who composed the famous 'women's battalion.'"[126] He believed that women had shown themselves to be the stronger sex in Russia and commended them for being "truer to their purpose, more faithful to what they conceive to be their duty."[127] Ross contrasted devoted and hard-working women, in offices, fields, and factories, with Russian men, who he believed had become lazy and idle, shirking their duty to the nation. He lauded the nation for making extensive use of women's talents, as demonstrated by the use of women as *zemstvo* (local administration) doctors, and he even believed that patriarchy was waning in Russian families.

Although Ross's picture of the status of women in Russia may have been overly optimistic, his comments reveal that he believed conditions were sufficiently different in Russia as to allow women to participate in male domains that were restricted in the West. Ross's feminism was of the form prevalent in the West in the late nineteenth and early twentieth centuries. He therefore betrays the difficulty of accepting women as soldiers, which was clearly outside the conception of femininity so closely tied to domesticity. Ultimately, he concludes that the gender-role transgression of Russia's women soldiers was too great a challenge to "civilization" as he understood it:

> What thoughtful man could watch without a lump in his throat the drilling of
> its awkward squad, the lines of girlish figures so tender and unmartial . . .
> so little suited to military exercises! The Bolsheviks, wisely enough,
> disbanded this battalion. Had Amazonism spread along the fronts on both
> sides, another great wing of our civilization would have collapsed. Think of
> the effect upon women of becoming accustomed to use of the bayonet and
> upon men of becoming habituated to deadly hand-to-hand combat with
> women![128]

While many observers were uneasy with the social implications of women taking part in such clearly male-specific behavior, a number of commentators thought women *were* biologically capable of acting as combatants. Dr. Dudley A. Sargent of Harvard University believed that women could handle the conditions of combat. Expressing an opinion that completely opposed the common contemporary attitude that labeled women "the weaker sex," Sargent was convinced that women were physically strong enough to perform the duties demanded of soldiers. In an interview with a London *Times* correspondent, he outlined his theory on the fitness of women for war:

> Pound for pound, the average normal woman in good health can endure more pain, discomfort, and fatigue and can expend more muscular energy than the average normal man of similar condition. Woman of necessity comes nearer the primitive type than man. She is biologically more of a barbarian and has, therefore, more physical endurance. She can undergo many strains that a man cannot. Withstanding cold or thirst or hunger or physical privation of any sort a woman can outlast a man. Nine times out of ten a woman, from the standpoint of physical endurance, should make as good a soldier as a man.[129]

Graeme Hammond, a neurologist from the New York Post-Graduate Medical School and medical examiner for the U.S. Army, was also convinced that women had the ability to carry out the duties required of soldiers. In fact, he thought military discipline and rigorous physical training would be good for most women, especially in the West, where they had grown lazy in their domesticity. Moreover, he asserted that women were actually more combative than men. "Women do not enjoy peace as men do. There is a streak . . . of innate disputatiousness in women," he affirmed.[130] Hammond expressed some doubt as to the biological capabilities of women in a war setting, as well as their ability to be controlled. "If women could acquire the physical strength and could be disciplined—(make a note of that) AND COULD BE DISCIPLINED—they would dominate the earth. I believe it would be easier for them to acquire the necessary strength than for them to subject themselves to the necessary discipline."[131] So despite their obvious misogyny, both these medical men essentially endorsed the idea that women would make capable warriors.

While many foreign observers extolled the heroism and courage of the volunteers who enlisted in the women's units, they recognized that their actions were born of necessity. The demand for women soldiers had been created by the extraordinary conditions of the world war and were the result of what was considered to be a failing on the part of Russian men. Therefore, much of the Western adulation of the women soldiers was, like that of Russian commentators, tempered by criticism of men. On the performance of the 1st Russian Women's Battalion of Death in the battle of Smorgon, an American journalist remarked,

From the most disgraceful page in the history of new Russia, as it will be written for posterity, will stand out one bright, flaming spot—the gallant stand of the Women's Regiment—"the Command of Death"—in the midst of an ebbing wave of cowardly, panic-stricken men. For pure courage and coolness the action of the Butchkareff [sic] detachment near Vilna on the terrible July day has seldom been equaled.[132]

Overall, however, it is important to note that most Western observers, like their Russian contemporaries, believed that the women who became soldiers were not truly representative of their sex. As one British writer described the women soldiers, they were "remarkable exceptions to a general rule."[133] There were certain aspects of gender roles that were perceived as universal. *"Even in Russia* women are not supposed to be soldiers" [emphasis added], another British journalist stated.[134] Standards of gendered behavior trumped national and cultural peculiarities, and warfare remained almost universally perceived as a masculine endeavor. Female participation in combat, therefore, in order to be acceptable, had to be framed in terms of either exceptionality of circumstance or exceptionality of the individual.

### The Western Military Reaction

Western military personnel who came into contact with Russia's women soldiers had strong feelings about the phenomenon. Many were unable to accept the presence of women in the ranks of the active army. John Morse, an Englishman who served in the Russian army from 1914 to 1915, was quite taken aback when he came in contact with female combatants. He hardly recognized them as women: "I saw some of these female soldiers—quite a score in all. There was nothing particularly romantic in the appearance of any them. Most of them had the appearance of big, lanky raw-boned boys; faces oval, features 'puddeny,' complexions pale."[135] He was particularly astonished and uncomfortable when he discovered that some of the women had achieved officer rank and was quick to express his disapproval:

Indeed I heard that one lady commanded a regiment of Cossacks! This seems to me on par with a general nursing a baby! . . . All I say is that I am glad the lady referred to was not the Colonel of any regiment under the wings which I fought; and I imagine that any "mere male" brought before a court-martial of Amazons would stand more danger of being spanked than shot.[136]

Morse's remarks not only betray his gender bias but also reveal a deep-seated belief that weakness and sexual animosity with men make women largely ineffectual as soldiers.

Many Western military men who witnessed the all-female military units were very impressed. The French colonel Luazon praised the battle readiness of the women.[137] Other Western military observers were simultaneously impressed and disturbed by their encounters with female combatants. They were awed by the women's military abilities but were uncomfortable with their presence in the ranks. The British military attaché in Petrograd, General Alfred Knox, declared that the women's unit he saw in the capital "made the best show of any soldiers I have seen since the Revolution." Later, however, he made a point of explicitly telling some Russian officers in no uncertain terms "that no nation except the Russian had ever allowed its women to fight, and certainly the British nation never would."[138]

Other foreign military personnel were less generous in their assessments of the women soldiers. General Edmund Ironside, who met Maria Bochkareva in Archangel in December 1918, described her as a "pathetic figure." Other British and American military personnel serving in the Northern Territories during the Civil War also encountered Bochkareva and derided her in similarly unflattering terms. They were repulsed by her, particularly because of her emulation of such male habits as smoking, drinking, and swearing. Despite this distaste for her lack of femininity, there was general recognition that her actions in the war had been valuable. As Ironside remarked, "I do not undertake to estimate the merits of Madame Bochkareva's services in the Russian Army. I consider that the shedding of her blood in the service of her country will be appreciated finally by the Central Government."[139] Certainly these advocates recognized the abnormality of the circumstances and appreciated the bravery and fortitude of such women. But in no way did they believe that accepting females into the armed services should be adopted as a permanent practice.

Enemy soldiers engaged in battle with Russian women combatants were stunned upon discovering that their foes were female. Reports indicate that the Germans fought with "extreme ferocity" and "preferred death to capture" when they knew their opponents included women soldiers. Upon discovery of the sexual identity of their attackers in the battle of Smorgon, German soldiers are reported to have cursed themselves for the disgrace of being taken prisoner by the "weaker sex."[140] One of the military communiqués describing the events of the battle stated that the "prisoners have a depressed look, displaying shocking hostility." As Richard Abraham posits, "one cannot help wondering whether the Germans did not fight harder, and resent capture more fiercely, because they knew they were being tested against women."[141]

## *Western Women's Views*

Upon the outbreak of war in 1914, most European women found themselves in
the patriotic camp, in keeping with the initial pro-war sentiments exhibited in
the warring nations. Most believed it was their duty to aid the homeland, especially in a time of crisis. Women in Western nations paid particular attention to
the activities of their Russian sisters and were enthralled by the actions of
women soldiers. Many greatly admired Russia's women soldiers for their willingness to sacrifice themselves for the good of the nation. They were particularly struck by the fact that numerous women were eager to give their lives for
the cause, while some men hesitated. In Great Britain and America, some
women were so inspired by the example of Russia's female combatants that
they implored their governments to organize similar units, or at least to accept
women into the armed forces.

The American journalists Louise Bryant, Rheta Childe Dorr, and Bessie
Beatty devoted significant portions of their books on Russia during the revolutionary year of 1917 to describing the women's units. Bryant, the wife of John
Reed, asserted that "no other feature of the Great War ever caught the public
fancy like the Battalion of Death composed of Russian women."[142] In fact, after
hearing so much about the battalion in the United States, it was one of the first
things she set out to investigate upon her arrival in Petrograd in June 1917. After witnessing what the women soldiers were capable of, Dorr and Beatty were
convinced that the female soldiers would "prove to be the element needed to
lead . . . the disorganized and demoralized Russian army back to its duty on the
firing line."[143] Some female observers asserted that it would be the women of
Russia who would save the nation. "A country that can produce such women
cannot possibly be crushed forever. It may take time to recover from its present
debauch of anarchism, but recover it will. And when it does it will know how to
honor the women who went out to fight when the men ran home."[144] Meriel
Buchanan, daughter of the British ambassador in Petrograd, observed that "the
women of Russia joined hands in a supreme act of self-sacrifice, a vain endeavor to save the honor of their country's manhood."[145]

Despite its traditionally pacifist stance, the women's movement in the West,
like that in Russia, expressed support for the war effort. Like the socialists of
the Second International, whose opposition to world war crumbled under the
pressure of nationalism, most feminists eventually rallied to their nation's colors. Western feminists and advocates of women's rights saw the Russian
women's military movement as an extreme example of women' devotion to their
nation and thereby significant in the broader struggle for women's liberation
and particularly in the battle for suffrage. One of the major objections

Maria Bochkareva and British suffragette Emmeline Pankhurst, who considered the participation
of Russian women soldiers in the war a step forward for all women (from Donald Thompson,
*Blood Stained Russia*)

presented in the case against granting women the vote was that they could not
bear arms. In Great Britain, accounts in the women's periodical *Britannia* designed to raise morale among British women involved in the war effort were
"unambiguous in supporting military values and asserting that women can
demonstrate them as well as men."[146]

British suffragette Emmeline Pankhurst was highly impressed with Russia's women soldiers and zealously commended them for their bravery, discipline, and will to action. She visited the all-female combats units in Petrograd and Moscow during a mission to boost morale and keep the Russians in the war. Crediting the female soldiers with tremendous importance for the cause of gender equality, she assured them that their participation in the war would do much to advance the cause of women's rights. Once women proved their abilities on the battlefield, they would no longer be subjugated by men, excluded from public activity, and relegated to the position of minors. Nina Krylova reported that in a speech to the members of Bochkareva's battalion, Pankhurst exclaimed, "I greet you in the name of the millions and millions of women's hearts who anxiously await the results of your heroic attempts to show that women have the right and CAN participate in society in any situation and can everywhere be on the same level as men."[147] According to Krylova, after the courageous actions of the 1st Russian Women's Battalion of Death at the front, Pankhurst sent a telegram to Britain in which she paid tribute to the women's bravery. Emphasizing that they had "earned undying fame" she contended that their "moral effect [was] great."[148]

Despite the clear implications for women's equality and opportunity recognized by Western feminists, their exaltation for Russia's women soldiers was tempered by traditional conceptions of gender roles. As in Russian commentary, praise for patriotism, courage, and heroism was mixed with reservations about the wisdom of female involvement in the violence and destruction of war. In general, Western women viewed the actions of Russian women combatants as the result of the exigencies of war and, in particular, as being required by a failing on the part of Russian men.

Dorr wanted the Russian government to continue organizing all-female combat units "until the people got so excited over the tragedy of women being torn to pieces by German shot and shrapnel that they would have risen in wrath, taken hold of their army and their government, and created conditions which would relieve women from the dreadful necessity of fighting."[149] Even Pankhurst expressed regret that the men of Russia had allowed affairs to deteriorate so much that women felt obligated to use violence. Male control of the world, she proclaimed, had led to "war, revolution, social injustice, hunger, and terror." Women now had to set things right, but it was unfortunate that they had to do so in this manner. "When I looked at their tender young bodies I thought how terrible it was that they should have to fight, besides bringing children into the world. Men of Russia," she asked, "must the women fight? Are there men who will stay at home and let them fight alone?"[150] Beatty expressed similar reservations over the involvement of women in such a violent endeavor: "I shuddered at the idea that these girls with big eyes and clear open hearts were going out to kill; for I was among [those] whose pigeonholes held a fond faith in the coming of the day when women would bear neither arms nor soldiers, but a race of human beings gifted in the fine art of living together in peace and amity."[151]

Women of the socialist camp tended to deemphasize the significance of the Provisional Government's all-female military formations and explain them as an attempt by reactionary forces to continue the war for their own benefit. Yet this did not mean that they did not support female participation in the armed forces. Bryant, who had clear Bolshevik sympathies, was nonetheless fascinated by the concept of women soldiers and presented a detailed description of those she encountered. She attributed the deficiency of the movement to sexual separation. "Women in Russia have always fought in the army," she maintained, and "in my opinion the principal failure of the women's regiment was segregation. There will always be fighting women in Russia, but they will fight side by side with men and not as a sex."[152] Bryant's opinion may indeed hold some veracity, considering that the most vehement opposition to women as soldiers came only when the all-female units were formed. Socialist Sylvia Pankhurst, in an account of her mother Emmeline's visit to Russia, described the Russian female volunteers as "ill-starred companies of women, fitly named 'Battalions of Death.'"[153] Sylvia, unlike her mother and sister Cristabel, did not support the war, regarding it as male folly.

Some Western women asserted that a woman should never support or condone war, for its violence and death could never be reconciled with the procreative power of the female. They wondered how women, as naturally creative and nurturing beings, could take part in its annihilation. Therefore, they condemned the women soldiers for promoting destruction. Others simply did not believe that women had the biological or psychological fitness for soldiering. Florence Farmborough, an English nurse working on the Russian front, treated some women soldiers she thought were part of Bochkareva's detachment.[154] This encounter sparked her interest in the "remarkable battalion," and later she learned of their exploits in battle from a Russian newspaper. The report indicated that some of the women, "to their honor," did go into the attack but that others "remained in the trenches, fainting and hysterical," and that still others "ran or crawled back to the rear." This misinformation confirmed what Farmborough already suspected, what she perceived to be the "great truth" that "women were quite unfit to be soldiers."[155]

Like many men, some Western women attributed the existence of so many female soldiers to the exceptionalism of Russian women and society. American journalist Madeline Doty asserted that killing did not come naturally to women, but she believed that in Russia women were exceptions to the general rule. In that country, women had participated equally in violent terrorism as revolutionaries, and so "it was natural when war came that such women should turn soldiers" and express their bravery by serving shoulder to shoulder with their men, which accounted for the formation of units like the 1st Russian Women's Battalion of Death.[156] Yet Doty was not convinced women were capable of being fighters even after the unit had proved itself in the trenches. She labeled the whole effort a failure and firmly stated that women did not make good soldiers. "The reason is fundamental," Doty explained. "In their [women's] body [*sic*] they bear new life. To abuse the body is to abuse the child of the future." Moreover, it was wrong for women to imitate the violent and destructive behavior of men. "Temporarily Russian women have gone on the wrong track," she remarked. "They are magnificent creatures, but they have not expressed themselves. They have copied men. This they must not do. Women must give gifts of their own to humanity. . . . They must be warriors of the spirit, not slayers of the body. . . . It requires greater courage to give life than to take it."[157]

By and large, the view of Russia as exceptional reveals why Westerners could applaud Russian women who fought while rejecting such activity for women in their own countries. Russia, in the eyes of Western observers, was a completely different kind of society. Furthermore, the circumstances of the war were even more complex and peculiar because by 1917 so many men hesitated or refused to continue fighting. When women began filling the roles of combatants that men had abandoned, Westerners saw their actions again in the context of extreme necessity: Had Russian men been sufficiently carrying out their duty as soldiers, there would have been no need for women to do so. War was still fundamentally conceived as a masculine endeavor, even in Russia.

This notion of exceptionalism seems key to understanding the public perception of the women soldiers in both Russia and the West. The idea of these women as exceptional to the rest of the female gender permeated Russian commentary regarding the women soldiers. The vast majority of Russian society, including the women soldiers themselves, largely viewed the actions of women in the military sphere as something beyond the norm. Individual women who fought in the ranks of the Russian army were seeking to transcend the social prescriptions of their lives, but not to redefine the parameters of the gender roles of Russian society in general. The women's military formations had come into existence as a matter of necessity, born of the particular circumstances of the war and revolution. Had the majority of Russian men been fulfilling their prescribed role as warriors, the women probably would never have taken it upon themselves to carry out that role. For most of their contemporaries, the women who served as soldiers were laudable for their courage and self-sacrifice, but women soldiers were not desirable as a permanent feature of society. What became acceptable was a temporary exchange of gender roles precipitated by the failure of many men to fulfill their traditional duty as defenders. And once the men returned to their defensive roles, women soldiers would no longer be required.

# 8

## CONCLUSIONS

The dissolution of the women's combat formations created under the auspices of the Provisional Government and the subsequent withdrawal of Russia from the hostilities of World War I did not signify the cessation of women's military participation in Russia. Women went on to fight on both sides of the conflict during the Civil War. Estimates of the number of women who took part in these hostilities range from 73,000 to 80,000 just on the side of the Bolsheviks.[1] Women fought as part of mostly male units and in all-female formations, such as the Communist Women's Combat Detachment and the Women's Proletarian Battalion. According to historian Richard Stites, "They fought on every front and with every weapon, serving as riflewomen, armored train commanders, gunners."[2] Women also fought in the White Armies and partisan detachments, but in considerably smaller numbers and only in predominately male units.[3] Those who entered the hostilities on the side of the Whites usually did so disguised as men, while in the Red Army they were usually accepted as women. In World War II, the number of women who served their country in combat increased dramatically. More than 1 million women served in the Soviet armed forces and as partisans during this conflict.[4] Entire women's regiments were formed, particularly of female pilots. The women who became soldiers during World War I reinforced and expanded the historical precedent of Russian women as warriors. As historian Reina Pennington asserts, "The most dramatic precedent for Soviet women in combat was set by the 'Women's Battalion of Death' commanded by Maria Bochkareva in 1917."[5]

The successful participation of women in combat roles did not, however, lead to general sexual integration of the Soviet armed forces. Rather, the precedent that was established is one based on exceptionalism. The exigencies of war, the type of women who became soldiers, the political circumstances of revolution—all were considered to be extraordinary. Only these factors, or particular combinations of factors, made it temporarily acceptable for women to fight in Russia and the Soviet Union. In times of peace and social stability, their involvement in military endeavors became undesirable.

Nor did women's military participation during World War I provide significant changes to conventional gender roles. The evidence of women's successful performance in combat could have altered notions of biological inferiority and possibly opened the door to female participation in a variety of male-dominated areas. But this did not happen. Even the extreme example of women carrying out what was considered an exclusively masculine role was insufficient to overturn deeply entrenched conceptions of separate sexual spheres. Following the return to peacetime conditions, women were expected to return to more traditional feminine activities. Although women had gained a number of rights and opportunities as a result of the revolutions of 1917, these changes were due to the overturning of a political system that had restricted the majority of the population, including men. By officially sanctioning, organizing, and sending women soldiers into battle, the Russian Provisional Government of 1917 made an explicit statement about acceptable gender roles, in essence endorsing women's emulation of male behaviors and actions. Yet this was not its intent; there was no desire to make this a permanent feature of Russian society. In fact, it was a tactic employed in an effort to demonstrate how wrong it was that such action was necessary, to point out the glaring inadequacy of male soldiers who refused to carry out traditional male role of combatant, and thereby restore the "proper" order of gendered activities.

Yet Russia's female soldiers of the Great War were important in relation to the early twentieth-century women's movement. They demonstrated that women could actively and successfully participate in the public sphere and that they could endure the most challenging and difficult conditions. They controverted arguments that women were the "weaker sex," indicating just the opposite: Women could be strong, independent, and powerful. Perhaps more importantly for such women, they showed men that they possessed a strong sense of civic responsibility and dedication to the state and that their strengths and energies could be applied for the benefit of the nation. Thus, they were a powerful example for feminists, in Russia as well as in the West.

This example, however, was simultaneously disturbing to many in the women's movement. Although the traditional pacifism of the feminist movement had buckled under the pressure of patriotism and the seduction of political rewards in return for support for the war effort, many women still found it difficult to accept that women were participating in destruction and killing.

Even some of the most radical feminists were made uncomfortable by women's emulation of such violent and destructive male behavior. Just because women could fight as well as men did not indicate that they should do so. Much of the impetus behind advocacy of women's rights and equality was to increase their influence in public affairs and to prevent what feminists perceived as misguided errors made by men. In particular, such women wanted to stop the male folly of war, which was so destructive to humanity. According to many early twentieth-century feminists, male control of public affairs had precipitated the Great War, and once it was started, men had proved incapable of ending it. They believed that women had to intervene in order to bring the war to a victorious conclusion. Once again, the circumstances were considered exceptional, and while it was temporarily admissible for women to become soldiers, it certainly was not welcomed as a permanent restructuring of gender roles.

The creation of military units composed of women soldiers was based not on their capabilities on the battlefield but on their value as instruments of propaganda in the Russian Provisional Government's campaign to continue the war. Women's spiritual power and moral influence had always been highly valued in Russian culture. Therefore, it was hoped that the presence of women in the trenches would either lift the spirits of the men and inspire them to follow or shame them into returning to what was their "natural" duty. This "was certainly the first instance in modern history in which women were used in all-female fighting units as models of military valor and performance."[6] But when the idea was put into practice, the results were less than encouraging. Although the women who went into battle performed extremely well and proved definitively that their sex was no barrier to such activities, the efforts of the women soldiers to inspire men to continue fighting were ultimately unsuccessful.

That female military units failed to achieve the goal of reinvigorating the Russian army should not, however, be seen as a particular shortcoming of the women. The social experiment of placing women in the traditionally male role of defender was rooted in a paradox. Essentially, the women were sent to show the male troops how to act like "real men." Such an action was highly illogical: It said to male soldiers that if *women* (who were inferior) could carry out this kind of action, certainly men could do the same, and the entire concept of a male's special task of defense lost its potency. Men were socialized as protectors of their country, which included women and children, in times of war. With women next to them in the trenches, men were likely to question what they were defending. As a result, most men were left confused and threatened, while few were inspired to resume their masculine patriotic duty. The participation of

women in combat devalued it, made it "women's work," and many men refused
to serve with women. In particular, those who had no desire to fight any longer
were more than willing to let women take their places.

By late summer 1917, it had become clear that no amount of pleading, cajol-
ing, threatening, patriotic exhortations, or any other tactics on the part of the
Provisional Government and its supporters could get disintegrating army units
to fight as unified forces again. The creation of the women's military formations
clearly demonstrated how out of touch the elites were with the mass of war-
weary, conscripted peasants in the army. Appeals to the romanticized ideal of
the heroic, self-sacrificing male fell flat in the mass of exhausted, demoralized
peasant-soldiers, who expressed little interest in fighting for vague notions of
"nation" and "freedom." The Provisional Government's insistence on continuing the war would ultimately be its undoing, allowing the Bolsheviks to capital-
ize on promises of peace (as well as of bread and land) and obtain the support
of much of the peasant army.

The female soldiers of Bochkareva's battalion were sent to one of the "principal areas of mutiny"[7] on the Russian western front, where collapse of army
units was particularly advanced. There, soldiers were hostile to any effort to
continue the fighting. One can speculate that if the women had been introduced
at the front under different conditions, their assimilation could have been more
successful. This possibility is supported by the experiences of individual
women soldiers in this war and those of the women's units of subsequent wars,
wherein male military personnel quickly adjusted to the presence of women in
the ranks, once the women demonstrated their abilities to function successfully.

The concepts of patriotism and citizenship were essential parts of the idea of
using women soldiers to remind men of their duty to the homeland. Patriotism
is further significant to the women's military participation of World War I because, by and large, it was the primary motivation for most of the women who
became soldiers. The concept of patriotism was evolving and taking on new
meanings in Russia during the late nineteenth and early twentieth centuries.
Most historians would agree that in early twentieth-century Russia, the notion
was poorly developed compared to the countries of Western Europe and the
United States. There was some sense of loyalty to the state, as personified by
the tsar, which was exemplified by service to that state, a concept that Russian
rulers had worked to inculcate in their subjects since the time of Peter the
Great.

Yet beginning in the late nineteenth century, this patriotism had become increasingly separated from the state and the person of the tsar and more focused
upon the Russian people, the *narod*, particularly as members of Russian soci-

ety came to doubt that the former was really acting in the best interests of the latter. As Eric Hobsbawm convincingly argues, in the modern era patriotism has provided the basis for opposition to the existing state and for the conscious decision to form a nation based on mutual consent.[8] Therefore, the revolution that overturned tsarist rule in February 1917 was seen as a patriotic revolution, carried out for the good of the *narod*. The patriotism of the peasantry and working classes was also closely tied to the tsarist state, but it was little developed beyond the formulaic expression "For Faith, Tsar, and Fatherland." Yet as Nikolai Golovin states, "The loyalty of the common people to the throne has been exaggerated. . . . The swiftness with which the monarchy fell in February 1917 seems confirmation enough of this."[9] Thus, patriotism in Russia was a "complex and ambiguous phenomenon" that existed "along multiple axes." It could be simultaneously conservative in the traditional sense, supporting the status quo of the state and social order, and revolutionary in Hobsbawm's sense.[10]

Gender is an equally important part of patriotism, for notions of patriotic duty were decidedly different for men and women. Men were supposed to carry out patriotic obligations that consisted primarily of public service to the state, most importantly military service and, in times of war, defense of the nation. The nation included the Russian lands and its people, those who were unable to defend themselves, that is, women and children. For women, patriotic duty was defined in terms of "traditional" feminine roles and activities, which had recently been influenced by Western bourgeois values of domesticity. Motherhood was thus central to this conception, featuring caring and nurturing activities. This role was primarily a passive one: Women left the public action to the men and waited patiently at home. Increasingly, however, it had become somewhat acceptable for women to participate in certain public activities (although there were still those who opposed any form of women's involvement in the public sphere as morally damaging to society and family).

The Russian women's military movement of World War I is also significant to Russia's struggle to create a civil society during its period of modernization in the late nineteenth and early twentieth centuries, prior to the Bolshevik seizure of power. Some scholars believe that in this short period Russia was beginning to acquire the trappings of a society that could have, had it not been interrupted by the Soviet takeover, become a liberal democracy with a thriving middle class such as in Western European nations. With the toppling of the tsarist autocracy in 1917, there seemed even greater hope for further development in this direction. During this period of modernization, many charitable associations, political parties, clubs, grassroots organizations, and movements devoted to social and political change developed. A number of historians conclude that if that growth had been allowed to reach its fruition, it would have led to the kind of social and political climate necessary for the functioning of a liberal democracy.

The women's units were formed as part of this general effort by Russian elites to raise the level of civic responsibility among the population. Many of the volunteers in the women's units, as well as the women behind the organizational efforts, had a clear understanding that their actions were part of this conception of patriotic duty and citizenship, in which rights and opportunities provided by the state were coupled with responsibilities and obligations to that state. They recognized that the responsibilities of citizenship included the willingness to fight and die for one's country. Their patriotism often expressed this fundamental aspect of modern citizenship in the nation-state. Their understanding came from a new definition of citizenship and patriotism based upon equal rights and participation of the sexes.

The patriotic activity of the women soldiers transcended not only gender lines but those of class as well, since the volunteers came from varied socioeconomic backgrounds. Their patriotism is particularly striking when one considers that the nation had afforded them little in the way of rights and privileges but much struggle and hardship. It is also salient when placed against the background of an army of male soldiers, the majority of whom displayed none of the same enthusiasm for a war they considered not their own but, rather, forced upon them by a distant and self-serving government. The patriotism of those involved in the women's military movement who came from the upper social strata is somewhat easier to explain. First, it emanated primarily from a class of educated Russians who had a more developed sense of patriotic and civic duty. Second, it was consistent with a general resurgence of patriotic sentiment in Russian society following the February Revolution. And third, it was promoted by progressive women who believed they had something to gain from their service in the war effort.

Yet not all of the women who enlisted in the Russian army, as individuals or as part of the all-female military units, were representatives of the women's movement or even of the educated classes. In fact, many came from the peasantry and working classes. It is the patriotism of these women that is even more remarkable. Russians of the lower classes did not display the same outburst of zeal with which the educated classes greeted the outbreak of war in 1914, nor did they generally share in the renewed support for the war following the February Revolution (although they were mostly pleased about the end of the oppressive tsarist regime). Most tended to view the war as something being fought for the benefit of the ruling elites, and they did not identify with or even understand the government's war aims. Nor did they believe that they had anything to gain but suffering by participating in the conflict. Although there was little resistance to mobilization, most scholars would agree that the Russian masses went to the battlefield because they were used to following directives issued by the authoritarian government. As Allan Wildman asserts, most "responded with sullen resignation."[11] Moreover, the Russian lower classes had never developed the fundamental conception that patriotic duty included obligatory military service.[12] Instead, they viewed military service as an odious task and conscription as akin to a death sentence.

The Russian peasantry did have a general sense of loyalty to the tsar and to the religious and national values for which he stood, but this sentiment had its limitations. When the war began in 1914, the majority of Russians responded to the notion that Germany was an aggressive menace threatening Mother Russia, a notion fueled by propaganda characterizing the Germans as evil, bloodthirsty Huns. After all, the Germans had attacked first. This was clearly understood by the Russian masses. But this kind of patriotism was limited as well. The loyalties of the Russian masses tended to be local or regional rather than national. Many viewed themselves as members of a village community, which they could perceive as part of a larger region or province but rarely as part of a vast empire covering one-eighth of the earth's landmass. It was not uncommon for peasant soldiers to make comments such as "We are from Tambov—or Penza. The enemy is far from our province. What is the use of fighting?"[13] This is not to say that Russian peasants did not feel a sense of devotion to Mother Russia and to Russian Orthodoxy. Yet they were reluctant and, as the war dragged on, increasingly unwilling to fight and die for the cause of the war, which they did not believe truly represented the interests of either.

It is therefore striking when one encounters numerous examples of women from the peasantry and working classes who left the safety of their homes and traveled great distances in order to join the fighting. Nearly all expressed the desire to defend Russia. These women displayed a more developed sense of civic responsibility than their male counterparts and chose to perform traditionally male patriotic duty instead of offering their services to the nation in a more acceptably "feminine" way.

One of the most important factors in accounting for the actions of these women was marital and social status. Most of those who became soldiers were young, unmarried, and childless. Therefore they did not have the domestic responsibilities that wives and mothers had. Nor did they have the burdens of familial support shouldered by many male conscripts.[14] Many of the women who became soldiers had experience living or working in urban environments, which undoubtedly gave them more independence and freedom to make choices about the directions of their lives. They may have been "superfluous" daughters, those who were not essential to the survival of the family, often sent to work outside of the home, or even outside the village, without dowries and with dim prospects for marriage. Like their upper-class comrades in arms, they may have been looking for a way to be useful—useful to their country if not to their families. And they may have been searching for a sense of identity that they transmitted through patriotic duty. More importantly, as peasants and workers, these women would have been accustomed to hard, physically demanding labor. In fact, in an interesting commentary on women's roles in Russian society, many of the women who went into battle noted that trench warfare was "not the most difficult or the most disagreeable work they had ever done" and maintained that "it was less arduous if a little more dangerous than working in a harvest field or a factory."[15] Therefore, their entrance into the world of combat was seemingly less drastic a transition than one would assume.

Stepping into the void created by men who failed to fulfill their traditional patriotic role, Russia's women soldiers of World War I lead us to a reconsideration of gendered conceptions of patriotism. With so many women displaying the characteristics previously attributed only to men, they not only rejected the passivity assigned to them but also developed a new patriotic role for themselves and redefined the notion of the national defender, which had previously been assigned an exclusively male gender. Although the traditional roles centering on motherhood and on the caring and nurturing aspects of femininity were not replaced, they were augmented by an increased role in the public sphere. It was now acceptable, although granted only under the extreme circumstances of war, for women to assume the patriotic role of defender. Such actions were generally unwelcome during peacetime. The fact that these women were emulating masculine characteristics would, under other circumstances, make them social deviants. But their patriotic motivations, the fact that they were acting for the good of the nation rather than for their own benefit, made their actions acceptable, even laudable, even if only under certain circumstances and only temporarily during wartime. Thus, the image of the Russian patriotic woman was forever changed, and World War I was the catalyst for this change.

# EPILOGUE

Information on the subsequent fate of most of the women who served as soldiers during World War I in Russia is very sparse. There are records pertaining to barely a handful of these women. A number went on to fight during the Civil War, on both sides of the conflict. Maria Bocharnikova made her way south to the Don, where she joined the 1st Kuban Infantry Regiment and served as a sergeant major during the Civil War.[1] Eventually, she emigrated to France, where she wrote her memoirs in the 1960s, and then came to the United States and lived in New York.

Others emigrated as well, including Nina Krylova and Magdalena Skrydlova. Krylova and her husband, an officer in the Russian army, went to western Europe after the war. They settled in Belgium and raised a son. She met Skrydlova there as well. During World War II, Krylova was arrested and imprisoned by the Germans. While in prison, she met Boris Solonevich, to whom she related her experiences during the previous international conflict. She was deported from Belgium to Germany in 1944. There is no further information about her after that date, but Solonevich, who recorded her story, heard rumors that both she and Skrydlova had been killed in Allied bombings.[2]

We have the most information regarding Maria Bochkareva. After her battalion was disbanded in December 1917, she returned to Petrograd, where she was detained by the Bolsheviks. She was brought to Smolny, where, she claims, Lenin and Trotsky tried to convince her to join them. She refused and they released her, furnishing her with a train ticket to Tomsk so that she could be reunited with her family. The trip was difficult, as she was in terrible pain from a leg injury received during the fighting and she was harassed by soldiers who recognized her. After a month's convalescence, she returned to Petrograd in January 1918, after receiving a telegram from General Anosov, chairman of the St. George's Committee, who asked for her assistance in reaching Kornilov.[3] Disguised as a Sister of Mercy and furnished with a false passport, she made her way to Kornilov's headquarters at Novocherkassk in the Caucasus. Refusing Kornilov's offer that she might join his forces, Bochkareva left his headquarters in an attempt to reach Kislovodsk, where her former volunteer, Princess Tatuieva, resided and had invited her to visit.

On the way, she was caught by the Bolsheviks and was to be executed. She was rescued by a soldier who recognized her from her days as Yashka. She had saved his life in 1915, and he convinced the Bolsheviks to stay her execution. She was taken to Moscow to appear before a military tribunal, which, after holding her for several weeks, eventually released her and issued her a new passport. She then decided to go to the United States and Great Britain in order to solicit aid in the struggle against the Bolsheviks. The British Consulate gave her 500 rubles for the journey. She traveled to Vladivostok by train and then boarded the steamship *Sheridan* in April 1918.

After arriving in San Francisco, she went to New York and then to Washington, D.C., where she was received by the Russian ambassador, Boris Bakhmetev. In the United States, Bochkareva was sponsored by Florence Harriman, a wealthy socialite and women's rights activist. Harriman reported that all who met the female soldier were greatly impressed with her and were taken with her magnetism.[4] Bochkareva, along with a translator, met with Secretary of State Robert Lansing and Secretary of Defense Newton Baker. She also met with President Wilson on July 10. A State Department official who was present at the meeting with Wilson recounted the experience as the most dramatic scene he had ever witnessed. Through her translator, Bochkareva emotionally recounted the hardship and devastation that war-torn Russia was suffering. In the course of her account, she began to sob, dropped to the floor, and threw her arms around the president's knees, begging him to send American aid before Russia was totally destroyed. The president responded with his own tears and promised to do what he could.[5] On July 17, 1918, she met with a group of senators and congressmen, and once again urged the Allies to send a military expedition to Russia. In the United States, Bochkareva also met Isaac Don Levine, who had been asked by Harriman and Emmeline Pankhurst to write a biography of the "Russian Joan of Arc." She related the story of her life to Levine, who published it as a serialization in the *Capital Journal* with financial assistance from Teddy Roosevelt. It was published in book form in 1919.

After leaving the United States, Bochkareva went to Great Britain, where she visited her friend and supporter Pankhurst in Manchester. She then went to London and met with the British minister of war, and she was also given a brief audience with King George. The king advised her to return to Russia, where she would be of most use to her people. She managed to convince the British

War Office to fund her trip back. Arriving in Archangel in August 1918, she attempted to organize a detachment in an effort to raise a Russo-Allied army, but she was unsuccessful. She then went to Allied headquarters at Shenkursk, where she lingered for several months, proving to be something of a pest to Allied military personnel. One American officer reported that she was a heavy drinker and smoker, and that she had ballooned to 250 pounds.[6]

After nearly three months, Bochkareva was seen by General Edmund Ironside, commander in chief of the Allied forces, who sent her to General V. V. Marushevskii. In December, she appealed to Marushevskii for an assignment, but he refused and told her to remove her uniform and go home. The general sent this order to the Provisional Government of the Northern Territories, which, in April 1919, decided to supply Bochkareva with 750 rubles a month provided that she leave the region. She returned to Tomsk and there sought out Admiral Kol'chak, offering her services to him. Kol'chak suggested that she organize a women's medical detachment, but before she could complete this task, the Red Army took the region and the admiral and his staff fled. In January 1920, Bochkareva was arrested by the Bolsheviks and sent to Krasnoiarsk. She was interrogated for four months. After admitting to her activities in connection with Kornilov, Kol'chak, and other White and Allied forces, she was found guilty of being a "hostile and evil enemy of the worker-peasant republic." She was sentenced to execution and was shot on May 16, 1920.[7]

# APPENDIX A

## Russian Women's Military Organizations of 1917

| City | Name of Unit | Initiated by | Date |
|------|--------------|--------------|------|
| Petrograd | 1st Russian Women's Battalion of Death*† | Maria Bochkareva and the Women's National Military Union of Volunteers | May 1917 |
| Petrograd | 1st Petrograd Women's Battalion*† | Women's National Military Union of Volunteers | June 1917 |
| Moscow | 2nd Moscow Women's Battalion of Death*† | R. P. Slug and the All-Russian Women's Union to Aid the Motherland | June 1917 |
| Ekaterinodar | 3rd Kuban Women's Shock Battalion*† | M. L. Zalesskaia | June 1917 |
| Minsk | Minsk Women's Separate Guard Militia* | Minsk Women's Legion | July 1917 |
| Saratov | Saratov Women's Shock Battalion*† | Organizational Committee of the Saratov Women's Shock Battalion | June 1917 |
| Kiev | Kiev Women's Military Detachment*† | Unknown | June 1917 |
| Kiev | Women's Kuren of Death | Unknown | July 1917 |
| Mariupol' | Mariupol' Women's Battalion of Death | Private Novitsin, 24th Infantry Regiment | June 1917 |
| Baku | Baku Women's Battalion of Death | E. K. Petrova (local schoolteacher) | August 1917 |
| Viatka | Viatka Women's Battalion | Viatka Women's Union | Unknown |
| Poltava | 1st Detachment of Volunteer Women Scouts | Lieutenant Ilovaiskii | Unknown |
| Simbirsk | Simbirsk Women's Legion of Death | Unknown | May 1917 |

| Ekaterinburg | Ekaterinburg Women's Battalion of Death | Union for the Defense of the Motherland and Ms. Tiusheva | June 1917 |
| Tashkent | Unknown | Tashkent Women's Union | June 1917 |
| Odessa | Ukrainian Women's Battalion | Ms. Lebedeva (veteran woman combatant) | August 1917 |

*Source:* RGVIA, f. 29, op. 3, d. 1603; f. 1300, op. 1, d. 239; f. 2000, op. 2, d. 1557; f. 3474, op. 1, d. 1; f. 16173, op. 1, d. 4.

*These units were officially sanctioned.

†These units were brought under the authority of the military administration and incorporated into the regular army.

# APPENDIX B

Russian Women! Mothers and Sisters!

We write these lines with the blood of our hearts . . . listen to us.

Mothers and wives, maidens and sisters, abandoned families, orphaned children, do not forget about the millions of valiant warriors whose bones were crushed on the field of struggle in the first years of the war, your tears are converted into blood. . . . And with this blood we now write these words.

Listen to us, go with us in the name of the dear memory of our fallen heroes. They were soldiers. They knew what the motherland was. They loved the homeland. They were not cowards, remember how proudly they went to their deaths. In rank formation they went to war, in rank formation they threw their bodies onto the field of battle. Now they are forgotten. . . . Out of shame and dishonor their bones are strewn in the dust and in their brotherly graves.

Russian women, is it possible that these heroes did a shameful deed when they accepted terrible death for the motherland, for their families, for the future happiness of their children, for the glory of Russia? Is it possible that they would have been honorable if then they had traded bread, meat, kasha and sugar in the enemy trenches?

Russian women! Where are your heroes, who dry your tears, who heal the wounds of Russia, who proudly stand up for her? Where are your eagles, your falcons?

You, valiant warriors, our soldiers of free Russia, you who still maintain honor in your souls, and shame, and courage. To you we make this address: when will you finally raise up your powerful voices and silence the cowardly lips of disgraceful traitors of Russia, dressed in soldiers' coats? Either you wait for when we no longer can distinguish you from the traitors of the motherland, or when all the soldiers indiscriminately compel us to brand them with scorn.

You, dear soldiers, entwined in party conversations, it is you whom we address. Do you know that each day of your fruitless inaction at the front costs the motherland 50 million rubles? You are destroying the motherland. Do you know just what this is called? Do you know that the last hope in you is becoming dim in our hearts and we, weak women, are being transformed into tigresses in order to defend our children from disgrace, to defend the freedom of Russia? Sorrowful you will be when we will brand you with contempt.

And how will we treat you, soldiers who are cowardly and traitorous, like Judases who have sold Russia for thirty silver pieces, trading in the blood of their own fathers, selling the bread of our children to the Germans?

Soon, soon, it would be better for you to meet ten German bayonets with your chests rather than one tigress, us, who curse you. You who fight without annexations and reparations, but who starve your hometowns and dine on the motherland, rouse yourselves from your stupor!

In answer to your friendly call for general brotherhood, the enemy continues to fight on our soil. Is this not clear treason in the form of fraternization? The enemy laughs at you. Only bayonets will bring us close to peace. Only then will we heal the wounds of our native land, only then will the sun shine on Russia. Now you must keep the ranks, repel the enemy, go into their cities with flags waving on bayonets, overthrow the throne of Wilhelm—then we will believe the sincerity of your words, then we will bow before your greatness. And until then we will have no other name for you than cowards, traitors, Judases.

Among us, your mothers, wives, and sisters, there is only one party: the freedom and glory of great Russia. Yes, she will be great in brotherhood and her light shall shine on all peoples! And one platform: motherland, family and the happiness of our children. Forward against the enemy, we go to die together with you!

### To the Peoples of the Allied Nations

We, Russian women, appeal to you, valiant allies. The wave of your indignation at the "treason" of the Russian people has reached us and we openly respond to you: you are not correct.

We understand your fearful and anxious feelings, but do not accept your accusations, because they are not just, because you do not know the multifaceted nature of the Russian soul, which most of all strives for brotherhood with the entire world.

When it is necessary to die, we know how to die, and we have proved this throughout history, yes, and in this war as well, when on numerous occasions during these years we have taken upon ourselves deathly blows that were directed at you.

Perhaps you are right, it may be, that we do not struggle for national pride and do not boast about it, but we have something else: national strength, love for humanity, faith in its best ideals, hope in its general realization. Love comes before hatred in the Russian nature. Where there is love the elements of hate fall away and are replaced. Russians do not love to be treasonous. To this day, Russians have not forgotten those who have done kindly by them. And you can be assured: Russia will never forget the role of the allies in the general battle against German imperialism, and you will be repaid a hundredfold.

Those who lie about the reliability of Russia will always be punished fatally. And part of the punishment for Germany, particularly in terms of the reliability of the simply souled Russian people, will soon be evident.

No force will save Germany; she will be fatally divided by Russia with your courage and assistance. Russia buzzes like a beehive, and you, allies, see only the work of one bee, flying around, but the internal life you don't see and you cannot see.

The work is difficult, hard; Rus' is ready not only for the construction of one life, but for a reevaluation of all aspects and ideas of all of humanity. Just have patience, bravery, and strength to hold up for now with us. Show kindness to us, understand us and support us in our own work for the good of the whole.

### Appeal to the Russian Workers from the
### Women's National Military Union

Citizen Worker!

Our union of volunteers has only existed for several days, practically hours, and hundreds of entries, hundreds of letters, from every corner of the country by women ready to go to their deaths for its defense, testifies to our strength and our right to speak openly about all that weighs heavily on our souls.

Comrade Worker!

"Why are you looking at the splinter in the eye of your brother, when you have a log in your own?"

Comrade Worker, either you do not see that you already bow before a golden calf and in the church of freedom you trade your honor, or you do not see that in wrath the true scourge of God has already entered your head and if you do not repent you will be driven from the church in disgrace? Or you do not feel that your wounded comrades who have been called up for service, sitting in the trenches and in the mud for 3 years, have not laid down their bones for your freedom, that you are in the right not to go to fight, as their families sink into poverty, and you, remaining on the books, enrich yourselves.

Where then is the freedom, in that brotherhood and equality for which you call? Not in the increased wages and decreased profits of the capitalists, nor in the full destruction, of yours and well as others, of the saviors of Russia. You are on the books. You are obligated for conscription. Let all persons and enterprises be obligated for conscription. Let no one, even soldiers, receive pay or profits, but have shoes and food, and blood, while the war continues. As the Germans now act, so you cover your hearts and your eyes. Remember, consider, the general good, display your higher spirit. For the freedom of Rus' go further into the struggle; we ourselves are hungry to do so. We ourselves go to die for the benefit of Russia.

Long live sincere liberty, equality and fraternity!

*Source:* "Zhenskii Voenno-Narodnyi Soiuz Dobrovol'stev—Manifest," *Novoe vremia,* June 8, 1917: 5.

# APPENDIX C

## Personnel of the 1st Russian Women's Battalion of Death Who Took Part in Battle on July 9–10, 1917, at Novospasskii Forest near Smorgon

| Number and Rank | Name | Status and Notes |
|---|---|---|
| 1. Sublieutenant | Bochkareva, Maria | By her own initiative led her detachment into the counterattack and the entire time was in the front lines. Suffered concussion. |
| 2. Private | Prokhorova, Olga | During the counterattack was in the front lines. Killed in action. |
| 3. Private | Kalapoig, Tul'da | At the time of the counterattack was killed by an enemy grenade |
| 4. Private | Osipova, Valentina | Suffered concussion, remained in the ranks |
| 5. Private | Kravetz, Zinaida | Wounded |
| 6. Private | Klepatskaia, Valentina | Seriously wounded [Bochkareva reported she was killed.] |
| 7. Private | Minenkova, Evdokiia | Wounded |
| 8. Private | Nediavetskaia, Elena | Seriously wounded |
| 9. Private | Nikolaieva, Anna | Suffered serious concussion |
| 10. Private | Polshavtseva, Nina | Seriously wounded |
| 11. Private | Poplavskoiia, Rima | Wounded |
| 12. Private | Stupina, Efosin'ia | Wounded |
| 13. Private | Fedorova, Elena | Wounded |
| 14. Private | Tsvanugocher, Natasha | Wounded |
| 15. Private | Tsvetkova, Liubova | Wounded |
| 16. Private | Shanovalova, Varvara | Wounded |
| 17. Private | Shuksto, Evdokiia | Wounded |
| 18. Private | Iasimovskaia, Aleksandra | Suffered concussion |
| 19. Private | Iatsipo, Maria | Wounded |
| 20. Private | Iakovskaia, Evgeniia | Seriously wounded |

| 21. Private [actually senior NCO and commander's adjutant] | Skrydlova, Maria | Suffered concussion remained in ranks |
|---|---|---|
| 22. Private | Arsen'eva, Maria | Ill |
| 23. Private | Belokurova, Maria | Suffered concussion |
| 24. Private | Ginshunaia, Aleksandra | Suffered concussion, remained in ranks |
| 25. Private | Vasileva, Pelagaia | Suffered concussion |
| 26. Private | Vasileva, Nina | Suffered concussion |
| 27. Private | Dubchenko, Anastasia | Suffered concussion |
| 28. Private | Eremina, Anna | Suffered concussion |
| 29. Private | Konalova, Anna | Ill |
| 30. Private | Matveeva, Anis'ia | Suffered concussion, remained in ranks |
| 31. Private | Polonskaia, Leonina | Suffered concussion |
| 32. Private | Romanova, Evgeniia | Suffered concussion |
| 33. Private | Solov'eva, Lidia | Suffered concussion |
| 34. Private | Troshpova, Elena | Suffered concussion |
| 35. Medical Assistant | Tsurlang, Ekaterina | Suffered concussion |
| 36. Private | Maslennirova, Evgeniia | Suffered concussion |
| 37. Private | Nemkevicha, Nadezhda | Suffered concussion |
| 38. Private | Kunetsova, Sofia | Suffered serious concussion |

## The Following Women Participated in the Battle, Each Fulfilling Her Role and When Possible, Stopped Others from Running Away

| Number and Rank | Name | Notes |
|---|---|---|
| 39. Private | Kubash', Sofia | Participated in battle |
| 40. Private | Adel'to, Anna | Participated in battle |
| 41. Private | Antonova, Klavdia | Participated in battle |
| 43. Private | Andrushenko, Aleksandra | Participated in battle |
| 44. Corporal | Anlaeva, Aniia | Participated in battle |
| 45. Private | Barigrin, Galina | Participated in battle |
| 46. Private | Boitsova, Alrafena | Participated in battle |
| 47. Private | Bondareva, Anna | Participated in battle |
| 48. Private | Byp', Natasha | Participated in battle |
| 49. Private | Beckman, Elena | Participated in battle |
| 50. Private | Bakhmutova, Elena | Participated in battle |
| 51. Private | Budrina, Liubov' | Participated in battle |
| 52. Private | Brobina, Alevtina | Participated in battle |
| 53. Private | Biliariants, Anna | Participated in battle |
| 54. Private | Vasileva, Tatiana | Participated in battle |
| 55. Private | Vasileva, Maria | Participated in battle |

| 56. Private | Vasileva, Ekaterina | Participated in battle |
|---|---|---|
| 57. Private | Vasileva, Evgeniia | Participated in battle |
| 58. Private | Vorobleva, Aleksandra | Participated in battle |
| 59. Private | Vonovets, Iushenia | Participated in battle |
| 60. Private | Voronyna, Doina | Participated in battle |
| 61. Private | Guzhevich, Elena | Participated in battle |
| 62. Private | Guzhevich, Zinaida | Participated in battle |
| 63. Private | Gasilina, Matrena | Participated in battle |
| 64. Private | Ermailova, Nina | Participated in battle |
| 65. Private | Emel'ianovskaia, Dorotia | Participated in battle |
| 66. Private | Ekech, Raisa | Participated in battle |
| 67. Private | Grofeeva, Natasha | Participated in battle |
| 68. Private | Gavadepaia, Olga | Participated in battle |
| 69. Private | Zubkova, Anna | Participated in battle |
| 70. Private | Gakharova, Pelagaia | Participated in battle |
| 71. Private | Il'shevich, Anna | Participated in battle |
| 72. Private | Ivanova, Ekaterina | Participated in battle |
| 73. Private | Il'ina, Fedal'ia | Participated in battle |
| 74. Private | Ivanova, Evgeniia | Participated in battle |
| 75. Private | Gavrilova, Maria | Participated in battle |
| 76. Private | Kariachanova, Lidiia | Participated in battle |
| 77. Private | Kulakova, Anna | Participated in battle |
| 78. Private | Kopilova, Maria | Participated in battle |
| 79. Private | Kizul', Emiliia | Participated in battle |
| 80. Private | Kolesnikova, Vera | Participated in battle |
| 81. Private | Kuzmanoi, Natasha | Participated in battle |
| 82. Private | Kal'e, Liubov | Participated in battle |
| 83. Private | Kozel', Antonina | Participated in battle |
| 84. Private | Kakorana, Antonina | Participated in battle |
| 85. Private | Kirilova, Tatiana | Participated in battle |
| 86. Private | Kibardina, Nadezhda | Participated in battle |
| 87. Private | Kashina, Lidiia | Participated in battle |
| 88. Private | Komarova, Zinaida | Participated in battle |
| 89. Private | Lind, Ekaterina | Participated in battle |
| 90. Private | Lurin, Teplia | Participated in battle |
| 91. Private | Lupinkova, Anna | Participated in battle |
| 92. Private | Lokteva, Dariia | Participated in battle |
| 93. Private | Leliukhina, Kseniia | Participated in battle |
| 94. Private | Los'eva, Tatiana | Participated in battle |
| 95. Private | Levitznaia, Nina | Participated in battle |
| 96. Private | Morozova, Anisiia | Participated in battle |
| 97. Private | Mikhailova, Olga | Participated in battle |
| 98. Private | Mal'nina, Elizaveta | Participated in battle |
| 99. Private | Mertsanova, Lidiia | Participated in battle |
| 100. Private | Luk'ianova, Evgeniia | Participated in battle |
| 101. Private | Meisr, Maria | Participated in battle |

| 102. Private | Mansonova, Maria | Participated in battle |
|---|---|---|
| 103. Private | Zvaltseva, Ekaterina | Participated in battle |
| 104. Private | Murad'eva, Maria | Participated in battle |
| 105. Private | Minina, Pelegaia | Participated in battle |
| 106. Private | Ol'shchevskaia, Aleksandra | Participated in battle |
| 107. Private | Ogluzdina, Khariessa | Participated in battle |
| 108. Private | Orlova, Aleksandra | Participated in battle |
| 109. Private | Petrova, Valentina | Participated in battle |
| 110. Private | Petrova, Evgeniia | Participated in battle |
| 111. Private | Popkova, Anastasia | Participated in battle |
| 112. Private | Pilinova, Maria | Participated in battle |
| 113. Private | Parkholova, Maria | Participated in battle |
| 114. Private | Prakor'eva, Valentina | Participated in battle |
| 115. Private | Soberg, Al'ma | Participated in battle |
| 116. Private | Somanova, Liudmila | Participated in battle |
| 117. Private | Pervianova, Aleksandra | Participated in battle |
| 118. Private | Pigurina, Irina | Participated in battle |
| 119. Private | Pazukina, Malin'ia | Participated in battle |
| 120. Private | Prokhorova, Maria | Participated in battle |
| 121. Private | Pogenko, Aleksandra | Participated in battle |
| 122. Private | Puzen', Iuliia | Participated in battle |
| 123. Private | Starosel'skaia, Maria | Participated in battle |
| 124. Private | Smol'skaia, Maria | Participated in battle |
| 125. Private | Stargin, Aposhnariia | Participated in battle |
| 126. Private | Skorobogashva, Anna | Participated in battle |
| 127. Private | Stepanova, Anna | Participated in battle |
| 128. Private | Savich, Natasha | Participated in battle |
| 129. Private | Smolina, Anastasia | Participated in battle |
| 130. Private | Spetanina, Paraskeva | Participated in battle |
| 131. Private | Sidorova, Anastasia | Participated in battle |
| 132. Private | Stepanova, Elizaveta | Participated in battle |
| 133. Private | Teodorovich, Tatiana | Participated in battle |
| 134. Private | Trei, Al'vina | Participated in battle |
| 135. Private | Filippova, Anna | Participated in battle |
| 136. Private | Fingenova, Fedal'ia | Participated in battle |
| 137. Private | Khamunova, Maria | Participated in battle |
| 138. Private | Kharina, Zoe | Participated in battle |
| 139. Private | Khlopunova, Klavdiia | Participated in battle |
| 140. Private | Khuskevavze, Sofia | Participated in battle |
| 141. Private | Chaplinena, Evdokiia | Participated in battle |
| 142. Private | Chaplina, Elizaveta | Participated in battle |
| 143. Private | Shpeider, Kseniia | Participated in battle |
| 144. Private | Shtepan, Vera | Participated in battle |
| 145. Private | Shtai, Ekaterina | Participated in battle |
| 146. Private | Shupko, Aleksandra | Participated in battle |
| 147. Private | Idina, Marianina | Participated in battle |

| | | |
|---|---|---|
| 148. Private | Izhorskaia, Anna | Participated in battle |
| 149. Private | Trenke, Sofia | Participated in battle |
| 150. Private | Chonova, Chetin'ia | Participated in battle |
| 151. Private | Matskevich, Iuliia | Participated in battle |
| 152. Private | Guvannova, Ekaterina | Participated in battle |
| 153. Private | Sipelitseva, Darina | Participated in battle |
| 154. Private | Shestova, Zinaida | Participated in battle |
| 155. Private | Por'ze, Tamara | Participated in battle |
| 156. Private | Il'vina, Nina | Participated in battle |
| 157. Private | Levasheva, Aleksandra | Participated in battle |
| 158. Private | Gubileva, Anastasia | Participated in battle |
| 159. Junior NCO | Pal'tsina, Antonina | Participated in battle |
| 160. Private | Orlova, Ksenia | Participated in battle [She was the standard-bearer and was killed in action.] |
| 161. Medical Assistant | Kalishpinova, Aleksandra | Incessantly gave help to the wounded under artillery fire |
| 162. Medical Assistant | Pomitsur', Zinoviia | Incessantly gave help to the wounded under artillery fire |
| 163. Medical Assistant | Tret'iakova, Anastasia | Incessantly gave help to the wounded under artillery fire |
| 164. Medical Assistant | Goryntseva, Olga | Incessantly gave help to the wounded under artillery fire |
| 165. Medical Assistant | Zhidkova, Olga | Incessantly gave help to the wounded under artillery fire |
| 166. Doctor | Skoropisava, Leonina | Located in the trenches the whole time giving aid to the wounded |
| 167. Private | Mal'sheva, Olga | Missing in action |
| 168. Private | Shlashas', Agniia | Missing in action |
| 169. Private | Golubeva, Maria | Participated in battle [actually wounded] |
| 170. Private | Zhrebchikova, Aleksandra | Participated in battle |

## List of Instructors from the 525th Kiuruk-Dar'inskii Regiment Assigned to the Women's Detachment of Death and Who Participated in the Battle

| Number and Rank | Name | Notes |
|---|---|---|
| 1. Senior NCO | Solov'ev, Nikolai | Wounded during the time of the counterattack by a grenade |
| 2. Junior NCO | Smalnei, Petr | Wounded in reconnaissance |
| 3. Junior NCO | Mal'shenko, ? | Wounded in the counterattack |
| 4. Junior NCO | Shevchenko, Andrei, 1st Company | Held their positions the whole time and reassured their comrade soldiers, went into |
| 5. Junior NCO | Labachev, Aleksei, 2nd Company | counterattack twice |

| 6. Corporal | Morozov, Iakov,<br>4th Company | The entire time he supplied the women with cartridges. |

*Source:* "Imenoi spisok lits I zhenskoi komandoi smerti, uchastvovavshchikh v boi, 9 July 1917," RGVIA, f. 2277, op. 1, d. 368, L. 9. While only 170 women's names appear on the list, the detachment is reported to have had over 200 members. The explanation for the reduced number of names may lie in the fact that not all the women took part in the battle, some were assigned to the command of other units, others may have gone missing, and still others were killed and wounded in the artillery exchanges that the unit participated in prior to the battle proper. Since the army did not have any official personnel list before the battle, it may not have known the names of these women in order to include them on this list. Conspicuously absent from the list, however, are Nina Krylova, Princess Tatuieva, and the daughter of General Dubrovskii.

# APPENDIX D

## Staff List of the 2nd Moscow Women's Battalion of Death

### Officers

| Number | Post | Rank |
|---|---|---|
| 1 | Battalion Commander | Colonel or Lt. Colonel |
| 1 | Chief of Economic Section | Captain |
| 4 | Company Commanders: | Captains |
| | 1 Battalion Adjutant | |
| | 1 Commander of Machine-Gun Crew | |
| | 1 Commander of Scout Detachment | |
| | 1 Commander of Sapper Detachment | |
| 9 | Junior Officers | Various |

### Military Functionaries

| Number | Post | Rank |
|---|---|---|
| 1 | Doctor | Senior Officer |
| 1 | Doctor | Junior Officer |
| 1 | Quartermaster and Paymaster | Undetermined |
| 1 | Clerk of Economic Section | Undetermined |
| 1 | Master-at-Arms and Gunsmith | Undetermined |

### Noncommissioned Officers and Soldiers

| Number | Post | Rank |
|---|---|---|
| 5 | Combat Duties | Sergeants Major |
| 22 | Platoon Commanders | Senior NCOs |
| 6 | Quartermasters | Sergeants |
| 71 | General Duties | Junior NCOs |
| 1 | Battalion Bugler | Junior NCO |
| 8 | Company Buglers | Undetermined |

| 90  | Combat Soldiers | Corporals |
| 880 | Combat Soldiers | Privates |

*Noncombatants*

| Number | Post |
|---|---|
| 1 | Senior NCO |
| 1 | Battalion Clerk |
| 2 | Senior Clerks |
| 2 | Junior Clerks |
| 3 | Junior Aides-de-Camp (Officers' Attendants) |
| 1 | Senior Medical Officer |
| 1 | Junior Medical Officer |
| 4 | Company Medical Attendants |
| 1 | Veterinarian |
| 1 | Supervisor of the Infirm |
| 2 | Infirmary Attendants |
| 1 | Tailor |
| 2 | Senior Craftsmen |
| 5 | Junior Craftsmen |
| 2 | Cooks |
| 3 | Kitchen Workers |
| 55 | Transport Drivers |
| 7 | Miscellaneous |

## Staff of the Communications Crew

| Number | Post | Rank |
|---|---|---|
| 1 | Telephone Operator | Senior NCO |
| 1 | Telephone Operator | Junior NCO |
| 4 | Telephone Operators | Privates |
| 1 | Mounted Messenger | Junior NCO |
| 4 | Mounted Messengers | Privates |
| 2 | Cyclists | Privates |

## Staff of Mounted Reconnaissance (Scout) Detachment

| Number | Rank |
|---|---|
| 1 | Commander of Detachment |
| 1 | Senior NCO |
| 3 | Corporals |
| 27 | Privates |
| 1 | Orderly |

## Staff of Sapper Detachment

| Number | |
|---|---|
| 1 | Commander of Detachment |
| 1 | Senior NCO |
| 2 | Junior NCOs |
| 3 | Corporals |
| 25 | Privates |
| 1 | Orderly |

## Drivers of One-Horse Transport Carts

| Number | Post | Rank |
|---|---|---|
| 8 | For Cartridge Bearers | Privates |
| 1 | For Pharmaceutical Supplies | Private |
| 1 | For Telephone Equipment | Private |
| 1 | For Medical Supplies | Private |
| 8 | For Officers' Belongings | Privates |
| 20 | For Economic Goods | Privates |
| 4 | For Ill and Wounded | Privates |
| 4 | For Field Kitchen, Artillery Type | Privates |
| 3 | For Reserve Horses | Privates |

## Drivers of Transport for Machine-Gun Crew

| Number | Post | Rank |
|---|---|---|
| 2 | For Economic Goods | Privates |
| 1 | For Field Kitchen, Cavalry Type | Private |
| 2 | For Reserve Horses | Privates |

### *Staff of Battalion Companies*

| Number | Post | Rank |
|---|---|---|
| 1 | Company Commander | Sergeant Major |
| 4 | Platoon Commanders | Senior NCOs |
| 1 | Quartermaster | Sergeant |
| 16 | Squad Leaders | Junior NCOs |
| 2 | Buglers | Undetermined |
| 20 | General Duties | Corporals |
| 180 | Combatants | Privates |
| 8 | Porters | Privates |
| 2 | Cooks | Privates |

| | | |
|---|---|---|
| 2 | Kitchen Workers | Privates |
| 3 | Orderlies | Privates |

## Staff of Machine-Gun Crew

| Number | Post | Rank |
|---|---|---|
| 1 | Commander of Crew | Sergeant Major |
| 1 | Platoon Commander | Senior NCO |
| 1 | Machine Gunner | Senior NCO |
| 1 | Quartermaster | Sergeant |
| 3 | Machine Gunners | Junior NCOs |
| 4 | Spotters and Gun Layers | Corporals |
| 4 | Reserve Spotters and Gun Layers | Privates |
| 8 | Ammunitions Carriers | Privates |
| 8 | Drivers of Ammunitions Carts | Privates |
| 4 | Machine Gunners | Privates |
| 4 | Ammunitions Carts | Privates |
| 2 | Managers of Reserve Horses | Privates |
| 2 | Orderlies | Privates |

## Staff of the Separate Communications Detachment

| Number | Post | Rank |
|---|---|---|
| 1 | Commander of Detachment | Senior Officer |
| 1 | Adjutant | Junior Officer |
| 2 | Combatants | Senior NCOs |
| 2 | Combatants | Junior NCOs |
| 7 | Telephone Operators | Corporals |
| 69 | Telephone Operators | Privates |
| 1 | Motorcyclist | Corporal |
| 5 | Motorcyclists | Privates |
| 1 | Quartermaster | Senior NCO |
| 1 | Medical Officer | Senior Officer |
| 1 | Veterinary Medical Attendant | Senior Officer |
| 1 | Craftsman | Senior Rank |
| 1 | Craftsman | Junior Rank |
| 1 | Cook | Junior Rank |
| 1 | Kitchen Worker | Junior Rank |
| 2 | Drivers of Telephone Carts | Privates |
| 1 | Driver of Field Kitchen Cart | Private |
| 2 | Drivers of Economic Goods Carts | Privates |
| 1 | Driver of Two-Horse Cart | Private |

Source: Various personnel lists in RGVIA, f. 3474, op. 2, d. 10, ll. 3–4, 14, 16; f. 3474, op. 2, d. 11, l. 97.

# APPENDIX E

## Members of the 2nd Moscow Women's Battalion of Death Chosen to Become Cadets of the Aleksandrov Military College

| Name | Age | Graduate of |
|------|-----|-------------|
| Alekseeva, Anna Kuz'minichna | 20 | Mariupol' Women's Gymnasium |
| Barkhash, Tatiana Levovna | 20 | Moscow Commercial Gymnasium |
| Biriukova, Aleksandra | ? | Bogorod Women's Gymnasium/Petrograd Agricultural Courses |
| Videnek, Anna Aleksandrovna | 26 | Moscow Mariinskii Diocese College |
| Gotgart, Zinaida | ? | Moscow Mariinskii Women's Gymnasium |
| De-Bog, Sofia Nikolaevna | 21 | Petrograd Smolny-Nikolaev Institute |
| Zharina, Veronika Mikhailovna | 28 | Moscow Women's Gymnasium (Zhiti) |
| Zaborskaia, Nadezhda | ? | Second Moscow Women's Gymnasium |
| Zubakina, Olga Veniaminovna | 21 | Simbirsk Women's Gymnasium/Moscow Medical Courses |
| Ivankova, Vera | ? | Okhansk Women's Gymnasium |
| Klimovskaia, Tat'iana | ? | Moscow Mariinskii Women's Gymnasium |
| Kochergina, Antonina Mikhailovna | 24 | Moscow Women's Gymnasium (Gel'b) |
| Kremianskaia, Maria | ? | Moscow Women's Gymnasium/Higher Courses in France |
| Mers'e, Maria Feliksovna | 19 | First Moscow Women's Gymnasium |
| Mers'E, Vera Feliksovna | 21 | First Moscow Women's Gymnasium |
| Neudachina, Olga Gavrilovna | 19 | Second Roslavl' Women's Gymnasium |
| Nikolaeva, Olga Ivanovna | 22 | Ekaterinoslav Commercial School/Moscow Commercial Institute |
| Pankrat'eva, Aleksandra | ? | Tashkent Women's Gymnasium |
| Platunova, Maria | ? | Moscow Mariinskii Women's Gymnasium |
| Pylaeva, Iuliia Vladimirovna | 18 | El'ninsk Women's Gymnasium |
| Reformatskaia, Zinaida Nikolaevna | 23 | Kuril (Kurmshysk?) Women's Gymnasium |
| Svirchevskaia, Zinaida Benedictovna | 23 | Kostroma Women's Gymnasium |
| Semenova-Feoktistova, Natalia | ? | Moscow Women's Gymnasium (Ezhovoi) |
| Tikhomirova, Evgeniia Sergeevna | 20 | Moscow Elizavetskii Women's Gymnasium |
| Chernopiatova, Maria Grigorevna | 21 | Moscow Gus'kov Boarding School |

*Source:* "Attestantsionyi spisok iunkerov Moskovskago Zhenskago Batal'ona Smerti," RGVIA, f. 725, op. 54, d. 489, l. 19; "Report," RGVIA, f. 3474, op. 2, d. 11, l. 97.

# APPENDIX F

## Volunteers of the 1st Women's Naval Detachment

| No. | Last Name, First Name, and Patronymic | Trade |
|-----|----------------------------------------|-------|
| 1 | Mikhailova, Vera Terent'evna | Medic/Nurse |
| 2 | Stankevich, Aleksandra Fedorovna | Clerk-typist |
| 3 | Stankevich, Maria Fedorovna | Graduate of Pokrovskii Gymnasium |
| 4 | Art'teva, Nadezhda Vassil'evna | Printing press worker |
| 5 | Petrova, Evgeniia Feofilaktovna | Childcare worker/Nanny |
| 6 | Korobina, Zoia Konstaninovna | Telephonist |
| 7 | Zakharova, Ekaterina Nikoleavna | Tailor |
| 8 | Kosik, Pelagea Konstantinovna | Nurse |
| 9 | Shopshina, Vera Iakovlevna | Domestic servant |
| 10 | Zhiriakova, Efrosiniia Osipova | Agricultural worker |
| 11 | Ponomareva, Evdokiia Tikhovna | Nurse/Domestic servant |
| 12 | Bachishche, Anna Fedorovna | Unskilled laborer |
| 13 | Zakharina, Tatiana Matveevna | Agricultural worker |
| 14 | Mamaeva, Feodora Nikolaevna | Agricultural worker |
| 15 | Chelomova, Evdokiia Savvatievna | Agricultural worker |
| 16 | Nikoforova, Ul'iana Ivanovna | Agricultural worker |
| 17 | Osipova, Anna Ivanovna | Office clerk |
| 18 | Iofa, Mirka Mendeleevna | Can type a little |
| 19 | Nikitina, Vera Fedorovna | Tailor-seamstress |
| 20 | Makarova, Maria Emel'ianovna | Cook |
| 21 | Antonova, Antonina Ivanovna | Office clerk |
| 22 | Kapitonova, Marfa Kapitonovna | Server in a tavern |
| 23 | Pebrova, Maria Viktorovna | Typist |
| 24 | Dikhtiareva, Tatiana Afanas'evna | Completed 4th level of gymnasium |
| 25 | Lavrenova, Vera Vasil'evna | Tailor |
| 26 | Klekova, Felka Kuz'minishna | Served as a cook on a steamship |
| 27 | Roriakova, Elizaveta Osipova | Seamstress |
| 28 | Skvortsova, Evdokiia Merkur'evna | Teacher-pedagogue |
| 29 | Apfel'baum, Ida Iur'evna | Tailor-seamstress |
| 30 | Kisliakova-Stepanova, Anastasia Kharitonovna | Hospital orderly (cleaner) |

| 31 | Zimina, Pelagia Andreevna | Tailor-seamstress |
| 32 | Bogdanova, Ekaterina Alekseevna | Office clerk |
| 33 | Vau, Ida Martovna | Office clerk |
| 34 | Bol'shova, Evdokia Pavlovna | Officer worker |
| 35 | Kobiakova, Agrapina | Cook/Servant |

*Source:* "Spisok dobrovolits Morskoi Uchebno-Strelkovoi Komandy," RGAVMF, f. 417, op. 4, d. 6571, l. 27.

# NOTES

## INTRODUCTION

1. This number is based on the more than 5,000 women who enlisted in the all-female military units created in 1917 and the hundreds of individuals who served in male units prior to the formation of women's units.

2. Brian Crim, "Silent Partners: Women and Warfare in Early Modern Europe," *A Soldier and a Woman: Sexual Integration in the Military*, ed. Gerard DeGroot and Corinna Peniston-Bird (London: Longman, 2000), 19.

3. Margaret H. Darrow, "French Volunteer Nursing and the Myth of War Experience in World War I," *American Historical Review*, 101, no. 1 (February 1996): 81.

4. Alfred G. Meyer, "The Impact of World War I on Russian Women's Lives," in *Russia's Women: Accommodation, Resistance, Transformation*, ed. Barbara Evans Clements, Barbara Alpern Engel, and Christine D. Worobec (Berkeley and Los Angeles: University of California Press, 1991), 208–209.

5. Linda Grant De Pauw, *Battle Cries and Lullabies: Women in War from Prehistory to the Present* (Norman: University of Oklahoma Press, 1998), 15.

6. Nicole Ann Dombrowski, "Soldiers, Saints, or Sacrificial Lambs? Women's Relationship to Combat and the Fortification of the Home Front in the Twentieth Century," in *Women and War in the Twentieth Century: Enlisted with or without Consent*, ed. Nicole Ann Dombrowski (New York: Garland, 1999), 3.

7. Penny Summerfield, "Gender and War in the Twentieth Century," *International History Review* 19, 1 (February 1997): 3.

8. George L. Mosse, *Nationalism and Sexuality: Respectability and Abnormal Sexuality in Modern Europe* (New York: Howard Fertig, 1985), 115.

9. Susan Grayzel, *Women and the First World War* (London: Pearson Education, 2002), 12.

10. Barbara Alpern Engel, "Transformation versus Tradition," in *Russia's Women: Accommodation, Resistance, Transformation*, ed. Barbara Evans Clements, Barbara Alpern Engel, and Christine D. Worobec (Berkeley and Los Angeles: University of California Press, 1991), 144.

11. Grayzel, *Women and the First World War*, 106–109.

12. Arthur Marwick, *The Deluge: British Society and the First World War* (London: Bodley Head, 1965), 93 et passim.

13. Joanna Bourke, *Dismembering the Male: Men's Bodies, Great Britain and the Great War* (Chicago: University of Chicago Press, 1996), 1 et passim.

14. Darrow, "French Volunteer Nursing and the Myth of the War Experience," 97.

15. Summerfield, "Gender and War in the Twentieth Century," 5.

CHAPTER ONE. THE RUSSIAN CONTEXT

1. Barbara Alpern Engel, "Transformation versus Tradition," in *Russia's Women: Accommodation, Resistance, Transformation,* ed. Barbara Evans Clements, Barbara Alpern Engel, and Christine D. Worobec (Berkeley and Los Angeles: University of California Press, 1991), 136.

2. Barbara Evans Clements, Barbara Alpern Engel, and Christine D. Worobec, introduction to *Russia's Women,* 3.

3. Christine Worobec, "Accommodation and Resistance," in Clements, Engel, and Worobec, *Russia's Women,* 19.

4. Richard Stites, *The Women's Liberation Movement in Russia: Feminism, Nihilism, and Bolshevism, 1860–1930* (Princeton, NJ: Princeton University Press, 1978), 17.

5. Jane McDermaid and Anna Hillyar, *Women and Work in Russia, 1880–1930: A Study in Continuity through Change* (London: Longman, 1998), 11.

6. Jessica Tovrov, "Mother-Child Relationships among the Russian Nobility," in *The Family in Imperial Russia,* ed. David Ransel (Urbana: University of Illinois Press, 1978), 17.

7. Worobec, "Accommodation and Resistance," 24.

8. Engel, "Transformation versus Tradition," 135–136.

9. Mary Matossian, "The Peasant Way of Life," in *Russian Peasant Women,* ed. Beatrice Farnsworth and Lynn Viola (New York: Oxford University Press, 1992), 22–24; Barbara Alpern Engel, *Between the Field and the City: Women, Work, and Family in Russia, 1861–1914* (Cambridge: Cambridge University Press, 1994), 7–33.

10. Worobec, "Accommodation and Resistance," 20.

11. Natalia Pushkareva, *Women in Russian History: From the Tenth to the Twentieth Century,* trans. Eve Levin (London: M. E. Sharpe, 1997), 233.

12. Ibid., 25.

13. Ibid., 145–149.

14. Richard Stites, "M. L. Mikhailov and the Emergence of the Woman Question in Russia," *Canadian Slavic Studies* 3, 2 (1969): 178–179.

15. Karen Petrone, "Family, Masculinity, and Heroism in Russian War Posters," in *Borderlines: Genders and Identities in War and Peace, 1870–1930,* ed. Billie Melman (New York: Routledge, 1998). 95.

16. See Engel, *Between the Field and the City.*

17. See Rose Glickman, "The Russian Factory Woman, 1880–1914," in *Women in Russia,* ed. Dorothy Atkinson, Alexander Dallin, and Gail Warshofsky Lapidus (Stanford, CA: Stanford University Press, 1977), 63–82.

18. Barbara Clements, "Introduction: Accommodation, Resistance, Transformation," in Clements, Engel, and Worobec, *Russia's Women,* 8–9.

19. Laura Engelstein, *The Keys to Happiness: Sex and the Search for Modernity in Fin-de-Siècle Russia* (Ithaca, NY: Cornell University Press, 1992), 3–4.

20. Vera S. Dunham, "The Strong Woman Motif," in *The Transformation of Russian Society*, ed. Cyril Black (Cambridge, MA: Harvard University Press, 1960), 462.

21. Dorothy Atkinson, "Society and Sexes in the Russian Past," in Atkinson, Dallin, and Lapidus, *Women in Russia*, 9.

22. I. Kharlamov, quoted in Cathy A. Frierson, *Peasant Icons: Representations of Rural People in Late Nineteenth Century Russia* (New York: Oxford University Press, 1993), 167.

23. Barbara Heldt, *Terrible Perfection: Women and Russian Literature* (Bloomington: Indiana University Press, 1987), 12.

24. Ibid.

25. Dunham, "The Strong Woman Motif," 468.

26. Frierson, *Peasant Icons,* 167–168.

27. Dunham, "The Strong Woman Motif," 468.

28. Atkinson, "Society and Sexes in the Russian Past," 3.

29. Lawrence Osborn, "The Women Warriors," *Lingua Franca* 7, 10 (December 1997–January 1998): 23.

30. Barbara G. Walker, *The Woman's Encyclopedia of Myths and Secrets* (San Francisco: Harper and Row, 1983), 24–27.

31. John T. Alexander, "Amazon Autocratrixes: Images of Female Rule in the Eighteenth Century," in *Gender and Sexuality in Russian Civilisation,* ed. Peter I. Barta (London and New York: Routledge, 2001), 33–54.

32. Evgenii Anisimov, "Slovo i delo russkoi zhenshchiny," afterword to *Svoeruchnye zapiski kniagini Natal'i Borisovny Dolgorukoi docheri fel'marshala grafa Borisa Petrovicha Sheremeteva* (St. Petersburg: Khudozhestvennaia literatura, 1992), 122.

33. Alfred G. Meyer, "Women Soldiers in Russia and the Soviet Union," in *The Modern Encyclopedia of Russian and Soviet History,* 60 vols. (Gulf Breeze, FL: Academic International Press, 1976–2000), 55:21.

34. Iu. N. Ivanova, "Zhenshchiny v istorii rossiiskoi armii," *Voenno-istoricheskii zhurnal* 3 (1992): 86.

35. Jeannine Davis-Kimball, "Warrior Women of Eurasia," *Archeology* 1 (January–February 1997): 40–41.

36. Ivanova, "Zhenshchiny v istorii rossiiskoi armii," 87–88.

37. Ibid., 88.

38. Durova's memoirs were originally published in periodical format, then as a separate book titled *A Cavalry Maid: It Happened in Russia* (although Durova herself requested the memoirs be published as "A Russian Amazon, known by the name of Aleksandrov"). Soviet editions call the book *Notes of a Cavalry Maid.* There are two English translations: *The Cavalry Maiden: Journals of a Russian Officer in the Napoleonic Wars,* trans. Mary Zirin (Bloomington: Indiana University Press, 1988), and *Cavalry Maid: The Memoirs of a Woman Soldier of 1812,* trans. J. Mersereau and D. Lapeza (Ann Arbor: University of Michigan Press, 1988).

39. "Durova, Nadezhda Andreevna," in *The Modern Encyclopedia of Russian and Soviet History,* 60 vols. (Gulf Breeze, FL: Academic International Press, 1976–2000), 10:66–67.

40. L. A. Churilova-"Charskaia," *Smelaia zhizn': Podvigoi zagadochnogo geroia,* 1st ed. (Moscow, 1908); 2nd ed. (St. Petersburg: M. O. Vol'f, 1910).

41. Mary Zirin, "Translator's Introduction," in Durova, *The Cavalry Maiden,* xxix.

42. A. Saks, *Kavalerist-devitsa: Shtabs-rotmistr A. A. Aleksandrov (Nadezhda Andreevna Durova)* (St. Petersburg: Vestnik russkoi konnitsy, 1912).

43. The works based on Durova's memoirs published during World War II were *Kama Foundling,* a novel, and *Nadezhda Durova,* a play, as well as a short biography of Durova. Reina Pennington, *Wings, Women and War: Soviet Airwomen in World War II Combat* (Lawrence: University Press of Kansas, 2001), 64.

44. J. S. Curtiss, "Russian Sisters of Mercy in the Crimea, 1854–1855," *Slavic Review* 25 (March 1966): 84–100.

45. Ivanova, "Zhenshchiny v istorii rossiiskoi armii," 86.

46. "Warrior Women," *Literary Digest* 55 (June 19, 1915): 42.

47. Stites, *The Women's Liberation Movement in Russia,* 141.

48. Ibid., 147.

49. Diana Condrell and Jean Liddiard, *Working for Victory: Images of Women in the First World War, 1914–1918* (London: Routledge and Kegan Paul, 1987), 41. Sandes, who went to Serbia as a Red Cross nurse, ended up fighting with the Serbian army after being separated from her unit. She participated in the Serbian advance of 1916 and was awarded the Order of Karageorge and promoted to the rank of lieutenant for her bravery.

CHAPTER TWO.

INDIVIDUAL WOMEN SOLDIERS, 1914–1917

1. Susan R. Grayzel, *Women and the First World War* (London: Pearson Education, 2002), 3.

2. Michael J. Lyons, *World War I: A Short History* (Englewood Cliffs, NJ: Prentice Hall, 1994), 220–228. In France, Austria-Hungary, and Russia, significant numbers of women went to work in war industries beginning in 1914 and 1915; in Great Britain, they had become a large part of the labor force by June 1916. In Germany, however, there was less of an influx of women into industrial production.

3. Nikolai N. Golovin, *The Russian Army in the World War* (New Haven, CT: Yale University Press, 1931), 49; Lewis H. Siegelbaum, *The Politics of Industrial Mobilization in Russia, 1914–17* (London: Macmillan, 1983), 152.

4. Linda H. Edmondson, *Feminism in Russia, 1900–1917* (Stanford, CA: Stanford University Press, 1984), 162.

5. Alfred G. Meyer, "The Impact of World War I on Russian Women's Lives," in *Russia's Women: Accommodation, Resistance, Transformation,* ed. Barbara Evans Clements, Barbara Alpern Engel, and Christine Worobec (Berkeley and Los Angeles: University of California Press, 1991), 214–216.

6. Richard Stites, *The Women's Liberation Movement in Russia: Feminism, Nihilism, and Bolshevism, 1860–1930* (Princeton, NJ: Princeton University Press, 1978), 281.

7. Ibid., 287.

8. Meyer, "The Impact of World War I on Russian Women's Lives," 214.

9. Ibid., 215.

10. Ibid., 222.

11. Grayzel, *Women and the First World War*, 102–103.

12. Barbara Alpern Engel, *Women in Russia, 1700–2000* (Cambridge: Cambridge University Press, 2003), 128.

13. Edmondson, *Feminism in Russia, 1900–1917*, 158.

14. As translated by Stites in *The Women's Liberation Movement in Russia*, 283, taken from *Zhenskoe delo*, August 15, 1915: 1–2.

15. See issues of *Damskii mir, Zhenskoe delo, Zhenskii vestnik*, and other Russian women's journals beginning in September 1914 and continuing through the war, and A. K. Iakovleva, "Prizyv k zhenshchinam," *Zhenshchina i voina* 1 (March 5, 1915): 3.

16. Stites, *The Women's Liberation Movement in Russia*, 280.

17. *Zhenshchina i voina*, whose first issue was dated March 5, 1915.

18. Meyer, "The Impact of World War I on Russian Women's Lives," 221.

19. *Russkii invalid*, May 25, 1917: 4.

20. Meyer, "The Impact of World War I on Russian Women's Lives," 220.

21. Ibid.

22. Tikhon Polner, *Russian Local Government during the War and the Union of the Zemstvos* (New Haven, CT: Yale University Press, 1930), 255.

23. "E. P. Samsonova," *Zhenshchina i voina* 1 (March 5, 1915): 5–6.

24. Ibid., 7.

25. Nikolai Ardashev, *Velikaia voina i zhenshchiny Russkiia* (Moscow: F. Ia. Prigorina, 1915), 13.

26. Christine White, introduction to *A Dance with Death: Soviet Airwomen in World War II*, by Anne Noggle (College Station: Texas A&M University Press, 1994), 4.

27. "Zhenshchiny geroi," special issue, *Voina* 24 (1915).

28. See articles in *Zhenskaia zhizn'* 1 (January 7, 1915): 7; 2 (January 22, 1915): 2; 4 (February 22, 1915): 3; 7 (April 7, 1915): 11; 15 (August 7, 1915): 10; 18 (September 22, 1915): 8; 20 (October 22, 1915): 11; 24 (December 22, 1915): 11.

29. See chapter 7 for examples and analysis of commentary by such observers.

30. "Warrior Women," *Literary Digest* 55 (June 19, 1915): 1460.

31. Ann Eliot Griese and Richard Stites, "Russia: Revolution and War," in *Female Soldiers: Combatants or Noncombatants? Historical and Contemporary Perspectives*, ed. Nancy Loring Goldman (Westport, CT: Greenwood, 1982), 67.

32. Research on the American Civil War has yielded at least 250 cases of women serving in combat, but scholars estimate that there were probably many more, perhaps closer to 400, many of whom were not recognized as women. See DeAnn Blanton and Lauren Cook, *They Fought Like Demons: Women Soldiers in the Civil War* (New York: Vintage, 2002), 7. Approximately 6 million men fought in the Civil War. Thus, it seems entirely reasonable that in Russia during World War I, where approximately 15 million men were mobilized, approximately 1,000 women served as soldiers.

33. V. Yermilova, "Zhenshchina—Sud'ia," *Zhenskaia zhizn'* 2 (January 22, 1915): 2;

"Odna iz mnogikh," *Zhenskoe delo* 2 (January 15, 1915): 19–20; Florence Farmborough, *Nurse at the Russian Front: A Diary, 1914–18* (London: Constable, 1974), 300.

34. Meyer, "The Impact of World War I on Russian Women's Lives," 219. Numerous Russian and foreign periodicals contain reports of such women, which will be detailed below.

35. See *Rossiiskii gosudarstvennyi voenno-istoricheskii arkhiv* (Russian State Military-Historical Archive, Moscow, Russia; hereafter RGVIA), f. 2003, op. 2, d. 28, ll. 23, 45, 71–72, 131, for numerous examples of petitions sent to the Russian high command by women requesting permission to enlist in the active army.

36. Maria Botchkareva [*sic*], *Yashka: My Life as Peasant, Officer and Exile,* as told to Isaac Don Levine (New York: Frederick A. Stokes, 1919). Her story will be told in detail in Chapter 4.

37. Quoted in and translated by Joshua Sanborn, "Drafting the Nation: Military Conscription and the Formation of a Modern Polity in Tsarist and Soviet Russia, 1905–1925" (Ph.D. diss., University of Chicago, 1998), 412–413.

38. Tatiana Alexinsky [Aleksinskaia], *With the Russian Wounded,* trans. Gilbert Cannan (London: Fisher Unwin, 1916), 84.

39. "Zhenshchiny-dobrovol'sty," *Zhenshchina* 21 (November 1914): 10.

40. Hubertus F. Jahn, *Patriotic Culture in Russia during World War I* (Ithaca, NY: Cornell University Press, 1995), 166 et passim.

41. "A. A. Krasil'nikova (Zhenshchina Georgievskii kavalier)," *Zhenshchina i voina* 1 (March 5, 1915): 11.

42. Ibid.

43. Quoted in Rheta Childe Dorr, *Inside the Russian Revolution* (New York: Macmillan, 1917), 75.

44. "Odna iz mnogikh," 20.

45. "Young Girls Fighting on the Russian Front," *Current History,* May 1916: 366.

46. Ibid.

47. Her medal was awarded under the name Evgenii Makarov, the male pseudonym she used to enlist. See Iu. N. Ivanova, "Prekrasneishchie iz khrabrykh," *Voenno-istoricheskii zhurnal* 3 (1994): 94.

48. "Young Girls Fighting on the Russian Front," 366.

49. Ibid., 367.

50. "Devuskha-voin'?" in "Zhenshchiny geroi," special issue, *Voina* 24 (1915): 5

51. "Zhenshchiny i voina," *Zhenskii vestnik* (March 1915): 73

52. "Warrior Women," 42.

53. "Zhenshchiny i voina," *Zhenskii vestnik* 4 (April 1915): 93.

54. "Partizanki-zhenshchiny," in "Zhenshchiny geroi," special issue, *Voina* 24 (1915): 6.

55. Ibid., 7.

56. Ibid., 5, 8.

57. Princess Kati Dadeshkeliani, *Princess in Uniform,* trans. Arthur Ashton (London: G. Bell and Sons, 1934).

58. Ibid., 96.

59. Ibid., 97.

60. Ibid., 96.

61. "Zhenshchiny geroi," special issue, *Voina* 24 (1915): 8.

62. "Girl Made Lieutenant," *New York Times*, April 26, 1915: 3.

63. "Warrior Women," 42; "Russia: Women and the War," *Jus Suffragi* 9 (July 1, 1915): 322.

64. "L. P. Tychinina," in "Zhenshchiny geroi," special issue, *Voina* 24 (1915): 4; "Odna iz mnogikh," 19; and "Voina i mir: Kursistka Tychinina," *Zhenshchina* 3 (February 1, 1915): 32. There is a slight discrepancy in the account presented in this last journal, which reports that Tychinina enlisted as "Aleksandr Nikolaev" rather than "Anatolii Tychinin," as reported in the other two sources.

65. *Zhenshchina i voina* 1 (March 5, 1915): 14; "Girl Wins War Honor," *New York Times*, February 7, 1915: 3. Natalia also used the name Antolii Tychinin to enlist.

66. "Zhenshchiny i voina," *Zhenskii vestnik* 4 (April 1915): 93–94.

67. "Voina i mir: Devushka-geroi," *Zhenshchina* 3 (February 1, 1915): 32.

68. "Odna iz mnogikh," 19–20.

69. "Devuskha-dobravol'tsa," in "Zhenshchiny geroi," special issue, *Voina* 24 (1915): 5–6.

70. Igor Kobzev, "'Kavelerist-Devitsa' iz Cheka," *Rodina* 8–9 (1993): 75–77.

71. "Odna iz mnogikh," 20, and "Zhenshchiny geroi," special issue, *Voina* 24 (1915): 6.

72. "M. N. Isaakova," in "Zhenshchiny geroi," special issue, *Voina* 24 (1915): 4.

73. *Times* (London), September 1914: 8; "Odna iz mnogikh," 19.

74. "Girls Don Uniforms, Fight as Soldiers," *New York Times*, November 3, 1915: 3.

75. "Russia: Women and War," *Jus Suffragi*, February 1, 1917: 74.

76. V. V. Brusianin, *Voina, zhenshchiny i deti* (Petrograd: Mechny Put', 1917), 64.

77. "Razvedchik Alekseev," in "Zhenshchiny geroi," special issue, *Voina* 24 (1915): 8–9.

78. "Zhenshchiny i voina," *Zhenskii vestnik*, April 1914: 94.

79. "Zhenshchiny-Dobrovol'sty," 10.

80. *Jus Suffragi*, November 1914: 190; "Russia: Women and the War," *Jus Suffragi*, May 1, 1915: 290.

81. *Zhenskoe delo* 9 (May 1, 1915): 9.

82. *Zhenskii vestnik* (January 1916): 21.

83. "Zhenshchiny i voina," *Zhenskii vestnik* (January 1916): 21.

84. "Russia: Women and War," *Jus Suffragi*, February 1, 1917: 74.

85. Maria Bochkareva, M. N. Isaakova, Princess Kudasheva, Margarita Kokovtseva, Elena Choba, and Tatiana Kaldinkhina, to name a few.

86. Shane O'Rourke, "Women in a Warrior Society: Don Cossack Women, 1860–1914," in *Women in Russia and Ukraine*, ed. Rosalind Marsh (Cambridge: Cambridge University Press, 1996), 46–50.

87. "Dobrovolets-Kazachka," in "Zhenshchiny geroi," special issue, *Voina* 24 (1915): 6; "Girls Don Uniforms, Fight as Soldiers, 3."

88. "Zhenshchiny i voina," *Zhenskii vestnik* 11 (November 1915): 21.

89. "Warrior Women," 42. This report claims that Kokovtseva held the rank of colonel, in command of the 6th Ural Cossack Regiment, but that is highly unlikely.

90. "Russkaia Amazonka," in "Zhenshchiny geroi," special issue, *Voina* 24 (1915): 12.

91. Ibid.

92. Ibid., 13.

93. Ibid.

94. Marina Yurlova, *Cossack Girl* (New York: Macaulay, 1934).

95. Ibid., passim.

96. Ibid., 185.

97. Ibid., 140.

98. Botchkareva, *Yashka*, 81–83.

99. Ibid., 106.

100. The English nurse Florence Farmborough, serving with Russian forces during the war, reported having treated several women soldiers serving with male units during the summer of 1917, even after the all-female military formations had been created. See Farmborough, *Nurse at the Russian Front*, 204.

CHAPTER THREE.
RUSSIA'S FIRST ALL-FEMALE COMBAT UNIT

1. Of the women who enlisted in these sexually segregated formations, only those whose units maintained records that were preserved are known. More than 5,000 women became members of these official military formations. To this number must be added those in the many units that were formed unofficially by grassroots women's organizations, as well as those who were part of official units with incomplete or missing personnel lists.

2. William Henry Chamberlin, *The Russian Revolution, 1917–1921*, vol. 1 (New York: Macmillan, 1935), 73.

3. During the Revolution of 1905, members of the Russian workers' movement organized councils, called "soviets," to represent the interests of workers. The most important of these was the St. Petersburg Soviet, created in the capital and headed by Lev Trotsky.

4. Sheila Fitzpatrick, *The Russian Revolution, 1917–1932* (Oxford: Oxford University Press, 1990), 34.

5. John M. Thompson, *Revolutionary Russia, 1917* (New York: Charles Scribner's Sons, 1981), 33.

6. Ibid., 30.

7. Richard Abraham, *Alexander Kerensky: The First Love of the Revolution* (New York: Columbia University Press, 1987), 192–193.

8. "Resolution of the All-Russian Conference of the Soviet of Workers' and Soldiers' Deputies," in *Documents of Russian History, 1914–1917*, ed. Frank Alfred Golder, trans. Emanuel Aronsberg (New York: Century, 1927), 332.

9. See John Bushnell, *Mutiny amid Repression: Russian Soldiers in the Revolution of 1905–1906* (Bloomington: Indiana University Press, 1985).

10. Allan Wildman, *The Old Army and the Soldiers' Revolt (March–April 1917)*, vol. 1 of *The End of the Russian Imperial Army* (Princeton, NJ: Princeton University Press, 1980), 35.

11. See Wildman, *The Old Army and the Soldiers' Revolt*, 77–78, 178, 182–191, 229–230, and 377–378; Nikolai N. Golovin, *The Russian Army in the World War* (New Haven, CT: Yale University Press, 1931), chaps. 10 and 11; Louise Erwin Heenan, *Russian Democracy's Fatal Blunder: The Summer Offensive of 1917* (New York: Praeger, 1987), chap. 7, for discussions of soldiers' attitudes about the war.

12. Joshua Sanborn, "Drafting the Nation: Military Conscription and the Formation of a Modern Polity in Tsarist and Soviet Russia, 1905–1925" (Ph.D. diss., University of Chicago, 1998), 87.

13. Wildman, *The Old Army and the Soldiers' Revolt*, 100–101.

14. Ibid., 236.

15. W. Bruce Lincoln, *Passage through Armageddon: The Russians in War and Revolution, 1914–1918* (New York: Simon and Schuster, 1986), 350.

16. N. G. Ross, "Popytka sozdaniia ruskoi revoliutsionnoi armii (Mai–Iiun' 1917 g.)," *Novyi chasvoi* 1 (1994): 76.

17. Heenan, *Russian Democracy's Fatal Blunder*, xiv.

18. Quoted in Allan Wildman, *The Road to Soviet Power and Peace*, vol. 2 of *The End of the Russian Imperial Army* (Princeton, NJ: Princeton University Press, 1987), 74.

19. Wildman, *The Old Army and the Soldiers' Revolt*, 362–363.

20. Ross, "Popytka sozdaniia ruskoi revoliutsionnoi armii," 75.

21. Heenan, *Russian Democracy's Fatal Blunder*, xii.

22. "The Soviet and War Aims," in Golder, *Documents of Russian History, 1914–1917*, 331.

23. Alexander F. Kerensky, *The Catastrophe: Kerensky's Own Story of the Russian Revolution* (New York: D. Appleton, 1927), 195.

24. "Resolution of the All-Russian Congress of Workers' and Soldiers' Deputies," 332.

25. A. S. Senin, *Voennoe ministerstvo Vremennogo pravitel'stva* (Moscow: Privately published, 1995) 173.

26. "Telegramma gen. Brusilova Verx. Glavnokomanuiushchemu," May 16, 1917, in *Razlozhenie Armii v 1917 godu*, ed. N. E. Kakurin and Ia. A. Iakovlev (Moscow: Gosudarstvennoe izdatel'stvo, 1925), 64.

27. "Plan formirovaniia revoliutsionnykh batal'onov iz volunterov tyla," June 13, 1917, in Kakurin and Iakovlev, *Razlozhenie Armii v 1917 godu*, 73.

28. "Doklad Vseross. ts. i. k. po organizatsii dobrovol'cheskoi revoliutsionnoi armii," June 30, 1917, in Kakurin and Iakovlev, *Razlozhenie Armii v 1917 godu*, 71.

29. "Telegramma gen. Kornilov," in Kakurin and Iakovlev, *Razlozhenie Armii v 1917 godu*, 75.

30. "Telegramma gen. Alekseeva Glavnokomanduiushchemu Zapadnym frontom," May 18, 1917, in Kakurin and Iakovlev, *Razlozhenie Armii v 1917 godu*, 65.

31. Viktor Shklovsky, *A Sentimental Journey: Memoirs, 1917–1922*, trans. Richard Sheldon (Ithaca, NY: Cornell University Press, 1970), 30.

32. Ibid.

33. "Prikraz No. 561 armiiam Iugo-Zapadnogo fronta," May 22, 1917, in Kakurin and Iakovlev, *Razlozhenie Armii v 1917 godu*, 68–69.

34. Wildman, *The Road to Soviet Power and Peace*, 79.

35. "Prikraz No. 561 armiiam Iugo-Zapadnogo fronta"; and "Prisiaga revoliutsionogo-voluntera," in Kakurin and Iakovlev, *Razlozhenie Armii v 1917 godu*, 68–69.

36. Kakurin and Iakovlev, *Razlozhenie Armii v 1917 godu*, 68–69.

37. General Brusilov's directive of May 22, 1917, quoted in Wildman, *The Old Army and the Soldiers' Revolt*, 79.

38. "Prisiaga revoliutsionogo-voluntera," 69–70.

39. Melissa K. Stockdale, "'My Death for the Motherland Is Happiness': Women, Patrio-

tism, and Soldiering in Russia's Great War, 1914–1917," *American Historical Review* 1 (February 2004): 92.

40. Bernard Pares, *My Russian Memoirs* (London: Jonathan Cape, 1935), 449–451, quotation on 449. The British, as well as the other Allies, were keenly interested in ensuring that Russia remained in the war, and Britain sent a variety of missions to Russia to help to see to this.

41. "Voennyi soiuz Lichnago Primera," *Petrogradskii listok*, June 9, 1917: 5.

42. "Vozzvanie," in Kakurin and Iakovleva, *Razlozhenie Armii v 1917 godu*, 69.

43. Pares, *My Russian Memoirs*, 473.

44. Report on the program activities of the Women's Volunteer Committee of the Military League, RGVIA, f. 366, op. 1, d. 90, l. 50.

45. This appeal appeared in *Russkoe slovo*, June 2, 1917: 3; *Russkii invalid*, June 4, 1917: 4; and *Iskry* 23 (June 18, 1917): 183. See appendix B for another example of such appeals published in prominent periodicals of the day.

46. *Russkie vedomosti*, June 16, 1917: 4.

47. *Russkii invalid*, May 7, 1917: 3.

48. V. Poznakhirev, "Zhenskaia gvardiia Kerenskago," *Sovietskii patriot* 41 (October 1991): 12.

49. "Zhenshchiny geroi," special issue, *Voina* 24 (1915): 9.

50. Valentina Kostyleva, "Nashi Amazonki," *Zhenskaia zhizn'* 19 (October 1, 1914): 24.

51. Richard Stites, *The Women's Liberation Movement in Russia: Feminism, Nihilism, and Bolshevism, 1860–1930* (Princeton, NJ: Princeton University Press, 1978), 292.

52. *Ogonek* 25 (July 2, 1917): 397.

53. "Organizatsiia bol'nykh i ranenykh voinov v Petrograde," *Russkii invalid*, May 25, 1917: 4.

54. Stites, *The Women's Liberation Movement in Russia*, 294.

55. "Zhenshchiny idut na front!" *Petrogradskii listok*, May 26, 1917: 2; "Zhenskii Voenno-Narodnyi Soiuz Dobrovol'stev—Manifest," *Novoe vremia*, June 8, 1917: 5; Sofia Zarechnaia, "Amazonki velikoi voiny," *Zhenskoe delo* 14 (July 1, 1917): 10–11.

56. "Vozzvanie Zhenskogo Soiuza," *Rech'*, May 28, 1917: 6.

57. "800 Amazonok," *Petrogradskii listok*, May 28, 1917: 4.

58. "Pismo zhenschshiny-doborvol'tsa Voennomu Ministru," in Kakurin and Iakovlev, *Razlozhenie Armii v 1917 godu*, 70.

59. "Zhenshchiny-soldaty," *Petrogradskii listok*, May 25, 1917: 13.

60. Report of the Organizational Committee of the Women's Military Unit to the minister of war, Alexander Kerensky, RGVIA, f. 2000, op. 2, d. 1557, l. 3.

61. "Zhenskie marshevye otriadi," GUCSh, Department of Organization and Service of Troops, RGVIA, f. 2000, op. 2, d. 1557, l. 4.

62. Telegram to the minister of war from the All-Russian Women's Military Union to Aid the Motherland, RGVIA, f. 2000, op. 2, d. 1557, ll. 15 and 194.

63. "Zhenshchiny-voiny," *Novoe vremia*, June 1, 1917: 2.

64. Maria Botchkareva [sic], *Yashka: My Life as Peasant, Officer and Exile*, as told to Isaac Don Levine (New York: Frederick A. Stokes, 1919). Sergei Drokov provides more accurate information about Bochkareva's life in works including "Organizator zhenskogo batal'ona smerti," *Voprosy istorii* 7 (1993): 164–169; "Yashka: O komandire zhenskogo

batal'ona smerti," *Ogonek* 24 (June 1992); and "Protokoly doprosov organizatora Petrograd-skogo zhenskogo batal'ona smerti," *Otechestvennye arkhivy* 1 (1994): 50–66.

65. Drokov, "Protokoly doprosov organizatora Petrogradskogo zhenskogo batal'ona smerti," 51.

66. Botchkareva, *Yashka*, 45.

67. Ibid., 28.

68. Ibid., 81.

69. Ibid., 83, 87–88, and 144.

70. Other women were awarded the St. George's Cross, but the majority were either disguised as men or were serving in medical capacities.

71. Botchkareva, *Yashka*, 126.

72. Ibid., 135.

73. Nicoletta Gullace, "White Feathers and Wounded Men: Female Patriotism and the Memory of the Great War," *Journal of British Studies* 36, 2 (April 1997): 184 et passim.

74. Maurice Richards, ed., *Posters of the First World War* (London: Evelyn, Adams and McKay, 1968), 10.

75. Gullace, "White Feathers and Wounded Men," 184.

76. Botchkareva, *Yashka*, 156–161.

77. This conspicuous absence in the writings of these men, who were intimately involved with the project, may seem suspicious to the reader, but as the creation of the women's unit was controversial and failed to accomplish the goal of improving troop morale, they may have been embarrassed or otherwise reluctant to speak of a failed efforts. This is particularly poignant in light of views that considered the Provisional Government so weak and desperate that it was forced to turn to women for its defense.

78. "Pismo voennomu ministru ot dobrovol'tsa-mladshego unter-of. 28 Polotskago Polka, kavaliera Geor. Kresta i 3 medalei, Marii Bochkarevoi," RGVIA, f. 366, op. 1, d. 90, l. 4.

79. Telegram to the chief of staff of GUGSh from the Office of the Minister of War, May 31, 1917, RGVIA, f. 366, op. 1, d. 90, l. 5.

80. Boris Solonevich, *Zhenshchina s vintovkoi: Istoricheskii roman* (Buenos Aires: Privately published, 1955) (the "slightly fictionalized memoirs" of Nina Krylova), 34.

81. Ibid., 40.

82. The only official personnel lists for this unit that have been located deal with its composition at the front following its first participation in battle. Both Bochkareva and Krylova assert that 2,000 women enlisted initially, although there is some discrepancy between their accounts of the recruitment meetings. Krylova says the assembly she attended was held at the Cinizelli Circus at 11:00 AM on May 21, 1917, where 3,500 women signed up to join the unit, but only 2,000 actually showed up the next day for registration. Bochkareva speaks only of a meeting at the Mariinskii Theater on the same day, in the evening, where 1,500 were recruited, and notes that an additional 500 enlisted the next day.

83. Solonevich, *Zhenshchina s vintovkoi*. Krylova's account is the only other by a member of Bochkareva's unit, and although the accuracy of the text is questionable in places, the work largely corroborates Bochkareva's and provides insight into many aspects of the unit's life that only a firsthand participant would be able to relate. Therefore it is a valuable source in reconstructing the history of this pioneering unit.

84. Botchkareva, *Yashka*, 164.

85. "Zhenskie marshevye otriadi."

86. Solonevich, *Zhenshchina s vintovkoi*, 54; "Zhenshchiny idut na front," 2; "Zhenskii Batal'on Smerti," *Niva* 26 (June 30, 1917): 394.

87. "Zhenshchiny voennye," *Petrogradskii vistok*, 6 August 1917: 3.

88. Rheta Childe Dorr, *Inside the Russian Revolution* (New York: Macmillan, 1917), 56.

89. "Zhenskii Batal'on Smerti," *Ogonek* 23 (June 28, 1917): 360; Solonevich, *Zhenshchina s vintovkoi*, 54.

90. Dorr, *Inside the Russian Revolution*, 56–57, and Bessie Beatty, *The Red Heart of Russia* (New York: Century, 1919), 100–101. Dorr and Beatty were among a number of American journalists in Russia during the revolutionary year. They both expressed great interest in the women soldiers, spending time with them in training and devoting significant portions of their books to them.

91. Dorr, *Inside the Russian Revolution*, 56.

92. "Zhenskii Voenno-Narodnyi Soiuz Dobrovol'stev—Manifest," 5; Beatty, *The Red Heart of Russia*, 101–102.

93. Dorr, *Inside the Russian Revolution*, 58.

94. Solonevich, *Zhenshchina s vintovkoi*, 62.

95. Poorly fitting uniforms were not uncommon in the Russian army, even for male soldiers.

96. Solonevich, *Zhenshchina s vintovkoi*, 48.

97. Ibid., 56. The tremendous public interest in the women soldiers will be explored in detail in chapter 7.

98. "Zhenskii Batal'on Smerti," *Ogonek* 23 (June 28, 1917): 360.

99. Solonevich, *Zhenshchina s vintovkoi*, 51.

100. Ibid., 58.

101. Quoted in ibid., 50.

102. "800 Amazonok," 4.

103. Botchkareva, *Yashka*, 164–168.

104. Ibid.

105. A number of these women would eventually join another, more democratic women's unit, the 1st Petrograd Women's Battalion, formed in the capital shortly after the formation of Bochkareva's battalion. For details regarding this unit, see chapter 5.

106. Solonevich, *Zhenshchina s vintovkoi*, 65.

107. L. Borobevskii, "Batal'on smerti," *Rabochii i Soldat* 7 (July 30, 1917): 3–4.

108. Botchkareva, *Yashka*, 195–196.

109. For more complete coverage and analysis of public opinion, see chapter 7.

110. Quoted in Solonevich, *Zhenshchina s vintovkoi*, 75.

111. Botchkareva, *Yashka*, 169.

112. Solonevich, *Zhenshchina s vintovkoi*, 85.

113. Ibid., 184–186.

114. Abraham, *Alexander Kerensky*, 218.


## CHAPTER FOUR. THE WOMEN'S MILITARY MOVEMENT

1. "Vopl' zhenshchin iz derevni," *Birzhevyia vedomosti*, May 18, 1917: 5. This poem was

posted around the city of Novgorod in mid-May 1917, calling for women "from the country-side" to join the war effort.

2. These include two infantry units and two communications detachments formed in Petrograd, one infantry unit and two communications detachments formed in Moscow, one infantry unit in Ekaterinodar, five communications detachments in Kiev, and two communications detachments in Saratov.

3. These include units of various sizes and designations formed in Kiev, Tashkent, Baku, Mariupol', Odessa, Perm, Minsk, Viatka, Poltava, and Simbirsk.

4. "Zhenskii dobrovol'cheskii komitet," *Armiia i flot svobodnoi Rossii*, July 2, 1917: 3.

5. "Ustav Vserossiskago voennago zhenskago soiza 'Pomoshchi Rodine,'" RGVIA, f. 2000, op. 2, d. 1557, l. 194.

6. Senin, "Zhenskie batal'ony i voennye komandy v 1917 godu," *Voprosy istorii* 10 (1987): 177.

7. "Dokladnaia zapiska voennomu ministru iz Organizatsionogo Komiteta Zhenskei Armii," RGVIA, f. 2000, op. 2, d. 1557, l. 48.

8. "Zhenshchiny-voiny," *Novoe vremia*, June 1, 1917: 2.

9. Coded telegram from the military agent in England, OGENKVAR, August 1, 1917, RGVIA, f. 2000, op. 2, d. 1557, l. 62.

10. "Zhenshchiny-soldaty," *Petrogradskii listok*, May 25, 1917: 13.

11. "Zhenskii 'Batal'on Smerti,'" *Utro Rossii*, June 2, 1917: 4; "Zhenskiia Voennyia Organizatsii: Soiuz aktivnoi pomoshchi rodine," *Utro Rossii*, June 6, 1917: 6.

12. Telegram from the quartermaster general of Stavka to the commander of the southwestern front, in *Razlozhenie Armii v 1917 godu*, ed. N. E. Kakurin and Ia. A. Iakovlev. (Moscow: Gosudarstvennoe izdatel'stvo, 1925), 72.

13. "Zhenskii 'Kuren' Smerti,'" *Utro Rossii*, July 22, 1917: 5.

14. Telegram to the minister of war from the commissar of the Kuban Oblast, Ekaterinodar, RGVIA, f. 2000, op. 2, d. 1557, l. 22.

15. Ob"iavlennie: "Zhenshchiny-Grazhdanki!" RGVIA, f. 2000, op. 2, d. 1557, l. 75.

16. "Ob organizatsii zhenshchin-dobrovol'tsev," from *Listok voiny* (Ekaterinodar), June 17, 1917, 4, in RGVIA, f. 2000, op. 2, d. 1557, l. 77.

17. "Protokol organizatsionnago sobraniia zhenshchin volonterok," RGVIA, f. 2000, op. 2, d. 1557, l. 73.

18. Letter to the minister of war from the Organizational Committee of the Saratov Women's Shock Battalion, July 14, 1917, RGVIA, f. 2000, op. 2, d. 1557, l. 46.

19. Letter to the minister of war, RGVIA, f. 2000, op. 2, d. 1557, l. 9.

20. Evgeniia Piatunina, "Russkie Zhanny d'Ark: Vospominaniia udarnitsy zhenskago batal'ona," *Nezavisimaia gazeta*, March 4, 2000: 2.

21. "Batal'ony smerti," *Russkoe slovo*, July 15, 1917: 4.

22. Telegram to GUGSh, Petrograd, from Odessa, RGVIA, f. 2000, op. 2, d. 1557, l. 112.

23. Telegram to the chief of staff from Tashkent, June 16, 1917, RGVIA, f. 2000, op. 2, d. 1557, l. 23.

24. "Simbirskii zhenskii 'batal'on smerti,'" *Ogonek* 29 (July 30, 1917): 454.

25. Telegram to Minister of War Kerensky from Ekaterinburg, June 14, 1917, RGVIA, f. 2000, op. 2, d. 1557, l. 24.

26. Telegram from the 6th Section to the 1st Section of the Department of Organization

and Service of Troops, GUGSh, RGVIA, f. 2000, op. 2, d. 1557, l. 104; Telegram from the Mobilization Department to the Department of Organization and Service of Troops, RGVIA, f. 2000, op. 2, d. 1557, l. 106.

27. Kakurin and Iakovlev, *Razlozhenie Armii v 1917 godu,* 73.

28. Telegram to Minister of War Kerensky from Mariupol', June 30, 1917, RGVIA, f. 2000, op. 2, d. 1557, l. 40.

29. "Zhenskii batal'on smerti v gorode Baku," *Ogonek* 33 (August 27, 1917): 520.

30. Memorandum from GUGSh, RGVIA, f. 2000, op. 2, d. 1557, l. 79.

31. Telegram from Pavlgrad to Petrograd, June 15, 1917, RGVIA, f. 2000, op. 2, d. 1557, l. 20.

32. Telegram from the adjutant general of the commander in chief of Western Front to the chief of staff of the Tenth Army, July 8–9, 1917, RGVIA, f. 2277, op. 1, d. 368, l. 81; Telegram to the chief of staff of the Western Front, RGVIA, f. 2003, op. 2, d. 349, l. 42.

33. This and the following quotation are from "Polozhenie o Minskoi otdel'noi karaul'noi druzhine iz zhenshchin-dobrovol'tsev," RGVIA, f. 2003, op. 2, d. 349, l. 44.

34. Ibid.

35. Ibid.

36. This and the following quotation are from Telegram from the duty officer (adjutant general) of the staff of the commander in chief of the Army of the Western Front to the chief of staff of the Tenth Army, July 8–9, 1917, RGVIA, f. 2277, op. 1, t. 368, l. 81.

37. Telegram to GUGSH, Petrograd, from Odessa, RGVIA, f. 2000, op. 2, d. 1557, l. 112.

38. Telegram from the chief of staff of the Petrograd Military District, Mobilization Department, to the chief of staff of the Department of Organization and Service of Troops in GUGSh, July 24, 1917, RGVIA, f. 2000, op. 2, d. 1557, l. 59.

39. "Dokladnaia zapiska po Glavnomu Upravlenniiu Generalnago Shtaba o formirovanii voiskovykh chastei iz zhenshchin-dobrovol'tsev," RGVIA, f. 2000, op. 2, d. 1557, l. 8.

40. Telegram from the Department of Organization and Service of Troops, June 12, 1917, RGVIA, f. 2000, op. 2, d. 1557, l. 14.

41. "O formirovanii voiskovykh chastei iz zhenshchin-dobrovol'stev," June 18, 1917, RGVIA, f. 2000, op. 2, d. 1557, ll. 29–32. The ruble was worth approximately $0.51 U.S. in June–July 1917. The information on pay for male soldiers can be found in RGVIA, f. 29, op. 3, d. 1613, l. 12.

42. Order from GUGSh, RGVIA, f. 2000, op. 2, d. 1557, l. 8.

43. "Zhenskaia Armiia," *Novoe vremia,* June 2, 1917: 3.

44. "Zhenskiia Voennyia Organizatsiia: Soiuz aktivnoi pomoshchi rodine," *Utro Rossii,* June 6, 1917: 6.

45. Report from the chairman of the Women's Military Union in Petrograd, June 27, 1917, RGVIA, f. 2000, op. 2, d. 1557, l. 54.

46. Extract from the journal of the Main Council of the Military League: Report on the project activities of the Volunteer Women's Committee, June 29, 1917, RGVIA, f. 366, op. 1, d. 90, l. 50.

47. "Conscription of Women for War Work," in *Documents of Russian History, 1914–1917,* ed. Frank Alfred Golder, trans. Emanuel Aronsberg (Gloucester, MA: Peter Smith, 1964), 422.

48. Ibid.

49. Report by the chairman of the Central Executive Committee on the Formation of Revolutionary Battalions under Stavka, September 7, 1917, RGVIA, f. 2003, op. 2, d. 349, l. 31.

50. Report to the Main Directorate of the General Staff, June 25, 1917, RGVIA, f. 2000, op. 2, d. 1557, l. 51.

51. "Dlia soobshcheniia v pechati," RGVIA, f. 2000, op. 2, d. 1557, l. 52; "Zhenshchin-dobrovol'tsev," *Petrogradskii listok*, June 28, 1917: 3.

52. Report of GUGSh, RGVIA, f. 29, op. 3, d. 1603, l. 15.

53. Secret report of the Military Council, August 16, 1917, RGVIA, f. 2000, op. 2, d. 1557, l. 114.

54. Ibid.

55. "Po voennym obstoiatel'stvam o sformirovanii zhenskogo batal'ona iz zhenshchin-dobrovol'tsev v gorode Ekaterinodare," July 31, 1917, RGVIA, f. 2000, op. 2, d. 1557, l. 100.

56. Memorandum from GUGSh, July 31, RGVIA, f. 2000, op. 2, d. 1557, l. 79.

57. Ibid.

58. Ibid.

59. Ibid.

60. Telegram from the adjutant general of the commander in chief of the Western Front to the chief of staff of the Tenth Army, July 8–9, 1917.

61. Louise Erwin Heenan, *Russian Democracy's Fatal Blunder: The Summer Offensive of 1917* (New York: Praeger, 1987), 118.

62. Richard Abraham, *Alexander Kerensky: The First Love of the Revolution* (New York: Columbia University Press, 1987), 218.

63. Bessie Beatty, *The Red Heart of Russia* (New York: Century, 1919), 103.

64. Krylova says that the use of the word "detachment" (Russian *komanda*) rather than "battalion" was a technical error and that although the women soldiers were highly offended by it, nothing was done about it. Boris Solonevich, *Zhenshchina s vintovkoi: Istoricheskii roman* (Buenos Aires: Privately published, 1955) (the "slightly fictionalized memoirs" of Nina Krylova), 85.

65. There are numerous accounts of this event: Maria Botchkareva [*sic*], *Yashka: My Life as Peasant, Officer and Exile*, as told to Isaac Don Levine (New York: Frederick A. Stokes, 1919), 189–190; Beatty, *The Red Heart of Russia*, 103–104; Solonevich, *Zhenshchina s vintovkoi*, 85; and a number of contemporary periodical accounts: "Zhenskii Batal'on Smerti," *Niva* 26 (June 30, 1917): 394–395; "Shestvie zhenskoi komady smerti," *Petrogradskii listok*, June 22, 1917: 3; "Batal'on smerti," *Iskry* 25 (July 2, 1917): 198. The story in *Iskry* even reported (inaccurately) that Olga Kerenskaia would be going to the front with Bochkareva's unit as a nurse.

66. "Sbor v polzu zhenskogo batal'iona smerti," *Russkii invalid*, June 23, 1917: 4.

67. "Shestvie zhenskoi komandy smerti, *Petrogradskii listok*, June 22, 1917: 3.

68. There is some discrepancy on the date of the unit's departure for the front. Drokov and a number of contemporary periodicals list the date as June 23, Dorr, Bochkareva, and other press sources give the twenty-fourth, and Krylova, the twenty-fifth.

69. "Docheri otechestva: Batal'on smerti—na front," *Petrogradskii listok*, June 24, 1917: 3. It is curious that the Russian Orthodox Church seems to have sanctioned the women's unit, despite the deeply entrenched patriarchy and misogyny of the institution. However, the

church had also traditionally been a staunch supporter of the state and therefore may have given its blessing (literally) as a way of helping shore up the government.

70. Botchkareva, *Yashka*, 192–193; Rheta Childe Dorr, *Inside the Russian Revolution* (New York: Macmillan, 1917), 60–62; Solonevich, *Zhenshchina s vintovkoi*, 95.

71. Telegram from the chief of staff of the Petrograd District to the chief of staff of Supreme High Command, June 6, 1917, in Kakurin and Iakovleva, *Razlozhenie Armii v 1917 godu*, 72.

72. Dorr, *Inside the Russian Revolution*, 65; Botchkareva, *Yashka*, 193–194.

73. Botchkareva, *Yashka*, 195–196.

74. Dorr, *Inside the Russian Revolution*, 70; Botchkareva, *Yashka*, 201.

75. Botchkareva, *Yashka*, 202–203.

76. Ibid., 208.

77. The reactions of male military personnel to the women soldiers will be explored in depth in chapter 7.

78. Report of July 5, journal of the military actions of the 132nd Infantry Division from July 1 to August 31, 1917, RGVIA, f. 2445, op. 1, d. 53, l. 2.

79. "Boevoi prikaz no. 11, 7-go Iulia 1917," battle orders of the 525th Kiuruk-Darinskii Infantry Regiment, RGVIA, f. 3058, op. 1, d. 4, l. 1.

80. Telegram to the general quartermaster of the army, chief of staff of the corps, July 6, 1917, RGVIA, f. 2277, op. 1, d. 102, l. 31.

81. Solonevich, *Zhenshchina s vintovkoi*, 107.

82. "Boevoi prikaz no. 11, 7-go Iulia 1917"; "Posledovatelnoe opisanie voennykh deistvii," journal of military actions of the 525th Kiuruk-Darinskii Regiment, RGVIA, f. 3058, op. 1, d. 11, l. 1.

83. "Boevoi prikaz no. 11, 7-go Iulia 1917."

84. Solonevich, *Zhenshchina s vintovkoi*, 209.

85. Telegram: operational correspondence of the I Siberian Army Corps with the staff of the Tenth Army, RGVIA, f. 2277, op. 1, d. 102, l. 33.

86. Botchkareva, *Yashka*, 211.

87. Telegram from the chief of staff of the I Siberian Army Corp on the actions of the Women's Battalion of Death in the battle of July 9, 1917, at Novospasskii forest, RGVIA, f. 2277, op. 1, d. 1, l. 1; Solonevich, *Zhenshchina s vintovkoi*, 125–126.

88. Telegram to the chief of staff of the Tenth Army, July 9, 1917, RGVIA, f. 2277, op. 1, d. 102, l. 79 ob.; telegram to the chief of staff of the army, July 11, 1917, RGVIA, f. 2277, op. 1, d. 102, l. 105.

89. Reports from July 8–10, journal of the military actions of the 132nd Infantry Division from July 1 to August 31, 1917, RGVIA, f. 2445, op. 1, d. 53, ll. 3–6.

90. Bochkareva claims that they captured 100 German prisoners, and Krylova claims 200 captives, but the number listed in the journal of military action of the 525th Kiuruk-Darinskii Regiment is 24. "Posledovatel'noe opisanie voennykh deistvii," RGVIA, f. 3058, op. 1, d. 11, l. 1.

91. Solonevich, *Zhenshchina s vintovkoi*, 129; Dorr, *Inside the Russian Revolution*, 74.

92. "Imenoi spisok lits I-oi zhenskoi komandoi smerti, uchastvovavshchikh v boi, 9 July 1917," RGVIA, f. 2277, op. 1, d. 368, l. 9. Bessie Beatty and Louise Bryant, who claimed

they received their information from highly reliable sources, say 6 were killed and between 21 and 30 were wounded. This is fairly consistent with the official record. Bochkareva put these numbers somewhat higher, claiming 50 dead or wounded. Krylova gives an altogether unrealistic report of more than 100 dead, 192 wounded, and 8 missing. See appendix C for a list of personnel who participated in the battle.

93. Botchkareva, *Yashka*, 213.

94. Report from the chief of staff of the I Siberian Army Corps, July 13, 1917, RGVIA, f. 2277, op. 1, d. 368, l. 68.

95. Report from the chief of staff of the I Siberian Army Corps on the actions of the Petrograd Women's Battalion in the battle of July 9, 1917, at Novospasskii Forest, RGVIA, f. 2277, op. 1, d. 368, l. 1.

96. Telegram to the commander of the 525th Regiment from the commander of the 6th Company, Sublieutenant Kervich, RGVIA, f. 3058, op. 1, d. 8, l. 4.

97. Report from the commander of the 132nd Infantry Division to the chief of staff of the I Siberian Army Corps, July 13, 1917, RGVIA, f. 2277 op. 1, d. 368, l. 66.

98. Telegram from the Commander of the 1st Siberian Division, RGVIA, f. 2277, op. 1, d. 368, l. 1.

99. Ibid.

100. Telegram from the Command Staff of 132nd Infantry Division to the chief of staff of the I Siberian Army Corps, July 13, 1917, RGVIA, f. 2445, op. 1, d. 74, l 6.

101. Ibid.

## CHAPTER FIVE. THE OFFICIAL WOMEN'S COMBAT UNITS

1. See chapter 6 for a detailed account of the women's involvement in the siege of the Winter Palace.

2. Papers of Maria Bocharnikova, Bakhmeteff Archive, Columbia University Rare Book and Manuscript Library, New York.

3. Battle orders of the 525th Infantry Regiment, RGVIA, f. 3058, op. 1, d. 5; telegram to the commissar of the western front from the commissar of Supreme High Command, October 25, 1917, RGVIA, f. 2015, op. 1, d. 28, l. 29; Maria Botchkareva [*sic*], *Yashka: My Life as Peasant, Officer and Exile*, as told to Isaac Don Levine (New York: Frederick A. Stokes, 1919), 262; Boris Solonevich, *Zhenshchina s vintovkoi: Istoricheskii roman* (Buenos Aires: Privately published, 1955) (the "slightly fictionalized memoirs" of Nina Krylova), 150.

4. From notes and documents on the 1st Petrograd Women's Battalion, RGVIA, f. 16173, op. 1, d. 4, l. 29.

5. List of the staff of the Reserve Company of the 1st Petrograd Women's Battalion, RGVIA, f. 2000, op. 2, d. 1557, l. 188.

6. Maria Bocharnikova, "V zhenskom batal'one," Papers of Maria Bocharnikova. Bocharnikova also published an account of her participation in the defense of the Winter Palace: Maria Bocharnikova, "Boi v Zimnem Dvortse," *Novyi zhurnal* 68 (1962): 215–227.

7. The manuscript, entitled "Gorod Viatka i ego obyvateli," was compiled by Aleksandr

Prozorov and is located in the State Archive of Kirov Oblast. The story of volunteer S. was printed in Evgeniia Piatunina, "Russkie Zhanny d'Ark: Vospominaniia udarnitsy zhenskago batal'ona," *Nezavisimaia gazeta,* March 4, 2000: 2.

8. Overhead list, July 26, 1917, "Matters Concerning the Arms Master of the First Petrograd Women's Battalion," RGVIA, f. 16173, op. 1, d. 3, ll. 14 and 17; Telegram from the Main Artillery Administration to the commander of the 1st Petrograd Women's Battalion, August 18, 1917, RGVIA, f. 16173, op. 1, d. 3, l. 1.

9. Piatunina, "Russkie Zhanny d'Ark," 2.

10. Explanatory note regarding the liquidation of the files of the 1st Petrograd Women's Battalion because of its disbandment, RGVIA, f. 16173, op. 1. d. 1, l. 3.

11. "Prazdnik zhenskago batal'ona," *Petrogradskii listok,* August 1, 1917: 4; "Miting 1-go zhenskago voennago soiuza," *Birzhevyia vedomosti,* July 31, 1917: 4.

12. Senin, "Zhenskie batal'ony i voennye komandy v 1917 godu," *Voprosy istorii* 10 (1987): 181n.

13. Bocharnikova, "V zhenskom batal'one," 8.

14. Kapitan Shagal, "Zhenskii batal'on," *Voennaia byl'* 95 (January 1969): 5.

15. Volunteer S. calls her "Kocheryshkina" and describes her as energetic and demanding. Piatunina, "Russkie Zhanny d'Ark," 2.

16. Bocharnikova, "V zhenskom batal'one," 1.

17. Piatunina, "Russkie Zhanny d'Ark," 2.

18. Bocharnikova, "V zhenskom batal'one," 4.

19. Piatunina, "Russkie Zhanny d'Ark," 2.

20. Bocharnikova, "V zhenskom batal'one," 7.

21. Ibid., 19–20.

22. Ibid., 15.

23. Ibid., 20.

24. Shagal, "Zhenskii batal'on," 8.

25. Bocharnikova, "V zhenskom batal'one," 11.

26. Telegram from the quartermaster general of the Headquarters of the Petrograd Military District to the chief of the Department of Organization and Service of Troops at GUGSh, October 17, 1917, RGVIA, f. 2000, op. 2, d. 1557, l. 203.

27. Telegram from Stavka to GUGSh, RGVIA, f. 2003, op. 2, d. 349, l. 50.

28. The story of the 1st Petrograd Women's Battalion will be completed in chapter 6.

29. "Zhenskiia voennyia organizatsiia: Soiuz aktivnoi pomoshchi rodine," *Utro Rossii,* June 6, 1917: 6.

30. "Soiuz 'Zhenshchina za otechestvo,'" *Vremia,* June 28, 1917: 2.

31. "Zhenskii 'batal'on smerti,'" *Utro Rossii,* June 2, 1917: 4.

32. "Zhenskii batal'on," *Russkoe slovo,* June 17, 1917: 4.

33. Telegram to the chief of staff of the Moscow Military District from Petrograd, June 20, 1917, RGVIA, f. 3474, op. 2, d. 10, l. 2.

34. "Ot Komandira zhenskogo batal'ona," *Vremia,* June 26, 1917: 2; Order no. 2, RGVIA, f. 3474, op. 2, d. 5, ll. 5–6.

35. Order no. 1 of the 2nd Moscow Women's Battalion of Death, June 22, 1917, RGVIA, f. 3474, op. 2, d. 12, l. 7

36. Documents of the 2nd Moscow Women's Battalion of Death, Orders no. 1–124, RGVIA, f. 3474, op. 2, d. 5, passim.

37. See appendix D for the tables of organization of the 2nd Moscow Women's Battalion of Death.

38. Telegram from the chief of staff of the Moscow Military District to the Office of the District Quartermaster General and the commander of the Aleksandrov Military College, June 18, 1917, RGVIA, f. 3474, op. 2, d. 10, l. 1.

39. Order no. 2 to the 2nd Moscow Women's Battalion of Death, June 28, 1917, RGVIA, f. 3474, op. 2, d. 5, l. 5.

40. Ibid.

41. Order no. 3 to the 2nd Moscow Women's Battalion of Death, June 29, 1917, RGVIA, f. 3474, op. 2, d. 5, l. 7.

42. "Attestantsionyi spisok iunkerov Moskovskago Zhenskago Batal'ona Smerti," RGVIA, f. 725, op. 54, d. 489, l. 19.

43. Order no. 2 to the 2nd Moscow Women's Battalion of Death, June 28, 1917, RGVIA, f. 3474, op. 2, d. 5, l. 5.

44. Order no. 3 to the 2nd Moscow Women's Battalion of Death, June 29, 1917, RGVIA, f. 3474, op. 2, d. 5, l. 7.

45. See appendix E for a list of the women enrolled in officer training.

46. Personal documents of the women volunteers of the Battalion of Death, 1917, RGVIA, f. 3474, op. 1, d. 13, passim.

47. "Zhenskii 'batal'on smerti," Utro Rossii, June 28, 1917: 5.

48. Ibid.

49. Documents of the 2nd Moscow Women's Battalion of Death, RGVIA, f. 3474, op. 2, d. 5, l. 7.

50. "Blagoslovenie zhenskogo batal'ona," Vremia, June 28, 1917: 2; "Moskovskii Zhenskii 'Batal'on Smerti,'" Ogonek 28 (July 23, 1917): 443.

51. "M-ss Pankhurst v Moskve," Russkoe slovo, August 6, 1917: 4.

52. Botchkareva, Yashka, 222.

53. "Zhenskii batal'on," Russkoe slovo, August 1, 1917: 4.

54. "Miting i sbor dlia zhenskago batal'ona," Vremia, June 23, 1917: 2; "Zhenskii batal'on," Vremia, June 27, 1917: 2.

55. Louise Bryant, Six Red Months in Russia: An Observer's Account of Russia before and during the Proletarian Dictatorship (New York: George H. Doran, 1918), 211–212.

56. Resolution of the company committees of the 2nd Moscow Women's Battalion of Death, RGVIA, f. 3474, op. 1, d. 61.

57. See chapter 7 for more complete analysis of reactions to the women soldiers.

58. "Zhenskii udarnyi batal'on," Vremia, August 11, 1917: 2.

59. Telegram from the duty general of the southwestern front, October 4, 1917, RGVIA, f. 2003, op. 2, d. 349, l. 39.

60. Documents of the 2nd Moscow Women's Battalion of Death, Orders no. 95, 98, 100, 101, 103, 110, 111, and 115, RGVIA, f. 3474, op. 2, d. 5, ll. 163, 167, 171, 172, and 175.

61. Documents of the 2nd Moscow Women's Battalion of Death, Orders no. 105, 107, 117, and 124, RGVIA, f. 3474, op. 2, d. 5, ll. 177, 179–182, and 199.

62. Telegram from the chief of staff of the Headquarters of the Armies of the Western Front to the adjutant general of the Supreme High Command, November 1, 1917, RGVIA, f. 2003, op. 2, d. 349, l. 54.

63. Ibid.

64. Senin, "Zhenskie batal'ony i voennye komandy v 1917 godu," 182.

65. Announcement put out in the Kuban Oblast, "Women Citizens," RGVIA, f. 2000, op. 2, d. 1557, l. 75.

66. Report from the representative of the Organizational Bureau of the Kuban Women's Shock Battalion to the minister of war and navy, RGVIA, f. 1300, op. 1, d. 239, l. 3.

67. "Po voennym obstoiatel'stvam o sformirovanie zhenskogo batal'ona iz zhenshchin-dobrovol'tsev v gorode Ekaterinodare," RGVIA, f. 2000, op. 2, d. 1557, l. 100.

68. Memorandum to the minister of war from the chairwoman of the Organizational Bureau of the Kuban Women's Shock Battalion, citizen of the Kuban Oblast, Ekaterinodar, Matriona Leontevna Zalesskaia, August 3, 1917, RGVIA, f. 2000, op. 2, d. 1557, l. 69.

69. Correspondence from the Committee of the 3rd Kuban Women's Shock Battalion to the Headquarters of the commander in chief of the Caucasian Army, October 15, 1917, RGVIA, f. 1300, op. 1, d. 239, l. 1.

70. Report from the representative of the Organizational Bureau of the Kuban Women's Shock Battalion to the minister of war and navy, RGVIA, f. 1300, op. 1, d. 239, l. 3.

71. Ibid.

72. "K organizatsii zhenshchin-volonterok," Listok voiny, June 17, 1917: 4.

73. Telegraph from Zalesskaia in Ekaterinodar to the Headquarters of the Military District, September 16, 1917, RGVIA, f. 1300, op. 1., d. 239, l. 37.

74. Copy of communication with GUGSh, Department of Organization and Service of Troops and the chief of Military Headquarters of the Kuban Caucasian Forces, September 26, 1917, RGVIA, f. 1300, op. 1, d. 239, l. 9.

75. Telegram from the Committee of the 3rd Kuban Women's Shock Battalion to the Headquarters of the commander in chief of the Caucasian Army, October 15, 1917, RGVIA, f. 1300, op. 1, d. 239, l. 1.

76. Copy of the reported correspondence from the organizer of the 3rd Kuban Women's Shock Battalion, M. L. Zalesskaia, to the Headquarters of the Kuban Military District from October 21, 1917, RGVIA, f. 1300, op. 1, d. 239, l. 25.

77. Memorandum to the chief of the Office of the Supreme Commander of the Caucasian Military District, October 24, 1917, RGVIA, f. 1300, op. 1, d. 239, l. 31.

78. Telegram to the Ekaterinodar Troop Headquarters from the Mobilization Department, December 27, 1917, RGVIA, f. 1300, op. 1, d. 239, l. 57.

79. Telegram to the duty general of the Headquarters of Supreme High Command of Troops of the Caucasian Front from the senior adjutant of the Mobilization Department, December 27, 1917, RGVIA, f. 1300, op. 1, d. 239, l. 87.

80. Telegram to the Ekaterinodar Troop Headquarters, February 26, 1918, RGVIA, f. 1300, op. 1, d. 239, l. 99.

81. Committee of the Circle of Women's Labor for the Motherland, "Russian Women Unite," letter to the commander in chief of the Petrograd District, re-sent to the Main Naval

Headquarters and the Ministry of the Navy, July 1, 1917, *Rossiiskii gosudarstvennyi arkhiv voenno-morskogo flota* (Russian State Archive of the Navy, St. Petersburg, Russia; hereafter RGAVMF), f. 417, op. 4, d. 6571, l. 3.

82. Telegram to GENMOR Goncharov from Rybaltovskii, July 30, 1917, RGAVMF, f. 417, op. 4, d. 6571, l. 20.

83. Order to the navy and naval military authorities in Petrograd, July 12, 1917, no. 397, RGAVMF, f. 417, op. 4, d. 6571, l. 1.

84. Ibid.

85. Report of the commander of the Naval Infantry Training Unit to Main Naval Headquarters, July 19, 1917, RGAVMF, f. 620, op. 1, d. 406, l. 1.

86. Telegram from the Ministry of the Navy, Main Naval Headquarters, 2nd Department to the chief of the Naval Infantry Training Unit, July 28, 1917, RGAVMF, f. 620, op. 1, d. 406, l. 2.

87. Note to the Office of the Naval Infantry Training Unit no. 25, July 31, 1917, RGAVMF, f. 620, op. 1, d. 406, l. 3.

88. Order to the navy and naval military authorities in Petrograd, July 12, 1917, no. 397, RGAVMF, f. 417, op. 4, d. 6571, l. 1.

89. "Spisok dobrovolits Morskoi Uchebno-Strelkovoi Komandy," RGAVMF, f. 417, op. 4, d. 6571, l. 27.

90. "Rospisanie: Zaniatyi s dobrovolitsam Zhenskoi Morskoi Komandy pri Morskoi Uchebno-Strelkovoi Komandy," RGAVMF, f. 620, op. 1, d. 406, ll. 4–5.

91. Report of the commander of the Naval Infantry Training Unit to Main Naval Headquarters, July 19, 1917, RGAVMF, f. 620, op. 1, d. 406, l. 1.

92. Order no. 1004, August 16, 1917, RGAVMF, f. 620, op. 1, d. 519, l. 218.

93. "O formirovanii 'Zhenskikh Morskikh Komand,'" resolution adopted by the General Meeting of Sailors of the Naval Infantry Training Detachment, August 1, 1917, RGAVMF, f. 620, op. 1, d. 413, l. 172.

94. Proceedings of the extraordinary meeting of the detachment committee of the Naval Infantry Training Detachment of August 11, 1917, RGAVMF, f. 620, op. 1, d. 413, l. 179.

95. See appendix F for a list of personnel of the 1st Women's Naval Detachment.

96. Memorandum, from the Ministry of the Navy, Main Naval Headquarters, 2nd Department, to the Naval General Staff, August 16, 1917, RGAVMF, f. 418, op. 26, d. 2688, l. 436.

97. Copy of a telegram to Lieutenant Vladimirtsov from the Main Naval Headquarters, RGAVMF, f. 620, op. 1, d. 406, l. 14.

98. Telegram from the Ministry of the Navy, Main Naval Staff, 2nd Department, to the commander of the Naval Infantry Training Detachment, RGAVMF, f. 620, op. 1, d. 406, l. 16.

99. Telegram from the Ministry of the Navy, Main Naval Headquarters, 2nd Department, to the commander of the Petrograd Military Port, September 11, 1917, RGAVMF, f. 620, op. 1, d. 406, l. 20.

100. Note from the Central Committee of the All-Russian Navy to the Coastal Committee of the Infantry Training Detachment in Oranienbaum, September 14, 1917, RGAVMF, f. 620, op. 1, d. 413, l. 211.

101. Statement from a volunteer of the Women's Naval Detachment, Mira Iofa, to the Detachment Committee of the Naval Infantry Training Detachment, RGAVMF, f. 620, op. 1, d.

413, l. 221; report no. 53—Meeting of the Detachment Committee of the Naval Infantry Training Detachment, September 19, 1917, RGAVMF, f. 620, op. 1, d. 413, l. 222.

102. Telegram from the Ministry of the Navy, Administration of Medical Units of the Fleet, to the Naval Training Detachment (Oranienbaum), August 23, 1917, RGAVMF, f. 620, op. 1, d. 406, l. 21; order no. 1062, September 3, 1917, RGAVMF, f. 620, op. 1, d. 519, l. 228.

103. Order no. 1113, September 19, 1917, RGAVMF, f. 620, op. 1, d. 519, l. 238 ob.

104. Order no. 1110, September 19, 1917, RGAVMF, f. 620, op. 1, d. 519, l. 238.

105. Order no. 1122, September 21, 1917, RGAVMF, f. 620, op. 1, d. 519, l. 240.

106. Order no. 1146, September 28, 1917, RGAVMF, f. 620, op. 1, d. 519, l. 244.

## CHAPTER SIX. THE FATE OF THE MOVEMENT

1. "Po voennym obstoiatel'stvam o sformirovanie zhenskogo batal'ona iz zhenshchin-do-brovol'tsev," July 31, 1917, RGVIA, f. 2000, op. 2, d. 1557, l. 100.

2. "Vserossiskii zhenskii voennyi s'ezd," *Novoe vremia*, July 13, 1917: 4.

3. "Zhenskii voennyi s'ezd," *Russkoe slovo*, August 2, 1917: 2.

4. Maria Bocharnikova, "V zhenskom batal'one," Papers of Maria Bocharnikova, Bakhmeteff Archive, Columbia University Rare Book and Manuscript Library, New York, 6–7.

5. Richard Stites, *The Women's Liberation Movement in Russia: Feminism, Nihilism, and Bolshevism, 1860–1930* (Princeton, NJ: Princeton University Press, 1978), 299.

6. "Zhenskii voennyi s'ezd," *Rech'*, August 2, 1917: 3; "Zhenskii voennyi s'ezd," *Russkoe slovo*, August 2, 1917: 2.

7. "Zhenskii voennyi s'ezd," *Rech'*, August 2, 1917: 3.

8. Ibid.

9. "Zhenshchiny-voiny (zakrytie zhenskago voennago s'ezda)," *Petrogradskii listok*, August 6, 1917: 3; "Zhenskie voennyi s'ezd v Petrograd," *Niva* 32 (August 12, 1917): 493.

10. "Zhenskii voennyi s'ezd," *Rech'*, August 2, 1917: 3.

11. Report by GUGSh, October 17, 1917, RGVIA, f. 2000, op. 2, d. 1557, l. 211.

12. Aleksandr Solov'ev, *Zapiski sovremennika: V nogu s pokoleniem* (Moscow: Sovietskii pisatel', 1964), 183–190.

13. Report by GUGSh, October 17, 1917, RGVIA, f. 2000, op. 2, d. 1557, l. 211.

14. Ibid.

15. Journal of the Commission on the Reduction of Staff of the Army, August 22, 1917, RGVIA, f. 2015, op. 1, d. 28, l. 2.

16. Information from the Department of Organization and Service of Troops, GUGSh, September 17, 1917, RGVIA, f. 2000, op. 2, d. 1557, l. 190.

17. Ibid.

18. A. S. Senin, "Zhenskie batal'ony i voennye komandy v 1917 godu," *Voprosy istorii* 10 (1987): 179.

19. Informational report from the Department of Organization and Service of Troops, RGVIA, f. 2000, op. 2, d. 1557, l. 136.

20. Memorandum from the minister of war to the Provisional Government, RGVIA, f. 2000, op. 2, d. 1557, l. 127.

21. Resolution of the Provisional Government, RGVIA, f. 2000, op. 2, d. 1557, l. 134.

22. Telegram to the chief of the Military Department, RGVIA, f. 2000, op. 2, d. 1557, l. 148.

23. Senin, "Zhenskie batal'ony i voennye komandy v 1917 godu," 179.

24. Telegram from the chief of the Military Department of the Administration of the Chinese Eastern Railway, October 14, 1917, RGVIA, f. 2000, op. 2, d. 1557, l. 206.

25. Telegram from the Commission on Women's Labor Conscription to the minister of war, July 18, 1917, RGVIA, f. 2000, op. 2, d. 1557, ll. 83 and 91.

26. Memorandum from the minister of war to the Provisional Government, RGVIA, f. 2000, op. 2, d. 1557, l. 84; resolution of the Provisional Government, RGVIA, f. 2000, op. 2, d. 1557, l. 85.

27. Report of the Commission on Women's Labor Conscription to the chief of the General Staff, September 11, 1917, RGVIA, f. 2000, op. 2, d. 1557, l. 169.

28. Report by GUGSh, October 17, 1917, RGVIA, f. 2000, op. 2, d. 1557, l. 211.

29. Telegram to the commander of the I Siberian Army Corps, RGVIA, f. 2277, op. 1, d. 368, l. 105.

30. Maria Botchkareva [sic], Yashka: My Life as Peasant, Officer and Exile, as told to Isaac Don Levine (New York: Frederick A. Stokes, 1919), 218–219 and 239–245; Boris Solonevich, Zhenshchina s vintovkoi: Istoricheskii roman (Buenos Aires: Privately published, 1955) (the "slightly fictionalized memoirs" of Nina Krylova), 100–104.

31. Information from the Department of Organization and Service of Troops, GUGSh, RGVIA, f. 2000, op. 2, d. 1557, l. 190.

32. "Voennaia odezhda dlia zhenshchin-voinov," Vremia, October 20, 1917: 2.

33. "Protiv zhenskikh 'batal'on smerti,'" Armeiskii vestnik, August 22, 1917: 4.

34. "Appeal of the Soldiers' Section of the Poltava Soviet of Workers' and Soldiers' Deputies to the Minister of War," September 11, 1917, in Razlozhenie Armii v 1917 godu, ed. N. E. Kakurin and Ia. A. Iakovleva (Moscow: Gosudarstvennoe izdatel'stvo, 1925), 73.

35. Informational report from the Department of Organization and Service of Troops, September 27, 1917, RGVIA, f. 2000, op. 2, d. 1557, l. 190.

36. Ibid.

37. Telegram from the duty general of the southwestern front, October 4, 1917, RGVIA, f. 2003, op. 2, d. 349, l. 39.

38. Letter from the All-Russian Central Committee for the Organization of Volunteers for the Revolutionary Army, to the chief of the Mobilization Department of GUGSh, June 26, 1917, RGVIA, f. 2000, op. 2, d. 1557, l. 38.

39. Report by GUGSh, October 17, 1917, RGVIA, f. 2000, op. 2, d. 1557, l. 211.

40. Ibid.

41. Report by GUGSh, October, 4, 1917, RGVIA, f. 2003, op. 2, d. 349, l. 39.

42. Ibid.

43. Bocharnikova, "V zhenskom batal'one," 22–30; Maria Bocharnikova, "Boi v Zimnem dvortse," Novyi zhurnal 68 (1962): 215–227; Ariadna Tyrkova-Williams, "The Women's Battalion," Englishwoman, January 1919: 4–8, and February 1919: 60–64; Louise Bryant, Six Red Months in Russia: An Observer's Account of Russia before and during the Proletarian Dic-

*tatorship* (New York: George H. Doran, 1918), 212–219; "Rasskaz ofitsera o zashchite Zimnego dvortsa," in *Oktiabr'skoe vooruzhennoe vosstanie v Petrograde,* ed. I. A. Bulygin and G. N. Golikov (Moscow: Akademiia Nauk SSSR, 1957), 425.

44. Rex Wade, *Red Guard and Workers' Militias in the Russian Revolution* (Stanford, CA: Stanford University Press, 1984), 189.

45. Rex Wade, *The Russian Revolution, 1917* (Cambridge: Cambridge University Press, 2000), 229.

46. Alexander Rabinowitch, *The Bolsheviks Come to Power: The Revolution of 1917 in Petrograd* (New York: W. W. Norton, 1976), 244.

47. W. Bruce Lincoln, *Passage through Armageddon: The Russians in War and Revolution, 1914–1918* (New York: Simon and Schuster, 1986), 443–445.

48. "Telefonogramma nachal'nika shtaba Petrogradskogo voennogo okruga generala Ia. Bagratuni komandiru 1-go Petrogradskogo zhenskogo batal'ona o nemedlennom pribytii so stantsii Levashovo v g.Petrograd," Document no. 345 in Bulygin and Golikov, *Oktiabr'skoe vooruzhennoe vosstanie v Petrograde,* 281.

49. Bocharnikova, "V zhenskom batal'one," 23; Kapitan Shagal, "Zhenskii batal'on," *Voennaia byl'* 95 (January 1969): 10.

50. Major General Ia. G. Bagratuni, quoted in Senin, "Zhenskie batal'ony i voennye komandy v 1917 godu," 181.

51. Bryant, *Six Red Months in Russia,* 216.

52. Bocharnikova, "V zhenskom batal'one," 23.

53. Lincoln, *Passage through Armageddon,* 447–448.

54. "Zasedanie 3 noiabria," *Stenograficheskie otchety zasedanii Petrogradskoi gorodskoi dumy sozyva 1917 g., Gosudarstvennaia publichnaia bibliotekta imina Saltykova-Shchedrina* (Saltykov-Shchedrin State Public Library, St. Petersburg, Russia; hereafter GPBSS), Manuscript Section, 1957, l. 36.

55. Bocharnikova, "Boi v Zimnem dvortse," 215–227; Bocharnikova, "V zhenskom batal'one," 22–30; Evgeniia Piatunina, "Russkie Zhanny d'Ark: Vospominaniia udarnitsy zhenskago batal'ona," *Nezavisimaia gazeta,* March 4, 2000: 2.

56. Shagal, "Zhenskii batal'on," 9.

57. "Predpisanie shtaba Petrogradskogo voennogo okruga komandiru poty 1-go Petrogradskogo zhenskogo batal'ona ob okhrane mostov," Document no. 437, in Bulygin and Golikov, *Oktiabr'skoe vooruzhennoe vosstanie v Petrograd,* 332.

58. Bocharnikova, "Boi v Zimnem dvortse," 216.

59. Piatunina, "Russkie Zhanny d'Ark," 2.

60. Account of an officer on the defense of the Winter Palace, in Bulygin and Golikov, *Oktiabr'skoe vooruzhennoe vosstanie v Petrograd,* 425.

61. Norman Saul, *Sailors in Revolt: The Russian Baltic Fleet in 1917* (Lawrence: Regents Press of Kansas, 1978), 188; Orlando Figes, *A People's Tragedy: A History of the Russian Revolution* (New York: Penguin, 1996), 493.

62. Bocharnikova, "V zhenskom batal'one," 26–27.

63. Richard Abraham, "Mariia L. Bochkareva and the Russian Amazons of 1917," in *Women and Society in Russia and the Soviet Union,* ed. Linda Edmondson (Cambridge: Cambridge University Press, 1992), 130.

64. John Reed, *Ten Days That Shook the World* (New York: Boni and Liveright, 1919), 81–82.

65. Figes, *A People's Tragedy,* photo caption 61.

66. Bocharnikova, "V zhenskom batal'one," 37.

67. Ibid., 27; "Vospominania tov. A A. Ioffe, chlena Leningradskogo Voenno-Revoliutsionnogo Komiteta v dni Oktiabr'," *Krasnoarmeets* 78 (November 1925): 7; Sir George Buchanan, *My Mission to Russia and Other Diplomatic Memories* (Boston: Little, Brown, 1923), 208; Reed, *Ten Days That Shook the World,* 105–106.

68. Bocharnikova, "V zhenskom batal'one," 27.

69. Buchanan, *My Mission to Russia and Other Diplomatic Memories,* 208; "Zasedanie 3 noiabria," *Stenograficheskie otchety zasedanii Petrogradskoi gorodskoi dumy sozyva 1917 g.,* GPBSS, Manuscript Section, 1957, l. 39.

70. "Postanovlenie ob osvobozhdenii arestovannykh pervogo zhenskago udarnago batal'ona, 26 Okt., 1917," Document no. 172 in *Petrogradskii Voenno-Revoliutsionyi Komitet: Dokumenty i materiali,* ed. Dmitri Chugaev, 3 vols. (Moscow: Akademiia Nauk SSSR, 1966), 1:130.

71. Piatunina, "Russkie Zhanny d'Ark," 2.

72. Shagal, "Zhenskii batal'on," 10; Bocharnikova, "V zhenskom batal'one," 28.

73. There is some disagreement about the number of women who remained after being dismissed by Loskov. Bocharnikova says 600, while Tyrkova and Mandel'berg, sent by the Petrograd Municipal Council to investigate the conditions of the battalion, say approximately 200.

74. Kh. M. Astrakhan, "O Zhenskom Batal'one, zashchishchavshem Zimnii dvorets," *Istoriia SSSR* 5 (1965): 96.

75. "Predpisanie shtabu Krasnoi gvardii o vydache rasporiazheniia o svobodnom propuske dobrovolits 1-go Petr. zhen. Bat., 5 Noia, 1917," Document no. 276 in Chugaev, *Petrogradskii Voenno-Revoliutsionyi Komitet: Dokumenty i materiali,* 2:113 and 2:116.

76. "Postanovlenie o rasformirovanii Komiteta zhenskogo voennogo soiuz, 8 Noia, 1917," Document no. 604 in Chugaev, *Petrogradskii Voenno-Revoliutsionyi Komitet: Dokumenty i materiali,* 3:234.

77. Shagal, "Zhenskii batal'on," 10.

78. This may very well have been Bocharnikova, who in her memoirs reported having been hit on the back of the head.

79. "Zasedaniia 2.11.1917," *Stenograficheskie otchety zasedanii Petrogradskoi gorodskoi dumy sozyva 1917 g.,* GPBSS, Manuscript Section, 1957, ll. 23–30.

80. Bryant, *Six Red Months in Russia,* 214.

81. Bocharnikova, "V zhenskom batal'one," 40.

82. "O rasformironvanii voiskovykh chastei iz zhenshchin-dobrovol'tsev," November 19, 1917, RGVIA, f. 29, op. 3, d. 1603, l. 24.

83. Report of the Military Council, November 30, 1917, RGVIA, f. 29, op. 3, d. 1603, l. 26.

84. Report of the commander of the 1st Petrograd Women's Battalion to the chief of staff of the Revolutionary Field Forces, January 10, 1918, RGVIA, f. 16173, op. 1, d. 9, l. 1; Bocharnikova, "Boi v Zimnem dvortse," 227.

85. Bocharnikova, "V zhenskom batal'one," 47–57; Bocharnikova, "Boi v Zimnem dvortse," 227.

86. Shagal, "Zhenskii batal'on," 10.

87. Senin, "Zhenskie batal'ony i voennye komandy v 1917 godu," 180.

88. Copy of the journal of military activity, December 14–15, operations of the 27th Infantry Division, RGVIA, f. 2357, op. 1, d. 520, l. 8.

89. Botchkareva, *Yashka*, 263.

90. Telegram to the commissar of military-naval affairs of the Caucasian Commissariat, from the chief of staff of the Caucasian Military District, Mobilization Department, February 17, 1918, RGVIA, f. 1300, op. 1, d. 239, l. 97.

CHAPTER SEVEN. IMAGING THE WOMAN SOLDIER

1. Most of the information in this section is derived from contemporary publications, particularly periodicals. Many of these are somewhat problematic as historical sources. Many reports, including those made by eyewitnesses, contain glaring inaccuracies and exaggeration. Hyperbole and sensationalism were quite common in media reports; "yellow journalism" was mixed with factual reporting in even the most reputable publications. Moreover, some of the women soldiers themselves euphemized, exaggerated, and even falsified certain aspects of their lives. Such errors contributed to the formation of contemporary perspectives of the female soldiers, and thus the commentary cannot be dismissed despite the presence of misinformation.

2. See issues of popular and widely circulated newspapers such as *Birzhevyia vedomosti, Novoe vremia, Petrogradskii listok, Rech', Russkoe slovo,* and *Utro Rossii* and journals such as *Iskry, Niva, Ogonek, Sinii zhurnal,* and *20-yi vek* between May and October 1917.

3. "Dobrovolets-Kazachka," in "Zhenshchiny geroi," special issue, *Voina* 24 (1915): 6.

4. "Partizanki-zhenshchiny," in "Zhenshchiny geroi," special issue, *Voina* 24 (1915): 5.

5. Victor Marsen, "How the Women of Russia Helped," in *Women's War Work,* ed. Lady Randolph Churchill (London: C. Arthur Pearson, 1916), 102.

6. "800 Amazonok," *Petrogradskii listok,* May 28, 1917: 4.

7. "Provody pervogo zhenskago batal'ona," *Novoe vremia,* June 22, 1917: 4.

8. "Zhenskii bata'lon smerti," *Niva* 26 (June 30, 1917): 394.

9. *Ogonek* 25 (July 2, 1917): 398.

10. "Zhenshchina pod ruzh'em," *Sinii zhurnal* 31 (September 1917): 10.

11. B. Liubchev, "Batal'on smerti," *Sinii zhurnal* 21 (June 1917): 12.

12. "Zhenskii batal'on smerti," *Ogonek* 23 (June 18, 1917): 361.

13. Prince A. Lobanov-Rostovsky, *The Grinding Mill: Reminiscences of War and Revolution in Russia, 1913–1920* (New York: Macmillan, 1935), 236.

14. "Provody pervogo zhenskago batal'ona," 4.

15. "Miting i sbor dlia zhenskago batal'ona," *Vremia,* June 23, 1917: 2.

16. "Prazdnik zhenskago batal'ona," *Petrogradskii listok,* August 1, 1917: 4.

17. "Muzhchinyi k ochagam! Zhenshchinyi k oruzhiiu!" *Birzhevyia vedomosti,* August 1, 1917: 2.

18. "Voennaia odezhda dlia zhenshchin-voinov," *Vremia*, October 20, 1917: 2.

19. Boris Solonevich, *Zhenshchina s vintovkoi: Istoricheskii roman* (Buenos Aires: Privately published, 1955) (the "slightly fictionalized memoirs" of Nina Krylova), 107.

20. "O Russkoi zhenshchine," *Vremia*, July 13, 1917: 1.

21. "Zhenshchina pod ruzh'em," 10.

22. "Docheri otechestva (batal'on smerti—na front)," *Petrogradskii listok*, June 24, 1917: 3.

23. Maria Bocharnikova, "V zhenskom batal'one," Papers of Maria Bocharnikova, Bakhmeteff Archive, Columbia University Rare Book and Manuscript Library, New York, 15.

24. "Provody pervogo zhenskago batal'ona," *Novoe vremia*, June 22, 1917: 4.

25. Rheta Childe Dorr, *Inside the Russian Revolution* (New York: Macmillan, 1917), 76–77.

26. Richard Abraham, "Mariia L. Bochkareva and the Russian Amazons of 1917," in *Women and Society in Russia and the Soviet Union*, ed. Linda Edmondson (Cambridge: Cambridge University Press, 1992), 141.

27. Bozhena Viteitskaia, "Zhenskie batal'ony," *Damskii mir* 9–10 (September–October 1917): 2–3.

28. M. Berkut, quoted in Maria Ancharova, "Batal'on smerty," *Zhenskoe delo* 15 (August 1, 1917): 3.

29. "Shutka pro zhenshchine-soldatom," *Baraban* 11 (June 1917): 3.

30. Maria Botchkareva [*sic*], *Yashka: My Life as Peasant, Officer and Exile*, as told to Isaac Don Levine (New York: Frederick A. Stokes, 1919), 160.

31. "Zhenskii batal'on smerti," *Zhenskii vestnik* 6 (July–August 1917): 3.

32. "Krestianskii sovet o zhenskikh batal'onakh," *Rabotnitsa* 7 (July 19, 1917): 16.

33. Ibid.

34. Aleksander Solov'ev, *Zapiski sovremennika: V nogu s pokoleniem* (Moscow: Sovetskii pisatel', 1964), 183.

35. Quoted in Klara Zetkin, "Iz zapisnoi knizhki," in *O zhenskom voprose: K. Marks, F. Engel's, V. I. Lenin*, ed. Vera Bil'shai (Moscow: Izdatel'stvo politicheskoi literatury, 1971), 185.

36. L. Borobevskii, "Batal'on smerti," *Rabochii i soldat*, July 30, 1917: 3–4.

37. Ibid., 3.

38. Solov'ev, *Zapiski sovremennika*, 183.

39. Quoted in Abraham, "Mariia L. Bochkareva and the Russian Amazons of 1917," 130.

40. Borobevskii, "Batal'on smerti," 4.

41. "Russkaia amazonka," in "Zhenshchiny geroi," special issue, *Voina* 24 (1915): 13.

42. "Odna iz mnogikh," *Zhenskoe delo* 2 (January 15, 1915): 19–20.

43. Ann Eliot Griese and Richard Stites, "Russia: Revolution and War," in *Female Soldiers: Combatants or Noncombatants? Historical and Contemporary Perspectives*, ed. Nancy Loring Goldman (Westport, CT: Greenwood, 1982), 65.

44. Botchkareva, *Yashka*, 157.

45. Kapitan Shagal, "Zhenskii batal'on," *Voennaia byl'* 95 (January 1969): 8.

46. Botchkareva, *Yashka*, 222.

47. "Zhenshchiny idut na front!" *Petrogradskii listok*, May 26, 1917: 2.

48. Petr A. Polovtsev, *Glory and Downfall: Reminiscences of a Russian General Staff Offi-*

*cer* (London: G. Bell and Sons, 1935), 220–222. Interestingly, Polovtsev is one of the few involved in the formation of the women's battalion to have commented on it in his memoirs (in contrast to Kerensky, Brusilov, Rodzianko, and others).

49. Ibid., 222.

50. Botchkareva, *Yashka*, 196; Dorr, *Inside the Russian Revolution*, 69; Solonevich, *Zhenshchina s vintovkoi*, 105–106.

51. Botchkareva, *Yashka*, 201.

52. See chapter 5 for details of this praise.

53. Shagal, "Zhenskii batal'on," 8.

54. Quoted in Lord Edmund Ironside, *Archangel, 1918–1919* (London: Constable, 1953), 77.

55. Anton I. Denikin, "Ocherki russkoi smuty," *Voprosi istorii* 10 (1990): 113.

56. Quoted in Dale Ross, "The Role of the Women in Petrograd in War, Revolution, and Counter-Revolution, 1914–1921" (Ph.D. diss., Rutgers University, 1973), 253.

57. "Zhenskii batal'on smerti," *Zhenskii vestnik* 6 (July–August 1917): 4.

58. "Docheri otechestva (batal'on smerti—na front)," 3.

59. Dorr, *Inside the Russian Revolution*, 69.

60. "Protiv zhenskikh 'batal'on smerti,'" *Armeiskii vestnik*, August 22, 1917: 4.

61. "Matrosy o 'zhenskikh morskikh komandakh,'" *Armeiskii vestnik*, August 19, 1917: 3.

62. Viktor Shklovsky, *A Sentimental Journey: Memoirs, 1917–1922*, trans. Richard Sheldon (Ithaca, NY: Cornell University Press, 1970), 30.

63. "Obrashchenie soldatskoi sektsii Poltavskogo S. R. i S. Deputatov k voennomu ministru," in *Razlozhenie Armii v 1917 godu*, ed. N. E. Kakurin and Ia. A. Iakovlev (Moscow: Gosudarstvennoe izdatel'stvo, 1925), 73.

64. Botchkareva, *Yashka*, 195.

65. See chapter 4 for a more detailed description of the experiences of Bochkareva's unit at the front and their relations with male soldiers.

66. Botchkareva, *Yashka*, 190.

67. "Iz deistvuiushchii armii," *Ogonek* 42 (October 29, 1917): 661.

68. "Prazdnik zhenskago batal'ona," 4.

69. Quoted in Viteitskaia, "Zhenskie batal'ony," 2.

70. "O zhenshchinakh-dobrovolits," *Armeiskii vestnik*, August 16, 1917: 4.

71. *Russkie vedomosti*, June 6, 1917: 3.

72. V. Ermilova, "Zhenshchina—sud'ia," *Zhenskaia zhizn'* 2 (January 22, 1915): 2.

73. "Odna iz mnogikh," 20.

74. Ibid.

75. Valentina Kostyleva, "Nashi amazonki," *Zhenskaia zhizn'* 19 (October 1, 1914): 24.

76. Ibid.

77. Valentina Kostyleva, "Zhenshchina, voina, i sem'ia," *Zhenskaia zhizn'* 17 (September 1, 1914): 28.

78. "Zhenskii batal'on smerti," *Zhenskii vestnik* 6 (July–August, 1917): 4.

79. Viteitskaia, "Zhenskie batal'ony," 2.

80. "Docheri otechestva (batal'on smerti—na front)," 2.

81. Kostyleva, "Nashi amazonki," 24.

82. Viteitskaia, "Zhenskie batal'ony," 2.

83. Sofia Zarechnaia, "Amazonki velikoi voiny," *Zhenskoe delo* 14 (July 1, 1917): 10.

84. Ibid.

85. Countess Olga Putiatina, in *War and Revolution: Excerpts from the Letters and Diaries of Countess Olga Poutiatine,* ed. and trans. George Lensen (Tallahassee, FL: Diplomatic Press, 1971), 74–75.

86. Zarechnaia, "Amazonki velikoi voiny," 11.

87. "Zhenshchiny idut na front!" 2; "800 Amazonok," 4.

88. Linda Edmondson, "Mariia Pokrovskaia and *Zhenskii vestnik:* Feminist Separatism in Theory and Practice," in *An Improper Profession: Women, Gender, and Journalism in Late Imperial Russia,* ed. Barbara Norton and Jehanne Gheith (Durham, NC: Duke University Press, 2001), 211.

89. "Zhenskii batal'on smerti," *Zhenskii vestnik* 6 (July–August 1917): 4.

90. A. Tyrkova, "Zhenskaia Povinnost'," *Rech',* June 10, 1917: 3.

91. "Vozzvanie zhenskogo soiuza," *Rech',* May 28, 1917: 6.

92. Ancharova, "Batal'on smerty," 1.

93. "Zhenskii batal'on smerti," *Zhenskii vestnik* 6 (July–August 1917): 4.

94. Zarechnaia, "Amazonki velikoi voiny," 10.

95. Quoted in Edmondson, "Mariia Pokrovskaia and *Zhenskii vestnik,*" 211.

96. "Muzhchiny k ochagam! Zhenshchiny k oruzhiiu!" *Birzhevyia vedomosti,* August 1, 1917: 2.

97. Sofia Zarechnaia, "Amazonki Velikoi Voiny" *Zhenskoe delo* 14 (July 1, 1917): 11.

98. Quoted in Alfred Meyer, "The Impact of World War I on Russian Women's Lives," in *Russia's Women: Accommodation, Resistance, Transformation,* ed. Barbara Evans Clements, Barbara Alpern Engel, and Christine Worobec (Berkeley and Los Angeles: University of California Press, 1991), 220.

99. Ancharova, "Batal'on smerty," 1.

100. Ibid.

101. Ibid., 2.

102. Ibid.

103. Countess Kleinmichel, *Memories of a Shipwrecked World: Being the Memoirs of Countess Kleinmichel,* trans. Vivian Le Grand (New York: Brentano's, 1923), 267.

104. Aleksandra Kollontai, "Zhenskie batal'ony," *Rabotnitsa* 6 (June 28 1917): 7–8.

105. See *New York Times,* November 3, 1914: 2; January 10, 1915: 2; February 4, 1915: 2; February 7, 1915: 3; April 11, 1915: 11; April 26, 1915: 3; June 19, 1915: 2; August 7, 1915: 2; and October 2, 1915: 2; *Times* (London), September 5, 1914: 8; September 13, 1914: 3; September 14, 1914: 8; December 2, 1914: 8; February 18, 1915: 10; February 26, 1915: 8; March 27, 1915: 7; February 8, 1916: 7; and February 26, 1916: 3; *Literary Digest,* June 19, 1915: 1460; *Delineator,* November 1915: 19; *Collier's,* March 6, 1915: 13; and *Jus Suffragi,* October 1, 1914: 1; November 1, 1914: 190; January 1, 1915: 224; February 1, 1915: 241; March 1, 1915: 253; April 1, 1915: 277; May 1, 1915: 290; June 1, 1915: 300; July 1, 1915: 322; and October 1, 1915: 9.

106. Herman Axelbank Film Collection, reel 19, segment 1 (June–July 1917), Hoover Institution Archives, Stanford, California.

107. Marsen, "How the Women of Russia Helped," 102.

108. Ibid.

109. Leonid I. Strakhovsky, *American Opinion about Russia, 1917–1920* (Toronto: University of Toronto Press, 1961), passim.

110. Bernard Pares, *My Russian Memoirs* (London: Jonathan Cape, 1931), 289–291.

111. Robert Scotland Liddell, *On the Russian Front* (London: Simpkin, Marshall, Hamilton, Kent, 1916), 231.

112. "Warrior Women," *Literary Digest* 55 (June 19, 1915): 42.

113. John Morse, *An Englishman in the Russian Ranks: Ten Months' Fighting in Poland* (London: Duckworth, 1915), 69.

114. Charles E. Beury, *Russia after the Revolution* (Philadelphia: George W. Jacobs, 1918), 69.

115. Richard Stites, *The Women's Liberation Movement: Feminism, Nihilism, and Bolshevism, 1860–1930* (Princeton, NJ: Princeton University Press, 1978), 297n.

116. "Those Russian Women," *Literary Digest* 55 (September 29, 1917): 48.

117. Ibid.

118. Liddell, *On the Russian Front*, 231.

119. "Warrior Women," 42.

120. Pares, *My Russian Memoirs*, 473.

121. Quoted in Ross, "The Role of the Women of Petrograd in War, Revolution and Counter-Revolution," 264.

122. "Root Lauds Russian Women" *New York Times*, August 7, 1917: 2.

123. Quoted in Robert V. Daniels, *Red October: The Bolshevik Revolution of 1917* (New York: Charles Scribner's Sons, 1967), 137.

124. "Muzhchiny k ochagam! Zhenshchiny k oruzhiiu!" 2.

125. W. G. Shepherd, quoted in "The Women Soldiers of Russia," *Times*, July 30, 1917: 7.

126. Edward Alsworth Ross, *Russia in Upheaval* (New York: Century, 1918), 237.

127. Ibid., 254.

128. Ibid.

129. "Women's Fitness for Soldiering" *Times* (London), October 9, 1917: 10.

130. George MacAdam, "When Women Fight: Dr. Graeme M. Hammond Discusses 'The Female of the Species,' Her Warlike Qualities and Limitations," *New York Times Magazine*, September 2, 1917: 3.

131. Ibid., 14.

132. "Those Russian Women," 49.

133. Marsen, "How the Women of Russia Helped," 102.

134. "Warrior Women," 1460.

135. Morse, *An Englishman in the Russian Ranks*, 69.

136. Ibid.

137. "M-ss Pankhurst v Moskve," *Russkoe slovo*, August 6, 1917: 4.

138. Quoted in Abraham, "Mariia L. Bochkareva and the Russian Amazons of 1917," 138–139.

139. Ironside, *Archangel*, 77. This prediction never came to fruition, however, for the Soviet government was not inclined to celebrate the heroism of a counterrevolutionary, regardless of her sex.

140. Solonevich, *Zhenshchina s vintovkoi*, 129.

141. Abraham, "Mariia L. Bochkareva and the Russian Amazons of 1917," 129–130.

142. Louise Bryant, *Six Red Months in Russia: An Observer's Account of Russia before and during the Proletarian Dictatorship* (New York: George H. Doran, 1918), 210.

143. Dorr, *Inside the Russian Revolution*, 50.

144. Ibid., 51.

145. Meriel Buchanan, *Petrograd: The City of Trouble, 1914–1918* (London: W. Collins Sons, 1919), 126.

146. Abraham, "Mariia L. Bochkareva and the Russian Amazons of 1917," 128.

147. Quoted in Solonevich, *Zhenshchina s vintovkoi*, 74–75.

148. Abraham, "Mariia L. Bochkareva and the Russian Amazons of 1917," 128.

149. Dorr, *Inside the Russian Revolution*, 76.

150. Quoted in David Mitchell, *Women on the Warpath: The Story of the Women of the First World War* (London: Jonathan Cape, 1966), 68.

151. Bessie Beatty, *The Red Heart of Russia* (New York: Century, 1919), 98.

152. Bryant, *Six Red Months in Russia*, 212.

153. Quoted in Abraham, "Mariia L. Bochkareva and the Russian Amazons of 1917," 128.

154. In reality they were probably not members of the Battalion of Death, because Farmborough was working near Broskautsky, on the Romanian front, and the women's unit was stationed near Molodechno, on the western front. They could have been members of the Moscow Women's Battalion, who were dispatched unofficially to the Romanian front just prior to the disbanding of the unit.

155. Florence Farmborough, *Nurse at the Russian Front: A Diary, 1914–18* (London: Constable, 1974), 302–305, quotation on 305.

156. Madeline Z. Doty, "Women Who Would A-Soldiering Go," *World Outlook*, September 1918: 7.

157. Ibid.

## CHAPTER EIGHT. CONCLUSIONS

1. Richard Johnson, "The Role of Women in the Russian Civil War (1917–1921)," *Conflict* 2, 2 (1980): 213; Ann Eliot Griese and Richard Stites, "Russia: Revolution and War," in *Female Soldiers: Combatants or Noncombatants? Historical and Contemporary Perspectives*, ed. Nancy Loring Goldman (Westport, CT: Greenwood, 1982), 67.

2. Richard Stites, *The Women's Liberation Movement in Russia: Feminism, Nihilism, and Bolshevism, 1860–1930* (Princeton, NJ: Princeton University Press, 1978), 318.

3. There are no formal figures on the number of women who fought with the White Armies, and no studies have been conducted.

4. Kazimira Jean Cottam, "Soviet Women in Combat in World War II: The Ground Forces and the Navy," *International Journal of Women's Studies* 3, 4 (July–August 1980): 345.

5. Reina Pennington, *Wings, Women, and War: Soviet Airwomen in World War II Combat* (Lawrence: University Press of Kansas, 2001), 5.

6. Griese and Stites, "Russia: Revolution and War," 64.

7. Martin Gilbert, *Atlas of Russian History* (New York: Oxford University Press, 1983), 89.

8. E. J. Hobsbawm, *Nations and Nationalism since 1790: Programme, Myth, Reality* (Cambridge: Cambridge University Press, 1990), 87–88.

9. Nikolai N. Golovin, *The Russian Army in the World War* (New Haven, CT: Yale University Press, 1931), 206.

10. Hubertus F. Jahn, *Patriotic Culture in Russia during World War I* (Ithaca, NY: Cornell University Press, 1995), 4.

11. Allan Wildman, *The Old Army and the Soldiers' Revolt (March–April 1917)*, vol. 1 of *The End of the Russian Imperial Army* (Princeton, NJ: Princeton University Press, 1980), 77.

12. Golovin, *The Russian Army in the World War*, 8.

13. Ibid.

14. Male heads of households were supposed to be called only when all other men had been drafted, but in World War I, irregularities in the way the draft was carried out, coupled with the extreme need for manpower, meant that many such men were called, and this was a highly unpopular policy.

15. Rheta Childe Dorr, *Inside the Russian Revolution* (New York: Macmillan, 1917), 78.

## EPILOGUE

1. Maria Bocharnikova, "V zhenskom batal'one," Papers of Maria Bocharnikova, Bakhmeteff Archive, Columbia University Rare Book and Manuscript Library, New York, 47–57; Bocharnikova, "Boi v Zimnem dvortse," *Novyi zhurnal* 68 (1962): 227.

2. Boris Solonevich, *Zhenshchina s vintovkoi: Istoricheskii roman* (Buenos Aires: Privately published, 1955) (the "slightly fictionalized memoirs" of Nina Krylova), 150n.

3. Sergei Drokov, "Yashka: O komandire zhenskogo batal'ona smerti," *Ogonek* 24 (June 1992): 22.

4. Florence Jaffray Harriman, *From Pinafores to Politics* (New York: Henry Holt, 1923), 279–281.

5. Jerome Landfield to Secretary Breckenridge Long, July 13, 1918, Department of State communiqué, Long Papers, box 38, Manuscript Division, Library of Congress, Washington, DC.

6. Drokov, "Yashka," 23.

7. Sergei Drokov, "Organizator zhenskogo batal'ona smerti," *Voprosy istorii* 7 (1993): 168.

# BIBLIOGRAPHY

The sources for this study are extremely varied. They include the personal accounts of some of the women soldiers themselves, including published memoirs and unpublished papers, some of which have never before been studied. Accounts by eyewitnesses and reports from the contemporary media also provide rich source material, as observers were fascinated by the women and the press covered their exploits extensively. Perhaps most significantly, this is the first major work in English, and the first work of length in any language, to utilize archival documentation relating to the women's military units and their activities. Such sources are invaluable, providing much previously unknown factual information, and without them the story of Russia's women soldiers of World War I could not be told. Extensive governmental and military documents were used, many of which were being viewed by Western eyes for the first time. These included the records of the Ministry of War and its agencies, the documents of various army groups and organizations, and the correspondences between these elements, located in the Russian State Military-Historical Archive (*Rossiiskii gosudarstvennyi voenno-istoricheskii arkhiv;* RGVIA) in Moscow and the Russian State Archive of the Navy (*Rossiiskii gosudarstvennyi arkhiv voenno-morskogo flota;* RGAVMF) in St. Petersburg. The Russian military authorities kept extensive records, contained in separate files scattered through different collections, of the formation, training, and activities of the women's units under their command. Most of the units had their own *fondy* (collections) dedicated to their activities, but there was also much duplication of documentation found in other more general collections or in the *fondy* pertaining to the larger regimental units to which the women's units were assigned.

Archival documents, like all other sources, are not free of a certain degree of bias. Government and military officials often intentionally omitted important elements or used imprecise or ambiguous language in order to avoid any possible culpability. Moreover, the authors of such documents possessed varying degrees of education, and many authors, especially those of army records, were only marginally literate, making the task of translation even more daunting for the nonnative speaker of Russian. Similarly, some of the memoir material was written in highly colloquial and idiomatic language. The best effort was made to retain the original style and connotation of the sources, except where doing so resulted in a loss of meaning.

Other official sources include materials in the State Archive of the Russian Federation (*Gosudarstvennyi arkhiv Rossiiskoi Federatsii;* GARF) in Moscow, which contains records of the Provisional Government. The most significant aspect of these collections was the relative sparsity of the Provisional Government's documentation of the women's units, which affirms the lack of importance the civilian authorities assigned to the matter of women combatants. The manuscript section of the Saltykov-Shchedrin State Public Library in St. Petersburg (*Gosudarstvennaia publichnaia bibliotekta imena Saltykova-Shchedrina*) contains the records of the Petrograd City Duma (city council) pertaining to its investigation of events following the taking of the Winter Palace and the capture of the women soldiers who participated in its defense. Other unpublished materials, including the manuscripts of Maria Bocharnikova, were obtained from the Bakhmeteff Archive of the Columbia University Rare Book and Manuscript Library in New York City and the Hoover Institution Archives in Stanford, California. Bocharnikova's account of the events surrounding the defense of the Winter Palace has provided us with an entirely new view of this pivotal event.

Many eyewitness accounts of the events of the revolutionary year of 1917 include at least brief descriptions of the women's battalions formed by the Provisional Government and thus were also valuable sources. Despite their value as eyewitness accounts and in showing opinions concerning the women soldiers, these sources have some serious shortcomings as well: Many are highly exaggerated and imbued with personal and political bias. Besides their lack of objectivity, other problems arise from inaccurate reporting amid a chaotic period. Much of the data collected at the time, as well as later, reflects this disorientation and lack of precision. Some sources neglect essential elements of the story, and some contradict other sources.

Numerous media sources were utilized as well. Both Russian and foreign newspapers and journals carried reports of the women soldiers. In particular, I relied heavily on media accounts for information concerning the individual women who enlisted in all-male units. There are no archival records for these women, so the media accounts are extremely important, but they too have flaws that generate serious concerns. Journalistic reporting of the time tended to be hyperbolized and flavored by the action-packed style of "yellow journalism." Therefore, all such sources had to be used with caution, and a concerted effort was made to verify all information in other sources. When this was impossible, it was often left to the author's discretion and basic common sense to decide what information to include and how to utilize it.

Russia's women soldiers have not been incorporated into the narrative history of the period. While there are a number of solid studies on the women who served their country during World War II, such as those by Jean Cottam (*Soviet Airwomen in Combat in World War II;* "Soviet Women in Combat in World War II: The Rear Services"; "Soviet Women in Combat in World War II: The Ground Forces and the Navy") and Reina Pennington (*Wings, Women, and War*), no serious or comprehensive examinations exist of the participation of Russian women soldiers in World War I. They faded into relative obscurity in the years following the October Revolution.

That there has been little scholarly investigation of the topic may be partially accounted for by the fact that Soviet historiography on World War I is much less developed than that of the West. The Soviets did not mythologize World War I, regarding it as an imperialist venture of the old regime, and therefore did not celebrate its heroes. In accounts of the history of the war and revolution, women soldiers received sparse, shallow, and often inaccurate treatment. They were pushed aside by subsequent historiography for a number of reasons, not least because they ended up on the losing side of the upheavals of 1917. Those who fought in the Imperial Russian Army were fighting for the autocracy; those who fought in the women's combat formations of 1917 were organized under the auspices of the Provisional Government and were thus associated with the "bourgeois" elements that the Bolsheviks were determined to crush. As a result, the women were ridiculed, maligned, dismissed, and ignored by most Soviet sources.

Some of the information pertaining to this episode in Russian history was not available to scholars because of their "anti-Soviet content." The memoirs of Maria Bochkareva, the commander of a women's combat unit, were prohibited from publication in the Soviet Union for this reason and only appeared in Russian in 1992. Although many Russians are aware of the existence of women soldiers during World War I, particularly of those who participated in the defense of the Winter Palace, their views are often distorted. Texts and films glorifying the Great October Socialist Revolution portrayed the women as foolish misfits and pawns of the bourgeoisie. As Richard Abraham comments, "We are asked by stereotype-ridden films and secondary literature to believe that the women who defended the Winter Palace were misguided, stupid and cowardly" ("Mariia L. Bochkareva and the Russian Amazons of 1917," in *Women and Society in Russia and the Soviet Union*, ed. Linda Edmondson, 130).

This attitude of derision penetrated the Western record as well, and as a result accurate and detailed coverage of the activities of these women is difficult to find. Sporadic references in encyclopedias and other reference works mention only the creation of a single unit of female soldiers, usually an amalgamation of the 1st Russian Women's Battalion of Death and the Petrograd Women's Battalion, without acknowledging the many other units that existed. A number of other Soviet and Western publications on the October Revolution include distorted accounts of the involvement of the small company of the Petrograd Women's Battalion in the defense of the Winter Palace. (For Soviet sources, see Mints, *Istoriia Velikogo Oktiabria*, 2:915, 919, 949; Temkin, *Bol'sheviki v bor'be za demokraticheskii mir,* 391; Startsev, *Krakh Kerenshchiny,* 173; *Oktiabr'skoe vooruzhennoe vosstanie v Petrograde,* 281; and "Zhenskii batal'on," 180. Western sources include Daniels, *Red October;* Rabinowitch, *The Bolsheviks Come to Power,* 261–262; *The Modern Encyclopedia of Russian and Soviet History,* 5:10, 10:21–23; and Jones, *The Military-Naval Encyclopedia of Russia and the Soviet Union,* vol. 2.) These sources have "ignored the origin and meaning of the women's military formations" (Stites, *The Women's Liberation Movement in Russia,* 289).

Moreover, it is significant that virtually none of the major male actors involved in the creation of the women's military formations in 1917 mention the phenomenon in their published or unpublished reminiscences of the period. Neither Mikhail Rodzianko, who "discovered" Maria Bochkareva and brought her to Petrograd to pitch the idea of all-female combat units, Alexander Kerensky, the minister of war who authorized the formations, or General Aleksei Brusilov, who promoted the women's military movement, includes any information about the women's units in their books or papers. This may have been the result of embarrassment or unwillingness to admit the level of desperation that led them to utilize women in combat. Or perhaps they did not believe the episode significant enough to record. Whatever the reason, the omission is important, as it underscores both the limited effect of the women's military movement on the ultimate outcome of the war and the revolution and the male tendency to regard women's actions as insignificant.

There are a few exceptions worthy of note, however, both among Russian and Western scholarship. Recently, a number of significant but brief works have appeared in Russia on the women's military formations of 1917, although there has been no detailed study of the individual women soldiers who entered the Russian army prior to 1917. The most solid and well-documented work on the all-female units is Alexander Senin's "Zhenskie batal'ony i voennye komandy v 1917 godu," based on archival materials from the RGVIA. In the mid-1990s the Russian *Journal of Military History* published a series of articles dealing with the participation of women in the Russian armies. These include Iu. N. Ivanova's articles "Zhenshchiny v rossiiskoi armii," "Prekrasneishie iz khrabrykh," and "Problem khvatalo i bez nikh no . . . ." Maria Bochkareva, the commander of the 1st Russian Women's Battalion of Death, undoubtedly the best-known of the women soldiers, has also received some scholarly attention. In particular, Sergei Drokov has produced the most authoritative works, including "Organizator zhenskogo batal'ona smerti," "Yashka," and "Protokoly doprosov organizatora Petrogradskogo zhenskogo batal'ona smerti." Kh. M. Astrakhan devoted an article to the involvement of women soldiers during the defense of the Winter Palace on October 25, 1917, "O Zhenskom Batal'one, zashchishchavshem Zimnii dvorets," but it is a considerably whitewashed version of the events and omits some important details.

The historiography in English on Russia's women soldiers is also thin, but it has grown in the last few decades. Even detailed studies of the Russian Army during 1917 such as Allan Wildman's *The End of the Russian Imperial Army* make only the briefest mention of the women soldiers. Richard Stites's seminal work on the Russian women's movement, *The Women's Liberation Movement in Russia*, opened the door to further scholarship by introducing the subject to the West. Stites writes briefly about the individual soldiers and includes important information about some of the women's units, but he relies solely on memoirs and contemporary periodical literature and does not use essential archival materials (which were not available to him at the time); as a result, he draws several inaccurate conclusions. Richard Abraham covered the topic more substantially in his article "Mariia L. Bochkareva and the Russian Amazons of 1917," in *Women and Society in Russia and the Soviet Union*, edited by Linda Edmondson. Although this is a more detailed and analytical study that addresses both the content and the meaning of the Russian women's military movement, without the benefit of archival sources it also misses significant aspects of the story.

The most comprehensive studies on both the individuals and the women's military units are my own works, based primarily on archival and other primary source materials. These include my unpublished 1995 master's thesis ("Russian Women in Combat: Female Soldiers of the First World War") and an article entitled "They Fought for Russia," in *A Soldier and a Woman*, edited by Gerard DeGroot and Corinna Peniston-Bird, as well as a number of shorter articles in the *Encyclopedia of Russian Women's Movements*, edited by Norma Noonan and Carol Nechamias, and *Amazons to Fighter Pilots*, edited by Reina Pennington. My doctoral dissertation, "They Fought for the Homeland," is the most complete and is the basis for this book.

An article by Melissa Stockdale focusing on patriotic aspects of the women soldiers of World War I, "'My Death for the Motherland Is Happiness,'" based largely on the sources utilized in my own works, is a very interesting assessment of how some of the women soldiers framed their service in terms of their patriotism and citizenship. Although Stockdale cites support from women's organizations and from the women's movement in general, she fails to explain their extensive involvement and support of the women soldiers and therefore misses one of the most important aspects of the phenomenon in terms of patriotism and citizenship. Perhaps more important, she fails to identity the creation of the women's military units as part of a larger social movement with the specific aim of expanding women's roles as citizens. She also incorrectly attributes the idea of the creation of women's military units to Bochkareva, accepting Bochkareva's own claim at face value without considering the various other individuals and groups that had already voiced the idea prior to Bochkareva's appearance in Petrograd in May 1917.

Although the historiographical record is sparse and in spite of official attempts to denigrate and obliterate their images, the legend of these women soldiers lived on among some members of Russian society. For Soviet women desiring to become soldiers, they served as a powerful and significant example (Pennington, *Wings, Women, and War,* 5). Furthermore, in recent years, the subject has begun to receive more public attention. Articles have appeared in the Russian popular media, in publications such as *Argumenty i fakty, Ogonek,* and *Moskovskii Komsomolets.* At the beginning of the 1990s, a Russian television program interviewed surviving women who served as soldiers in World War I. In the West interest has grown as well. Several encyclopedias and dictionaries devoted to female warriors specifically and to women's issues in general have included entries about the Russian women soldiers and the military movement of World War I (see texts such as Salmonson, *The Encyclopedia of Amazons;* Wheelwright, *Amazons and Military Maids;* Pennington, *Amazons to Fighter Pilots*). Maria Bochkareva was featured prominently in an award-winning series coproduced by PBS and the BBC entitled *The Great War,* which aired in 1996. Currently, a British production company is working on a film on her life for a major studio. Bochkareva's "as-told-to" memoirs have been used in university courses on women and war. As a result, the public is gaining greater access to information on this subject.

## PRIMARY SOURCES

### *Archival Sources*

RGVIA (*Rossiiskii gosudarstvennyi voenno-istoricheskii arkhiv*), Russian State Military-Historical Archive, Moscow, Russia

RGAVMF (*Rossiiskii gosudarstvennyi arkhiv voenno-morskogo flota*), Russian State Archive of the Navy, St. Petersburg, Russia

GARF (*Gosudarstvennyii arkhiv Rossiiskoi Federatsii*), State Archive of the Russian Federation, Moscow, Russia

Hoover Institution Archives, Stanford, California

Alekseev, Mikhail Vasil'evich, Papers, 1905–1956

Axelbank, Herman, Film Collection

Golovin, Nikolai Nikolaevich, Papers, 1912–1943

Kerensky, Aleksandr Feodorovich, Papers, 1917

Paley Collection (Papers of Princess Olga V. Paley: Memories of Russia, 1916–1919)

Pickett, Carrie, Collection

Rodzianko, Mikhail Vladimirovich, Papers, 1916–1923
Bakhmeteff Archive, Columbia University Rare Book and Manuscript Library, New York, New York
Bocharnikova, Maria, Papers
GPBSS (*Gosudarstvennaia publichnaia bibliotekta imina Saltykova-Shchedrina*), Saltykov-Shchedrin State Public Library, Manuscript Section, St. Petersburg, Russia
Long, Breckenridge, Papers, Manuscript Division, Library of Congress, Washington, DC


## Published Documents

Bil'shai, Vera, ed. *O zhenskom voprose: K. Marks, F. Engel's, V. I. Lenin.* Moscow: Izdatel'stvo politicheskoi literatury, 1971.

Browder, Robert P., and Alexander F. Kerensky, eds. *The Russian Provisional Government, 1917: Documents.* 3 vols. Stanford, CA: Stanford University Press, 1961.

Bulygin, I. A., and G. N. Golikov, eds. *Oktiabr'skoe vooruzhennoe vosstanie v Petrograde.* Moscow: Akademiia Nauk SSSR, 1957.

Chugaev, Dmitri, ed. *Petrogradskii Voenno-Revoliutsionnyi Komitet: Dokumenty i materiali.* 3 vols. Moscow: Akademiia Nauk SSSR, 1966.

Golder, Frank Alfred, ed. *Documents of Russian History, 1914–1917.* Trans. Emanuel Aronsberg. New York: Century, 1927; Gloucester, Mass.: Peter Smith, 1964.

Kakurin, N. E., and Ia. A. Iakovlev, eds. *Razlozhenie Armii v 1917 godu.* Moscow: Gosudarstvennoe izdatel'stvo, 1925.

*Leningradki: Vospominaniia, ocherki, dokumenty.* Leningrad: Lenizdat, 1968.

Lensen, George, ed. and trans. *War and Revolution: Excerpts from the Letters and Diaries of Countess Olga Poutiatine.* Tallahassee, FL: Diplomatic Press, 1971.

Richards, Maurice, ed. *Posters of the First World War.* London: Evelyn, Adams and McKay, 1968.

Solov'ev, Aleksandr. *Zapiski sovremennika: V nogu s pokoleniem.* Moscow: Sovietskii pisatel', 1964.


## Contemporary Periodicals

### Russian Newspapers
*Armeiskii vestnik*
*Armiia i flot svobodnoi Rossii*
*Birzhevyia vedomosti*
*Golos soldata*
*Listok voiny*
*Na strazhe*
*Novaia zhizn'*
*Novoe vremia*
*Petrogradskii listok*
*Pravda*
*Rabochii i soldat*

*Rech'*
*Russkiie vedomosti*
*Russkii invalid*
*Russkoe slovo*
*Soldatskaia pravda*
*Soldatskaia zhizn'*
*Utro Rossii*
*Vremia*

**Russian Journals**
*20-yi vek*
*Baraban*
*Damskii mir*
*Iskry*
*Krasnoe znamia*
*Letopis' voiny*
*Niva*
*Ogonek*
*Rabotnitsa*
*Rodina*
*Sinii zhurnal*
*Voina*
*Zhenshchina*
*Zhenshchina i voina*
*Zhenskaia zhizn'*
*Zhenskii vestnik*
*Zhenskoe delo*

**Western Newspapers**
*Daily Mail* (London)
*Graphic* (London)
*Independent* (London)
*London Morning Post*
*Manchester Guardian*
*New York Evening Sun*
*New York Times*
*Times* (London)

**Western Journals**
*Atlantic Monthly*
*Colliers*
*Contemporary Review*
*Current History*
*Delineator*
*Englishwoman*
*Good Housekeeping*

*Jus Suffragi*
*Ladies' Home Journal*
*New Statesman*
*Spectator*
*World Outlook*

### Books

Alennikova, N. S. *Dorogi dal'nie, nevozvratnye: Vospominaniia.* Paris, 1979.
Alexinsky, Tatiana [Aleksinskaia, Tatiana]. *With the Russian Wounded.* Trans. Gilbert Cannan. London: Fisher Unwin, 1916.
———. *Zhenshchina v voine i revoliutsii.* Petrograd: Knigoizdatel'svto Znanie-sila, 1917.
Anet, Claude. *Through the Russian Revolution: Notes of an Eyewitness, from 12th March–30th May.* London: Hutchinson, 1917.
Ardashev, Nikolai. *Velikaia voina i zhenshchiny Russkiia.* Moscow: F. Ia. Prigorina, 1915.
Beatty, Bessie. *The Red Heart of Russia.* New York: Century, 1919.
Beury, Charles E. *Russia after the Revolution.* Philadelphia: George W. Jacobs, 1918.
Botchkareva [Bochkareva], Maria. *Yashka: My Life as Peasant, Officer and Exile.* As told to Isaac Don Levine. New York: Frederick A. Stokes, 1919.
Breshko-Breskovskaia, Ekaterina. *Hidden Springs of the Russian Revolution.* London: Oxford University Press, 1931.
Brusianin, V. V. *Voina, zhenshchiny i deti.* Petrograd: Mechny Put', 1917.
Brusilov, Alexei A. *Moi vospominaniia.* Moscow: Gosudarstvennoe izdatel'stvo, 1929.
———. *A Soldier's Notebook, 1914–1918.* London: Macmillan, 1930.
Bryant, Louise. *Six Red Months in Russia: An Observer's Account of Russia before and during the Proletarian Dictatorship.* New York: George H. Doran, 1918.
Buchanan, Sir George. *My Mission to Russia and Other Diplomatic Memories.* Boston: Little, Brown, 1923.
Buchanan, Meriel. *The Dissolution of an Empire.* New York: Arno Press and New York Times, 1971.
———. *Petrograd: The City of Trouble.* London: W. Collins Sons, 1919.
Churchill, Lady Randolph, ed. *Women's War Work.* London: C. Arthur Pearson, 1916.
Churilova-"Charskaia," L. A. *Smelaia zhizn': Podvigoi zagadochnogo geroia.* 1st ed., Moscow, 1908; 2nd ed., St. Petersburg: M. O. Vol'f, 1910.
Crosley, Pauline S. *Intimate Letters from Petrograd.* New York: E. P. Dutton, 1920.
Dadeshkeliani, Princess Kati. *Princess in Uniform.* Trans. Arthur J. Ashton. London: G. Bell and Sons, 1934.
Dorr, Rheta Childe. *Inside the Russian Revolution.* New York: Macmillan, 1917.
Durova, Nadezhda. *Cavalry Maid: The Memoirs of a Woman Soldier of 1812.* Trans. J. Mersereau and D. Lapeza. Ann Arbor: University of Michigan Press, 1988.
———. *The Cavalry Maiden: Journals of a Russian Officer in the Napoleonic Wars.* Trans. Mary Zirin. Bloomington: Indiana University Press, 1988.
Ermeev, Konstantin S. *Plamia: Epizody oktiabr'skii dnei.* Moscow: Izdatel'stvo Federatsiia, 1928.

Farmborough, Florence. *Nurse at the Russian Front: A Diary, 1914–18.* London: Constable, 1974.

Fortescue, Granville. *Russia, the Balkans and the Dardanelles.* London: Andrew Melrose, 1915.

Gippius, Zinaida. *Siniaia kniga: Peterburgskii dnevnik, 1914–1918.* Belgrade, 1929.

Graham, Stephen. *Russia and the World.* London: Cassell, 1915.

Grow, Malcom C. *Surgeon Grow: An American in the Russian Fighting.* New York: Frederick A. Stokes, 1918.

Halsey, Francis Whiting, ed. *The Literary Digest History of the World War.* Vol. 7. New York: Funk and Wagnalls, 1919.

Harriman, Florence Jaffrey. *From Pinafores to Politics.* New York: Henry Holt, 1923.

Howe, Sonia E. *Real Russians.* London: Sampson, Low, Marston, 1918.

Il'in-Zhenevskii, Aleksandr F. *Ot Fevralia k zakhvatu vlasti: Vospominaniia o 1917 gode.* Leningrad: Priboi, 1927.

Ironside, Lord Edmund. *Archangel, 1918–1919.* London: Constable, 1953.

Kerensky, Alexander F. *The Catastrophe: Kerensky's Own Story of the Russian Revolution.* New York: D. Appleton, 1927.

Kleinmichel, Countess. *Memories of a Shipwrecked World: Being the Memoirs of Countess Kleimichel.* Trans. Vivian Le Grand. New York: Brentano's, 1923.

Knox, Sir Alfred. *With the Russian Army, 1914–1917.* 2 vols. London: Hutchinson, 1921.

Kollontai, Aleksandra. *Rabotnitsa za god revoliutsii.* Moscow: Kommunist, 1918.

Levine, Isaac Don. *Eyewitness to History: Memoirs and Reflections of a Foreign Correspondent for Half a Century.* New York: Hawthorn Books, 1973.

Liddell, Robert Scotland. *On the Russian Front.* London: Simpkin, Marshall, Hamilton, Kent, 1916.

Lobanov-Rostovsky, Prince A. *The Grinding Mill: Reminiscences of War and Revolution in Russia, 1913–1920.* New York: Macmillan, 1935.

Long, Robert Crozier. *Russian Revolution Aspects.* New York: E. P. Dutton, 1919.

McCormick, Robert R. *With the Russian Army: Being the Experiences of a National Guardsman.* New York: Macmillan, 1915.

Morse, John. *An Englishman in the Russian Ranks: Ten Months' Fighting in Poland.* London: Duckworth, 1915.

New York Times. *Current History: The European War.* Vol. 7. New York: New York Times, 1917.

Pares, Bernard. *My Russian Memoirs.* London: Jonathan Cape, 1931.

Polovtsev, Petr A. *Glory and Downfall: Reminiscences of a Russian General Staff Officer.* London: G. Bell and Sons, 1935.

Price, M. Philips. *My Reminiscences of the Russian Revolution.* London: George Allen and Unwin, 1921.

Reed, John. *Ten Days That Shook the World.* New York: Boni and Liveright, 1919.

Rodzianko, Mikhail V. *Gosudarstvennaia Duma i Fevral'skaia 1917 g. revoliutsiia.* Arkhiv Russkoi Revoliutsii. Berlin, 1922.

Ross, Edward Alsworth. *Russia in Upheaval.* New York: Century, 1918.

Saks, A. *Kavalerist-devitsa: Shtabs-rotmistr A. A. Aleksandrov (Nadezhda Andreevna Durova).* St. Petersburg: Vestnik russkoi konnitsy, 1912.

Semina, Khristina D. *Tragediia Russkoi armii pervoi velikoi voiny, 1914–198 gg.: Zapiska sestry miloserdiia kavkazkogo fronta.* 2 vols. New Mexico, 1964.

Shklovsky, Viktor. *A Sentimental Journey: Memoirs, 1917–1922.* Trans. Richard Sheldon. Ithaca, NY: Cornell University Press, 1970.

Sinegub, Aleksandr. *Zashchita Zimnego dvortsa: 25 Oktiabr'–7 Noiabr' 1917 g.* Archiv Russkoi Revoliutsii. Berlin, 1922.

Solonevich, Boris. *Zhenshchina s vintovkoi: Istoricheskii roman.* Buenos Aires: Privately published, 1955 (the "slightly fictionalized memoirs" of Nina Krylova).

Sorokin, Pitrim A. *Leaves from a Russian Diary—and Thirty Years After.* Boston: Beacon Press, 1950.

Tyrkova-Williams, Ariadna. *From Liberty to Brest-Litovsk: The First Year of the Russian Revolution.* London: Macmillan, 1919.

Washburn, Stanley. *Field Notes from the Russian Front.* London: Andrew Melrose, 1915.

Williams, Albert Rhys. *Through the Russian Revolution.* London: Labour Publishing, 1923.

Yurlova, Marina. *Cossack Girl.* New York: Macaulay, 1934.

———. *The Only Woman.* New York: Macaulay, 1937.

## Articles

"A. A. Krasil'nikova (Zhenshchina Georgievskii kavalier)." *Zhenshchina i voina* 1 (March 5, 1915): 11–13.

Ancharova, Maria. "Batal'on smerty." *Zhenskoe delo* 15 (August 1, 1917): 1–3.

Bocharnikova, Maria. "Boi v Zimnem Dvortse." *Novyi zhurnal* 68 (1962): 215–227.

Denikin, Anton I. "Ocherki russkoi smuty." *Voprosy istorii* 10 (1990): 98–121.

"Dobrovolets-Kazachka." In "Zhenshchiny geroi." Special issue, *Voina* 24 (1915): 6.

Doty, Madeline Z. "Women Who Would A-Soldiering Go." *World Outlook*, September 1918.

"E. P. Samsonova." *Zhenshchina i voina* 1 (March 5, 1915): 5–7.

Ermilova, V. "Zhenshchina—sud'ia," *Zhenskaia zhizn'* 2 (January 22, 1915).

Iakovleva, A. K. "Prizyv k zhenshchinam." *Zhenshchina i voina* 1 (March 5, 1915): 3.

"Iz deistvuiushchii armii," *Ogonek* 42 (October 29, 1917).

Kollontai, Aleksandra. "Zhenskie batal'ony." *Rabotnitsa* 6 (June 28, 1917): 7–8.

Kostyleva, Valentina. "Nashi Amazonki." *Zhenskaia zhizn'* 19 (October 1, 1914): 24.

———. "Zhenshchina, voina, i sem'ia." *Zhenskaia zhizn'* 17 (September 1, 1914).

"L. P. Tychinina." In "Zhenshchiny geroi." Special issue, *Voina* 24 (1915): 4.

"M. N. Isaakova." In "Zhenshchiny geroi." Special issue, *Voina* 24 (1915): 4.

"Odna iz mnogikh." *Zhenskoe delo*, January 15, 1915: 19–20.

"Partizanki." In "Zhenshchiny geroi." Special issue, *Voina* 24 (1915).

"Russkaia amazonka." In "Zhenshchiny geroi." Special issue, *Voina* 24 (1915): 12.

"Russkaia zhenshchina i voina." *Zhenskoe delo*, May 1, 1915: 6–7.

Shagal, Kapitan. "Zhenskii batal'on." *Voennaia byl'* 95 (January 1969): 5–11.

Strievskaia, S. I. "Smol'nyi, komnata 43." In *Leningradki: Vospominaniia, ocherki, dokumenty.* Leningrad: Lenizdat, 1968.

"Those Russian Women." *Literary Digest* 55 (September 29, 1917).

Tyrkova-Williams, Ariadna. "The Women's Battalion." *Englishwoman*, January 1919: 4–8; February 1919: 60–64.

Viteitskaia, Bozhena. "Zhenskie batal'ony." *Damskii mir* 9–10 (September–October 1917).
"Voina i mir: Devushka-geroi." *Zhenshchina* 3 (February 1, 1915): 32.
"Voina i mir: Kursistka Tychinina." *Zhenshchina* 3 (February 1, 1915): 32.
"Vospominania tov. A A. Ioffe, chlena Leningradskogo Voenno-Revoliutsionnogo Komiteta v dni Oktiabr," *Krasnoarmeets* 78 (November 1925): 5–7.
"Warrior Women." *Literary Digest* 55 (June 19, 1915): 42.
"Young Girls Fighting on the Russian Front." *Current History,* May 1916: 365–367.
Zarechnaia, Sophia. "Amazonki velikoi voiny." *Zhenskoe delo* 14 (July 1, 1917): 1916.
"Zhenshchiny i voina." *Zhenskii vestnik,* January 1915: 21; March 1915: 73–74; April 1915: 93–95; November 1915: 21; January 1916: 21–22.
"Zhenskii batal'on smerti." *Ogonek* 23 (June 28, 1917): 360.
"Zhenskii batal'on smerti." *Zhenskii vestnik* 6 (July–August 1917): 3–4.

SECONDARY SOURCES

*Unpublished Sources*

Ross, Dale. "The Role of the Women of Petrograd in War, Revolution, and Counter-Revolution, 1914–1921." Ph.D. diss., Rutgers University, 1973.
Sanborn, Joshua. "Drafting the Nation: Military Conscription and the Formation of a Modern Polity in Tsarist and Soviet Russia, 1905–1925." Ph.D. diss., University of Chicago, 1998.
Stoff, Laurie. "Russian Women in Combat: Female Soldiers of the First World War." Master's thesis, University of Kansas, 1995.
———. "They Fought for the Homeland: Russia's Women Soldiers of the First World War." Ph.D. diss., University of Kansas, 2002.

*Books*

Abraham, Richard. *Alexander Kerensky: The First Love of the Revolution.* New York: Columbia University Press, 1987.
Addis, Elisabetta, Valeria Russo, and Lorenza Sebesta. *Women Soldiers: Images and Realities.* New York: St. Martin's Press, 1994.
Atkinson, Dorothy, Alexander Dallin, and Gail Warshofsky Lapidus, eds. *Women in Russia.* Stanford, CA: Stanford University Press, 1977.
Barta, Peter I., ed. *Gender and Sexuality in Russian Civilisation.* London and New York: Routledge, 2001.
Bil'shai, Vera. *Reshchenie zhenskogo voprosa v SSSR.* Moscow: Politizdat, 1959.
Black, Cyril, ed. *The Transformation of Russian Society.* Cambridge, MA: Harvard University Press, 1960.
Blanton, DeAnn, and Lauren Cook. *They Fought Like Demons: Women Soldiers in the Civil War.* New York: Vintage Books, 2002.
Bolt, Christine. *The Women's Movement in the United States and Britain from the 1790s to the 1920s.* Amherst: University of Massachusetts Press, 1993.
Bourke, Joanna. *Dismembering the Male: Men's Bodies, Great Britain and the Great War.* Chicago: University of Chicago Press, 1996.

Bushnell, John. *Mutiny amid Repression: Russian Soldiers in the Revolution of 1905–1906.* Bloomington: Indiana University Press, 1985.

Chamberlin, William Henry. *The Russian Revolution, 1917–1921.* Vol. 1. New York: Macmillan, 1935.

Chapkis, Wendy. *Loaded Questions: Women in the Military.* Amsterdam: Transnational Institute Press, 1981.

Clements, Barbara Evans, Barbara Alpern Engel, and Christine D. Worobec, eds. *Russia's Women: Accommodation, Resistance, Transformation.* Berkeley and Los Angeles: University of California Press, 1991.

Clements, Barbara Evans, Rebecca Friedman, and Dan Healy, eds. *Russian Masculinities in History and Culture.* New York: Palgrave, 2002.

Condrell, Diana, and Jean Liddiard. *Working for Victory: Images of Women in the First World War, 1914–1918.* London: Routledge and Kegan Paul, 1987.

Cottam, K. Jean. *Soviet Airwomen in Combat in World War II.* Manhattan, KS: MA/AH, 1983.

Crisp, Olga, and Linda Edmondson, eds. *Civil Rights in Imperial Russia.* Oxford: Clarendon Press, 1989.

Curtiss, John Shelton. *The Russian Revolutions of 1917.* New York: Van Nostrand Reinhold, 1957.

Daniels, Robert V. *Red October: The Bolshevik Revolution of 1917.* New York: Charles Scribner's Sons, 1967.

DeGroot, Gerard, and Corinna Peniston-Bird, eds. *A Soldier and a Woman: Sexual Integration in the Military.* London: Longman, 2000.

De Pauw, Linda Grant. *Battle Cries and Lullabies: Women in War from Prehistory to the Present.* Norman: Oklahoma University Press, 1998.

Dombrowski, Nicole Ann, ed. *Women and War in the Twentieth Century: Enlisted with or without Consent.* New York: Garland, 1999.

Edmondson, Linda H. *Feminism in Russia, 1900–1917.* Stanford, CA: Stanford University Press, 1984.

———, ed. *Women and Society in Russia and the Soviet Union.* Cambridge: Cambridge University Press, 1992.

Engel, Barbara Alpern. *Between the Field and the City: Women, Work, and Family in Russia, 1861–1914.* Cambridge: Cambridge University Press, 1994.

———. *Mothers and Daughters: Women of the Intelligentsia in Nineteenth Century Russia.* New York: Cambridge University Press, 1983.

———. *Women in Russia, 1700–2000.* Cambridge: Cambridge University Press, 2003.

Engelstein, Laura. *The Keys to Happiness: Sex and the Search for Modernity in Fin-de-Siècle Russia.* Ithaca, NY: Cornell University Press, 1992.

Farnsworth, Beatrice, and Lynn Viola, eds. *Russian Peasant Women.* Oxford: Oxford University Press, 1992.

Figes, Orlando. *A People's Tragedy: A History of the Russian Revolution.* New York: Penguin, 1996.

Fitzpatrick, Sheila. *The Russian Revolution, 1917–1932.* Oxford: Oxford University Press, 1990.

Frierson, Cathy A. *Peasant Icons: Representations of Rural People in Late Nineteenth Century Russia.* New York: Oxford University Press, 1993.

Frenkin, Mikhail S. *Russkaia armiia i revoliutsiia 1917–1918.* Munich: Logos, 1978.

Gaponenko, L. *Soldatskie massy zapadnogo fronta v bor'be za vlast' sovetov (1917).* Moscow: Gospolizdat, 1953.

Gilbert, Martin. *Atlas of Russian History.* New York: Oxford University Press, 1983.

Glickman, Rose. *Russian Factory Women: Workplace and Society, 1880–1914.* Berkeley and Los Angeles: University of California Press, 1984.

Goldman, Nancy Loring, ed. *Female Soldiers: Combatants or Noncombatants? Historical and Contemporary Perspectives.* Westport, CT: Greenwood, 1982.

Golovin, Nikolai N. *The Russian Army in the World War.* New Haven, CT: Yale University Press, 1931.

Grayzel, Susan R. *Women and the First World War.* London: Pearson Education, 2002.

Gronsky, Paul P., and Nicholas Astrov. *The War and the Russian Government.* New York: Howard Fertig, 1973.

Grunt, A. Ia., and V. I. Startsev. *Petrograd-Moskva, Iiul'-Noiabr', 1917.* Moscow: Politizdat, 1984.

Halliday, E. M. *The Ignorant Armies: The Anglo-American Archangel Expedition, 1918–1919.* London: Weidenfeld & Nicolson, 1960.

Heenan, Louise Erwin. *Russian Democracy's Fatal Blunder: The Summer Offensive of 1917.* New York: Praeger, 1987.

Heldt, Barbara. *Terrible Perfection: Women and Russian Literature.* Bloomington: Indiana University Press, 1987.

Hirshfield, Magnus. *A Sexual History of the World War.* New York: Cadillac Press, 1934.

Hobsbawm, E. J. *Nations and Nationalism since 1790: Programme, Myth, Reality.* Cambridge: Cambridge University Press, 1990.

Ivanov, N. Ia. *Kontrrevoliutsiia v Rossii b 1917 godu i ee razgrom.* Moscow: Izdatel'stvo Mysl', 1977.

Jahn, Hubertus F. *Patriotic Culture in Russia during World War I.* Ithaca, NY: Cornell University Press, 1995.

Jones, David R., ed. *The Military-Naval Encyclopedia of Russia and the Soviet Union.* Vol. 2. Gulf Breeze, FL: Academic Press International, 1980.

Karpetskaia, N. D. *Rabotnitsy i Velikii Oktiabr.* Leningrad: Izdatelstvo Leningradskogo Universiteta, 1974.

Kirchberger, Joe H. *The First World War: An Eyewitness to History.* New York: Facts on File, 1992.

Koenker, Diana, William Rosenberg, and Ronald Suny, eds. *Party, State and Society in the Russian Civil War.* Bloomington: Indiana University Press, 1989.

Laffin, John. *Women in Battle.* London: Abelard-Schuman, 1967.

Lincoln, W. Bruce. *Passage through Armageddon: The Russians in War and Revolution, 1914–1918.* New York: Simon and Schuster, 1986.

———. *Red Victory: A History of the Russian Civil War.* New York: Simon and Schuster, 1989.

Lyons, Michael J. *World War I: A Short History.* Englewood Cliffs, NJ: Prentice Hall, 1994.

Marsh, Rosallind, ed. *Women in Russia and Ukraine*. Cambridge: Cambridge University Press, 1996.

Marwick, Arthur. *The Deluge: British Society and the First World War*. London: Bodley Head, 1965.

McDermaid, Jane, and Anna Hillyar. *Women and Work in Russia, 1880–1930: A Study in Continuity through Change*. London: Longman, 1998.

Melman, Billie, ed. *Borderlines: Genders and Identities in War and Peace, 1870–1930*. New York: Routledge, 1998.

Menning, Bruce W. *Bayonets before Bullets: The Imperial Russian Army, 1861–1914*. Bloomington: Indiana University Press, 1992.

Miller, V. I. *Soldatskoe komitety russkoi armii v 1917 g*. Moscow: Nauka, 1974.

Mints, I. I. *Istoriia Velikogo oktiabria*. Vol. 2. Moscow: Nauka, 1978.

Mitchell, David. *Women on the Warpath: The Story of the Women of the First World War*. London: Jonathan Cape, 1966.

*The Modern Encyclopedia of Russian and Soviet History*. 60 vols. Gulf Breeze, FL: Academic International Press, 1976–2000.

Mosse, George L. *The Image of Man: The Creation of Modern Masculinity*. New York: Oxford University Press, 1996.

———. *Nationalism and Sexuality: Respectability and Abnormal Sexuality in Modern Europe*. New York: Howard Fertig, 1985.

Noggle, Anne. *A Dance with Death: Soviet Airwomen in World War II*. College Station: Texas A&M University Press, 1994.

Noonan, Norma, and Carol Nechemias, eds. *The Encyclopedia of Russian Women's Movements*. Westport, CT: Greenwood, 2000.

Norton, Barbara, and Jehanne Gheith, eds. *An Improper Profession: Women, Gender, and Journalism in Late Imperial Russia*. Durham, NC: Duke University Press, 2001.

*Oktiabrem rozhdennye*. Moscow: Izdatel'stvo Politicheskoi Literatury, 1967.

*Oktiabr'skoe vooruzhennoe vosstanie v Petrograde*. Moscow: Nauka, 1957.

Pennington, Reina, ed. *Amazons to Fighter Pilots: A Biographical Dictionary of Military Women*. Westport, CT: Greenwood, 2003.

———. *Wings, Women, and War: Soviet Airwomen in World War II Combat*. Lawrence: University Press of Kansas, 2001.

Polner, Tikhon. *Local Government during the War and the Union of the Zemstvos*. New Haven, CT: Yale University Press, 1930.

Pugh, Martin. *Women and the Women's Movement in Britain 1914–1959*. New York: Paragon House, 1992.

Pushkareva, Natalia. *Women in Russian History: From the Tenth to the Twentieth Century*. Trans. Eve Levin. London: M. E. Sharpe, 1997.

Rabinowitch, Alexander. *The Bolsheviks Come to Power: The Revolution of 1917 in Petrograd*. New York: W. W. Norton, 1976.

Ransel, David, ed. *The Family in Imperial Russia*. Urbana: University of Illinois Press, 1978.

Rostunov, I. I. *Istoriia pervoi mirovoi voiny: 1914–1918*. Moscow: Nauka, 1975.

———. *Russkii front pervoi mirovoi voiny*. Moscow: Nauka, 1976.

Rutherford, Ward. *The Russian Army in World War I*. London: Gordon Cremonesi, 1975.

Sabrosky, Judith. *From Rationality to Liberation: The Evolution of Feminist Ideology*. Westport, CT: Greenwood, 1979.

Salmonson, Jessica A. *The Encyclopedia of Amazons*. New York: Paragon House, 1991.

Saul, Norman. *Sailors in Revolt: The Russian Baltic Fleet in 1917*. Lawrence: Regents Press of Kansas, 1978.

———. *War and Revolution: The United States and Russia, 1914–1921*. Lawrence: University Press of Kansas, 2001.

Schneider, Dorothy, and Carl Schneider. *Into the Breach: American Women Overseas in World War I*. New York: Penguin, Viking, 1991.

Senin, A. S. *Voennoe ministerstvo Vremennogo pravitel'stva*. Moscow: Privately published, 1995.

Siegelbaum, Lewis H. *The Politics of Industrial Mobilization in Russia, 1914–17*. London: Macmillan, 1983.

Skorodinskii, Nikolai A. *Poteria Rossii Zimnego dvortsa 25 Oktiabr 1917 g*. London, Ontario: Zaria, 1983.

Sobolev, G. L., and Iu. P. Smirnov. *Aleksandr Kerenskii, liubov i nenavist' revoliutsii: Dnevniki, stat'i, ocherki i vospominaniia sovremennikov*. Cheboksary: Chubaliskii University Press, 1993.

Startsev, V. I. *Krakh Kerenshchiny*. Leningrad: Nauka, 1982.

Stites, Richard. *The Women's Liberation Movement in Russia: Feminism, Nihilism, and Bolshevism, 1860–1930*. Princeton, NJ: Princeton University Press, 1978.

Strakhovsky, Leonid I. *American Opinion about Russia, 1917–1920*. Toronto: University of Toronto Press, 1961.

Temkin, Ia. *Bol'sheviki v bor'be za demokraticheskii mir*. Moscow: Gospolitizdat, 1957.

Thompson, John M. *Revolutionary Russia, 1917*. New York: Charles Scribner's Sons, 1981.

Tylee, Claire. *The Great War and Women's Consciousness*. Iowa City: University of Iowa Press, 1990.

Wade, Rex. *Red Guards and Workers' Militias in the Russian Revolution*. Stanford, CA: Stanford University Press, 1984.

———. *The Russian Revolution, 1917*. Cambridge: Cambridge University Press, 2000.

———. *The Russian Search for Peace, February–October 1917*. Stanford, CA: Stanford University Press, 1969.

Walker, Barbara G. *The Woman's Encyclopedia of Myths and Secrets*. San Francisco: Harper and Row, 1983.

Wheelwright, Julie. *Amazons and Military Maids: Women Who Dressed as Men in Pursuit of Life, Liberty and Happiness*. London: Pandora Press, 1989.

Wildman, Allan. *The Old Army and the Soldiers' Revolt (March–April, 1917)*. Vol. 1 of *The End of the Russian Imperial Army*. Princeton, NJ: Princeton University Press, 1980.

———. *The Road to Soviet Power and Peace*. Vol. 2 of *The End of the Russian Imperial Army*. Princeton, NJ: Princeton University Press, 1987.

Williams, William Appleman. *American-Russian Relations, 1781–1947*. New York: Rinehart, 1952.

*Zhenshchiny Russkoi revoliutsii*. 2nd ed. Moscow: Isdatel'stvo Politicheskoi Literatury, 1982.

Zinin, Iulian V. *Rossiia, revoliutsiia, grazhdanskaia voina v otsenkakh i vospominaniiakh sovremennikov.* Penza: Penzenskogo Gosudarstvennogo Pedagogicheskogo Instituta, 1993.

*Articles*

Anisimov, Evgenii. "Slovo i delo russkoi zhenshchiny." Afterword to *Svoeruchnye zapiski kniagini Natal'i Borisovny Dolgorukoi docheri fel'dmarshala grafa Borisa Petrovicha Sheremeteva.* St. Petersburg: Khudozhestvennaia literatura, 1992.

Astrakhan, Kh. M. "O Zhenskom Batal'one, zashchishchavshem Zimnii dvorets." *Istoriia SSSR* 5 (1965): 93–97.

Chickering, Roger. "'Casting Their Gaze More Broadly': Women's Patriotic Activism in Imperial Germany." *Past and Present* 118 (February 1988): 156–185.

Cottam, Kazimira Jean. "Soviet Women in Combat in World War II: The Ground Forces and the Navy." *International Journal of Women's Studies* 3, 4 (July–August 1980): 345–355

———. "Soviet Women in Combat in World War II: The Rear Services." *International Journal of Women's Studies* 5 (September–October 1982): 363–378.

Curtiss, John. "Russian Sisters of Mercy in the Crimea, 1854–1855." *Slavic Review* 25 (1966): 84–100.

Darrow, Margaret H. "French Volunteer Nursing and the Myth of the War Experience in World War I." *American Historical Review* 101, 1 (February 1996): 80–106.

Davis-Kimball, Jeannine. "Warrior Women of Eurasia." *Archeology* 50, 1 (January–February 1997): 40–41.

Drokov, S. V. "Mariia Bochkareva: *Yashka: Moia zhizn'. Krest'ianka, ofitser, ssyl'naia.* Literaturnaia zapis' Isaaka Don Levina." *Druzhba narodov* 6 (1993): 5–47.

———. "Organizator zhenskogo batal'ona smerti." *Voprosy istorii* 7 (1993): 164–169.

———. "Protokoly doprosov organizatora Petrogradskogo zhenskogo batal'ona smerti." *Otechestvinnye Arkhivy* 1 (1994): 50–66.

———. "Yashka: O komandire zhenskogo batal'ona smerti." *Ogonek* 24 (June 1992): 21–23.

Gullace, Nicoletta. "White Feathers and Wounded Men: Female Patriotism and the Memory of the Great War." *Journal of British Studies* 36, 2 (April 1997): 178–206.

Huston, Nancy. "The Matrix of War: Mothers and Heroes." *Women's Studies International Forum* 5, nos. 3–4 (1982): 119–136.

———. "Tales of War and Tears of Women." *Women's Studies International Forum* 5, nos. 3–4 (1982): 271–282.

Ivanova, Iu. N. "Prekrasneishchie iz khrabrykh." *Voenno-istoricheskii zhurnal* 3 (1994): 93–96.

———. "Problem khvatalo i bez nikh no . . . ." *Voenno-istoricheskii zhurnal* 6 (1994): 75–77.

———. "Zhenshchiny v istorii rossiiskoi armii." *Voenno-istoricheskii zhurnal* 3 (1992).

Johnson, Richard. "The Role of Women in the Russian Civil War (1917–1921)." *Conflict* 2, 2 (1980): 210–217.

Khristinin, Iu. N. "Ne radi nagrad, no rodnogo radu tokma narodu." *Voenno-istoricheskii zhurnal* 1 (1994): 92–93.

Osborn, Lawrence. "The Women Warriors." *Lingua Franca* 7, 10 (December 1997–January 1998): 50–57.

Piatunina, Evgeniia. "Russkie Zhanny d'Ark: Vospominaniia udarnitsy zhenskago batal'ona." *Nezavisimaia gazeta*, March 4, 2000: 2.

Poznakhirev, V. "Zhenskaia gvardiia Kerenskago." *Sovietskii Patriot* 41 (October 1991): 12.

Ross, N. G. "Popytka sozdaniia ruskoi revoliutsionnoi armii (Mai-Iiun' 1917 g.)." *Novyi chasvoi* 1 (1994): 75–87.

Rozental', Isaak. "Smertnitsy na fronte: Zhenskie batal'ony v semnadtsatom godu." *Argumenty i fakty* 720 (August 31, 1994): 7.

Senin, A. S. "Zhenskie batal'ony i voennye komandy v 1917 godu." *Voprosy istorii* 10 (1987): 176–182.

Stiehm, Julia Hicks. "The Protected, the Protector, the Defender." *Women's Studies International Forum* 5, nos. 3–4 (1982): 367–376.

Stites, Richard. "M. L. Mikhailov and the Emergence of the Woman Question in Russia." *Canadian Slavic Studies* 3, 2 (1969).

Stockdale, Melissa. "'My Death for the Motherland Is Happiness': Women, Patriotism, and Soldiering in Russia's Great War, 1914–1917." *American Historical Review* 1 (February 2004): 78–116.

Summerfield, Penny. "Gender and War in the Twentieth Century." *International History Review* 19, 1 (February 1997): 3–15.

"Zhenskii batal'on." *Velikaia Oktiabr'skaia sotsialisticheskaia revolutsiia Entsiklopediia*. 180. Moscow, 1977.

# INDEX